FIVE
O'CLOCK
ANGEL

FIVE O'CLOCK ANGEL

*Letters of
Tennessee Williams
to Maria St. Just*

1948-1982

With commentary by Maria St. Just

Preface by Elia Kazan

Alfred A. Knopf   New York   1990

THIS IS A BORZOI BOOK
PUBLISHED BY ALFRED A. KNOPF, INC.

Library of Congress Cataloging-in-Publication Data
Williams, Tennessee, 1911–1983.
Five o'clock angel : letters of Tennessee Williams to Maria St. Just,
1948–1982 / with commentary by Maria St. Just. — 1st ed.
p.   cm.
ISBN 0-394-56427-8
1. Williams, Tennessee, 1911–1983—Correspondence.
2. St. Just, Maria—Correspondence.
3. Dramatists, American—20th century—Correspondence.
I. St. Just, Maria. II. Title.
PS3545.I5365Z487   1990
812'.54—dc20   89-43354
[B]   CIP

Manufactured in the United States of America
First Edition

To James Laughlin

For this I hold
friendship is more than life,
longer than love
and it shall prove warm to the spirit
when the body is cold.

STEPHEN HAGGARD

Preface

W ho is Maria?

Most every author I've known has someone special that he or she looked to for a judgment-in-advance on his or her work. This might be a trusted editor but is less likely to be an intellectual than a person whose instinct the writer respects absolutely. In the case of Tennessee Williams, a man who would doubt praise when he thought it excessive and was equally able to shoulder off attacks and go on with his work, this one trusted person was Maria St. Just. Often the identity of such a person is kept secret by the author—who can easily yield that much power to another? But when Tennessee wanted a loyal, because absolutely true, reaction, he would turn to her. When he wrote what he called an autobiography, he sent it to her, then asked what she thought. Yes, she said, she had the book, and it was now where it belonged—in her wastepaper basket. Possibly Tennessee was hurt, but not for longer than a minute, and he was not alienated. He suspected that in very short order he might hold the same opinion of that book. It had happened before.

What he admired most about Maria was her unswervable, desperate grip on what she valued in life. It was what he admired in women, he would say, that they would fight with claws for what was essential for them as women and never be deflected. If you've read *Cat on a Hot Tin Roof,* you've read the author's portrait of Maria in Maggie—all the qualities he loved in Maria are highlighted there. To the end of his life, whatever distance separated them, he never lost touch with her, always counted on her when he was troubled or "lost." The truth saves. So does courage. He could count on her for both.

ELIA KAZAN
April 5, 1988

Acknowledgments

I would like to thank Vicky Wilson, my brilliant editor, whose encouragement, sharp eye and ear, and immense sense of the ridiculous has made *Five O'Clock Angel* into a book; Bob Gottlieb, who read the letters and was amused and moved, commissioned them and has been the father, mother, brother, cousin, uncle, aunt and friend to me and to Tennessee; Gore Vidal, who has always helped me so much in everything; Antoinette White, for her devotion to detail and hard work (and who is not distracted by nonsense); John Eastman, my co-trustee, for his cooperation, encouragement and help; and my two daughters, Pulcheria and Natasha, whose total lack of interest and enthusiasm spurred me on in blind fury.

And finally, I would like to say a very special thank you to Alexander Shouvaloff, for his tireless work in collating the letters with infinite patience and such care; and to Kit Harvey, whose energy, invaluable humor and spirit contributed so much to the narrative of the book.

Introduction

Shortly before the Russian Revolution a respectable English couple journeyed to visit a cousin, a Russian noblewoman who lived in St. Petersburg. On arriving at the house, they were greeted by her fifteen-year-old daughter.

This young lady announced that since her mother was out, she had arranged a divertissement to amuse the English cousins until her return. The Imperial Ballet, no less, was to give them a private performance, there in the house.

The visitors exchanged awed glances. The Russian ballet was famous worldwide for the quality of its classical dancers and its choreography. The young girl solemnly showed them into the ballroom. She perched them on two gilt chairs. She clapped her hands.

Into the room trooped, as they had done every day of their lives, the family serfs. They had rags tied bulkily to their feet, with which to polish the ballroom floor. On cue, they began gyrating, randomly and with great energy.

The English couple watched in reverent admiration. The silence was punctuated only by the grunts of the sweating serfs. At the conclusion, the English couple burst into grateful applause. The girl beckoned over the three least appetizing-looking dancers. "I would like you to meet my three brothers: your distant cousins."

Formalities done with, she led them through the dining room. She pointed out, on the sideboard, the silver dishes of *klukva*—sugar balls, like snowballs, filled with soft red berries that burst. "These are put out at the end of the meal," she said. "It is customary, in our country, to throw them as hard as you can at the hostess. It is a mark of appreciation." The English couple nodded gravely. They went upstairs to dress for a dinner that they would spend their lives trying to forget.

It comes as no surprise to those who know her that Maria Britneva, Lady St. Just, is the daughter of that little girl in the big house in St. Petersburg. The Tartar imperiousness; the theatrical panache; the dislike of the bourgeois, the stuffy, or the second-rate; above all, the savagely mordant sense of humor: the spirit is the same. It was that spirit which proved enduringly attractive to a man whose own character seemed very different—the American playwright Tennessee Williams.

"The element of vitality in such works as Maggie the Cat, in *Cat on a Hot Tin Roof*, and, recently, the Countess in *This Is*, were inspired by the volatile Russian spirit of Maria." So wrote Tennessee in 1976. He was also to describe Maria as "my closest friend." It was a friendship that they managed successfully to keep private for over thirty years.

Most of Maria's letters to Tennessee have not survived. Gore Vidal commented, "Ah, dear child! Tennessee was so sentimental. . . ."

During the Revolution, Maria's maternal grandparents fled with the White Russians to England and used much of their private fortune in order to evacuate the British consulate to safety. Their daughter was by now married to an eminent surgeon, Alexander Vladimirovitch Britnev, whose father had been physician-in-ordinary, with the rank of general, to Dowager Empress Maria Fedorovna at Tsarskoe Selo. The young couple remained in Leningrad, where Maria was born, the younger of their two children.

These were famine years, during which the Ogpu (secret police) began brutally "purging" what remained of the Russian nobility. For her children's safety, therefore, Madame Britneva decided to join her mother in London. The consulate arranged the passes: the family's English connections proved useful after all. Alexander Britnev, however, remained behind: men with his skills, he reasoned, were needed now more than ever. Shortly afterwards, he was shot by the Soviets.

"I had rickets," Maria remembers, "having been raised entirely on group potato-skins. Grandmother had sent us food parcels during the famine: Fortnum and Mason hampers containing handmade chocolates, caviar, pâté de foie gras—all the most ridiculous delicacies.

"We arrived off the boat at the London docks. I was immediately snatched by the Salvation Army, to bleats of 'Save the baby, save the baby!' I vanished for three hours, during which they stuck bottles into my mouth. When eventually they returned me to my distraught mother, I was copiously sick. We reached my grandmother's house. 'Honestly,' said my mother. 'Pâté de foie gras! You might have sent out food that was a little more practical!' My grandmother threw up her hands. 'But, my child! I wanted to adorn your life!' " Maria's grandparents, unlike many of the White Russians, had escaped with a certain amount of money, and Maria was expensively educated. After the death of Maria's grandfather, however, she and her mother were not well off.

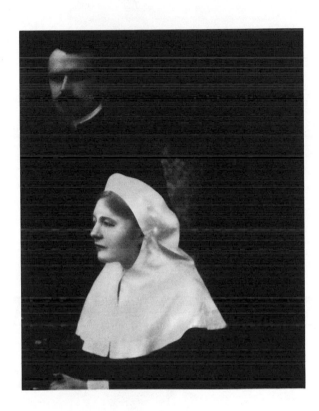

Maria Britneva's father, Alexander Vladimirovitch Britnev, and mother, Mary Britneva, 1917

"During the Second World War, my mother worked for the Foreign Office, screening Soviet deserters and displaced persons who had arrived in London, and teaching them English at home. One woman, an eminent scientist, began to cry when my mother announced her name. 'Britnevsky Dom!' she said again and again. The scientist explained that she had been born in the Britnevsky Dom, our family house in Russia, which was now turned into flats. 'Now I've come full circle—back to the Britnev house.' "

Maria began training for the ballet under Tamara Karsavina and quickly became her favorite pupil. She was nicknamed "the Little Grasshopper" because she could jump higher than anybody else.

Maria Britneva in costume for Balanchine's ballet *La Concurrence,* in which she performed with de Basil's Ballets Russes de Monte Carlo, Covent Garden, London, 1938

"I returned from school one day and said in bafflement to my grandmother, 'Babushka, I do believe that there is a girl at school who doesn't like me!' Grandmother was horrified. 'Not like you? But, my darling, how could anybody fail to *love* you? The poor girl is a fool. *Bock sniey*—God help her!' From that day on, I adopted the philosophy that anybody who didn't like me must be a fool."

When Colonel de Basil's Ballets Russes de Monte Carlo visited London, they needed a child dancer, and asked Karsavina to recommend someone. Karsavina smiled. "Not only do I have a child—I have a *Russian* child." So I danced for three seasons, in *La Concurrence*, in *La Boutique fantasque*, in *Le Beau Danube*, in *Le Coq d'or*, and in *Petrushka*. I danced with Toumanova, Danilova, Baronova, Massine, Fokine, Lichine.

"As I was under age, the London County Council insisted that I have a room of my own and not share it with anyone. However, Vera Zorina, who was at that time having an affair with Massine, was put into my room. I then became the messenger girl, passing secret notes from Massine to Vera.

"I recall dancing in *La Concurrence*, in the part of 'A Spoiled Child of Indulgent Parents.' My mother had, to the rage of my dresser, put my costume on back to front. We gathered onstage before every performance, to be blessed and told to go with God. Serge Grigoriev came to bless me and suddenly began to whine, 'Oh, God, we should have rehearsed her more, this child. She's got a big part. Supposing she forgets the steps?' Leon Woizikowski, the leading dancer, said, 'Don't worry, little Mary. I will stand in the wings opposite and give you all the steps with my hands'— which he did. At the end of my little performance, I got enormous applause and a huge bunch of carnations, one of which I broke off and handed grandly to Woizikowski. Exciting nights for a little grasshopper, hopping around the stage at Covent Garden."

Maria developed foot trouble and had to have an operation. It put an end to her dancing, but she was awarded a scholarship to train as an actress under Michel Saint-Denis at the Old Vic School in London. She was living for much of the time with her grandmother.

"We spent a great deal of time playing solitaire together. I once remarked that I never knew whether to choose the red or the blue cards. Grandmother seemed surprised at my dilemma. 'But you must always choose the red cards! The red cards make your hands look whiter!' "

Near Maria's grandmother's house, in New Cavendish Street, was the mansion of the Grenfell family, in Cavendish Square. Edward Grenfell, ennobled as Lord St. Just, was a partner of the American banker J. P.

Morgan. Together, they owned the banking house of Morgan Grenfell. Grenfell's only son, Peter, was a childhood friend of Maria's.

Madame Britneva was an accomplished writer, and translator of Chekhov's *The Three Sisters* and *The Cherry Orchard* for John Gielgud's company. It was this company that Maria joined on a tour of India, Singapore and Egypt, playing to the troops stationed there after the Second World War, in productions of Shakespeare's *Hamlet* and Coward's *Blithe Spirit*. Maria and Gielgud became, and have remained, great friends.

On their return to England, Gielgud arranged for Maria to be given a contract with H. M. Tennent Ltd. Under its directors, John Perry and Hugh Beaumont (known as "Binkie"), this company was the most powerful postwar producer in London. Employing the best directors, actors, designers and writers, Tennent was an unofficial national theatre, and a Tennent contract was a coveted prize. Its productions always had a recognizable mark of excellence, but, unsubsidized, they worked to a tight budget. The company found Maria very useful, not only in performing small parts but understudying in several theatres.

On June 11, 1948, Maria was one of the guests at a party given by John Gielgud at his house in London. Among the other guests were Laurence Olivier, Vivien Leigh, Noël Coward, and the American director Margo Jones, "the Texas Tornado."

"I've no idea why I was invited. I'd borrowed a frock from somewhere. It was far too big for me, and I had to keep hiking the thing up. After a while, I noticed a little man sitting on a sofa. He was wearing a blue sock on one foot and a red one on the other. He looked unassuming and vulnerable, and nobody was talking to him. I thought that he must be an understudy. I went up to him and asked him if he would like another drink. He seemed genuinely surprised at the interest I took. He looked at me with his blue eyes, blushed, and asked, 'Who brought you up?' 'My grandmother,' I replied. He said, wonderingly, 'My grandmother brought me up, too.' Very occasionally one meets someone with whom one feels an immediate, deep rapport. I'd still no idea who he was. He told me that Chekhov was his favorite playwright. He'd never met a live Russian before.

"Later that night, I told my mother that I'd met this poor young man, and that I'd arranged to meet him at his hotel the next day to bring him home for a meal, because he looked hungry."

The young man went with Maria to meet her mother, and her cousin Sandra—Alexandra Molostvova, the last direct descendant of Field Marshal Suvorov, who lived with them. (Sandra's mother had died of diabetes when

Sandra was only four; the two cousins were brought up as sisters.) Gradually, Maria introduced him to the White Russian colony: Auntie Vodka; Larky Boy, their Russian tutor; Klop the Bug (the father of Peter Ustinov); the Slug. . . . He spent all his time with them, fascinated by their accounts of pre-Revolutionary Russia.

Tennent was producing, at the Haymarket Theatre in London, the Broadway hit play *The Glass Menagerie.* It was to be directed by John Gielgud. The leading role of Amanda Wingfield was to be played by Helen Hayes. The play was to have a week's tryout in Brighton.

The shy man whom Maria had befriended was Tennessee Williams.

Unexpectedly, in the days before the opening, Tennessee disappeared to Paris. This is where the letters begin.

———

Tennessee Williams, Venice, 1952. "It was the first time Tenn took me to Venice. I was a tireless sightseer, but he loathed sightseeing. He just wanted to sit and eat ice cream."

FIVE
O'CLOCK
ANGEL

Irene Selznick, Tennessee and Elia Kazan on the set of *Streetcar* in 1947

[*Handwritten letter*]

Hôtel de l'Université
rue de l'Université
arr. 7
Paris

July 18, 1948

Dear Maria,

How strange Paris is after England, and not altogether better though more interesting to the outsider.

Darling, how thoughtful (characteristically) it was of you to send me what I most needed, the white handkerchiefs. I have the dress suit with me—but no pounds. Could you get 4 from the B.O. [box-office] at the Globe from my account—tell Johnny [Perry]—and pay Moss Brothers?

I must have the tuxedo on for the 28th—John G. [Gielgud] says I should *not* take a bow and just out of perversity, now, I am resolved to do so if there is even the faintest whisper of "Author!" in the house. See you then and there—

Love—Tenn.

IN THE EVENT, Tennessee never appeared on opening night. Maria had to meet his mother, Edwina, and his younger brother, Dakin, who had arrived from America.

"Mrs. Williams was a tiny little woman. Nobody dared ask her where her famous son was. John, Binkie, and I were left to entertain her. She remained very dignified throughout Tennessee's disappearance. Binkie never quite forgave him for missing his first night, mistakenly thinking that it was a case of bad manners.

"As it was, the opening was lukewarm. Helen Hayes was very well received, but the play was slammed.

"I took Mrs. Williams and Dakin to meet my mother. They seemed to get on remarkably well."

Hôtel de l'Université
22, rue de l'Université
Paris

July 30, 1948

Darling Maria:

It was sweet and thoughtful of you to let me know about the opening. Yours is the only communication that I have had from the front, save for a couple of long-distance calls at times when I was not here to receive them.

My absence from the opening was not deliberate. At least I don't think it was. I had been quite ill for several days previous and with my usual hypochondria thought I was even worse than I was. I had been over-working. It was mostly nerves but I had also had vomiting and diarrhoea, to be painfully factual about it, so I had to put off making a plane reservation until the last evening. Then could only get one for 7 o'clock the following morning. I tried to stay awake all night, remained in my clothes and drank coffee. I don't think I really fell asleep—just blacked out or something—and the hotel has no call-system. It was noon when I woke up, so I just said a little prayer for Helen [Hayes] and the players—and went back to work. I know, I know, it was not at all nice of me, but I once did something even worse than that. I went all the way to Washington for the command performance of the *Menagerie* [January 27, 1946] and then I slept in the Statler Hotel right through the reception at the White House because I had not understood what time it was.

The press is the worst the play has ever been given anywhere in Europe, which offers the distressing suspicion that it is better in other languages. How is the box-office? For Helen's sake I hope that the houses are good in spite of the press and that the London audiences are responsive. She worked so hard and gallantly on this production and I think her performance is a really great one. I hope she does not feel that I let her down. I stayed through the rehearsal period and in Brighton as long as there seemed to be any use for me at all. Because I have been working so hard, battering my way through the first draft of a play [*The Big Time Operators*] things are a bit cloudy to me and no doubt I have done a number of thoughtless and apparently negligent things which I had no idea of doing. I am so like John [Gielgud], he seems like a brother to me. The business about the bow was only a joke.

Our pathetic little dress-suit and shirt and patent leather slippers and tie! They are wadded up in the salesman's sample-case as they were when we got them, and I have not had them on once except at your party. What a nice party that was! The best time I had in England. In fact it is the afternoons with you, the walks, the teas, the companionship—the ability to talk to somebody—that I remember most happily about the English adventure.

Needless to say I am completely out of laundry and am wearing continually a midnight blue shirt which does not show the dirt. I shall be here until the fifth of August. Then I shall probably take the night-ferry to London so that I can sail from Southampton on the *Queen Mary* the 7th. It would probably not be worth while sending the laundry to me here. Somehow I cannot make plans or decisions about things like that so I will leave it to you to decide for me, if you will. What do you think we should do? I have great faith in your ability to solve this enormous problem! (Or ignore it!)

Love—Tenn

———

AFTER much reworking, *The Big Time Operators* eventually became *Sweet Bird of Youth.*

———

[*From Maria to Tennessee, a surviving handwritten letter*]

Darling Ten—

Read, mark and inwardly digest. Go to Caron, a scent shop in the place Vendôme (right bank) and buy a very pretty bottle of scent called Tabac Blanc for Miss Hayes, she'll be delighted, and say you got it for her first night. It's the sort of expensive good scent that I'm sure a woman like that would adore. Or get her Guerlain's L'Heure Bleue. Guerlain's shop is in the Champs-Elysées. I advise Tabac Blanc as it's more expensive and Caron has the best shop.

Wasn't I clever and sly about the laundry? So now the midnight blue shirt can be washed enfin. I'll meet you if you arrive Friday morning at Victoria. Only LET ME KNOW. Wire or telephone late in the evening. Then you can swim, or sleep, and see the *Menagerie* in the evening and have dinner with Pretty Missy. We might pop in and see J.G. or Perry. If you want to stay here, Mummy and me will hide all expensive well-bound books not to put you to temptation.

What has happened to your trunk? Is it still sitting sadly at the Savoy? Don't please forget [to] let me know when and if you arrive. Also the Olympic games are on here, booking might be difficult for a hotel, so try

Tennessee,
Irene Selznick
and Elia Kazan
at the *Streetcar*
cast party,
1947

From left: Elia Kazan, Jessica Tandy, Tennessee, Irene Selznick, Karl Malden and Kim Hunter celebrating a year's run of the New York production of *Streetcar*, 1948. Brando must have had his cake and eaten it.

and decide what you want me to do for you. And if your stomach is upset DON'T EAT food with a lot of fat and grease. And take those harmless Russian stomach disinfectant pills.

Hope to see you Friday morning at Victoria. Very much looking forward to seeing that pixie face from Missiisippie (I can't spell it)

Love, Maria

P.S. The booking for the *Menagerie* is excellent.

———

"MY MOTHER used to tease us: 'You and Tennessee, and your *amitié amoureuse!*' I'm not an intellectual, and have never pretended to be one. But we always had the most enormous fun together. I've read that Tennessee once said, 'I just need someone to laugh with.' And that's how we were, all the time; doubled up with laughter."

Staying at the same hotel in Paris as Tennessee was Gore Vidal, who had that year, at twenty-two, scored an enormous success with his novel *The City and the Pillar.* When Tennessee returned to England, he introduced Maria to Gore.

"He was the most beautiful young man I've ever seen. We were walking up the Strand after lunch, and Gore's eyes began to glitter at the sight of the bag of toffees which I was carrying. Quick as a flash, he crammed one into his mouth, and then let out a yelp of pain. He'd broken a tooth. He is as greedy as I am, so we became firm friends at once.

"In the nineteen-fifties, when the three of us were travelling from New York to Key West, Tennessee and Gore, who were both on diets, wistfully watched me tucking into an enormous ice-cream sundae. Gore turned to Tennessee and said through clenched teeth, 'Miss Pig strikes again!' The nickname stuck."

Tennessee felt that Maria was exploited by H. M. Tennent. He told her to give up her contract, and invited her to come to New York for the opening of *Summer and Smoke.* Maria sailed on the *Queen Mary* on September 8, 1948. She was met by Tennessee, who took her that evening to see his hit play *A Streetcar Named Desire,* in which Marlon Brando was starring. It was directed by Elia Kazan, nicknamed "Gadg," in whom Tennessee had enormous faith, and who directed most of his greatest successes.

Maria, however, complained that she found it very difficult to hear what Brando was saying.

The opening-
night party for
Summer and Smoke
at Tennessee's
apartment,
New York,
1948

Left to right:
Truman Capote,
Sandy Campbell,
Audrey Wood,
unidentified

Rear, left to right:
Margo Jones,
unidentified,
Maria Britneva,
Gore Vidal,
James Laughlin;
front row:
Frank Merlo and
Mrs. Williams,
Tennessee's mother

Marlon Brando and
Margaret Phillips

Eli Wallach,
Marlon Brando,
Margo Jones,
unidentified

Left to right:
unidentified,
Anne Jackson,
unidentified,
Gore Vidal,
unidentified,
Eli Wallach,
Marlon Brando

"Tennessee, with a glint of malice in his eye, said, 'Why don't you come backstage and tell him?' Which I did. Brando was absolutely delighted and took me to the Russian Tea Room immediately. The next evening, when I saw the play again, I could hear every word.

"Brando and I spent many evenings riding all over New York on his motorcycle. Irene Selznick, 'the Dame,' who was the producer of *Streetcar*, would ring me up each morning and beg me not to encourage him to ride that bike. Brando was too hot a property to risk losing that way.

"Brando was the toast of New York. But he was incredibly generous and unaffected towards his young fellow actors from the Actors Studio, for which I'd auditioned. I was in the group with Maureen Stapleton, Eli Wallach, Kevin McCarthy, James O'Rea, Anne Jackson, working on Tennessee's *American Blues*. Marilyn Monroe joined us later. Some of us used to turn up on payday in Brando's dressing room, and he would hand out five, two, or one-dollar bills, according to our needs. He never inquired as to what those needs were."

The first performance of *Summer and Smoke* was on October 6, 1948, at the Music Box Theatre, New York City, directed by Margo Jones, designed by Jo Mielziner, with Margaret Phillips as Alma Winemiller and Tod Andrews as John Buchanan, Jr. The music for it was composed by Paul Bowles, the author. He had also composed the score for *The Glass Menagerie*. Both Paul Bowles's and Tennessee Williams's work was published by New Directions, an important new publishing house. It had been founded by their great friend the poet James Laughlin, out of the fortune made by his family in steel. At the first-night party Maria met Laughlin. Later, they fell in love.

James Laughlin recalls an incident from the early days of their friendship.

"Tennessee was going to Chicago to see a performance of a play: I'm not sure which. Maria and I were having dinner in New York. She suddenly remembered that there was something important she had forgotten to say to Tennessee. I knew there were two night trains to Chicago: one from Pennsylvania Station and one from Grand Central Station. Both trains left at midnight, but they were parked in the stations so that people could go to bed before departure time. We rushed by taxi to Penn Station, found the Chicago train, and ran through the sleeping-cars shouting 'Tennessee!' No luck. I was ready to give up, but she insisted that we try the other train. There, we had no luck either—until the last car. Tennessee heard us, stuck his head out of the berth curtains. He was very surprised and pleased to see us; sleeping without pajamas, 'in the buff,' and struggling into his clothes. 'I forgot to say goodbye,' said Maria."

Gore Vidal with Tennessee on the Pincio, Rome, 1948

"James Laughlin at the time of our engagement, 1953; my mother used to call him 'le chevalier sans peur et sans reproche.' "

Gore Vidal and Maria Britneva, Coney Island, 1949

"Gore took me to Concy Island, where there was a terrifying, creaking roller coaster, which boasted a speed of ninety miles an hour. I said to Gore, 'Nothing on earth will get me onto that monstrous thing!' Gore narrowed his eyes and said in a slow, dreamy voice, 'I think I know something that will get you onto that roller coaster.' 'Nothing!' I repeated. Slowly and sweetly, he said, 'I'll write a little part for you in my next TV play.' I climbed onto the roller coaster."

[*Sent to New York City*]

American Express
Rome

February 7, 1949

Dear Maria:

I have been very very cross with you and that is why I have not written you since I sailed. I have however had reports of you from time to time, from various scouts, and am satisfied to hear that you continue to remain on the surface of the vortex of Manhattan society, although I should be, perhaps, justified in preferring to see you go under. You are a very naughty person, you know: at least the vocal part of you is astonishingly active. You seem to say all the things that discreet people only think. Oh, that tongue of yours! As one who was, and perhaps still is, inclined to like so much of the rest of you, including what I optimistically assume to be your heart, I do most earnestly advise and beseech you to curb it, like the fancy little dogs on Fifth Avenue. I can hear you innocently saying, But what have I said? And then, Tennessee, you are becoming paranoiac! Well, honey, you may be right that I am "Finit," as you so fastidiously put it. I have often thought so myself and everyone is sooner or later and perhaps my number is already up. Quite, quite possibly. But one cannot help being a bit of a crossington with a Cassandra who is crying one's own doom at the top of her sweet little voice. One thing I am sure of. The reason you give, and the only possible salvation that you perceive, are equally and totally irrelevant. Latitude of experience, range of association, diversity of interest are not what I lack. I won't go on with this any further as it sounds so patronizing and pompous, and it would take "the Old One" [John Gielgud] to deliver those lines properly. So let's get on to more cheerful subjects. We could always laugh together: something I could only do with you and Donnie [Windham] and Paul [Bigelow] in New York. I am a terrible dullington here in

Rome, especially now that Frank is visiting his relatives in Sicily. Don't see or talk to anybody. Work in the mornings, enjoy the sun in the afternoons, cruising dreamily about in the Buick which still hangs together after all its crossings so well that it is continually greeted by cries of Que [*sic*] Bella Macchina! Paul [Bowles] is still in Morocco. I miss him a lot more than I do Morocco, he will always be more interesting than any place he inhabits. Morocco might be wonderful *not* in the rainy season, but the rainy season is what we hit, there was no swimming, my nervous tension increased, I developed "vibrations": shipped out of Casablanca for the Riviera and Rome. This brings me up to date. Now how about you?

Love 10

"WHEREAS Tennessee's likes and dislikes mostly came from paranoia (as he would have agreed), mine were often the result of sheer passion, mostly protective of him. Throughout our relationship, Tennessee was constantly warning me against the arbitrariness of my reactions to people—and I now realize that he was from the very beginning trying to save me from a lot of pain caused by my sharp tongue.

"Paul Bigelow was a great friend of Tennessee's from the days of the Theatre Guild. I never really trusted him. His jaw was twisted permanently southeast. No one knew who he was or what he did. He simply loitered in the corridors of power. I asked Gore, 'Is Bigelow an arriviste?' 'Maria, dear, he never arrivéed!'

"Donald Windham, the writer, and his companion, Sandy Campbell, were extremely kind and hospitable to me. They were friends of Tennessee's from the early days."

Tennessee had met his Sicilian companion, Frank Merlo, in Provincetown, while writing *A Streetcar Named Desire*. "Frankie had educated himself on the gunning turrets as a GI. I christened him 'the Little Horse' because of the size of his teeth.

"Despite the inevitable initial resentments when I arrived on the scene, I became very fond of Frank Merlo, who was the only one of Tennessee's close companions who truly loved him for what he was. He was also the only one whom Tennessee really loved. He had great integrity, and great dignity. Tennessee used to show him work he had written. That was a measure of his regard for him: ordinarily, he was paranoiac about showing it to anybody. When I, or anybody else, came into the room, Tennessee would fling himself protectively across the typewriter, concealing what he'd

Frank Merlo,
affectionately called
the Little Horse
because of the size
of his teeth,
Key West, 1952.
Tennessee would
often recite a poem
he wrote:
"My name for him
is Little Horse./
I wish he had a
name for me."

Frank Merlo with Tennessee, Key West, 1955

written. Frankie would read Tennessee's manuscripts at a tremendous rate, his little horse-hoofs stabbing at the pages as he turned them."

———

[*Sent from Rome*]

March 5, 1949

Dear Maria:

Have I ever told you that I like Italians? Well, now let me tell you I do! They are the last of the beautiful young comedians of the world.

I am glad that we have made it up, for I enjoyed your letters enormously, especially the last one about your strange life in New York and the crack about Truman [Capote]'s voice being so high that only a dog can hear it. Even people who don't know Truman, and there are a few here who don't, get a terrific laugh out of that one. I guess it is so graphic it presents a complete image, all except the yards of Bronzini neckwear. I once told him he was going to die like Isadora Duncan who also wore one of those things and it got caught in the wheel of a car in which she was making a very grand departure and it promptly broke her neck. Ha ha! I knew that would please you, darling. You have the same risibilities as those characters of Charles Addams. None of the "Young American writers" have arrived here as yet despite your continual warnings of their approach, you Cassandra! Not one, not even Vidal. Have you dismembered their bodies in a bathtub and deposited them in the East River? If so I hope that Thelma Spellman, as we call the dear Cardinal, gave them a very gay blessing as their souls drifted out to Long Island Sound, probably to be washed up on what is called "Bare-ass Beach."

The Young Horse—do you know who that is?—has returned from Sicily where he had a case of galloping dysentery which was vastly complicated by the fact that none of his relatives had the ghost of a plumbing fixture amongst them. He has lost weight, is downright diaphanous, all eyes and nose. He said it was the goat's milk that did it. They brought the goat right into his bedroom and milked it beside the bed and handed him the milk and would not take no for an answer as the goat was a great prize. Soon as he has recovered sufficient[ly], and he is showing some signs of recovery now, we are going back down there together in the Buick. As I am too fat, the goat will do me no harm, and the reports of social life down there are fantastic. The girls are not allowed to speak to the boys till after marriage: a kiss has the same consequences as a pregnancy used to have in the backward

The Merlo family, New Jersey, 1960

communities of the South, and they must still have dowries, no matter how pretty. Frank gave his aunt ten thousand lire so that she could marry off a pretty young cousin of his who was practically going into a panic of frustration, she had so many things she wanted to say to a handsome young ragazzo. I am sure when she is finally at liberty to speak she will get her tongue twisted and babble so incoherently they will throw her, still inviolate, into the mad-house, for even Sicilians seem to get rather excited about Sicilians.

Last week I entered Roman society with a bang but probably made an almost simultaneous exit. I went to a big dinner at which everybody wore white ties and titles. There were exactly three duchesses, one of them had been a princess. She came to the top of the steps and announced in a loud voice that she could not advance a step further as she had arthritis. Everybody had to go up and kiss her hand. I wish you had been there to bite it. Perhaps you could have bitten off one of her diamonds. I got it halfway to my mouth and thought, My God, has it come to this! And I stopped and just shook a little, which did not seem to please her at all, especially as my tie was red, white and blue and very loosely knotted. One of the duchesses claimed an acquaintance with your mother. That one was the nicest one of the three and I sat next to her at dinner and yesterday she invited me to have cocktails and mentioned your name as "the little Britneva": wanted to know what you were doing: I said you were living in New York: she wanted to know a great deal more but that was all I told her: you see I do not have your faculty for making inspired conversation about my friends!

How long do you think you will last at your present residence? Judging by the labels you put on some of those bottles you are going to go through that place like the proverbial dose of solubles. I hope you land gently somewhere and that you will not let the entire season pass without seeing something besides *Death of a Salesman*. Do you know I got five complete sets of notices of that play, sent me by various well-meaning friends in New York? More than I ever got for any play of my own, including the *Menagerie* in London, when you picked them like flowers: or perhaps it would be better to say you gathered them like toadstools with the morning dew still on them.

Tomorrow we are leaving for Florence to visit an old schoolmate of mine, Bill Smith, who is a poet and is married to a young lady poet, and they both live in a villa on a hill, I suppose both of them writing mad sonnets about spring in Tuscany, but the wife is now pregnant so evidently the relationship is not strictly one of iambics. Her name is Barbara. Do you suppose I will get along with her at all? If you answer this quickly the address will be American Express in Florence: if later, the Roman address, as we are returning here before we branch out again. What is the news from the Globe?

Love from Tenn

———

NINA, the Duchess Colona di Cesaro, was indeed a great friend of Maria's mother. They had volunteered together as nurses to the front during the First World War. Her daughters, Simonetta and Mita, were a few years older than Maria and were her friends.

In Rome Tennessee was working on a number of plays and on the novel *The Roman Spring of Mrs. Stone*. The character of Karen Stone was based on his friend Eyre de Lannux.

"Frank Merlo's immediate relations were an enormous brood of first-generation Sicilian immigrants who had settled in New Jersey or some-where. His poor mother was tormented by the size and vociferousness of her family, and used often, after arguments, to climb the fig tree in the backyard and sulk, sometimes for hours on end. I remember Frankie telling us that after one particularly blinding row, she refused to come down. Having shouted at her, and pleaded with her, her sons eventually took an axe to the tree and brought the whole thing down, with her in it. Tennessee and I, hearing this story, were whimpering with laughter. Frankie was livid: he took her very seriously indeed."

In April Tennessee went to London for meetings about the English production of *A Streetcar Named Desire,* to be directed by Laurence Olivier, with Vivien Leigh as Blanche.

Maria went to Rome, and met up with Tennessee on June 9. During this time she briefly recorded her days with him in a school exercise book.

10 June

As we were sitting in the bar I looked at Ten I am worried about him. There is a curious listlessness and lack of spark in him. I do not think he is well and his eyes are puffy and tired tired tired. He said he felt "a hundred years old."

He seems very detached somehow, like something that is running down, unwinding itself. Maybe it's good—and if he rests and goes away—but I am concerned. I feel something overhanging us somehow, and I had such an urgent urgent feeling to get here. It is strange how dear and beloved he is, and what a feeling of peace he gives. There's never been anyone like Tenn for closeness

2:30 a.m.

We've just returned from a strange evening filled with conflict between 10 and Frank, over two strangers that came to dinner. Ten was tense and nervous, as I was aware, and wanted to dash to a cinema, and as night was beginning to fall, the first night, prima sera, we drove round St. Peter's.

I suppose one will never see anything more lovely in one's life, and a little lighted window where the Pope sits in his room.

We had dinner in the Aurora and then coffee in a beautiful square with a hideous all-woman band, and the loo was in the catacombs. Let the people off, and drove to a beautiful view. 10 and I walked and talked—it's good I'm here. He can talk to me about anything—his family, sister, self. I know he's not working well, and he was upset about being inadequate company tonight and cross with Frank for having strangers and not understanding why he didn't want them.

Then Frank went for a walk and 10 and I sat in a bar, with all the underworld of Rome and a one-legged whore was there with a horrid decadent-looking man.

I love my *Battle of Angels,* so beautifully bound by 10 for me. Tomorrow I go to the Colonas.

[*The diary breaks off at this point.*]

––––––

TENNESSEE had given Maria a copy of his early play *Battle of Angels,* which eventually was to become *Orpheus Descending.* He inscribed it: "Darling Maria, When you read this play remember that when I wrote it I was creeping and crouching about the attic of Clayton, Missouri, wretched as ten flies at the end of summer, had to borrow a dime for coffee. Then one morning the telephone rang. New York was calling! Ever—Tennessee"

Rose Williams, Tennessee's sister, was the most important person in his life and the inspiration for most of his work. He was constantly concerned about her, and guilty that he had done nothing to prevent her undergoing one of the first lobotomies, on their mother's instruction, in 1937. The operation had left her in need of constant institutional care.

"Whenever Tennessee talked about her he would burst into fits of loud, hysterical laughter, and roll his eyes round in embarrassment. He used to cry when he told the story of how, when they were children, he would tug at her ringlets, shouting 'Ding dong, ding dong!' He used to ask me, 'How could I have been so cruel?' Rose used often to write poetic postcards to her brother Tom—Tennessee's real name. She once wrote, 'Tell Tom I love him so much; he stole my heart away in the dark ages.'

"Tom was the name which only his immediate family used. Curiously enough, I've noticed that those who knew him the least, but who would want to appear to have been closer, call him Tom. His inner circle of friends would never dream of calling him anything but Tennessee."

––––––

[*Maria's diary resumes some days later.*]

Saturday night

I wonder how many emotions one can go through until one finally gives up. I felt for the first time the direct impact of homosexuality tonight and realized fully I think the inadequacy in myself to ever be able to do anything

Tennessee and Maria
arriving late to a
party in Rome, 1949,
during the time he
was writing *Cat*

Ever —
Tennessee,

Battle of Angels

Tennessee's
inscription in
a specially bound
first edition of
Battle of Angels

Darling Maria, when you read
this play remember that when I
wrote it I was creeping and
crouching about the attic of
Clayton, Missouri, wretched as ten
flies at the end of summer, had
to borrow a dime for coffee.
Then one morning the telephone
rang. New York was calling!

Tenn.

for maybe the one person that I want to do something for.—It is not pleasant, and destructive in the extreme to oneself.—Suddenly I was an outside person and glad to be, except that a great gap seemed to come between me and them. What the hell am I doing in Rome? Why do I run so frantically to the one person that I imagine can give me peace? I do not want to hinder or oppress, I do not want to possess or be possessed, I want to turn my head and smile and watch a child steal sugar from a bowl, and catch the eye of another that notices and have a quiet secret. I remember that tonight, and the exact feeling I have for Ten, and that I hold him in my heart's core—and guess I will always, if such a word exists as always. I don't think that I've ever been so tired of anything as I am of my face and myself. I want to wake up new like a daffodil.

What is your substance | Wherefore are you made | That millions of strange shadows on you tend . . . I could say that forever and ever. I wish I hadn't given my sonnets to Tennessee tonight. I want them now. And I believe I wrote a poem to him in the back. I hope I'm mistaken but I suddenly remembered. I must get them back tomorrow and tear it up.

———

MARIA, Frank and Tennessee went to Florence to see Luchino Visconti's production of *Troilus and Cressida*. There they met Oliver Evans, a lecturer in English at the University of Nebraska at Lincoln and a lifelong friend of Tennessee's. He was nicknamed "the Clown." Maria's schoolgirl diary records:

July 5, Monday

"You've learned something, which often makes one feel as though you've lost something"—GBS

Florence was incredible—not the town but the circumstances under which we went. I have never seen anything so frantic as the behavior of poor Oliver stopping and staring at every young Italian boy. My God, the lack of dignity—

Frank is very possessive which is silly. Friends are friends, lovers lovers, and without the deep bond of friendship, when the physical thing dies, very little remains except a kind of stale feeling like the smell of yesterday's cigarette butts. I'm glad that I have grown up emotionally.

We seem to get on so well and have just a wonderful companionship and laughter bursts from us almost simultaneously. How important it is to be

Franco Zeffirelli and Tennessee with Luchino Visconti in his garden, Rome, 1949

Rome, 1949

able to laugh and to have the same sense of humor. A bond forever. Never have we laughed so as at *Troilus and Cressida,* with Oliver drunk mad for the boys getting tangled in bushes, under horses' hoofs, deaf, half-crazy with desire and then at the end of it no happiness. It makes me sad.

Now I'm also worried about Ten, who spoke like from a tomb about himself saying *Streetcar* was his highest achievement and that he was getting weaker physically and as a writer.—This is complete nonsense as he is such a great and tremendous writer, so talented, what can one say to quiet this fear of his which is so unfounded?

Monday 11th

Frank is possessive and destructive of every relationship Ten has, which is bad, for an artist [like] Ten needs some impetus—happiness or unhappiness—not just the nervous reactions of a horse. Also when I think of the presumptuousness to dare to tell me what to do with my life, and then telling Ten I was in love with him just to ruin everything—if I don't know myself how the hell does Frank know so well what is going on in my heart, the fool. I was very cold with him this evening. I could have died in Rome for all he had bothered. Tomorrow I will buy flowers and figs and take them to make the room nice for Tennessee to welcome him when he returns. Now I sleep.

Thursday August 25th

Just returned [from] Mischa Auer [the Russian-born character actor]'s party at the [Hotel] Quirinale where we had champagne, talked Russian and in general enjoyed ourselves. I'm a bit tight now. The party at Allegra's was wonderful. Gérard Philipe [the French film actor] is really the most magnetic person I've ever seen or met. The whole evening was dominated by his personality. Tennessee seemed to be just in a dream.

[*The diary finishes here.*]

"Luchino [Visconti] was filming *La terra trema* in Sicily and invited Tennessee onto the set. Tennessee arrived at night, tired and sleepy. It was his first visit to Sicily. They were all living in a pokey little pensione in a small village, deep in the mountains. As Tennessee was gobbling up his pasta, he looked around the dining-room. Dangling perilously from rusty nails driven into the wall were some very cheap prints of churches. All the most celebrated cathedrals and basilicas in the world hung there: St. Paul's, London; St. Peter's, Rome; St. Basil's, Moscow; Santa Sophia, Constantinople; St. Patrick's, New York. Tennessee gazed at them. 'This looks like a really nice little town. I'd like to go and visit some of those churches tomorrow.' "

Tennessee returned to New York in September.

———

[*From New York City*]

October 9, 1949

Dear Maria:

I have not deliberately neglected you, nor have I been cross as two sticks. Life has just been too hectic, there hasn't been any let-up since we landed. In fact the night before we landed, for we ran into the tail of the hurricane. (The Horse turned a lovely green color, but I was cunning as ten flies and remained my usual peach-bloom.) We had two days here, seeing old friends, then we were whisked off to Hollywood, or rather, Burbank and Bel Air. I had to do the entire screenplay [*The Glass Menagerie*] all by myself but I think it turned out pretty well and as you must know, Gertie Lawrence is to do it. I met her but the meeting did not come off too well, I arrived twenty minutes late and she took a dim view of it. I brought her a corsage and she threw them right into the sink. You and I have an equal lack of rapport with leading ladies. The Dame [Irene Selznick] has been in a continual froth about the London *Streetcar*. Hardly a day has passed without a ten-page cable or letter insisting that I should stamp my foot about various things across the Atlantic. My typing is almost as bad as yours. Well, I am not in a very good condition. I have given up coffee and cigarettes, both, completely, to rest my nerves which were quite shaken by all the travelling and excitement. I feel dopey. That is, not too bright. Do you know what I mean? I never take a sleeping-pill before ten in the morning, however—that is, not until I have gotten out of bed and brushed my teeth—and I only have two boxes in my pocket when I go out, one of phenos and one of "Secs." Well, the town is blooming with British queens mostly connected in some way with the ballet. Bobbie Helpmann is to appear this evening as the fairy princess. I shall not go until Michael Somes does a turn. We are in the old Chelsea Hotel on West Twenty-third Street. Not at all chic. The lobby is always full of Polish refugees, but the rooms are quiet and sunny. Could not blast Buffie Johnson out of the old apartment I had last time, but anyhow we are buying a new Buick and taking off for Key

West, Florida, in a week or so, and then I shall go back on coffee and cigarettes and try to complete a play [*The Rose Tattoo*] for Gadg [Kazan]. He is such a doll. We had dinner with him and the Logans [Joshua and Nedda] and the Brooks Atkinsons a few nights ago, and it is now all set for Gadg to direct *Streetcar* on the screen. Poor Josh looked a wreck. I am sure he must have inherited Tom [Heggen]'s little bottles. Oh! Did you know that Donnie [Windham] has sold his novel [*The Dog Star*]? Yes, indeed, he sold it to Doubleday which is one of the big houses and he got a thousand-dollar advance. We are all very thrilled over this as it took so long to sell it, a whole year, and Donnie was getting discouraged. Jane and Tony are well. I gave her a pair of Chinese silk blouses that I found in Chinatown in Frisco. From Oliver [Evans] only a wretched little postcard saying that Ischia was not as good as Capri, which could only mean one thing. I suppose the Clown has resumed his duties at Nebraska, not omitting to drop by the bus-depot at odd moments, when classes are not in session. I miss him and hope he will visit me this winter. So far it appears to be a bad season in the theatre, few good plays coming up, most of the houses still vacant. But I shall certainly let you know if I hear of anything. Very cross with Margo [Jones]. Two sticks could not possibly be crosser. Her Chicago company which she praised so highly was a poor travesty of what it should have been. And I implied as much when I saw her, surrounded, as usual, by her gangsters and yes-men who insulate her against all unflattering contact with the world. Dakin has quit his job in St. Louis and is practicing independently. He has two clients both of whom are serving two-year sentences for robbery in the county jail. I suppose he goes and prays with them. They are his only clients thus far and I cannot imagine they are very lucrative ones unless they happened to be wealthy kleptomaniacs—a point of view, or supposition, too optimistic for anybody but Margo to maintain. My sister [Rose] continues to write to me. Oh, how happy she was with her shawl and her compact and some money I put in it! But she says she has some grey hairs. "I cannot decide whether to dye my hair jet black or snow white. Which would you prefer?" she says. She also says It is time for the children to return to school (hers!) and to give them her love as they are very dear to her! Otherwise the letter was quite normal and she had had, as usual, a chicken dinner and gave me the complete bill-of-fare. We are driving [to Nyack] out to Carson [McCullers]'s this evening, as she is giving a supper for Ethel Waters who is to appear in her play. I am so happy over the success of John Perry's [*Treasure Hunt*].

Love and good luck, Tenn

Tennessee's
beloved
grandfather,
the Reverend
Walter Dakin

A letter to
Tennessee
from his
grandfather

My dearest Tom:

  So glad you are in London. I wish I were with you.
I have been in Clarksdale over a month and enjoyed every minute
until I took sick. I am just out of the hospital where I was
for a few days. I received a blood transfusion and that was
no fun. Everyone was so good to me. My room was like a garden
so many sent flowers and cards and I had many callers. Hospitals
are expensive, especially when a transfusion is given, but it is all
paid for by me.

  Hope to go to Perry's for a few days next week.

  I am glad Mrs. Selznick is with you. I like her.
Remember me to her.

  I am longing to see you in America soon.

  Your mother enjoyed the Company the two weeks they were
in St. Louis - gave an after theatre party which she says all
enjoyed.

  Edwina wrote Rose is having a vacation. I am praying
hard for her.

  No news! Just love, love and desire to see you.

    Devotedly,

    Grandfather

May 9, 1949.

    Lots of love

———

BROOKS ATKINSON, the distinguished theatre critic of the *New York Times,* was a constant supporter of Tennessee.

Carson McCullers (nicknamed "Choppers" by Maria, since "her cheeks looked like two lamb chops") and her husband, Reeves, were old friends of Tennessee's. She had stayed with Tennessee while writing her play *The Member of the Wedding.*

Buffie Johnson was an artist from whom Tennessee subleased an apartment at 235 East Fifty-eighth Street. The architect-turned-sculptor Tony Smith and his wife, Jane, a singer, were great friends of Tennessee's. Tennessee had been best man at their wedding, and he and Tony had enormous respect for each other's work. Jane Smith recalls: "We met Maria and adored her. Tennessee would introduce her to people as 'my beloved Maria.' No one could understand her, of course, but the combination of the British accent and the Russian spirit was unique."

Maria was being pursued around New York by a peer in the Irish Guards. She wrote to Tennessee complaining that she was feeling a little seedy.

———

[Handwritten on letterhead Hotel George Washington, Jacksonville 2, Florida]

November 9, 1949

Darling Maria:

I hope you have gotten rid of your worms and have consumed enough raw beef to overcome the anemia. Perhaps the trouble with you is an overdose of Irish peers. Or could it be the lingering effects of too many American belles? We miss you, honey. I have not heard a word from Oliver. Last night, on the highway, I bought him a fancy silk pillow-slip with the picture of an alligator on it, with a wide-open mouth, and a lovely little verse, of tender sentiment, called "Florida Sweetheart." It remains to be seen in what spirit this gift will be received. The good humor of the Clown is not invariable, especially when he is confined to the stately halls of Nebraska.

No news. We have a house in Key West for six months, in which I shall finish a play [*The Rose Tattoo*]. Grandfather (now in his 93rd year) will arrive day after tomorrow for an indefinite stay. Talked to Mother on phone. She complains that all my brother's legal clients are in jail.

Dear love to you, my favorite little girl. Let me know how you are. The address is 1431 Duncan Street, Key West, Fla.

Tenn.

TENNESSEE later bought the house at 1431 Duncan, and it remained his only permanent address until his death.

Maria was offered work in London, in *The Boy with a Cart,* by Christopher Fry, directed by Gielgud, starring Richard Burton, and returned to England.

1431 Duncan Street
Key West, Fla.

November ?, 1949

Maria darling:

It is wonderful to know that you are once again in the ranks of the employed! I have noted your nylon size. This is a very tiny place and rather on the rough side and whiskey and rubber-goods are the only commodities that one can be at all sure of finding in stock. Is there anything you need in that line? But I will look around for nylons. I found a little jacket that I sent my sister for her birthday, made by the Indians of Guatemala, and perhaps I could send you one just like it for Xmas. I imagine that you would like the same things. I hear from the family that she made them a visit recently but declined to stay overnight as she said she felt more at home in the hospital. I expect I shall soon have another one of her inimitable little letters thanking me for the jacket. Have heard from Oliver. He sent me a beautiful montage made of the various snapshots and bits of postcards and bus-tickets and so forth that he had collected in Rome. The Clown did it quite beautifully. The allusion to the alligator pillow-case was very brief and ironic, saying that he had never had such a touching gift. It seems that the colored pictures have turned out well, especially the ones of the bicyclist encountered on the road to Brescia, and I am hoping that the Clown will send me some copies as the memory is one that we have in common.

We have a lovely little place here, [a] sort of Tom Thumb mansion, a snow white frame house of the Bahama type with a white picket fence and with lovely pink shutters and light green porch furniture. Grandfather has the whole downstairs to himself as the bellowing conversations in the morning between him and the maid make sleep impossible after her arrival at eight if you are on the same floor-level. He will not wear his hearing aid, is afraid to, and without it is stone deaf.

I have gone on a diet, only one meal a day, and have taken off 10

Key West, 1956

Maria's grand-
mother, Antonina
Pavlovna Mikoulina
Annovsky, in her
court costume,
St. Petersburg,
late 1870s

Tennessee's grand-
mother, Mrs. Walter
Dakin, with his
sister Rose. "Grand"
would slip five-
dollar bills in an
envelope for
Tennessee to keep
him going when
he was in dire need.

pounds. The face is not nearly so fishy—I hope. And the work goes well. I get out to the beach in the afternoons, with Grandfather and the Horse. We hope to leave for Europe in the late spring, providing my work is finished, and the plan is to go to England first, then Paris, then Copenhagen, then Stockholm and finally back down to Italy for the balance of the summer. Do you suppose I will finally get to see you on the stage?

With much love from your devoted, 10

MARIA was rehearsing with John Gielgud in London and living with her grandmother at the time.

On November 13, 1949, Maria's grandmother died unexpectedly.

"That morning, when I went up to say goodbye to Grandmama as usual, she asked me: 'When will I see you, my angel?' I replied: 'At five o'clock.'

"When I returned from the rehearsal, my grandmother was dead. On receiving the news, Tennessee asked me a question which only he would have asked: 'What were the last words your grandmother spoke to you?' 'Five O'Clock Angel' became Tennessee's pet name for me."

[*Handwritten on letterhead Key West, Florida, postmarked January 4, 1950*]

My dearest Maria:

I am deeply distressed for you by the news of your grandmother's death. By thinking of my own grandmother [Rose Dakin], who also died in January a few years ago [in 1944], on the day of Epiphany—I can understand your feelings. I was also out of the house when she was stricken ill but (perhaps unfortunately) returned during her last moments when I am sure that she, who would never admit even feeling not well, would not have wanted me there. But I am glad that you were in England to be close to her during her last months. She adored you and it will be a comfort to you, later, knowing that you were near her during that time.

She was an invalid, so you must not allow yourself to think of this as a tragedy and you must go on with your work and not go into mourning.

This week I am sending you the Gypsy dress that I mentioned, made by the Indians of Guatemala, and you must not hesitate to wear it because of the colors. Wear it in memory of your grandmother's warm Russian heart, which is yours!

With love—Tennessee.

———

TENNESSEE had loved the stories of Maria's grandmother's life in Tartary.

"The estates on the Volga had private landing stages, at which the riverboats would wait on their journey to Kazan. My great-grandmother received a telegram from her daughter in St. Petersburg: 'Come immediately. Baby Nina is going to be christened.' Great-grandmother, who must have been eccentrically unpunctual even for a Russian, replied, 'Marvellous, marvellous! I'll catch the first boat in the spring.' The boat remained hooting at the landing stage for days on end, with the peasants, who'd been there probably for weeks, bundled into the hold. Back came another telegram from St. Petersburg: 'Babushka, Babushka, come and see little Nina!' Spring, summer, autumn, the boats would remain whistling on the landing stage. Back and forth would come the frantic telegrams: 'I'll catch the last boat in the autumn.' The telegrams were sent regularly twice a year for twelve years. She missed all the boats for twelve years, and never saw her granddaughter."

———

[*Envelope marked Excelsior, Napoli*]

August 8, 1950

Maria darling:

I had every intention of coming over to London from Paris but the stay in Paris was very exhausting and I had to go directly to Rome to recuperate. My greatest regret is that I didn't get to see you. Rome is not nearly as nice as it was last summer. Mariella [Tennessee's previous landlady in Rome]'s apartment was rented to some embassy queen and we had to take a little flat over a motor-cycle garage that works twelve hours a day, sounding like the battle-front in Korea. The bedroom window faces the wrong way, so there is suffocating heat, and you can't sleep night or day. I have come here for a rest, to Positano, a little town built on a cliff between Sorrento and Amalfi. At first it appeared to be inhabited only by lesbians and goats, with the dikes predominating and the goats jumping over the cliff to avoid them. But this afternoon I went to a cocktail party and discovered there were a lot of interesting people, some completely bi-lingual Italians of the best class—that is, the cosmopolitan—and some women that must have been great beauties about twenty years ago and several boys from the Sadler's Wells Ballet. One boy wore only a pair of dainty white shorts and a diamond cross suspended from a heavy gold chain. When the hostess asked him to get somebody a drink, he was so cross at being asked to do anything that he threw the glass over the cliff! Luckily had a thermos of Scotch and water or I would never have made it. The Horse will have to come and fetch me out. He remained in Rome as we were expecting a cable. It is cool here and good swimming. I am reading the *Seven Pillars of Wisdom* which comes in handy as I have lost the habit of sleeping at night. Beside my bed I have a tray of cheese and fruit and a bottle of iced wine for any faint spells that may overtake me in the small watches.

Oliver is in Florida, Miami Beach, visiting the widow of the heir to the United Fruit fortune [Marion Vaccaro]. He died, the heir, rather abruptly and mysteriously a couple of years ago. He was an alcoholic with a glass eye who took ether when he gave up liquor and used to take out his glass eye and throw it at his mother-in-law, the widow of an Episcopal clergyman. The heiress (now a widow) is as big a queen as Oliver so they must be having a wonderful time together. Recently her diamonds were stolen by a sailor that turned "dirt" on her! As you may have heard, Oliver was badly injured in an auto smash-up. You remember how badly he drove in Italy, turning up that goat path on the road to Florence? I think his poems were pretty well received, although one notice was written by a rival poet whose poems consist entirely of punctuation and he took a dim view of Oliver's addiction to what he called "poems of statement."

Windham has fallen out with me, I am not sure why, just general principles I suppose. He does not answer my letters but I hear, indirectly, that he has gone from Sicily to Florence. His novel was brought out with no publicity or promotion and consequently had no sales, but I still think it is a great book, and will eventually be appreciated. Jane [Smith] remained in Paris and is studying for the opera while Tony stays in New York with several commissions for houses. We are leaving sometime late this month, going to Hollywood at Warner Brothers' expense [working on *Streetcar*], then back to Key West where I have bought the little house we occupied last winter. I still hope we can get over to London for a few days before we sail, if we sail from a French port.

Love, 10

P.S.—I am now in Naples. Positano was just a little too much. Having completely overwhelmed the goats, the dikes began to turn on the queens and the fur was flying! I took flight with a Dutch baroness who is part Javanese. She could not pay her bill at the Miramare so she gave the padrone a strong-box full of rocks and sea-shells, saying: "These are my jewels, all I have left in the world! I am afraid to leave them in the room while I'm gone!" As we left, he was examining the lock which was fortunately a combination lock that he will puzzle over for a long time!—Are there any new plays in London? Three of the Sadler's Wells boys were at Positano, cutting some fancy capers never seen on the stage at Covent Garden! I have a bag for you of peasant handicraft in bright Roman stripes which I will deliver to you if we sail out of Southampton.—I have been working so hard, and I am so dreadfully, dreadfully *tired*!—Oh, Maria, what *is* it all about?!!***?—Write me an immediate answer, Rome, American Express. We may be leaving in a few days now.

Much love as ever, 10
[*There is a drawing of a face in the 0 of the signature.*]

———

M A R I O N   V A C C A R O , née Black and nicknamed "the Banana Queen," and Oliver Evans became the prototypes of the characters in Tennessee's short story "Two on a Party," which eventually developed into *Sweet Bird of Youth*.

"I only met Marion Vaccaro, better known as 'the Banana Queen,' on two occasions. She was small, fair, fat, and drunk on both. Tennessee's immortal remark about her was that she created more problems than she solved as a travelling companion. I totally agreed. She and Oliver Evans were the original types for the short story 'Two on a Party.'"

Having shaken off the Irish peer, Maria was in love with a young man named Sebastian.

———

[*On letterhead Claridges, Brook Street, W.1., postmarked New York, September 6, 1950*]

Sunday-at-Sea

Maria darling!

I have just come from the Commodore's cocktail party: annoyed the old man quite visibly. He is mad about Churchill, regaled the company with endless anecdotes about him. I finally remarked that Churchill was really quite American, although only his mother came from Virginia.

The Horse has wired from New York. It seems that the plane was stranded in Newfoundland for eight hours! I suppose the Horse went out and grazed a bit on the tundra. I think that is what they call the vegetation in those bleak northern regions. He is now at the Algonquin, doubtless sucking his teeth as busily as ever the "Old One" [Gielgud] picked his nose.

I shall be waiting eagerly for news of matrimony. Somehow Sebastian seems very right to me. Even the occasional "nervous spells." I like the idea of you gracefully placing a handkerchief over his face now and then. But seriously, you and I have the same need of people who need us. And you would be happy with him. I do hope it works out! You could visit us in Key West for your honeymoon. And have the "master bedroom" with the sunporch.

Please don't forget to send me some Floral Cream for my hair which is in a sad state of disrepair. We will send you nylons if you will let me know the shade, size and thickness that you prefer. The Floral Cream is the only good hair-dressing I've ever found. It is made by Geo. F. Trumper, 9 Curzon Street, Mayfair, London. (The bottle being directly in front of me.)

The sea-air is stimulating, liquor available at all agitated moments and sleeping-pills holding out. I have done lots of work, investing the play [*The Rose Tattoo*] with mad comedy which I think you might like.

Have made one friend in the tourist section but we have a dreadful time getting through to each other. A regular steeplechase. By the time contact is established one is really too exhausted to care!

My address is care of Audrey [Wood], 551 Fifth Ave., for the time being. Give your mother my love and kiss Sebastian for me!

Love, Tenn

Thanks for everything in London!

———

"IN MARCH 1939, Molly Day Thacher, who was married to Elia Kazan, had been looking for plays for the Group Theatre. She offered a special prize of one hundred dollars to Tennessee for *American Blues,* a collection of one-act plays. She also sent them to Audrey Wood, an agent who had been a vaudeville dancer as a child. (There was a song at the time entitled 'Wee Audrey Wood,' a copy of which she showed me.) Audrey married her boss, the agent William Liebling, and managed what rapidly became the Liebling-Wood Agency. Shortly after that it became simply Audrey Wood. Audrey Wood was Tennessee's agent from 1939 to 1971."

———

[*Undated, November 1950*]

235 East 58th Street
N.Y.

Dear Maria:

You probably won't get a real honest to God letter from me for a couple of months, as I am up to my neck and down to my heels in putting on a play [*The Rose Tattoo*]. We got your long letter this morning and it brightened the day for us a great deal. I wish that you and Sebastian were closer to some conclusion but conclusions rarely occur in life, thank God. In fact, some people say they occur only once.

I think you were very wise in your choice of a hat for Sebastian's mother. Although I have never seen her, I accept your verdict regarding the desirability of obscuring her face. The Italian sun is very penetrating. I doubt that anything but a medieval helmet would be entirely effective. Does Sebastian take after her in appearance? This is a point we never covered, although you once told me you had to put a handkerchief over his face. Audrey Wood says this is cruel but I know you will appreciate realism.

Edith Sitwell is here and I am crazy about her. I think she is one old lady that you could tolerate. Edith Evans was not long for this world. That will please you. The Old One [Gielgud] must be here. We saw a picture of him descending from a plane with Fairy-Glum-from-Across-the-Ravine. [??] I guess you know who she is. There is a feeling here that his play will be a tremendous hit.

Oliver Evans is in New York. We have seen him every night. He was terribly dissatisfied with his classes. He has to teach freshman grammar to engineering students and is fighting violently with the head of his department as well as an elderly dowager of the first rank in financial and social circles who once made the mistake of trying to groom him for her spheres. He told her that she had the manners of a fishwife. In fact, she sent me a copy of the letter and says he'll never be allowed to enter her door. We shall still receive him. You might drop him a note of confidence c/o us and let us know if you improve on Sebastian's mother's disguise.

I might think of items of interest if I were not dictating this letter to you. It is a novel experience and a bit intimidating. The Horse is going to the dentist and God knows what will come of it.

Much love from us both, Tenn.

1 9 5 0

On December 29, 1950, *The Rose Tattoo,* directed by Daniel Mann, with Maureen Stapleton as Serafina Delle Rose and Eli Wallach as Alvaro Mangiacavallo had its first performance at the Erlanger Theatre, Chicago. The published version of the play is dedicated "To Frank in return for Sicily," and the name of the character Mangiacavallo means "eat a horse." The production transferred to the Martin Beck Theatre, New York City, on February 3, 1951. It was a commercial success, although some critics objected to the heavy-handed symbolism.

Edith Sitwell, on a lecture tour, had appeared as Lady Macbeth in a reading of Shakespeare's *Macbeth* at the Museum of Modern Art on November 16.

Edith Evans had taken a violent dislike to Maria on two counts. "First, I was foreign, and therefore unhealthy. Secondly, Gielgud and I got on so well together. In *Crime and Punishment,* in which Edith played the consumptive Mrs. Marmaladova, I played her daughter. She used to give me a vicious slap before curtain-up to get into character, and had inquired all through rehearsal as to how she should cough. As a Christian Scientist, she took pains to point out, she had never had a cough in her life. She learned to cough, however, loudly and clearly, all through John's speeches. There was a particularly difficult scene in which poor John was crouched on the floor in the corner of the stage, talking about blood on his bootlace—not an easy way to hold an audience. During this speech, Edith and I were to creep on in darkness to the other side of the set, and she was to have 'a mild itch in her throat.' I had to get a pillow and put it behind her head. Edith would then go into terrible fits of whooping cough, upstaging Johnny most awfully, drawing the audience's attention away from his scene to herself. He would wait in the wings afterwards and say, 'Can't you keep her quiet, darling?' He was too cowardly and too kind to say anything himself. After one particularly loud fit of choking, I lost my temper. I put the pillow over Edith's face and firmly held it down. I came off, and there was J.G. in the wings. 'Marvellous, darling. What did you do?' I said glumly, 'Nothing.' All hell broke loose. I was hauled up before Binkie and John in the morning. Binkie said quietly, 'We do not smother leading ladies if we wish to get on in the English theatre. We take them cups of tea.' Then, to cap it all, came one of King Wallah [Gielgud]'s bricks. Edith had an enormous death scene, center stage. Blocking it, Tony Quayle, the director, suggested I run offstage and fetch a glass of water. Gielgud cried out from the stalls, 'No, no! Everybody will be watching little Maria!' Edith said drily, 'I think I'll risk that.' "

———

1431 Duncan Street
Key West, Fla.

February 19, 1951

Darling Maria:

I have thought of you whenever I had a free and happy moment these last few months. Now that we have left New York, Chicago and Hollywood and returned to our little house in Key West, I hope those moments will happen more often. I know that they will. At the moment the house also contains Grandfather, Mother and Dinky Dakin (Dancing Daily!). Dinky Dakin is going back in the army. You guessed it, caught *again* in the draft! Mother is so upset that she fell down on her way home from church. Refused to get up and Frank had to fetch her in the car. Grandfather confided in me, "You don't know what I've been through with that tongue of hers!"—she has been keeping house for him while we were attending to professional matters in the North. Well, there is some hope that they will return to St. Louis on Wednesday. This is Monday. But we hope to survive. Grandfather, of course, will remain with us—until we go back to Europe in the late spring. Grandfather is hale and hearty. But when Dakin told Mother she fell down too often she said, "Ask Dr. Alexander about the state of my health!" But I am not too alarmed as she ate a very hearty "Shore Dinner" after the fall.

I am suffering from that vicious sort of cold called Virus X. Frank, Dakin and I went to the Bamboo Room tonight and I had two planter's punches, each containing a triple shot of rum, thinking it might help my cold, but I am afraid the help is only temporary. I have a fever, which I always like. It helps me with my writing. Windham returned. He gave me the ties and they were divided among us. We are all so pleased with the ones we selected, especially the Horse who got the best. Windham seems a bit morbid. He told me that he had heard that I had told *two* people that he was going *blind*! I think that's a little far-fetched. One-eyed Riley would not call the kettle black. Surely one can think of some better reason not to like me! But as far as I'm concerned we are still good friends. It is just that he looks at me with such a cold eye these days.

I am delighted to hear your mother is doing the new Chekhov translation. I hope it's *The Sea Gull* and that it will be running when we come back to Europe. We plan to leave early in May and want to visit England and

Copenhagen first, buy a small English car and drive down to Italy. A
bientôt!

Love, Tenn.

———

TENNESSEE called himself "one-eyed Riley." He had had several
operations for a cataract and he thought, self-consciously and wrongly, that
they had left him slightly wall-eyed.

Maria's mother, Mary Britneva, was in fact translating *The Three Sisters*.
Maria understudied the role of Irina in the production, directed by Peter
Ashmore, which opened on May 3, 1951, at the Aldwych Theatre, London,
with Ralph Richardson, Margaret Leighton, Celia Johnson and Renée
Asherson.

Madame Britneva was appalled at the size and redness of the actresses'
hands. In Russia, Madame Britneva and her sisters had been instructed by
their English governess, Miss Fanny, to hold up their hands and wave them
as guests were arriving at her parents' estate, all the while shouting, *"Gosti!
Gosti yedut!"* ("Guests! Guests are coming!"), until the blood drained into
their arms and their hands appeared whiter still.

Maria became ill with appendicitis. Although there were complications,
their seriousness was gravely exaggerated by Tennessee. Oliver Evans, who
had been suffering from increasing deafness, underwent surgery on his ear.

"Tennessee, as a rule, worked on several manuscripts at the same time;
it is not always possible to pinpoint exactly which plays or stories he is
referring to."

———

[*Envelope postmarked Rome, June 30, 1951*]

Dearest Maria:

I am looking forward to your joining us somewhere in Italy when the
show comes off. I am already getting a bit restless in Rome. For the first
two weeks here I wrote a great deal, but then the Roman languor or "febbre
Tevere" as they call it set in and now I can only knock out two or three
pages a day with effort. Unfortunately there are not really nice beaches
anywhere around Rome and the swimming pools, you remember how they
are—the water tepid and crowded and you'd rather not have to taste it. I've
been taking little excursions here and there in the Jaguar but haven't yet
found a place nearby that suits me. The Horse is delighted with Rome and
of course wants to stay here, but I do think I shall have to find a brisker

climate where I can get the essential exercise to keep my nerves in order. I'll wait till you're free to travel. Then perhaps we can make a really big jump to some place like the island of Mallorca or the Costa Brava of Spain!

Three of my dearest friends have had serious operations in the last few days: you, then Oliver, and now Audrey. Poor Audrey's I think is probably the most serious of you all. She had "several tumors" removed unexpectedly—thought it was just appendicitis! A letter from Oliver says his surgeon is practically certain that the ear-operation was a success, though he is still bandaged up and has to remain in Chicago for a while before he knows for absolutely sure. But he does hear sounds, so he knows the auditory nerve was not killed. That's the great danger in this operation. He was strapped to the table for *six hours,* my dear, while they were sawing away at his skull and making little adjustments! I do hope they removed the constant image of "trade!" while restoring the sense of sound. . . .

I have lots to tell you, but I don't want to tire you now. Such a sweet letter from Sandra [Molostvova]. Please give her my love and say that I will write when I am a little bit less exhausted. Remember, me, also, to your mother, and John Perry if he's about. I am pleased that he behaved as he did and had the talk with Paul; it bears out my impression of him.

Saluti, auguri, amore! 10

———

SANDRA (Alexandra) Molostvova's mother had died of diabetes in Florence when Sandra was four years old. Maria and Sandra had been brought up as sisters. Sandra herself contracted diabetes when she was about twelve. By 1951 her condition had deteriorated so much that she had to be hospitalized.

———

[*From Rome*]

July 12, 1951

Maria dear:

It has just occurred to me, suddenly, that you might not be going back to the play [*The Three Sisters*] for a few weeks and that you could meet me at St. Tropez for a rest on the sea. I probably need it as badly as you do. I was going up in the Jaguar. Frank would drive with me as far as Genoa, then go to Venice while I continued to St. Tropez. Now I am putting the trip off again, for I don't think I would really enjoy it all by myself, and the Horse cannot stand the seashore, not after the long stay in Key West where there was nothing else but the sea! And the Horse, for some reason, will *not* go into the water. You'd *almost* think that he was made of sugar. You can imagine his exasperation at the reversal of plans this morning, after he had done all the packing! Well, I shall go somewhere, but no place quite so far, at least not with the auto.

A wire from Oliver: "Operation brilliant success. Normal hearing restored to right ear." Isn't that splendid? But my other best friend in the States, Paul Bigelow, is going into the hospital to have one whole side of his jaw removed, my dear! Osteomyelitis, which he has had many years, now suddenly become acute and an immediate operation is necessary. Then Audrey, with her operation. She thought it was just an appendectomy but several "unexpected tumors" were discovered and she's had to leave the office for a long convalescence in the country. And your operation!—this has been the summer of operations. *Who will be next?*

I was so pleased with the Old One [Gielgud]'s great success in *Winter's Tale.* Should have wired him and Peter Brook but of course I didn't. The complications of sending telegraphic messages from Italy seem [*changed from* "are"] so enormous, and the hours they're open and the location of the offices are so inconvenient. Even mailing a letter seems a monumental undertaking in this Roman lassitude that I am falling into. Please thank Sandra for her letter. I hope she is out of the clinic and feeling well again. I wish that all of us were feeling well again!

You never told me the charges for the long distance call. I'm enclosing a check anyway, and if there's anything left over, take the little mother to the Ivy [Restaurant].

Love, Tenn.

[*From Rome*]

August 3, 1951

Dear Maria:

I busted up my car on the way to St. Tropez, drove it into a tree at seventy miles an hour and the whole side was bashed in. I have been a wreck ever since, although I wasn't seriously hurt in the crash. The shock was terrific. My typewriter flew out of the back seat of the car and hit me on the head. You should see the dent in the typewriter case! For some reason I only had a slight abrasion above the hairline.

The worse effect has been insomnia. I go three nights without sleeping more than a total of one or two hours, in spite of Seconals and liquid "calmatives." I hope I will slowly recover my equilibrium. I went to Munich and Venice by train but was not in any condition to enjoy them, so after two weeks I came back to Rome. It is now the "Solleone," the Lion Sun, and the heat barely credible but I try to keep on working.

The hair-dressing arrived. It was here when I returned and it is not the particular kind I had before but it is almost equally good and I am so thankful to have it. It was wonderful of you to remember it in the middle of all your little difficulties!

Don't you think it may really be good for you that you have to keep on working? Otherwise you might have too much time to brood about things? I find regardless of how I feel it is always better to keep myself occupied at something, and I think the reason the Horse is so nervy and temperamental is that he has absolutely nothing, but NOTHING, to do! I don't think I could stand another year without him being busy at something, and so I'm going to do everything in my power to get him to go to a secretarial school when we get back to the States. If not that, *both* of us to a good analyst!

I wish I had stayed in England this summer. The Cavendish and a good pool and the plays and our late suppers at the Ivy would have made a better time for me. . . .

Love, 10

———

"On his last trip to London, Tennessee had stayed at the Cavendish Hotel. The Cavendish had been given to the reputed mistress of Edward VII, Rosa Lewis, who charged the champagne consumed by her favorite clients to her richest. She was the model for Evelyn Waugh's Lottie Crump in *Vile Bodies*. The night porter at the hotel was called Mr. Moon. Later, Tennessee was to call his dog by the same name.

"Carson was also in London at the time. Tennessee and I used to have quiet little lunches at the back restaurant. There was a waitress there called Rose, who was very protective of Tennessee, particularly when Carson used to appear waving her walking-stick tipsily, grinning, chops hanging. We were having a particularly amusing meal when there was suddenly a wild cry from Rose, 'Look out, sir, she's coming!' Whereupon we both dived under the tablecloth.

"Tennessee immediately became stricken with remorse, and crawled out onto Carson's foot, bleating, 'Oh, Carson! I just dropped my napkin!' Carson looked at the two of us crouched on the floor. She had always been jealous of the fun we had together. 'And so did Maria,' added Tennessee.

"During our consequently glummer lunch, Choppers ate nothing, just drank and grinned. She'd had a slight stroke, and one of her hands was like a little hook. I was deeply mistrustful of this hand. We went upstairs to Tennessee's suite, where there was a piano. Carson sat down and ran an arpeggio down the keys with her good hand. 'Carson, why don't you play us a tune?', I said. She grinned, and before you could say Jack Robinson, the hook had descended and she was playing like Schnabel. I hissed at Tennessee, 'I told you so!' The music abruptly stopped. As abruptly, the hook re-appeared."

———

[*From Rome on letterhead Cavendish Hotel, 81 Jermyn Street, St. James's, S.W.1, with note in handwriting and arrow pointing to the address: "Can you reserve the suite again at?"*]

September 18, 1951

Dearest Maria:

I am still in Rome. I have been swimming every day at the Foro Italico pool instead of going to the beach, which is perhaps just as well. I am feeling better, more rested.

So far not a word from Peter Glenville, although I sent him a long wire. Last I heard was that rehearsals would start about October 10th, so I suppose I don't need to get back to London before the last week in September, and that they will hold off decisions on the smaller parts until then. [*Added in handwriting*] I shall do *all in my power* to get you "Nellie."

I do wish you would let me know if you have any more information. I sent them a lot of photographs of the Copenhagen sets for the play, which were lovely. I think the set is very important. The man who did them there is eager to do them in London. He is a fine designer and very, very nice.

The Jaguar is back and it looks like new and goes well. The Horse is behaving better. He was a great success in Copenhagen, they were mad for his dark charms! As a dishwater blond, I didn't do nearly so well.

Horse has just entered apartment. Gives me a quick glance over his shoulder, full of enigmas! He is reading *Nicholas Nickleby* in the public squares . . .

Says he is going to have complete new set of blankets made in London. When does your play [*The Three Sisters*] close? Why don't you meet me in Paris on my way back? We can do some shopping and fly over together. Audrey says I have francs there.

My love to the little mother, and much to little Sandra.

A letter from Peter [Glenville]. Says he plans to see you. I have just written him a very strong letter about you. The Horse is in bed, cross as two sticks—no, as five or six sticks! Claims to have a bad stomach. But I think the bad temper came first. What are we going to do with him?! Naturally no packing has been done, and nothing else. I have been working feverishly as the weather has been stimulatingly cool, but tomorrow I leave for three or four days on the beach. Then directly to Paris and a plane across the channel. John [Perry] says I should arrive early in October.

[unsigned]

————

THE BRITISH director Peter Glenville had been lined up by Tennent to direct the English production of *Summer and Smoke.*

Maria met Tennessee and Frank in Paris for the shopping spree. "We rushed into the bank, threw open a deposit box and stuffed our pockets full of francs. Frank bought himself several silk shirts, and I bought a suit by Jacques Fath. Tennessee lost most of his francs."

Sandra Molostvova went into a coma on September 27. Tennessee, despite his terror of flying, flew to London at the beginning of October to be with Maria. Sandra veered in and out of consciousness until her death on October 11.

"Sandra was spiritually the most extraordinarily developed person, and had total integrity. Her impact on those who met her was instant and unforgettable. When the Russian priest visited her in hospital, he urged her to make a full confession. She told him she was not going to curry favor with God; she was not afraid and did not feel like confessing. She turned him out of her room. Tennessee brought Sandra a beautiful antique cup with pink roses on it. When he came into her sick room, she was too ill to speak. She smiled and pointed to the cup. He was very touched.

"One day when he came with me to the clinic, I went in to Sandra's room and stayed for at least two hours. On emerging, to my astonishment, Tennessee was still sitting outside on a chair. 'Tennessee, I thought you'd gone back to your hotel!' Tennessee said, 'As long as I'm here, you'll never come out of that room alone.' And I never did."

Maria and her mother were with Sandra as she was dying. Tennessee went to fetch the Russian priest. "Tennessee spoke of the incident much later. He said, 'I'll never forget, when I brought the priest into the room, seeing you bending over little Sandra—you were holding the Russian cross to her lips.' "

After Sandra's funeral Tennessee wrote the following poem:

A WREATH FOR ALEXANDRA MOLOSTVOVA

For Maria Brit-Neva

It is well to remember, to celebrate and remember,
    how as we entered the shadowy vault of St. Phillip's,
bearing her roses among us,
    five tall solemn men
in the plain gray clothes of the street,
    burst into song,
and the reverence of candles . . .

It is well to remember those tall solemn men
    in the clothes they wore on the street,
their faces unweeping but solemn as a departure,
giving her praise as we bore her roses among them,
    and how chill it was till we entered,
and then it was warm, and the reverence of candles . . .

It is well to remember, to celebrate and remember
    the chant of her name, Alexandra,
its repetition and the solemnity of it,
    the name Alexandra,
as if an iron bell rang and continued ringing,
    the stately name Alexandra
and again, Alexandra . . .

It is well to remember the chill of the vault made warm
    by the entrance of roses
and the candles' reverence and those tall solemn men
    in the plain gray clothes of the street,
    chanting her name, Alexandra,
the incantation of her name, Alexandra . . .

But it is also well for you to forget,
    little sister, Maria,
to give her peace and forget,
to place in her hands this wreath and a silent white cross of
    Russia
    while saying farewell
and whispering, Sleep, Alexandra . . .

Maria was cast in the small role of Rosemary in the English production of *Summer and Smoke*. It was directed by Peter Glenville and designed by Reece Pemberton and William Chappell, with Margaret Johnston as Alma Winemiller and William Sylvester as John Buchanan, Jr. The production began with a tryout in Cambridge on November 5, moved to Brighton on November 12 and opened in London, at the Lyric Theatre, Hammersmith, on November 22.

————

[*On letterhead Cunard Line, R.M.S.* Queen Elizabeth, *envelope postmarked New York, November ?, 1951, sent to Maria c/o* Summer and Smoke *company, Theatre Royal, Brighton*]

Monday, 12:30 p.m.

Dearest Maria—

The voyage was easier and pleasanter than I had expected. Gadg is in a good mood and full of enthusiasm for the project [*Camino Real*]. He stimulated me to the point of a little rewriting. We arrive this afternoon, go to Gladstone Hotel first, then take a look at Oliver's selection of an apartment for us. A friend of yours, a Miss Marina Baistow or something like that, wrote me a letter from "Cabin Class" inviting me to have a drink with her, but I didn't reply till midnight when it appeared that Gadg might be able to use some female company. She didn't appear but sent us her telephone no. in New York. Should I call her?

We have a list of things for you, and we'll get them off "le plus vite possible," if not "tout de suite." The Horse bore up fairly well—except one day when he "threw up" five times, once while making a dash down the main lounge, quite spectacular.

Give Micky and Rupert my love.

Much to you, darling—Tenn

————

MISS MARINA BOWATER, as she was in fact named, was a friend of Maria's from childhood.

"Micky," Lady Rupert Nevill, wife of Lord Rupert Nevill, was another childhood friend.

————

1951

[*On letterhead Gladstone, 114–122 East 52nd Street at Park Avenue, New York City*]

November 17, 1951

Darling Maria:

There have been great goings-on here. Right now we are suspended in air, waiting breathlessly for Marlon Brando to make up his mind. He is the only one that seems right to play the male lead in both short plays, and he is interested but claims that he needs a week in which to consult his analyst about it and make the proper spiritual adjustment. He has been going to this analyst two years and still is confused! Meanwhile we are stuck in this hotel, just waiting, waiting! The Horse is twice as nervous as I am.

What happened at Brighton? The silence is ominous!

I am trying to work up the courage to call Donnie and deliver your prints [engravings] to him. Everyone is seething with malicious gossip here, tongues working at both ends against the middle, it all seems fantastic when you suddenly come back to it.

Please do something for me. See the editor of that magazine, Daniel Farson, 57 Beauchamp Place, and read the short story I gave him ["Two on a Party"]. I think it may be a mistake to bring it out before the play has opened, and I want a paragraph cut out of it (continuation of some dialogue) at the top of page fifteen. If that cut is made, I think it may be all right.

We have not yet had the time to go shopping but Frank has the list of things you want and we'll take care of it early this week. Thanks for the reviews you sent [of *Summer and Smoke* in Cambridge], they made me very happy. And do send the ones that we get in London, no matter what they may be. My sister is "on parole" from the sanitarium and Dinky Dakin is coming home for Thanksgiving. I'm going to visit them for a few days. Grandpa has fled to Memphis, his usual retreat at the Hotel Gayoso. Soon as we get settled we will send for him.

Love—Tenn.

[*Telegram sent December 18, 1951*]

DARLING MARIA IT'S AN ILL VAPORE [WIND] THAT BLOWS NO GOOD LOVE AND MORE LOVE TENNESSEE

AT THIS TIME, Maria's mother was beginning to show the symptoms of Parkinson's disease.

"Tennessee had given me a small Victorian good-luck ring of pearls and a tiny diamond. In *Summer and Smoke,* there is much talk of a ring. I was understudying Margaret Johnston as Miss Alma, and therefore imprecating the gods to let her fall and break her legs. She had the temerity to ask me if I would let her wear the ring during the run of the play. With my eyes narrowed to slits, I refused. The gods were on my side, for once—I eventually took over from her as Miss Alma.

"My performance as Miss Alma must have gone off moderately well. Margaret Johnston, to whom I was understudy, came scuttling back, despite a broken leg, a hacking cough, and a total lack of memory. She was begged by the management to continue her convalescence, but valiantly refused."

[*From New York City*]

December 22, 1951

Dearest Maria:

I wrote you a long, long letter while I was touring about the South with Gadg [working on *Camino Real*]. Left it in the Memphis hotel where I picked up Grandfather. It was forwarded to me, but I suspect it may have been intercepted by Liebling as I gave their office address for forwarding. I think it was not sealed and it contained some fairly unflattering comments on his capabilities as a producer, so I doubt that either of us will ever see it.

To shorten a long story, Liebling did not raise the money for the production. Irene [Selznick] bought a good new play and shot it to Gadg. *Camino Real* has been postponed till next season!

I'm rather glad about it, now, although I was fairly annoyed at the time. There was something inauspicious about the the whole thing, and the script needed lots more work. Next season we can get Eli Wallach. But meanwhile I had taken a four months' lease on an expensive apartment here. Now we are not going to occupy it. Grandfather and I are leaving for New Orleans Monday, we'll stay down there till the Jaguar arrives from England—it's still at sea!—and the Horse drives it south to join us in Key West. Oliver is going to New Orleans with me. I gave him the round trip for a Xmas present with the practical consideration that he might serve as some protection when I run into Valentina or Pancho down there. It's my first visit to New Orleans since 1947 and I'm very excited about it.

I'm also thrilled over the news that *Summer* is going into the Duchess, which I remember as a lovely little house, and of course by the news that you got to play Alma. Please tell me how that went off.

With so much going on, so much agitation and indecision and all, I did almost nothing about Xmas. But yesterday I did send Peter Glenville a charming antique silver cigarette-case that was made in Russia in about 1840. I hope it gets through customs okay and he likes it. Customs is so difficult, I thought it would be wiser to send you this check so you can get yourself something or just use the money. I know how you squander your salary! Out of it I wish you would purchase a little Christmas corsage for Margaret Johnston and a boutonniere for "John" [Perry].

You know the Key West address, don't you? It's 1431 Duncan Street, and we'll be there about January 7th. Gadg wants to make a film with me in the spring but I want to return in early April to Europe. Maybe it will work out both ways. [The] Oliviers are a sensational hit here, of course. The Dame has [George] Tabori's new play [*Flight into Egypt*] and it's far too good! I called her "treacherous!" in public. There were tears and protestations and lavish gifts for Christmas! But she got Gadg and I got what the little boy shot at. . . . When shall I see you, my angel?—Before five o'clock, I hope!———

Love & Love, 10

———

[*From Frank Merlo to Maria, from New York, handwritten on unheaded paper*]

Darling—

We have been rather busy. The play has been off and on so often I am happy the whole business is resolved finally and [illegible] it really comes off next fall—or at least that's what has been decided the last time we talked together. Gadg is now doing a play by George Tabori—an English writer. I must say the play is very exciting to read. Naturally Irene is doing it. We're looking to invest money in it; it is so good.

The holidays were a bore. Tenn left for New Orleans the day before Christmas and I am to meet him in Key West as soon as the car arrives from England this week. Oliver is with him and I can well imagine what they are doing down there without my nagging presence to restrain at least one member of that duo. Mr. Dakin, Tenn's grandfather, is along. One day I called him on the telephone and he pleaded with me most urgently to come down as soon as possible. Valentina is giving Tenn her house for a week.

How is the play going? Delighted that you played Alma for a few days. Wish it could be for all time. Love to your mother. Most fondly,

Frank (or) "One Who Wishes You Well"

―――――

"TENNESSEE was astounded that he had written me a letter, as Frankie never wrote to anybody.

"Part Russian, part Romanian, Valentina had appeared suddenly from under a stone, like an adventuress, with a lot of money. Her vulgarity was unparalleled. I remember one evening we'd all met for a drink at the Ritz in London, and she had a blinding row with the Horse. He insulted her in no uncertain terms. She screamed back at him, 'How dare you talk to me like that *in the Ritz!*' This became a catch-phrase between the three of us. Pancho had been a friend of Tennessee's before I knew him. He was extremely violent. I've been told that a lot of him surfaced in Stanley Kowalski, in *Streetcar.*"

―――――

[*Handwritten letter, envelope postmarked Key West, February 5, 1952*]

Dearest Maria:

When I finish work and am too tired to write letters, even to you, my five o'clock angel, the mere sight of the typewriter makes me gag. It was a shock to realize, today, that you must have already opened at the Duchess and in spite of your repeated warnings I had failed to wire the magnificent company. I can never praise them or thank them all enough for giving me back that play which the cruel failure in America had destroyed for me.

Grandfather, the Horse, and I are back in Key West, and I have two writing projects to complete before I can leave the country, a film script [*Baby Doll*] for Gadg and the re-write of *Camino.* I am so glad now that the play was put off, it was providential, for it would have failed in its original form, but I think the new version stands a better chance and Gadg has promised to produce it in the fall.

Frank is cooking for us, as the Swede servant can't even boil water. He is not satisfied with simple dishes but sits up till the wee hours poring over exotic cook books such as *Cordon Bleu* and each evening he devises some new astonishment in the kitchen, such as red snapper stuffed with spinach and codfish immersed in a sauce containing two kinds of wine. *Nothing* can be permitted to taste like what it is! Around four every p.m. Grandfather enquires in a tremulous voice, Are we eating *out* tonight? A negative response is likely to make him ask for a stiff drink.

We have a guest, the fabulous [Paul] Bigelow. I'm sure you've heard us speak of him. Since his recent jaw operation his face is slightly more symmetrical than it once was, but as you can see from the enclosed photo, snapped in a local bistro, he does not have features of classic regularity, even now. But he *is* a fantastic and rare character, you would love him. Valentina gave us her house in New Orleans, wouldn't even permit me to pay for the long distance calls. Oliver was with me. I gave him the trip for Xmas. He is well—won a $200 prize for best lyric poem published in '51.

Carson [McCullers] has sailed for Italy with her husband. We were at least formally reconciled. Poor dear girl, I hope she is happier there than she was in England, though I fear it is to be "grappa" instead of gin.

The film [*Rose Tattoo*] is to be shot on location in Mississippi and I will probably stay in States till it's completed in May. Then England, Sicily, Greece, and Helsinki for the Olympic Games.

I am worried about your precious little mother. What is wrong? Is she better now?

My love to all at the Duchess.

Grandfather celebrates his *95th* birthday in April—on Shakespeare's birthday.

Getting sleepy—

Love to you, my angel. It will soon be five, I hope.

Tennessee

———

MARIA could not find her next letter from Tennessee, which evidently contained disparaging remarks about Frank. *Summer and Smoke,* a revival of which would be the unexpected hit of the New York season, had finished an unexpectedly short run in London.

———

Hotel Monteleone
New Orleans 12, La., U.S.A.

March 29, 1952

Dearest Maria:

I am ashamed of that last letter I wrote you. I was crying into my gin instead of drinking it on the rocks with a little crushed mint and sugar as a southern gentleman should do.

My feeling about *Summer and Smoke* is entirely happy, for I saw it done better than I had ever hoped it could be done, but of course I am a little perplexed at the shortness of the run. I suppose people just don't care enough about the Almas and Roses and Sandras of this world as they ought to, or I was not able to put it into sufficiently eloquent words to make them care that much.

I have been in Hollywood, darling, for the past two weeks. A dreadful thing has happened about Gadg. It broke in one of the Hollywood columns that Gadg had once been a Communist, and almost immediately they put him in the deep freeze out there. It was timed exactly with our arrival for discussions with Warners about the new film script [*Baby Doll*]; consequently everything was stalled and obfuscated. They are waiting to see what will happen next. There is even the possibility of a jail sentence if he persists in his determination not to reveal names of other party members when he was in it. This I think very admirable of him, and very brave, and all decent people ought to respect his sense of honor about it. But of course most of them don't! Of course Gadg is not a Communist now and I know has absolutely no present sympathy with the system, but the red hysteria has reached such a pitch that this disclosure may very well wreck his career as a motion-picture director.

This also came at the same time as Gadg's first big failure on Broadway. The Dame [Irene Selznick]'s play, *Flight into Egypt* [by George Tabori], came a terrific cropper. I saw the final run-through, not the opening, and I must confess that Gadg and the actors did a bad job on it. It was a good play, but it was over-produced. The scenes were played too hard and heavy, so that the simple truth was lost in a lot of highly virtuoso theatricality. You couldn't see the characters for the staging! That's the sort of mistake that very good directors sometimes make—they get too imaginative for their material. I guess it happens more often here than in England.

Well, I'm stopping over in New Orleans for a couple of days on my way back to the Key where Grandfather and the Horse are waiting for me. Guess what happened to our friend Oliver? His father died and he has come into a very nice little inheritance. Even after taxes it may amount to about fifty thousand, and he has already bought a Cadillac and last night he took me out to dinner. One can only feel happy about it, as the father was a total imbecile and had been for months before his death.

Do take a holiday! We sail June 11th on the Liberté and if we don't see you in London will summon you to Paris. I say "we" as if I felt quite certain the Horse were going with me. Actually I don't know. He is going through some curious phase right now which I can't pretend to understand. I think

I am not at all clever about people unless they're people of my own invention. I no longer complain about the Horse's behavior. He has a perfect right to behave as he chooses, and I can't say that he has ever deliberately done anything to hurt me, and [he] has been very kind to Grandfather. Please forget my other letter!

Read a book by an English author [Walter Baxter] called *Look Down in Mercy*. Also a mad, mad play called *Ubu Roi* written by a Frenchman [Alfred Jarry] in 1896, the first surrealist work for the theatre and one of the funniest things ever written. It's printed by Gabberbochus Press in London and distributed here by New Directions. It would be wonderful for Peter Brook, but I don't suppose the censors would permit.

With love, Tenn.

Truman Capote's play, *The Grass Harp*, opened in New York Thursday. I've only seen one notice, the *Times,* which was a rave notice and I, of course, am insanely jealous! How I do hate myself for it!

JOSÉ QUINTERO successfully revived *Summer and Smoke* at the Circle in the Square in New York City on April 24, 1952, with Geraldine Page as Alma Winemiller and Lee Richard as John Buchanan, Jr.

"It made Geraldine Page's career, but she was to remark publicly, when we held a celebration at the Actors Studio for his life's work, that she 'didn't really like Tennessee.' The tastelessness of the remark on such an occasion enraged me. I ticked her off, just as publicly."

James Laughlin announced his intention to marry Maria when he was "free of other obligations." Maria told Tennessee but otherwise kept this a close secret.

[*?, New York City*]

May 27, 1952

Dearest Maria:

I am bursting with joy, purely unselfish joy, over the news in your letter, and you may trust me not to breathe a word of it to anyone but the Horse, who will share my happiness for you. J. [Laughlin] is the grandest person I have known in my life, the finest and purest, and just thinking about him does much to redeem my rather middling opinion of many of the other members of the human race. And that you who hold a similar place in my heart should be joined to him is just too wonderful! It seems like the old-time happy ending of fairy-tales; but, darling, when I think of the horrors of last summer, of Sandra, of your struggle against the coldness and indifference of Tennent's, of the awful business with Paul, it seems that nothing less wonderful than this could compensate for all that you have been through with so much endurance and strength and dignity. Oh, I really am very happy about it, and don't let anything spoil it, now. It is even more wonderful for Jay than it will be for you. J. needs someone of your nature to lighten and brighten his life, and someone of your grace and charm. I hope he knows it and doesn't forget it. As for J. being parsimonious, I quite agree. Almost everybody who knows him smiles over this eccentricity, which is so very odd in a man of such great wealth as J. must be. But J. is only mean about little things, never about big things, and he has great generosity of the heart which is far more important than the pocketbook, don't you agree? You will be happy together, I think. I know. And, oh, how happy it will make your precious little mother to know that you are settled and not just flopping around in the mischievous breezes of chance!

Will you still be in Italy this summer? Oliver hopes so, too.

Darling, *Summer and Smoke* is having a big success here in a revival at an "arena style" theatre and the girl doing it is even better than Maggie Johnston was, which was very good indeed, and the young director, José Quintero, is my new enthusiasm in the world of drama. If Gadg quits the theatre, which seems likely, now, Quintero will be, at last, another director that I could work with.

Do you think Peter Brook would be interested in doing a production of the new *Camino Real* in London, prior to its Broadway production? If he does it very well, and Gadg won't or can't, he could also do it on Broadway. I think it is a very exciting and highly plastic sort of thing now. No one has yet seen it. Poor Gadg may not be able to work again in New York as he "informed" about his Communist friends in Hollywood and most theatre people feel it was a betrayal of old friendships and there is great hostility toward him.

I take no attitude about it, one way or another, as I am not a political person and human venality is something I always expect and forgive. But I am not yet sure that Gadg will not disappoint me, personally, as he did with *Tattoo*. That remains to be seen. I haven't written his movie-script for him. I am very tired and can't wait to set foot on the Liberté June 11th. We will land at Le Havre. I would rather meet you in Italy than Paris this summer but we must certainly meet somewhere.

Much love, best wishes with all my heart! Tenn.

THE FIRST London production of *Camino Real,* with Denholm Elliott as Kilroy and Diana Wynyard as Camille, did not take place until April 8, 1957, at the Phoenix Theatre. It was directed by Peter Hall and established his reputation.

In July, Tennessee was in Rome for discussions about the film of *The Rose Tattoo* starring Anna Magnani.

Maria was working in Paris. She had a small part in the film *Moulin Rouge* directed by John Huston.

"Tennessee came onto the set of *Moulin Rouge,* and we'd sit up until three or four or five in the morning. John Huston would drink Pernod with us in the little bars. Huston refused to look at Zsa Zsa Gabor all through the movie, while he was directing her, and played poker through all of her scenes. Very occasionally he would glance in her direction and say, 'That's great, Zsa Zsa.' "

[*Envelope marked 45 Via Aurora, Rome, to Maria at Hôtel du Pont Royal, rue du Bac, Paris*]

July 2, 1952

Dearest Maria:

I meant to get this off to you yesterday but a *paralyzing* heat is over Rome, you can hardly creep through it, and nothing gets done. I don't think I will be able to stick it out for long, for one thing it makes work all but impossible, it's just like somebody had pumped you full of a stupefying drug, so I will take to my heels or the Jaguar pretty quickly and seek a cooler retreat. Fortunately I did finish my revisions on *Camino* before I got here. Saw Magnani on the street the first evening with her lover. She said she was going to the country for five days and would see me when she got back, she was very cordial and warm and I do think it terrible of them not to respond to my wire to the States. You might mention the situation to [John] Huston. He might be interested or know how to interest other people, such as Rank. Darling, I am sending this cheque post-haste, for I know you will want to remain in Paris while you're in touch with Huston and there is any prospect of a job. The Horse is going about constantly with a male whore here, and while I don't take a moral attitude, I do think this sort of company is very bad for him. The philosophy of such boys is so hard and cynical and association with them, constantly, is bound to have a corrupting effect. Also it's a public embarrassment, for when we sit down at a sidewalk table, the boy, Alvaro, is there and immediately his underworld associates begin to group about us and tell loud dirty stories and the Italians listen and stare. You simply can't get away with that sort of thing here, it has to be done very quietly and privately, then the Romans don't mind it, they only object when a public show is made of it. I can't talk to Frank about this without his flying off the handle and saying I am trying to run his life, etc.! That was one of the reasons I left Rome last summer, and will doubtless be one of the reasons I leave it this one. . . .

Please keep me informed how things are going. Did you mail my two letters, to Gadg and Cheryl [Crawford]? Do you know I am just too exhausted to mail my revisions of *Camino,* and the Horse is of course too preoccupied with his life in the "haut monde"!

Your snobbish but devoted friend, Tennessee

[*Added in handwriting*] P.S. Left my gabardine topcoat in Paris. *Will* you enquire? Will send you a story to sell for me (with commission) in London, wrote on the train.

————

CHERYL CRAWFORD was a founding member of the Group Theatre and a director, with Elia Kazan, of the Actors Studio. She produced *The Rose Tattoo* and *Camino Real.*

"Gadg, when I was in the Actors Studio, had once picked me out of the class and asked me to take the plans for the new Studio to Cheryl, who was waiting with the architect. He gave me five dollars—an enormous sum—for the taxi.

"I beckoned to my great chum Jimmy O'Rea and we left the building and, to Jimmy's astonishment, walked to Bloomingdale's. We bought me two pairs of nylon stockings, had a cream tea at Rumpelmayer's, and then took a bus and delivered the plans to Cheryl, who by this time was fit to be tied."

Maria travelled to Rome for a holiday. There, Tennessee organized, with deep trepidation, a meeting between Maria and Anna Magnani.

"Tennessee was convinced that we would not get on, and spent a lot of time sighing and rolling his eyes to heaven, and popping pink pills into his mouth. We met on the Via Veneto. Anna was dressed in black and wearing some very curious black shoes.

"We took one look at one another, and both adored each other. Anna at this time spoke very little English, and so we spoke French. For want of anything better to say, I said, 'What lovely shoes you have on!' Anna, with a yell of delight, took them off and gave them to me. I took mine off, threw them into the gutter, and donned Anna's, who walked barefoot."

———

45 Via Aurora
[Rome]

July 7, 1952

Dearest Maria:

I have been travelling and working and entertaining various visitors to the city, the latest of which is Dame Selznick. I gave a small cocktail party for her last night, and unlike some that I have given in the past, it was attended by a few of the ones invited, but it was a shambles. I did not have time to prepare for it and the Horse had vanished into the Casbah, as usual. Five minutes before the guests arrived I had to run out and purchase liquor and flowers and "solid refreshments." Then I discovered that Mariella had a single chunk of ice not much larger than the Dame's smallest diamond. We drank warm gin, passing the single chunk of ice back and forth among us like the single eye of the fatal sisters in the Perseus legend. Swiss cheese was served on great square crackers that made a terrific noise in the mouth, the carnations drooped, conversation expired, it was certainly the most brilliant affair of the season, and at the very height of it, that little Prince of yours, Boris de Rachewiltz, appeared at the gates and had to be admitted. I must say that I am not absolutely potty about the "piccolo Principe"! I gave [him] two huge slugs of my precious Scotch which made him quite drunk. He remained after the other guests had left in varying degrees of confusion. I had a dinner date at nine. At eight-fifty he was still there. When I turned my back for a moment, to put something in a desk-drawer, he finished off my Scotch. I didn't mind that, although Scotch is not easily obtained, but he forced me to violate the first and last principle of good manners, which is to outstay the guests. I had to get up and go, and I am surprised he was able to get down the steps unassisted. Either he is not used to liquor or his attitude to common-ers is extremely light. Of course I am joking a little, he is not as bad as all that! But I felt a little concern when I heard that he was expecting your mother as a guest at the Tyrolean castle.

As for the letters from J.! I have a feeling that J. is having a little sly fun with you. He simply can't be serious about this heavy seduction business, at least I prefer not to think so. I am almost sure that he is joking about it. You have your kind of humor and he has his, and you have not yet caught on to each other's. There is an undertone of delicate comedy in his importunities, and if I were you, I would treat them that way. He is not a villain, a "heavy," he simply could not play such a part in seriousness.

From Oliver a short and cold letter, announcing his arrival in Europe and giving his itinerary which does not include Rome or anywhere on the Italian peninsula. I think he has gone into one of his Welsh rages because I didn't answer a cable and letter he sent to American Express in Paris. I didn't call for mail there, as I wasn't expecting any, but Oliver will never accept that excuse. He wanted Carson's address so he could solicit a poem from her for an issue of a poetry magazine that he is guest-editor of. I'm sure he thinks I deliberately ignored the request out of professional jealousy. Actually the Paris mail was only forwarded to me last week, after Oliver had put to sea with silver buckles on his knee! I wrote him at Am. Ex. in Barcelona, his first port of call, giving him Sister-woman [McCullers]'s address and my apologies, but I am sure that nose is twitching like a scarlet horse-fly! The latest news about Sister-woman is that she is selling the "Ancien Presbytère" and that Reeves has been put in a clinic as she was threatening when we saw them in Paris. The poor mother, just out of a hospital, was advised not to come to Europe as Sister-woman will return to the States. I will send her the nice review from London. I already sent her one that I had found in a London paper, which was even more favorable than this one. It may cheer her up, I do hope so, for she was not one great big bundle of sheer animal exuberance when we last saw her at the Pont Royal, with all that talk of going downstairs through the window! When I told her, Honey, sit tight, we'll see you later tonight, and whisked off to see Anna Magnani in preference to the big jump, I realized just what a hopelessly heartless old cynic I have become! That's what comes of association with Tartars!

I want to ask you a favor. Will you please copy down for me those beautiful lines of Rilke's that little Sandra underlined in the [*Duino*] *Elegies,* the ones about "how strange it is to be no longer alive—putting off even our names like toys we have hardly grown used to . . ."—something like that, as I want to use it as a quotation in *Camino.* I can't find the book in Rome.

I am sure you'll get some work in *Moulin Rouge* and were wise not to tie yourself down with another part as understudy to a healthy girl like Pamela Brown unless you absolutely had to have a job. Flowers of arsenic in the tea of a star are likely to come to light at a post-mortem. And I am afraid that Jay's parcels to Wormwood-Scrubbs would consist mostly of remaindered copies of the New Directions anthologies of several years past. And one could not expect his passion, however incontinent it may seem at present, to endure for a twenty-year sentence, presuming you got off lightly.

Much love, Tenn.

I may go to Positano and Capri this next week. Will let you know. We have not yet made steamship reservations for a return to the States but will almost certainly be sailing from England as usual.

"CARSON'S 'Ancien Presbytère' I'd never visited, by choice; it was in France. Boris de Rachewiltz was then married to Ezra Pound's daughter, Mary: I'd met them through James Laughlin. We became friends, and they invited my mama to stay while I was there. She never went."

Maria sent Tennessee the lines from Rilke:

> True, it is strange to inhabit the earth no longer,
> to use no longer customs scarcely acquired,
> not to interpret roses, and other things
> that promise so much, in terms of a human future;
> to be no longer all that one used to be
> in endlessly anxious hands, and to lay aside
> even one's proper name like a broken toy.
> Strange, not to go on wishing one's wishes. Strange,
> to see all that was once relation so loosely fluttering
> hither and thither in space.

[*Telegram sent to Maria in London*]

VERY IMPORTANT LOCATE TENNESSEE WILLIAMS GRATEFUL ANY INFORMATION CAN GET IMMEDIATELY AUDREY LIEBSHOW

[*Handwritten on letterhead "Spirit of St. Louis," Pennsylvania Railroad*]

59 East 54th Street, N.Y.

October 25 [1952]

Dearest Maria:

Returning to N.Y. from a visit home. Dinky Dakin, sister Rose with attendant, Grandfather and Mother were all there, one big happy family! I am still alive. Grandpa was desperately anxious to leave with me but our plans are so uncertain that I couldn't take him. Cheryl and Gadg are at odds

Tennessee with his father
and his mother, 1913

Tennessee,
aged three,
and Rose,
aged five,
with their
adored nurse,
Ozzie, 1914

Tennessee, aged seventeen,
with his younger brother
Dakin, aged eleven, 1928

Rose and
Tennessee,
1930

Rose, aged
twenty-one,
1930

Tennessee with
his grandfather
on the steps of
the rectory, 1930

Tennessee's grandfather's rectory

[over *Camino Real*]. He demands an expensive production, she wants a modest one. I am sick of the whole thing and longing for Key West or Europe again. Gadg is still in Munich and I don't suppose the fate of the production will be decided till he gets back. Thanks for the lawyer's address. I'm sure Cheryl got in touch with him.

What news of the "Chevalier" [J. Laughlin]? I've heard nothing. The "Cheval" [Frank Merlo] has been on his *best* behavior. He was distressed because he feels you regard him as peasant. I assured him it was an honor. He is *very* fond of you, I think, and la petite mamouchka. How is *she*? Give her a big Russian hug for me. We have bought a dog, an English bull of high pedigree, still too young to leave his mother, but you shall see him at five o'clock, my angel.

I have a long story coming out in *New Yorker* November 2.

Can think of only *one* funny thing to tell you. Mother presented Sister, on her weekend visit, with a pair of slippers and asked her how she liked them, to which she replied, "They're good enough for a destitute old maid who is out of her mind." She was *not* turning in on the doctors this time!

I've been feeling ill and depressed or would have written you sooner.

All my love—Tenn

———

JAMES LAUGHLIN, who had been awarded the French Légion d'Honneur medal for publishing translations of the French classics, had been nicknamed "le Chevalier sans peur et sans reproche" by Maria's mother.

Tennessee sent Maria a draft poem, typed, and hand-marked "52":

A big storm blew
the wires down
so I ran screaming
through the town

Unclean, unclean!
and rang my bell
that lepers wear
to say, Not well!

And when my tongue
is blown away,
if there is more
I want to say,

I have an eyeball
that can stare
and a tuft of
sun-bleached hair

With which I'll make
a flag to wave
upon a staff of
splintered bone.

I'll wave it in
a field alone
as if to signal
all unknown

That people laugh at,
at whom they stare,
all shouting scarecrows,
skinny, bare

As buildings blasted,
crying dumb,
Cassandra's played
by Thomas Thumb. . . .

———

[Postmarked New York, December 3, 1952]

Dearest Maria:

I am in the middle of I don't know what! I worked so long and hard on *Camino* that now it seems to be slated for production it doesn't seem at all real to me. Gadg is being ominously angelic. He accepted half his usual fee and half his usual percentage. Our producer [Cheryl Crawford] is the female counterpart of the "Chevalier" in the hotly contested department of economy. I think they are running neck and neck in the stretch! But I suspect that Cheryl will pull out front by at least half a nose in the final plunge. She says that this is an "art production" and everyone must make sacrifices for it. I am taking "minimum royalties." Just why I am not at all sure. Perhaps if you work too long and hard on something it means that you should get paid half as much! She wants actors to perform for a couple of peanuts two or three times a week.

Grandfather is with us, here in New York, and we have a new member of the family, an English bull puppy named Mr. Moon, or "Moony." He is terribly spoiled by the Horse, and is incorrigible. Grandfather is cutting short his visit on this account. The dog will not let him alone, is constantly worrying his shoe-laces and trouser cuffs. The Horse will not discipline him at all, feeds him four huge meals a day, all kinds of between-meal snacks containing vitamins etc. which only increase his devilry.

I think Cheryl had some contact with Christine [Cromwell]'s lawyer but I don't know what came of it. Cheryl has had so many financial reverses in the theatre—her $350,000 musical *Paint Your Wagon* lost practically the entire investment, and *Tattoo* wound up about $40,000 in the red—that it is not going to be easy for her to get funds for *Camino*. I am supposed to read it aloud to a group of potential backers in a few days. Not many people seem to understand what it's about, and just reading it does very little good as most of its values are so plastic, pictorial and dynamic, that just listening to it or reading it is almost useless unless the listener or reader has a trained theatrical mind.

Darling, I wonder if you would like for me to send you a number of short-stories that you could sell in England to literary magazines? You might get some money for them, and I would want you to keep it if you did. Perhaps after "Two on a Party" nobody will publish my stories there, but on the other hand, they might be more interested in them. Binkie [Hugh Beaumont] informed Audrey he would not do *Tattoo* and she has now offered it to [Sam] Wanamaker who produced *Winter Journey* in London. So far no word from him. I hope he does it and that there will be something for you in that. Incidentally we have decided to cast a sixteen-year-old light Negro girl for the Gypsy's daughter in *Camino*. I know you will never agree with me and Gadg about this, but you are 100% wrong for Esmeralda and it would have been the opposite of a kindness to you or the play to pretend otherwise. There is something ineffaceably sensitive and cultivated about you, you are an aristocrat and a creature of unusual sensibility and whether you like it or not, that does come across in the theatre, and nobody in their right mind is going to cast you as a sort of mindless young animal, half primitive, and in her early teens. You *must* be realistic about what you should do and what you shouldn't do in the theatre. All the great leading-ladies know these things. When they have failures, such as Bankhead as Cleopatra, it is because they failed to recognize what was and wasn't right for them. Gadg is very impressed by you and fond of you, and he is keeping you in mind for whatever may seem right for you in anything that he does.

P.S. Had lunch with Don [Windham]. He's looking well but he and Sandy [Campbell] are having a tough time. Sandy is working as delivery boy for a liquor store now, Don says. It was wonderful to be seeing him again after the long lapse in our relations. I think now we will gradually grow closer together again, the critical time is past and we are both more adult than we were. He left me a bunch of mss. to read. I do hope they are as good as his writing usually is. Oh, I had a most unfortunate experience with Oliver. It is too much to write you about, I must tell you. He is no longer speaking to me. All on account of a ridiculous little mistake. I think he is just a wee bit off his rocker right now! He has left for New Orleans. I am not at all well, chest pains and breathless attacks, but I hope to see you again at five o'clock some day, my angel! The enclosed is a wee bit early for Christmas, but I know how seriously you take the season. To me it is a dreadful bore, but then in America we have more Santie Clauses and radio commercials and maudlin ballads about it. Soon as casting is completed I hope to spend about five weeks resting in Key West as rehearsals don't start till January 19th. Horse sends his love but will probably never write—it isn't [easy] to operate a pen with the hoof, you know.

Love, 10

CHRISTINE CROMWELL, a school friend of Maria's, had remained her great friend. Her father, James Cromwell, at one time United States ambassador to Canada, had married Delphine Dodge (Christine's mother) and, later, Doris Duke—two of the richest women in the world.

The Rose Tattoo was first produced in England at the New Shakespeare Theatrical Club, Liverpool, on November 4, 1958, with Lea Padovani as Serafina and Wanamaker, who directed, as Alvaro. The production moved to London on January 15, 1959.

[*Postmarked International Airport, Fla., December 19, 1952*]

Key West

Maria darling:

That's very funny about the cheque. What happened is I left the letter unsealed, intending to put the cheque in it, and the Horse trotted out with it, intending to be unusually useful, and deposited it in the mail box, one of his greatest undertakings in the past five years and one that must have left him quite exhausted! I am sorry it was so delayed in reaching you as I knew that you wanted to buy a lot of Xmas presents, not for quite the same reasons as the Chevalier sans peur. I just think it is a terrible bore and that most people have many more things than they ought to have, at least of the sort one can give them. I have no Yule-tide spirit, I think because Xmas was one of the holidays when my father was home and cast his enormous shadow upon the house, which the brightest Xmas tree in the world could not dispel.

Your letter put me in stitches. It arrived the morning I caught the train and I read it on the train soon as I got settled in my compartment and I think I was still laughing over the illustrations when we passed through Philadelphia. You have no idea what a mad scramble there has been for funds. Cheryl is so tight she hasn't even taken an option on the play [*Camino Real*], she has only signed one actor, the designer [Lemuel Ayers] has not received his fee and will not start to work and we are scheduled to go into rehearsals in mid-January. I had to read the play aloud to two assemblies of millionaires. Walter Chrysler [the car] magnate has now bought into the show and all but about $12,000 of the $125,000 is in Cheryl's purse but she is still not paying out. I had a terrible fight with Molly Kazan after the first reading. She is my bête-noir! I screamed at her all the four-letter words that I could think of, and Gadg just sat there and smirked. No. That's an exaggeration. I only used one bad word, but it was a very good one for the occasion. She then sent out "circulars" to everybody saying that I must cut 45 minutes out of the play and that if "we kept her with it we would have a play." I'm so glad you don't like her!

Christine [Cromwell]'s friend Mamie came to one of the readings but I never heard from her again! No word of Christine. Apparently Dodge motors are more cautious than Chrysler.

I think you will like the play and I am going to send you a copy soon as the script is final. I am still working on it.

I had a bottle of Graves for supper which made me think of you and the Cavendish and poor old Rosa Lewis. The witch Georgia Simmons is in New York and visited us unannounced a number of times. You and Frank are right about her, she is not very nice. She was attacking people cast in the play as "Reds," "nigger-lovers," etc. I was very put out and rather shocked by it.

I am in Miami waiting for Frank and Mr. Moon (the bull-dog) to arrive so we can drive down to Key West where Mother and Grandfather are occupying the little house. We will stay over the holidays, at least, and if Molly succeeds in talking Gadg out of the play, we'll remain till spring when we go back to Europe. I have been offered a lovely little house on the sea near Athens. It appears lovely in the pictures the owners showed me. It would be nice if we could all go there next summer, you and the Horse and I and Mr. Moon. Your mother too, if she is inclined to travel. That's good news about her job at Cambridge. Such a beautiful town, I'll never forget it. I think we ought to tie Molly Kazan and Binkie into the same sack and drop them off Thames Embankment or into Hoboken Sound, with a simple Protestant service and a sprinkle of salt.

Merry Xmas to you both and much love, 10

"GEORGIA SIMMONS was a malevolent and experienced troublemaker to whom Frankie and I had taken an instant dislike. Tennessee continued to whine how sweet she was, and that we did not understand her sensitive nature."

Madame Britneva took a job at Cambridge, teaching Russian. "My mother spoke, wrote and read perfect Russian, French, German and English. She'd been considered quite revolutionary in her time for daring to read the works of Tolstoy. Although she had never had to take or pass an examination in her life, the educational standard of the intelligentsia was so high in Russia that she was immediately accepted as a professor in England, without formal qualification.

"She told me a story of her grandmother, who was once browsing in a bookshop in Petersburg. The bookseller hovered, not daring to shut up shop. All the other customers had gone; the hours ticked by; still she went on browsing. Eventually, at about eleven o'clock at night, she told the bookseller, 'I really can't decide. Send everything in the shop to my estate.'

"Miss Fanny, her English governess, came back to England at the revolution and remained with the family, heartily and mutually loathed by the younger generation. She would bar people of whom she disapproved at the door of the house in Rosary Gardens, while the family waved merrily from the balcony, Miss Fanny resolutely denying that there was anybody at home. After thirty-five years in Russia, Miss Fanny had learned to speak appalling Russian, addressing princes in the familiar and speaking to dogs in tones of highest formality. She'd refer to her great gnarled feet in their vast black boots using the Russian diminutive; 'my little feetikins.'

"But the Russian text used in Cambridge textbooks at the time was still more perplexing to my mother. In one I remember, *Hugo's Russian,* were translations of 'useful Russian phrases': 'Question: What is the noise in the next-door room? Answer: It is my grandmother eating cheese.' Or: 'The postillion has been struck by lightning.' "

―――――――

[*Envelope postmarked Grand Central Station, New York, February 11, 1953*]

Dearest Maria:

So much has been going on I don't know where to begin, especially in my present state of tension and fatigue, so this is a very scrappy little bulletin. Actually things are going rather well, to everyone's surprise. Gadg is on his very best behavior, he is working brilliantly and if he continues at this pace, *Camino* will probably be his most remarkable piece of staging. It is an almost superhuman job, the play is so full of bizarre turns and twists that have to be woven into a fantastic but somehow congruous pattern and whole, it has to be done in its own completely new style, and I believe that Gadg, and possibly Peter Brook and [Peter] Glenville, are the only English-speaking directors I know who could handle it, and Gadg probably the best. He considers it (he says) my best play but when I think how tired and half-ill I was most of the time while I was working on it I find that hard to believe, but at least I do think it may have the most in spirit. Incidentally, that letter of yours with the unpleasant references to Molly "Catch-as-Catch-Can" [Kazan] was lying open on my front room table when he was over a few nights ago and all of a sudden I glanced up and he was browsing through it. He caught my horrified eye and grinned and said, "Can I read Maria's letter?" It was much too late to stop him, so I had to brazen it out and say, "Oh, please, do! She writes the funniest letters I've ever received." He started chuckling over the illustrations but I am not sure how he took the bit about Molly. Actually Molly is a pain in his derriere but he has to make a public show of loyalty to her as the Mother of His Four Children, and so forth, while he puts on her more horns than cab-drivers blow in Paris! I think he has a little spot in his heart for you. There are continual references such as, "Isn't this like little Maria? Isn't this how little Maria would do it?" He is always talking about the "little Marias" of the world. To him you have become a symbol, an archetype, of the "rebellious spirit" at bay. I thought I would let you know this, for once Gadg's imagination is caught by some quality in a person, he is really devoted. Some people think he is false for the same reason that they think I am insincere, simply because he lives under great pressure and can't be consistently attentive to so many things at one time. Only in his case the pressure is more diverse and greater. With me, it is only writing.

Michael Redgrave delivered the lovely wool ties by messenger, I didn't get to see him as no address was given. I guess he was very involved. What *does* annoy me is *Binkie*! He has been in New York several weeks, perhaps is still here, I don't know, staying at Dame Selznick's. I saw him exactly *once* and then by chance. Ran into him with the Dame at opening of [Peter Ustinov's *The Love of*] *Four Colonels*. The Dame suggested they join us at Sardi's for a drink, which they did for a perfunctory ten minutes. Wouldn't you THINK that having produced three of my plays, one of which was a great hit in London, he would have the modicum of good taste to call me, at least to say "Hello, how are you"? *NO*. He is much too grand for any such nonsense. . . .

On the other hand perhaps I should have called HIM. But I was never informed by him or the Dame of his presence in America.

HERE IS THE BIG NEWS! The Chevalier and Dyepot have PFFFT! as Walter Winchell puts it. I enquired about her and he said he hadn't seen her in a month or two and she isn't with New Directions anymore! FANCY THAT! The last line of *Hedda Gabler,* I believe. . . .

I do feel dreadfully sorry for Dyepot, really and truly. Don't you? "The gentleman named Ping" was a big shot with the Ford Foundation. The Chevalier took us all to one of the least expensive restaurants on the East Side but he did pick up the check with no *visible* anguish. However, the wine was served us by the glass rather than having a bottle on the table to encourage excess! I was terrified of the "Ping." He had the air of a Gestapo investigator, kept asking pointed questions about my politics, etc. I think the Knight has gone over to "Big Business" with a vengeance and his poor little publishing house and Dyepot and you and me are Banquo's ghost at the banquet. Of course I may be wrong! I *HOPE* SO! We have so little left to believe in now.

It seems that we will very likely have a little house on the sea island of Portos (near Athens) for at least one month of the summer. It is said to be a most heavenly place and I trust you can join us. I'm not sure which month the house will be available but we have no reason to return early to the States this time and I have accepted an invitation to Helsinki, Finland, the end of October so we should remain over at least that long this time.

Well, I must get to rehearsal before they quit for the day. Do burn a candle for me in the lovely Russian church, along with one for Sandra, and be a good girl and take care of your mummy.

Enclosed is a Key West snapshot, the gentleman to my left is Mr. Moon, the one to my right is Grandfather, who is patiently waiting for us in Key

West. The flat-eared picture looks a bit like the Chevalier at the sight of an approaching wine steward. Really we must stop making jokes about the Chevalier's thrift!

With much love, Tenn

[*Added in handwriting*] Enclosing a wee token of affection so you can pin some flowers on your lapel.

Mary Britneva's infamous comment to Tennessee when he proudly showed her this photograph of his grandfather. "I never knew that dogs wore white peaked caps in America."

W H E N Tennessee was in London, Maria's mother looked for a long time at the snapshot he had enclosed with this letter and then in a dreamy voice said: "Tennessee, I never knew that dogs wore white peaked caps in America." Tennessee was outraged, uncertain whether Maria's mother had genuinely confused his grandfather with the dog or was teasing. He replied stonily: "It is perfectly evident which is the human face, Madame Britneva." He never totally forgave her.

James Laughlin took a position in the cultural section of the Ford Foundation. "Dyepot" was the implausibly blond cover editor at New Directions, who had been Laughlin's long-standing *liaison dangereuse*.

[Part of a surviving letter from Maria to Tennessee, whom she called "Coco" when he was in favor: undated, but probably early March 1953]

Darling Coco—

What's new? How is the play? I've just put another huge 6d. candle in church for you, so it should be alright.

The party at John [Perry]'s was quite fun. Binkie told me he had dinner with you in N.Y. I looked so amazed that he corrected himself and said, "Well, actually, they were dining and we had a drink with them." So I said, "And how does Tenn look?" And Binkie said, "Good—thinner." Then I said, "Did you see Gadg?" At which Binkie's eyes closed from the bottom upwards like lizards' eyes do and he looked outraged at the idea and said "Oh NO, MISSY!" Has a big black cat run across the path, do you reckon?

I've just come out of church again as the news is that Stalin is dying—I put a fat big candle for him to die *quickly*—so we can all go to Russia, won't it be wonderful, Coco? I am longing to take you.

[The letter breaks off here.]

———

THE FIRST performance of *Camino Real* was at the National Theatre, New York City, on March 19, 1953, directed by Kazan, with Eli Wallach as Kilroy and Barbara Baxley as Esmeralda.

"At the first night of *Camino* in London, Tennessee, having just arrived from the airport, was very tired. He begged me to keep him awake but kept falling asleep. He woke up abruptly when shots were fired onstage. From then on I would tease him about having to write gunshots into his plays to keep himself awake—a joke which did not greatly please him." *Camino* was directed by Peter Hall, with Diana Wynyard and Denholm Elliott, at the Phoenix Theatre.

———

Write c/o Audrey Wood
551 Fifth Avenue

April 22, 1953

Dearest Maria:

I don't write you so much as spring advances since I know that I will probably soon see you. Also I knew that J. had given you a full report on the play and also I was simply so exhausted I didn't want to lift one unnecessary finger. I am not one penny richer, in fact quite a few pennies poorer, for the two years' labor. Of course soon as the notices came out Mother Crawford took us off royalties and we've never gotten back on, so practically everybody, author, director, composer, choreographer and designer, worked mostly for nothing. The actors have taken big cuts. She is hoping, as usual, to scrape along by such economies as lighting the stage by fire-flies and a smokey old kerosene lamp, substituting a bit of percussion on an old washtub for a five-piece band, etc., but even so the prospects for an extended run are but dim. I haven't seen the play since the various economy measures went into effect but it was very beautiful when it opened and I know that you would have loved and understood it. Gadg did a superlative job and I have been flooded with letters about it from the passionate minority that it did touch.

Donnie's been staying with me the past two weeks. He has written a lovely play [*The Starless Air*], and I am going to direct it in Houston, Texas, before we sail for Europe June 5th. I gave him my studio while he was here. He did some good work on the play and I think it will have a good chance on Broadway next season. If both of us are convinced that I can direct it, I may do it again in New York. Anyway it was wonderful to re-establish the old friendship between us which had languished sadly in the last few years. The Houston producer, Joanna Albus (a former girl-friend of Margo [Jones]'s), also came here. She and Donnie left yesterday. I was supposed to go to N.Y. with them to cast the play but since tomorrow is Grandfather's 96th birthday—and I am afraid the last one—I felt obliged to stay here. But I will fly to Houston early next week, unless in the meantime they decide to engage another director for it.

A few last golden days in the Key West studio! It is so lovely! A sky-light with delicate bamboo curtain, palms, banana trees and fern-like Australian pines through the windows in all four walls, a Japanese lantern over my head with glass-pendants that tinkle in the constant trade-winds, a silver ice-bucket, gin, and oranges for pauses in occupation. Wonderful sounds, the palms and banana trees make, like ladies running barefooted in silk skirts downstairs, a constant flickering of light and shadow, a table that's five feet long, theatrical posters stuck all over the lemon yellow walls, my own bathroom, a comfortable little bed, driftwood, a fan that belonged to Hart Crane, shells, solitude, peace! I would be content to stay right here forever, but the Horse is restless. He is rather moody. I think he longs to parade along the Via Veneto with Mr. Moon in Prima Sera! And hear the admirers say, Che brutto cane! Ah, che brutto cane!

I am also diverting myself with a little painting in oils and if one comes out well, I may bring it to you. I have done a (male) flamenco dancer for

Oliver's new house in New Orleans. I talked to him recently long-distance and he was very blue. Said the house was a terrible fraud, there wasn't a single sound piece of wood in it! He is having to re-construct it almost entirely and won't get to Europe, probably, till mid-summer. I shall stop over in New Orleans on my way to Houston to have a look at him. He sounded quite red in the face and pop-eyed with rage.

We sail June 5th on the *United States* and will land in France. I hope there will be some royalties waiting from the French production of *Rose Tattoo*. You could help us spend them in Paris. I am awfully sorry about the dislocated disks. What *have* you been up to?

Affectionate greetings to your little mother.

Much love, Tenn.

"HART CRANE was a favorite poet of Tennessee's. Tennessee stipulated in one of his wills that he be buried at sea, off Key West, as near as possible to the place where Hart Crane had drowned himself. Blanche says it in her last major speech in *Streetcar*: 'And I'll be buried at sea sewn up in a clean white sack and dropped overboard—at noon—in the blaze of summer—and into an ocean as blue as the blue of my first lover's eyes.' "

The Starless Air was first produced at Joanna Albus's Playhouse Theatre in Houston on May 13, 1953. It never made the move to Broadway.

Tennessee and Frank left for Europe on June 5, as they had planned.

[*11 Via Firenze, Rome*]

June 29, 1953

Dearest Maria:

I am worried about you. I dreamed last night that you ran up to me on the street and that one of your arms had been amputated and the wrist and hand sewed up in a sort of crêpe-de-chine sling! What do you make of it?

I've been working all day so I can't write you much of a letter but wanted you to know that I will probably be leaving this week for Barcelona and will wire you from Madrid, when I get there, in case you would like to join me for a couple of weeks in Spain. I'm not sure whether I'll take the car over (by boat from Naples) or rent one there, probably the latter.

Sorry [I] tore this page, it's too narrow for the machine. What happened about summer rep? Please talk to Binkie or Sam Wanamaker about [Lila]

Kedrova and my desire to direct the play [*Rose Tattoo*] in London, that is, if you have a chance to. I will also write Wanamaker a letter and have already written Audrey [Wood] how much I liked her [Kedrova] in *Tattoo* [in Paris].

We have an apartment with a fine terrace here in Rome. Frank and the Froggy Coachman will stay here while I go to Spain but may join me later in Tangier.

Love to your mama, and you, Tenn

———

M A R I A ' s family, curiously, already knew Lila Kedrova, the famous Russian-French actress. "After the Revolution, a famous male-voice quartet was formed in Paris by Lila's father, called the Kedrov Quartet. They were part of the entertainment at the famous Chauve-Souris, in which Lila played the child parts. In London they used to come and sing in our house, at one or two in the morning, after the theatre; people stopped outside in the streets to listen to them. We seemed never to sit down less than eighteen to twenty to a meal at home. . . ."

———

11 Via Firenze
Rome

July 25, 1953

Dearest Maria:

I did not actually get away from Barcelona till Wednesday as the planes were booked up till then. Paul Bowles went ahead by car and I flew over with his Arab companion, Ahmed. I'm glad you didn't come. The city was hell and I barely lived through it. Rome seems like heaven, especially since Paul is here and the Horse is back on his good behavior.

Truman Capote has invited us to Portofino but will not extend his hospitality to Mr. Moon as he has a female dog of approximately the same species. Anyway I'm not at all sure I would like to share a house with that one, as there would be more than one bitch under the roof, that's for sure. But as soon as the Jaguar is back in condition (it's now in a garage for repairs) I'll probably take off for the sea-coast. Portofino is said to have wonderful swimming and is very smart, which you would enjoy. If it didn't suit us we could travel along the coast till we found some place that did. Of course at this season the sea-resorts are heavily booked but I will write Truman to see if he can get us a couple of rooms at Portofino early in August. I'll wire you as soon as I've heard from him.

Phil Brown is very eager to do some one-acts of mine in London and I've just written him to give me more detailed account of the plans and to enquire if he would like me to direct one myself, say, in September or early October. Wouldn't it be nice if they could be done at the Lyric-Hammersmith? But I do think I should be around as the idiom is so southern and the quality difficult for English actors to catch without southern direction.

The water-pressure has failed in the building, we can't bathe, and the Arabs are smoking kif. Moon has fleas. . . .

The old dog in the white peaked cap is now in the mountains of East Tennessee. I'm working and feeling well again.

Much love, 10

———

PHIL BROWN had played Tom in the London production of *The Glass Menagerie.*

Maria was in Vicenza working with Tennessee on the revisions to the English script of the film *Senso,* directed by Visconti. The film was shot in two languages, English and Italian. The only actor to speak in English was Farley Granger. Visconti had asked Tennessee to write the script. Tennessee did not want to do it and suggested Paul Bowles instead. When Visconti was not satisfied with Bowles's script, Tennessee agreed to revise parts of it, principally the scenes in English with Granger. He did so on the condition that Maria assist him.

"I'd no idea about writing a script: I'm a halfwit. I didn't even know which way up it should go. But Visconti knew that if I did it, he could rest assured that Tennessee would oversee it, and at least (since Tennessee spoke no Italian and Visconti no English) I could interpret for Visconti in French. As it was, I spent most of the time having fun with Farley and with Franco Zeffirelli, who was Visconti's first assistant. Visconti used in temper to call Franco and me 'i due cretini'!

"While working on the script, Tennessee and I stayed in rooms which shared a balcony. Every morning at five, Tennessee would be rapping on my French windows: 'Come on, time to get up! Get to work!' His self-discipline was astonishing."

Tennessee came to the *Senso* set in Rome.

"I had met many young actors desperate to get their resumés typed up, in order to help them get jobs. 'I know a typist,' I would say, and would fly round to the Via Aurora, and Tennessee would patiently type them for me. It got annoying, he kept stopping and saying, 'I don't like this phrase, let's change it.' 'Oh, hurry up, Tennessee, stop fussing!' And his fat little banana fingers would bang away at the keys. He was an excellent typist."

———

[*Letter sent to Vicenza, Italy*]

Hotel Rembrandt
Tangier

October 15, 1953

Maria darling:

I have an intuitive feeling, woke up with it this morning, that something important is going on in your life. Please write me at once, here at the Hotel Rembrandt (room 413) in Tangier. We'll be sailing from Gibraltar soon as we can get booked onto something. The earliest possibility is the 27th on the *Andrea Doria* which bore our lovely lady ambassador to Italy last spring and must be still permeated by the fragrance of her spirit—however, Mr. Moon will take care of that if we obtain a passage. Did you get the prison scene that I mailed from Barcelona? I suspect you wrote me a second letter to Madrid. I hated that city and we left soon as repairs on Paul [Bowles]'s car had been completed. We arrived here for the beginning of the rainy season but today is still and clear and I'm going out on the beach, much too tired to work, too stupid even to write a decent letter. We have such a lovely little apartment here, the bedroom has an enormous window that overlooks two continents and the two seas and the ships sailing east and west through the narrow straits and also the white hill of the Casbah, so if one has to be totally exhausted, a better place for it couldn't be discovered.

Audrey wrote me a devastatingly negative reaction to that ms. 1 we mailed her in Rome. I believe she thinks that I have "flipped my lid" and will be waiting for me at the docks with a strait-jacket behind her back as she waves sweetly with the other hand. Then today, adding insult to injury, comes the following long cable, undoubtedly charged to my account: "Carson desperately eager to know whether possible you pick up in Paris various household items and some clothes now with American Embassy. She is so terribly concerned would appreciate your wiring if you will be in Paris before return home. Advise where I can reach you by letter rest of month. Love Audrey Wood."—Imagine!—a cable to Tangier asking me to collect Carson's old brooms, mops, bottles, pants and mackintoshes in Paris! I never knew Audrey had such a keen sense of humor. Carson's sense of the ridiculous was already well-established without this extra bit.

Horse is getting up now and we must trot out to Cook's before lunch and the beach. Miss you, Pretty Missy! Give my love to Luchino and Franco and I do hope they have the new material and it isn't too awful to use. I was rather pleased with the scene in the prison but have no faith in my own opinions.

Molto amore! Tenn

[*Added in handwriting*] Just now got your letters—so glad you liked *Camino*—hope I do.

———

THE MANUSCRIPT Tennessee had sent Audrey, to which she had reacted so negatively, was a new play—*Cat on a Hot Tin Roof.* Audrey could not understand its plot, which Maria had to explain to her.

———

[*Envelope postmarked Tangier, Morocco, October 25, 1953*]

Saturday

Darling Maria:

We are sailing on the *Andrea Doria* the 27th of this month which is next Tuesday and we'll be in Gibraltar the day before at the Rock Hotel there, and God, the wait here seems to be interminable, I just don't see how I can get through another day of it. I can't imagine how Bowles has stood it all these years. The city has no beauty, no charm, it is just like Miami Beach thrown in the middle of some ghastly slums. The Arabs are inscrutable, you could never get to know them if you lived here a hundred years and they dislike and despise all Christians. The Americans and Europeans here are a sort of last-ditch Bohemians. When the weather is good, which is sometimes, not today, I swim at an outdoor pool which is icy cold, the rest of the time I lie in bed and read with nothing much in the way of books. We take every meal at the same restaurant and the food is more monotonous than Giovanni's. Everything is cheap. Perhaps that is the charm of the place, I don't know, and everything can be had, if you want it. Unfortunately we'll have to come back here for the car next spring but we certainly won't linger. The more I see of other places the more I love Rome. I actually cried a little when I left it this time. I went out at dusk to buy a thermos bottle, and crossed the Piazza [dell'] Esedra and the great square in front of the station and could not bring myself to go home till it was quite dark, wondering if I would see it ever again. The Horse was stamping when I got back as we had to start out after dark. But it was nice seeing Jane and Tony [Smith] again those last few days. Did I tell you

Jane is pregnant, expecting a baby in January? I gave them the lire that I had left in the Rome bank and both have written me lovely letters as they said it made the trip much easier for them, they were travelling third class and Jane standing up for long over-night journeys or sleeping on wooden benches. Seeing people like that again is almost like having a transfusion of fresh strong blood, it revives your life and your faith in it again. That fat slug the Signora kept our 120,000 lire deposit and then had the nerve to call Alvaro and say that we had left without paying a small light bill. But it is hard, now, to remember anything unpleasant about Rome and will be increasingly hard to when we get back Stateside.

After being well all summer, Grandfather had a violent bilious attack soon as he returned home to Clayton and Mother writes that she was afraid for several days that he wouldn't recover but that "today he came down-stairs." She has always been gloomy about the old man's prospects. When I arrived in Key West where she had been keeping house for him I found she had written the undertaker's telephone number on the scratch pad on the living-room desk, right after the doctor's number and over the laundry, grocery, taxi and other quotidinal necessaries. I am sure he will revive as soon as he knows that we are back on American soil.

Dear love to Luchino and Franco, a kiss for Farley Warley [Granger], tell him that "music had charms to soothe the savage breast" but even if it is the food of love, it should not be played on and on and on and on. I find that a couple of ten-inch records and a stiff drink will turn the trick if the trick can ever be turned. Much love to you, Little Sister.

Tenn

TENNESSEE and Frank Merlo returned to New York and soon went south to New Orleans, where they stayed till mid-January 1954, when they moved back to Key West.

Maria's friend from childhood, Peter Grenfell, who had inherited the title of Lord St. Just at the age of nineteen, had wanted to marry Maria for some time. Meanwhile, James Laughlin's divorce from his first wife had by now been finalized, and he had extricated himself from his recent liaison with "Dyepot."

"There was a letter from Tennessee which is now lost. He wrote it after J. had invited him out to lunch and sounded him out about me. I remember that the letter began, 'Hold on to your hat, honey, the man's intentions are serious!' Tennessee said that he was so *bouleversé* that he quite forgot to beg J. for another glass of wine.

"J. came over to Italy during *Senso* and we became engaged. And then suddenly Peter St. Just appeared and he, too, proposed. When I told him that I was about to marry J., Peter told me I'd be miserable living in America and that I was going to marry *him*. Peter was absolutely ruthless, and would wait in the hotel foyer for me. Understandably, J. was livid, and totally confused, imagining that I was holding mysterious *renseignements*."

Maria and Laughlin invited Tennessee to be one of the twelve men who hold the crown over the bride and groom during the Russian Orthodox wedding service.

[*Telegram sent from Key West to Hôtel Pont Royal, Paris*]

DEAREST MARIA AND JAY YOUR LETTER MADE ME CRY WITH HAPPINESS FOR YOU BOTH SOMETHING BRIGHT AND BEAUTIFUL IN A DARK TIME OF COURSE I WILL COME AND HOLD THE CROWN OR ONLY TO HEAR THE MUSIC ALL MY LOVE AND DELIGHT TENNESSEE

LAUGHLIN departed on business for the Ford Foundation, and Visconti and Zeffirelli gave Maria an engagement party with the *Senso* company.

[*Handwritten letter from James Laughlin to Madame Britneva*]

c/o American Express Co., Rome, Italy

January 18, 1954

Dear Mme Britneva,

I'm sure you'll be glad to hear Mary is very well and in good spirits although working very hard on her film at the studios. It is wonderful to see her again. I have missed her so much.

In part, to get right to the point of this letter, I have missed her so much that I would like not to be parted from her in the future. If she cares for me enough, and if you too can accept me, I hope that she will marry me. This I have told her, and she has promised to think about it, as of course she must.

I have felt very close to Maria ever since the first time I met her with Tennessee in New York, and she has never been far from my thoughts. We get along so well together. Now I am at last free from all other obligations, and I feel certain that my happiness lies with her. There has never been

Pierino Tossi,
Luchino Visconti
and Maria in
Vicenza during the
filming of
Senso, 1953

Tennessee on
the Lido during
the filming of
Senso, 1953

With Farley Granger
outside St. Basil's in
Venice, 1953

Truman Capote
visiting the *Senso* set,
Verona, 1953

Maria with
Farley Granger,
Zeffirelli and
Visconti at
a trattoria,
Verona, 1953

Maria with Paul Bowles
and Tennessee on the *Senso*
set in Verona, 1953

"Ahmed takes my
place as I snap him
(center) with Paul
and Tennessee."

Frank and Maria

anyone who seemed to understand me so well, or was a more loyal unselfish friend. I do love her very much, and want to make her as happy as I know she can make me. I can promise you that I will be good to her and take care of her properly.

I feel a great responsibility to my two children. I know that Mary would be a wonderful second mother to them when they are with me in the summer. I would like them to copy her character and her sweet gaiety.

I can imagine that the thought of her going as far away as America to live may depress you, but I can assure you that you would always be most welcome in my home. Indeed, if you could bear to leave London, I would like you to come to live with us. But even if you cannot do that, you would see her often, because my work brings me to Europe every year, sometimes twice, and she would come with me.

I feel very humble and inadequate in asking you for Mary. I know my faults and they are many. But Mary has always inspired me, and I think with her love and help I can grow as a person and be what she would want me to be.

I shall be coming soon to London and perhaps then can tell you more about my feelings and my situation. But I wanted to let you know at once that I have spoken to Mary in these terms because I understand how close you are to each other and how unwilling she would be to take any steps which would not have your blessing.

With hopes and love, J.

[*Envelope postmarked Key West, February 16, 1954*]

Dearest Maria:

I am all ears! What's new?

The Horse and I are simply agog with excitement—even the Froggy Footman is walling his eyes with more than usual sense of something portentous. I am really very happy over what has happened and I feel so strongly that it will turn out well.

Dyepot called me long distance and wrote me, and was very sweet both in the phone conversation and [in] the letter. She wanted to know if what she had heard was true. I didn't know what to say, I was quite speechless, but she seemed to understand my inability to make any honest statement, for after all, it is hard to tell someone you like that you are happy over their misfortune, though it is hard for me to really believe that it will not be fortunate for all concerned in the long run, since it is obvious that J. is not truly in love with her and no relationship can be built on duty or fondness. It would be doing her an injustice, and I think Dyepot is not the sort of person who would be happy as an obligatory partner. She said that she had just resigned from New Directions and the Ford Foundation, both, that day, and I do hope that J. will not be upset and that she'll be soon reconciled to what was fated.

No news except that Grandfather, known to your mother as the dog in the peaked cap, had one of his last remaining teeth extracted and the extraction was so painless that he said "Ready!" when the tooth was out several minutes and the poor dentist was trying to persuade him to get out of the chair.

"Miss Priss" had a short stay in Key West, for she failed to curtail her nocturnal activities. She says she suffers from "alcoholic amnesia." Something happened one night in the "after hours" place called "The Jockey Club." She thinks it involved a shrimp fisherman and a bar-maid and a plain-clothesman but she doesn't recall the nature of the experience, only that the next day when she started mincing down the main street, the officer came up to her and said, "I thought you said you'd be out of town tonight." She caught the midnight bus for Miami. We call it "the lavender bus" as the ones advised to leave for such reasons take it. I got a wire from her today from Havana reporting favorably on things there and urging me to fly over. Soon as I finish my work I may do so, as Miss Priss is one of my favorite people despite your dim view of her, and Frank's. The Horse goes into "shock" when he sees her or hears her name mentioned!

Was the film [*Senso*] really any good? I long to hear about it. I wired you both in Rome and [in] London, the same wire, as I didn't know where to reach you, saying how happy I was and am over the really wonderful news.

Give J. my very, very fondest regards and congratulations and much love to you.

Tenn.

"MISS PRISS was a tweezer-lipped acquaintance of Tennessee's—totally humorless and profoundly, if inexplicably, conceited. His real name I mercifully never knew."

[*Handwritten letter from Madame Britneva to Tennessee, undated*]

20 Tennyson Mansions
Queen's Club Gardens
London W.14

Dear Tennessee,

I am so glad to know that you are pleased about Maria's engagement. I too am delighted because I like J. so much, and I am sure that Maria will be a good wife for him. It is also such a relief to know that you will be in America, because I am afraid it is going to be very difficult for her to adjust herself to a new country with foreign people.

To be quite frank with you I am rather disturbed about J.'s liaison with this American woman; particularly as he assured me that this affair was finished on both sides and no question of marriage had ever arisen.

However, your letter which came yesterday worries me very much, as I feel that whilst it is completely finished from J.'s side, it appears that possibly from hers it is not.

But these may be only a mother's worries and this is why I am so happy that you will be within reach, and I do ask, as I feel sure you will, to do your utmost to help by discouraging this woman from having any contact with little Mary and thus ensure that she and J. start their married life without shadows.

Looking forward very much to seeing you at the wedding (and holding the crown!)

                                   Yours affectionately, Mary Britneva

––––––

LAUGHLIN and Maria travelled to London, where the engagement was announced in the *Times*.

J., a passionate skier, invited Maria and her mother to go skiing with him in St. Moritz. Madame Britneva thought it unsuitable that they should travel together before the marriage, and so he went with friends.

––––––

[*On letterhead The Robert Clay, Miami, Florida*]

1431 Duncan, Key West, Fla.

March 16, 1954

Dearest Maria:

I wrote you a long, long, long, long letter which is still reposing on the six-foot work-table in my Key West studio, so I'm dashing off this note in Miami where I've gone to consult a specialist about my feet—they suddenly started swelling up and turning numb so that I felt I was walking on a couple of sponges. I am worried about it. It seems like one of those little "R.S.V.P's" from the five o'clock angel, but maybe it is only a quarter past four, who knows, and I am determined to climb that gang-plank May 15th to sail back to Rome. I have finished two plays, a re-write of the re-write of *Battle of Angels* [*Orpheus Descending*] and a shorter, but not short, play [*Cat on a Hot Tin Roof*] that I was also working on last summer in Rome, and I've also done the film-script [*Baby Doll*] for Gadg, finally finished it, and I only have to do the film-script for *Rose Tattoo*—it is now all set that Magnani will make it next fall in America. This summer I will rest for the first time in many years, really and truly rest, if I do succeed in getting up that gang-plank on the *Andrea Doria*—oh, how I long to make it! Remember me in thy orisons day and night. I do so hope you won't be in Japan or some place equally remote, whether married or still my favorite spinster. By the way, which are you? Bigelow arrived here last night as if some intuition had dispatched him, and he says he heard from J.'s office, when he called about something, that J. was not in London but India. He thinks perhaps you've *both* gone. But [Robert] MacGregor, Jay's assistant [at New Directions], said nothing to indicate this in his letter a few days ago. Please relieve my suspense: *what's going on?*

I am going to answer Miss Mary [Britneva]'s letter, which was very sweet, when I get back to Key West. We will be in New York again about April 1st and be there till we sail. But please do write me in Key West before we go, and if you'll let me know the time of the nuptials, I want to celebrate them in some fashion though I will not be present.

Much love, Tenn.

———

ON DECEMBER 30, 1940, *Battle of Angels* was first produced at the Wilbur Theatre in Boston. It was not a success. Soon afterward, Tennessee revised the play for a proposed production at the New School in New York City.

On hearing of her son's engagement, Mrs. Laughlin in Pittsburgh sent him a frantic letter saying, "Jamesie! A RUSSIAN! Can't you find a nice American girl who knows our ways?"

———

[*1431 Duncan Street, Key West, Fla.*]

March 27, 1954

Dearest Maria:

I am disturbed by your last two letters, not only because J. has left London for India and Japan but also because it appears to me that you are behaving about as cleverly as that famous "London Brick Factory" otherwise known as "the Old One" [John Gielgud]. . . .

Darling! Nobody loves honesty more than I, but honey! there are times, there are situations, there are circumstances in which the head must not rule the heart but at least act in collaboration with it. You seem to be doing and saying or thinking all the wrong things. The concern of J.'s family is something you must understand. Isn't it the same as your mother's concern for you? After all, they have never seen you and know nothing of you. His experience with Margaret, that disastrous marriage, has naturally made them terribly concerned over a second alliance. You must try to understand that. J.'s assistant at New Directions, Bob MacGregor, was just here, and he tells me that J.'s family has been terribly upset over his "romantic connections" prior to the present one with you, so you mustn't feel that you alone are being put on the spot. I know how trying, how humiliating, it must be to feel that you are being subjected to this sort of scrutiny but you *must* understand it, and you should not be afraid of it. If you're not hostile to them, they are bound to *love* you! This also applies to whatever friends, or emissaries, they may dispatch. After all, marriages in these spheres are comparable to royal matches in old Europe. And you know how they were made. Princesses royal were lined up like criminals under a hot spot and they stood there and sweated and smiled and smiled and smiled! Personally I can't imagine how they endured it, but it seemed to come with the trade, and they did, they endured it, and sometimes it must have worked out fairly well in the end.

I think you should go on working and living as if none of this had happened, and if J. loves you and you love J., I do believe in both "ifs," all this confusion will clear up shortly. Oh, well. "Life is not easy, it calls for Spartan endurance. . . ." (Amanda Wingfield [in *The Glass Menagerie*]).

We've had a host of visitors here. Bigelow lingers on. Kazan is expected.

My feet are still like a couple of old dry sponges, very peculiar feeling to walk on them, but I am taking huge doses of vitamin B12 and B2 by capsule and injection, and except for the feet I feel better.

Grandfather just took a spill on the porch, opening the door, the door came out of its hinges and door and Grandfather fell flat on the floor of the porch, he must be made of India rubber. He got up and told me to see if his watch had broken. . . .

He is now having bourbon and sugar. He'll be 97 next month on Shakespeare's birthday. Yesterday I was—guess what?—No, I won't tell you, it's *too* awful!

Any news of our picture [*Senso*]? We sail May 15th on the *Doria*. I can't come sooner as I have to finish the picture of *Tattoo* for Magnani before I leave, also Gadg's picture, also a play.

I long to see your smile and hear your gay Russian laughter, Nitchevo, nitchevo. . . .

Love, Tenn.

––––––––

LAUGHLIN went to India, and thence to Japan. After a period, it seemed apparent to Maria that the engagement was over.

When they met again, after Tennessee's death, J. admitted to Maria that he had been gravely disturbed by an incident that had occurred while they were in Florence together.

"I was so bored with seeing J. in the same tie, day in, day out, that I went out shopping, and returned triumphantly with eight silk ties—one for every day of the week and two for Sundays. J. was paralyzed by this extravagance, even though I explained to him that I'd bought them with my own salary. 'My God! What are you going to do with all *my* money?' I was genuinely surprised. 'Why, have you *got* any?—I'll spend it, of course!'"

––––––––

[*Envelope postmarked Tangier, sent to Beirut as Maria was on a cruise*]

[Hotel Rembrandt]

May 22, 1954

Dearest Maria:

I was afraid that something had gone wrong so the letter that reached me in "Gib" shocked me but didn't surprise me. It shocked me because I can't reconcile J.'s conduct toward you with anything I have ever seen or known about him. In our professional and friendly relations he's always been the soul of honor and always so kind and so gentle, he has never even told me that anything I have written is bad! I have trusted him so much that I recently named him executor of my will. So of course I am terribly shaken by what you tell me. It does seem unfair and worse than that, unkind, because it has placed you in the most embarrassing position, and I feel even sorrier for your little mother as I know how desperately she has longed to see you settled and cared for and happy. Most of all it seems so foolish, so pitiably foolish, of J. because you would have made him a perfect wife and would have given him a faith in himself, as a poet and as a person, both, which he needs so badly, broken the bonds of self-doubt and morbid humility which have held him back as an artist which he primarily is. I suspect that this little boy, six foot seven inches tall, is simply terrified at the mere sight of happiness!—because he doesn't feel equal to it, doesn't feel he can live up to it. . . . You could have solved that dilemma for Jay and given him pride in himself and his art and his work and the freedom to do it. It's such a pity. But so many things are. . . .

Perhaps I am being a Pollyanna for a change (I'm usually such a gloom-pot) but I do believe that he loves you and will continue to love you and that the bad time will pass. I remember the lunch in Rome and the shy, anxious, loving way he talked and questioned me about you, wanting me to confirm his hopes, his intuitions about you. What on earth can have happened to throw him into this panic? A belated concern for Dyepot? Intimidation by family? Just childish fear of taking a forward step into something unknown? I just can't understand and I can't guess!

For the time being, let's drop the subject. We will be in Rome by the time you finish the trip and we would love to have you join us again this summer, and we won't be wearing black chiffon or broken hearts on our sleeves, but enjoy the golden city in the golden summer. We are picking up the Jaguar here in Tangier, where we left it last fall, and then going on to Rome. I may go through Spain to see a bull-fight or two while the car goes by boat to Italy. I have managed to bring two plays [*Cat* and *Orpheus*] close to completion this year but I haven't yet succeeded in pushing them over the last couple of hurdles.

Would you ask Jennie to look for an apartment for us in Rome? She spoke of having a lovely one we might be able to take there. Tell her we can pay $200 a month. I would like two bedrooms and bath and a terrace and *not* in the ugly new part of town, and we could all live together in it.

By the way, we lost poor Mr. Moon. He passed away quite suddenly on

Easter Sunday. We don't know what it was. He just stopped eating the day before he died. Was silent and stood in a corner looking at the wall. Just five minutes before he died he uttered a heartbreaking cry and dropped dead. He has been interred in a canine cemetery and has a little stone tablet. We bought a new bull right away. I think the Horse would have gone to pieces if we hadn't. Actually he is cuter, in appearance, than Moon, his name is Signor Buffo, he is white and fawn, mischievous, ill-tempered and constantly complaining but very cute.

Much, much love from us both. Tenn.

"JENNIE CROSS was a daughter of Robert Graves who had married the Reuters correspondent in Rome. They had a wonderful flat overlooking the old Forum. We visited it after Paul Bowles had given me kif for the first time, which, since I never smoke and don't know how to inhale, had absolutely no effect whatever. The pale Paul Bowles went even whiter with rage. After enough kif to kill a herd of elephants, he went to the kitchen and gave me a jam sandwich packed with the stuff. This did have a magical effect. We went off to the party at Jennie's and the Horse was very solicitous of my welfare. He never left my side. I remember going down streets that seemingly never ended, until Frank took me back to the hotel and instructed them, after I'd awoken from my hashish dreams of floating on clouds, to give me a large bacon-and-egg breakfast. Tennessee was very annoyed with Paul for giving me the hashish, and even more with me for eating it."

Tennessee invited Maria to join Frankie and him in Rome. Again, Maria kept a sketched diary of her summer with them.

27th July

Yesterday we went down to Anna Magnani's place in Circeo. It was a series of misfortunes. We tried to start early, but Tenn and I ran into Franco Zeffirelli, and as this was the first time we had seen each other since my return and ill-fated engagement party there was much to talk about. We only got back home at two o'clock. Frankie was waiting and not as cross as we'd expected, although he had full right to be, I thought. And we set off.

Tennessee in front, the Horse driving, and Mr. Buffo and me behind. Buffo tried to eat my toes until I gave him such a kick on his silly bull nose, he grunted disconcertedly and started eating Tennessee's new play instead.

Tenn complained, so the Horse with a deep sigh took off his best coat, and Buffo settled quickly and quietly for once to chew that. Then everyone seemed satisfied.

We lunched just outside Rome, drove until six o'clock. The village of Circeo is beautiful and there was a fiesta with colored flags and a loud band. We had a swim, even Buffo for the first time. He was very funny and brave. Both Tennessee and I wanted to stay the night, but the Horse kicked up such a fuss at the idea that we were too exhausted and bored to argue, although as things turned out it would have been far wiser to stay.

Drove over a very bad road and got to Magnani's villa. We were greeted by five vicious dogs. Tenn immediately became very shy and so Frankie and me had to do most of the talking. She looked extraordinary, with a rather dirty greasy face and shorts and her jacket open to the waist showing (rather unfortunately, I thought) her bosoms. I suppose because I have a rather large bosom myself I always feel self-conscious when other people parade theirs. She was most charming and pleased to see us. Tenn was in his dream-world catching forty winks. The Horse was nervous. We dined at the best hotel, drove off at midnight. Then the engine started stalling, so we stopped and were picked up by five locals who arranged for us to be towed into the next village, where there were no hotel rooms, and we took a taxi to Rome. Apparently one of Anna's sharp stones had torn the crankcase, so we were driving without oil. Hope the car is alright. Well, the cat will mew and Horse will have his way.

Rome, still 30th July

Left Rome in chaos as usual. Had coffee with Nina, Duchess Colona di Cesaro, Mita Corti and Dada Ruspoli who was so drugged and boring. Tennessee and I missed Meat Block, the stewardess we had to Vienna who took an instantaneous dislike to Tenn. He was so suspicious he accused her of poisoning his water. He sipped it and then very mysteriously passed it to me, saying "Does this taste like water to you?" I laughed till I cried.

Barcelona, August 1, Hotel Colon

We arrived here—it is so alive, this city. Washed and then Tenn and me went down to the bar where we had one of our long serious conversations for which this summer has been remarkable. Tenn talks more freely and openly to me than ever before—about fear. All neurotics are frightened and he thinks that more than 75% of his energy and creative force goes into fighting his fears of not being able to bring off his writing, so his strength ebbs away. He thinks he has intuition and powers of sensitivity and feeling far above his intellectual powers, and from these alone he has much to say in the world.

Maybe if he went to a psychiatrist he would be released and put all his time to writing freely—I told him that if he had a faith, any faith, it would release him because his writing would not then be so important to him, for now it is everything to him, and thereby he would also get relieved. He agrees. He says his grandfather is a really religious old man and believes in his God—I'm longing to meet him, and intend to do so when I go to America this autumn.

Sitges

Arrived today alone at three. That fool Oliver mucked it all up. I had to go with Oliver to meet his boy Sebastian who is much too good for him. I don't know why I went except Tennessee let him down in not going, so I felt I had to go for Tennessee.

I do love Tennessee and don't think there is anyone alive who is more sweet and gentle, kind and generous and so full of talent. He has been so wonderful to me all these weeks. His companionship and support are what I value now most in my life.

August 6

Went to Montserrat to see the Black Madonna. This is the first time in my life I have been deeply moved by a religious miraculous statue. I felt quite different when I prayed to her, so free and released. I prayed for J. of course, for him to have faith and strength and to come back to me IF HE WANTS.

I prayed for Mummy, for her not to get worse, and for Tsapy [Maria's brother, Vladimir Britnev] to get a job for her sake, and of course for my beloved Tennessee, his work, and for him to have a success and to get better physically. I am so concerned over his state but I don't want him to feel that. If only he would stop taking those sedative pills in the day and not drink so much. Dr. Gourewitsch says he must as his condition is serious. I don't want him to go to an analyst, but if I go to the States I will try and get him organized under a nerve specialist without frightening him—but it's important to do it now and not leave it. He has great strength of will, so maybe he can overcome these claustrophobic fits himself with intelligent guidance and help—I so hoped he would have confidence in Gourewitsch but I'm afraid not.

August 9

We have now been to five bullfights, and reading Hemingway's book gives one a wonderful added concern and understanding of everything. It makes the theatre pallid.

Last night Tenn and I walked around after dinner hand in hand round the Ramblas into the whore district. We couldn't find the streets for a long time, and finally came there. It was very wild as the U.S. Navy was leaving—SEVEN BATTLESHIPS, their last night. I've never seen anything so sordid and horrible. Went to a little café and two Spaniards were playing, one the mandolin and the other the guitar, and three men singing in turn. Tenn and me sat there fascinated. We were the only foreigners. We had two glasses of wine which cost one peseta (2d.!!). 10 popped into the whorehouse and I had to stay outside which was most embarrassing. He described what he saw—the fat old whores trying to lure me in, parading in mad costumes fanning themselves, one in a short chiffon ballet skirt. She was pregnant, and kept flinging her skirt up to show her swollen belly.

We came home around two and had dinner at the Colon. Food excellent. Tenn thinks Hemingway is really queer as he has an unnatural concern about queens—and, Tenn says, writes uninterestingly about women. So I said, if that were true, it proved he, 10, was normal, as he can only write interestingly about women. 10 laughed, and had no answer.

Madrid Friday 13th August 1954

This morning Tennessee came into my room saying he was unable to fly to Madrid as he hadn't slept. I already knew that as last night I heard him in our adjoining rooms ordering mineral water. So I set off on my own. I felt sure the plane would crash, 13th a Friday. Babushka died on 13th January, Friday.

Tennessee clings to life and longs to live. He is certainly much more delicate and I worry about him and how he will continue. He talks so often of death, and fears it.

Madrid 14th [August]

Went to the Prado and spent the morning there. Ran into Vivien Leigh. I do like her so much. She is charming and beautiful. Bought a nice wallet for Tennessee and some gloves for Mummy. Wish this hotel wasn't so expensive.

Rome 25th August

The other evening for the first time I really realized about 10's claustrophobia which in spite of Frankie telling me existed I had never come across. We were in the cinema, and he suddenly left. I never noticed him going. When we came out, we saw him in a bar opposite. Frankie said for me to go in as 10 didn't like being disturbed when he had claustrophobia. So I went in and his eyes were all red and he told us to drive up to Rosatti's and we would be able to take the car. However, when I told the Horse he flew into a rage and said he wanted to go and see the whores at the station.

So we left 10 rather against my will and the Horse and I talked by the station. I was most touched by him. He is really so intelligent and good, but unfortunately very coarse. But in his understanding and sensitivity he's helped me a great deal with my problem over J. and I'm most grateful to him and really am terribly fond of him. I would hate to see him and 10 break up, but I don't believe they ever will because they both love each other. And tonight I realized what a difficult position it is living with 10—who is a genius but with these strange suspicions of things no one could ever even think of.

[Alcide] De Gasperi [the Italian premier] died aged 72 from heart. Apparently every reference poor Frankie unwittingly made Tennessee interpreted as being a dig at him and his approaching death. He described an evening at Capriccio's when Frank said, "You look very strange tonight. Have you heard about De Gasperi's death?"

Of course I assured him it was sheer nonsense. However, to make matters worse, both Frankie and I went to see De Gasperi lying in state at the church near here. Came home to find 10 in bed and we told him. Then I found his whiskey flask in my handbag and offered to put it by his bed, which he also took as malice on my part.

However, thank God I insisted on getting to the root of the trouble the very next day, and he told me everything and asked me not to tell Frank, so I haven't. He also described the terror of claustrophobia he gets, and how frightening it is, and how he has to be left alone and his heart pounds and pounds and he feels as though he were suffocating and panics, and so has to have a drink to relax.

In Spain all this summer we have been having very intimate conversations. He is obviously haunted by his sister, and something he once said to her when she was already beginning to lose her mind and she sneaked on him to their mama. So he saw her standing in the doorway and he shouted out as he went downstairs, "I never want to see your ugly old face again." And she shrank away from him.

Also his fear of dying soon is a very real fear. [Tennessee, from what I recall, had the suspicion that Frankie wanted him to die, and our innocent remarks were interpreted as a Borgian conspiracy.]

We went to a nightclub, a horrid place called Bricktop's, and a fat singer, Spivvy, sang a very vulgar song in English about two queens, and one was a cream puff, "like you know who," [someone] who I am particularly fond of. The song was written by Paul Bigelow. I was horrified, and when Spivvy came to our table, I very nicely said, "Don't you think it would be nicer not to use anybody's name?" Whereupon 10 said I was being fussy, but Spivvy agreed and said that she would change the lyrics. The Horse paid the bill and we left. Ten was a bit tight, and consequently quarrelled with Frankie about the bill. And then we talked about the song, and he said I embarrassed everyone at the table. And so I said, How would you like me not to have protested if it had been "Tennessee Williams, that cream puff" instead? Whereupon he lost his temper and said, "You really hate homosexuals." I just said quietly, I'm leaving tomorrow, Tenn. And as we were driving along, he put his arms around me and apologized to me. He said he got drunk. I know he doesn't really think I hate him.

Another evening with Sam Spiegel who invited us on his yacht and to Venice and to dinner. We had a drink with Magnani first, and Hal Wallis [who was producing the film version of *The Rose Tattoo*], which was a strain. Then Frank very selfishly said he was going to see Charlie Chaplin in *City Lights* and not go to Spiegel's. This upset 10. When we got to Spiegel's, Frank had a drink and got up to leave. Spiegel's girl Betty Boo said she wanted to see the film. Then 10 did. So against the wishes of the hosts, we went to the film. Then Frank again insisted on taking us to the Taverna Romana where Magnani and Wallis were eating, and Spiegel didn't want to go. And then Spiegel said to 10, "I know you haven't had a success since *Streetcar*."

[*Added in handwriting*] Tenn—Hotel Rembrandt, Tangiers, till May 27, then American Express, Rome.

[*The diary breaks off here.*]

Left to right: Unidentified, Sam Spiegel (Maria called him Spieglie-Wieglie), Maria and Tennessee having dinner at the Lido on the Champs-Elysées in Paris, 1952

Frank Merlo, 1950

Tennessee, Maria
and Professor
Oliver Evans,
called the Clown
because of his
unceasing antics,
Naples

Tennessee and Anna Magnani (with unidentified man)
at Les Naturistes in the Palais Royal, Paris, 1952

———

ON SEPTEMBER 2, Maria decided to go down to Bari, to San Giovanni di Rotonda, to see Padre Pio, a monk and seer who had the stigmata. Tennessee wanted to go with Maria, but she refused to allow it, saying that he would start whining and spoil everything.

———

[*Letter never sent*]

323 East 58th Street
[New York City]

October 17, 1954

Dearest Maria:

Never had a quiet moment since we landed here till la Magnani took off by plane for Hollywood. Then *Cat on a* [*Hot*] *Tin Roof* was typed and Audrey and Gadg are both hot for it and a production is being formulated, with great tensions and contentions. Of course Audrey wants Liebling to produce it as [she] is reluctant to let it out of their hands. Cheryl and the Dame are both maneuvering for a glimpse. The only thing I want is Kazan. The thing I don't want is Liebling. But anyhow it will all come to a head this week and I suspect it will be Cheryl again with possibly Kazan and I co-producing and maybe Liebling creeping in somehow as a silent, I hope, partner. The trouble is that silence and Liebling are about as incompatible as any two elements since fire and water.

We leave for Key West in about a week. They are going to start shooting the exteriors of *Tattoo* there November 3. Till Nov. 17th. I have to pick up Grandfather in St. Louis and fly him down. I am supposed to stop off in New Orleans for a day or two to lend a hand in preparations for the opening of Raffaello's opera in that city. May need police protection with Oliver in town! I have never answered his card. Frank says not to.

I had lunch with your former fiancé day before yesterday. Kept on my dark glasses and didn't mention your name till he brought it up, when lunch was nearly over, after I had demanded a small bottle of domestic Burgundy. He kept dropping his silver in acute state of nerves. I played it cool. Same old dismal story—too much vitality, [he] doesn't want children, "just got scared," and so forth. Only a few nights before I had seen him at the theatre with you know who [Dyepot], sitting in the most expensive seats, so I maintained a slightly skeptical air when he renewed his protestations that this was "tutto finito" in his life. I felt embarrassed and sad the whole time and I think he did, too. He suffers from the most obvious and terrible sort of inner confusions but I still don't think he is justified in victimizing others.

Doll, I have mobilized the city in an all-out campaign to find "WORK FOR MARIA!" THAT IS THE CRY! Thaddeus Suski is particularly optimistic about the prospects and since he is terribly fond of you, I think he will very likely come up with something. So if things are stout in London, don't despond or despair. *Orpheus* is off till next fall.

Gadg just called. We are to meet in Sam Spiegel's suite at the Hotel Madison in twenty minutes for I don't know what nefarious purpose. Sam still has the same girl he had with him in Rome.

Give Little Mother my love. I'll write you again from the South.

Love ever, Tenn.

———

"As Audrey Wood's husband (whom she always called Liebling) was lying in his infant cradle, the Ugly Fairy must have given him a walloping great clout with her wand. He was the most extraordinary-looking man, with long ears which dangled well below his knees, and a wrist-alarm which clanged noisily and inappropriately, terrifying everybody, including himself. Tennessee had never been overly fond of him. Liebling had been an agent, but had never produced anything. And as Tennessee's mistrust grew, so Liebling became the scapegoat for any situation, however far removed, which went awry. If Tennessee lost his mackintosh, he'd still snarl beneath his breath, 'It's all Liebling's fault!'

"Tennessee's grandfather was longing to escape, having very reluctantly been living with his daughter, Edwina, all this time. He would sit on the porch of the house in St. Louis, fully dressed with panama hat and suitcase, shouting to the passing cars, 'ONE HUNDRED DOLLARS to anybody who will take me to the station!' "

Maria taught Tennessee some words of London Cockney rhyming slang. "At it like knives" meant, euphemistically, an orgy; "knife laid aboard" means a seduction. Rhyming slang particularly caught Tennessee's imagination: "Out like stout. In like Flynn."

"I notice that fewer and fewer people are Flynn."

———

October 29, 1954

Dearest Maria:

This must be a very sketchy sort of a letter as there's too much to cover and not enough time. Frank and I are in St. Louis. A very sad thing has happened: Grandfather has had a slight stroke just two days before we got here, probably from the excitement of his imminent escape. So now he can't make it. His left side is slightly paralyzed, and that, together with his 97 years, makes it too difficult to consider moving him to Key West as he dreamed and longed for all summer long. Evidently he had a dreadful summer. He says Mother gave him "four lectures a day, always winding up with a eulogy for herself," as he describes it. He fell down repeatedly but the last fall couldn't get up. Whether or not it was an actual stroke the doctor isn't sure. He has use of the arm and fingers, better than Carson, but has to be cared for like a baby at the present time. Today we transferred him from the hospital to a nursing home, frightfully expensive, but pleasant, full of dotty old people who wander about, from room to room, paying social calls on each other. One old fellow dropped in and said he was in one nursing home and he put his wife in another, because she thought he was keeping another woman in the house and made it so miserable he had to sell the house and go to separate infirmaries to relieve the situation; another that lay in bed shouting "Goodbye, goodbye!" incessantly and waving to everyone that passed in the corridor. Others are not loony, just noisy or cranky or enfeebled by years. I had hoped that Grandfather would not live to become helpless as he now is: it is very depressing, of course. Seeing *Rose Tattoo* filmed right next door to him in Key West would have been such a thrill for the old man. The film starts November third. We have to leave here tomorrow to arrive on time. They are doing all the exteriors, the school and church scenes, in Key West, then going back to Hollywood for the long interior scenes.

Kazan had committed himself (verbally) to do *Cat on a [Hot] Tin Roof*, starting rehearsals February 1st. We'll return about Xmas to begin casting. He is genuinely enthusiastic about the script but of course he had suggestions which I have been trying to follow and that has kept me busy as a "Cat on a Tin Roof"! We literally had engagements for every waking hour in New York, some overlapping and of course a great many forgotten, but I feel better, despite this turmoil, than I did when I left Italy. Perhaps I am geared for excitement. On the other hand, perhaps I will suddenly fall apart altogether, like the one-horse shay. Did I say Horse?

Gore Vidal, Tennessee and Maria at the Key West opening
of the movie *The Rose Tattoo,* 1955

Magnani seemed to adore New York, she got more and more frantic, till
finally one evening when we called on her, she came prancing out of the
bedroom in just a pair of transparent nylon panties, holding one finger over
each nipple, and did a sort of Cossack dance in this costume. She had a crush
on Johnny Nicholson, our gay landlord. She has a genius for the wrong
attachments, it seems. Knife was not laid aboard! He fled in acute apprehension. But I heard from Hollywood that she is somewhat interested now in
Hal Wallis.

I know you are just waiting for me to tell you all about lunch with J.,
that annual lunch we have at his club. Well, this time I had the nerve to
order a pint of imported Burgundy, but I cut down on my food to make
up for it. I did not mention you once. He got to the end of the lunch before,
in a weak, shaky voice, he said to me, "How is Maria?" (This is what is
known as a "Cat and Mouse Game.") I said, "Maria? Oh, fine! She's doing
a film in Rome, I think, and having a wonderful time." Then immediately
changed the subject. I did not want to discuss you with him at all. If I must

tell you the reason—I had seen him only two evenings before with you know who [Dyepot], occupying a divan in the most expensive orchestra section of the Tallulah Bankhead play, so I really did not think it suitable to talk about you to him. Tell me if I am wrong, but I felt that you would prefer for me not to under those circumstances. Anything that I said about you might be interpreted as making some sort of a plea, which is certainly not what you want. Despite my reserve, my silence, he began to explain and justify his behavior with the usual rigmarole about taking fright of your vitality, your desire for children, which he thinks are not right for him now, and winding up, lamely, with the admission that he "just got scared." As usual, I felt sorry for him. I think I feel even sorrier for Dyepot. It is really and truly a terrible mess for both of them to be in, "Don't you fink so, Mary?"

Your registered letter is being forwarded to Key West. We'll find it there. The Horse was too busy to call for it at the post-office in New York.

We called Dinky Dakin last night at his army post in Big Springs, Texas. He was drunk as a fiddler's bitch, wild screams were echoing from a party in progress, and he informed Mother that he would be out of the Air Force in one month! This surprised me, but Mother says she had observed some "disturbing signs" the last time he was home on leave. "Per qualità!"

We leave tomorrow for Florida and I'll write you from there. Remember my address, 1431 Duncan Street, Key West. Several people are looking for work for you in the States, especially that nice Polack, Thaddeus Suski.

Much love, 10

———

THE FILM of *The Rose Tattoo*, with Anna Magnani as Serafina Delle Rose and Burt Lancaster as Alvaro Mangiacavallo, directed by Daniel Mann and produced by Hal Wallis, was released in December 1955.

———

[Envelope postmarked Key West, November 7(?), 1954]

"Sweet Miss Mary (sweeter than you know!)"

I found your long letter including the checks waiting for me here in Key West. I am rather cross with you for returning the traveller's checks. I guess it was my fault, though. I never know how much money I have in the bank, am always afraid to enquire, and I had a morbid idea last summer that I was near destitution. When I got back to the States I was agreeably surprised, for I had quite a large sum left in my account and my expenses had not been at all excessive. I am sorry I didn't know about this earlier, for we could have had much more fun and stayed longer in Venice and so forth. All Americans, I'm afraid, have this pathological concern with cash. I am quite well off this year. It would distress me keenly if you did not let me know if you needed money. You should feel absolutely no embarrassment about it. I regard you, and I hope you do me, as a close relation. So I am sending the hundred bucks right back to you. I also intended, of course, for you to keep whatever was left from the deposit on the apartment, thought I made that clear on the boat when we were sailing. I realize full well that the sort of help you truly want is encouragement as an artist. Some day I am going to direct you in a play. Maybe soon. Maybe in London this spring or summer. Cheryl is planning to produce *Tattoo* herself in London with Eli [Wallach] and perhaps Maureen [Stapleton] and she wants me to direct it. I don't believe you're quite young enough for Rosa (at least as a child) but I think you could play Estelle Hohengarten (the other woman) beautifully, poetically, as it ought to be played, so let's keep that in mind. I could not offer you the female lead in *Cat on a [Hot] Tin Roof* in the States but I think I could get you role as understudy of the lead, and that if Gadg worked with you, you might be able to play it on tour or in England because I think it is a part that would fit you and please you. I think a lot of you has gone into the writing of it. Wit and gallantry etc. I finished my re-write on it this morning. I'm sending it off Monday and will soon know if Gadg is sufficiently satisfied with it to go ahead this season. It's getting late. They may want to put it off till the next. I hope not! My heart and my life hang suspended when I don't have a play. They've been shooting *Tattoo* for four days now and all is going promisingly well. But Anna and "Big Nat" [Natalia Murray] are coming to dinner tonight and we will hear a tale of woe, for so far Anna has only had a chance to do little bits of her role and is like a hungry tigress with a big juicy hunk of raw meat dangled outside her cage. They're only shooting exteriors here and the big scenes for Anna will come at the studio on the West Coast. Christopher Isherwood is here with the youngest-looking boy I have ever seen outside of school. They say he is twenty but he looks so young he has to order a Coca-Cola in bars: somewhat embarrassing . . . They've been together two years so I guess it's okay. Chris you would love! He's so funny, and so wise and simple. Horse is cooking dinner. I must now dash off a letter to Grandfather. We try to write him every day now that he's in the nursing-home in St. Louis.

Much love, Tenn

NATALIA MURRAY, the girlfriend of Janet Flanner, the well-known Paris correspondent to *The New Yorker,* lived at the Hotel Continentale in Paris. Christopher Isherwood's friend, Don Bachardy, was twenty at the time. He became a celebrated Hollywood portraitist.

Tennessee's beloved grandfather, the Reverend Walter Edwin Dakin, died on February 14, 1955.

"I met Grandfather only once. Tennessee took me to St. Louis especially to meet him, and we got him drunk on ginger wine, which we'd smuggled in past the nurses. Tennessee introduced me with great pride, shouting, 'Grandfather, here is Maria.' Grandfather, stone deaf, yelled back, 'She's just come from Korea?' Tennessee was furious with his poor grandfather, flew into a terrible rage. 'I said "Maria, Maria"! I told you about her—I have just written a play about her.'

"Grandfather asked, 'What is it called?'

"Tennessee said, '*Cat on a Hot Tin Roof*!'

"Grandfather gave a muffled groan and yelled, 'Cats don't come half past eight,/Tap, tap, tapping at the garden gate.'

"Tennessee went into total decline and hissed through his teeth at me. 'This is a bad omen. The curtain always rises at half past eight. This means there will be no audience.' I had a difficult time trying to cheer him up, calm him down, and get him back to his mother's in one piece."

Jane Smith remembers a story Tennessee told her. "When Grandfather died, Tennessee rang Maria, whining that the funeral was in Missouri, and that he was busy with *Cat,* and that he was exhausted, and that anyway, Grandfather would understand if he didn't go. Maria replied icily, 'Grandfather might understand, but I don't!'—and slammed the phone down. Tennessee went to the funeral."

The first performance of *Cat on a Hot Tin Roof* was at the Morosco Theatre, New York City, on March 24, 1955. It was directed by Elia Kazan, with Barbara Bel Geddes as Maggie, Ben Gazzara as Brick, and Burl Ives as Big Daddy.

"A lot of people, Tennessee included, have said that I was the inspiration for Margaret, Maggie the Cat. Tennessee had shown me the manuscript and with a sly, sideways glance had told me, 'Read this. You're in it.'

"I was terribly thrilled at first. But I read the thing with mounting fury. I exploded, 'But I wouldn't have said that! Tennessee, she isn't even *Russian*!' Tennessee said, 'But honey! I'm writing about your spirit—your tenacity to life.'

"It's silly to say that I was his inspiration. Artists don't work like that. Maggie is like all the rest, a composite, from within Tennessee. There are bits of me in her, of course: my daughters, seeing *Cat* much later, were doubled up with the laughter of recognition. But if Tennessee had never met me, it wouldn't have made any difference. His only real inspiration was Rose: everlastingly so."

Maria was with Tennessee at the first night.

"In his usual state of nerves, Tennessee kept muttering loudly to no one in particular during the performance: 'You see, people are talking all the way through my play,' and 'It's absolutely disgraceful,' and 'They're talking, you see,' and 'They're spoiling my play.' All round us the audience was saying 'Shh! Shh!' Eventually I had to snap at Tennessee savagely: 'You're the one who's talking—you're spoiling your own play!' At the interval I felt obliged to remove him from the theatre and stop him having a fight with himself. We went across the road to a sort of semi-strip bar, where we gloomily sat, Tennessee convinced that the whole evening was a disaster.

"We returned and stood at the back of the theatre during the last scene. It finished with an enormous ovation for Tennessee and the cast. Tennessee was still unconvinced. He succeeded in having a blinding row in the middle of the first-night party with Audrey Wood, who had done no harm to anyone. He told her she had ruined the play, and that it was all Liebling's fault, anyway! They made up during the party, and we all went off as usual to Times Square, waiting for the notices to come out.

"The play was a triumph."

Tennessee responded to a critic in an article, which he sent to Maria for safekeeping—something he was to do increasingly. The extent to which Maria's "spirit" was the inspiration for Maggie is indicated in this piece.

————

ABOUT EVASIONS

In his reviews of *Cat on a Hot Tin Roof* Mr. Walter Kerr has spoken of an "evasiveness" on my part in dealing with certain questions in the play, pertinent mostly to the character of the young male protagonist, Brick Pollitt. This is not the first time that I've been suspected of dodging issues in my treatment of play-characters. Critics complained, sometimes, of ambiguities in *Streetcar*. Certainly there were many divergent ideas of Blanche's character, and many widely differing interpretations in the playing of her character among the many productions I saw at home and abroad. She was often referred to as a prostitute; often as a dipso or a nympho or a liar. The truth about human character in a play, as in life, varies with the variance of experience and view-point of those that view it. No two members of an audience ever leave a theatre, after viewing a play that deals with any degree of complexity in character, with identical interpretations of the characters dealt with. This is as it should be. I know full well the defenses and rationalizations of beleaguered writers—a defensive species—but I still feel that I deal unsparingly with what I feel is the truth of character. I would never evade it for the sake of evasion, because I was in any way reluctant to reveal what I knew of the truth. But ambiguity is sometimes deliberate and for artistically defensible reasons. I can best answer Mr. Kerr's objection by a quote from the manuscript of the play which is not yet available to readers but will be in a few weeks.

Here is a long note which occurs in the second act, at the point where Big Daddy alludes to the charge of abnormality in Brick's relation with his dead friend Skipper:

Brick's resolute detachment is at last broken through. His heart is accelerated, his forehead sweat-beaded, his breath becomes more rapid and his voice hoarse. The thing they're discussing, timidly and painfully on the side of Big Daddy, fiercely, violently on Brick's side, is the inadmissible thing that Skipper and Brick would rather die than live with. The fact that if it existed it had to be disavowed to "keep face" in the world they lived in, a world of popular heroes, may be at the heart of the "mendacity" that Brick drinks to kill his disgust with. It may be at the root of his collapse. Or it may be only a single manifestation of it, not even the most important. The bird that I hope to catch in the net of this play is not the solution of one man's psychological problem. I'm trying to catch the true quality of experience in a group of people, that cloudy, flickering, evanescent—fiercely charged!—interplay of live human beings in the thundercloud of a common crisis. Some mystery should be left in the revelation of character in a play, just as a great deal of mystery is always left at the revelation of character in life, even in one's own character to himself. This does not absolve the playwright of his duty to observe and probe as clearly and deeply as he *legitimately* can: but it should steer him away from "pat" conclusions, facile definitions, which make a play just a play, not a snare for the truth of human existence.

This I believe states clearly my defense of these so-called ambiguities of character in my plays. The point is, of course, arguable. You may prefer to be told precisely what to believe about every character in a play, you may prefer to know precisely what will be the future course of their lives, happy or disastrous or anywhere in between. Then I am not your playwright. My characters make my plays. I always start with them, they take spirit and body in my mind, nothing that they say or do is arbitrary or invented. They build the play about them like spiders weaving their web, sea-creatures making their shell. I live with them for a year and a half or two years and I know them far better than I know myself. But still they must have that quality of life which is shadowy. Was Blanche DuBois a liar? She told many lies in the course of *Streetcar* and yet at heart she was truthful. Was Brick homosexual? He probably—no, I would even say quite certainly—went no further in physical expression than clasping Skipper's hand across the space between their twin-beds in hotel-rooms and yet—his sexual nature was not innately "normal." Did Brick love Maggie? He says with unmistakable conviction: "One man has one great good true thing in his life, one great good thing which is true. I had friendship with Skipper, not love with you, Maggie, but friendship with Skipper. . . ."—But can we doubt that he was warmed and charmed by this delightful girl, with her vivacity, her humor, her very admirable pluckiness and tenacity, which are almost the essence of life itself? Of course, now that he has really resigned from life, retired from competition, removed his hat from the ring, now that he wants only things that are cool, such as his "click" and cool moonlight on the gallery and the deadening of recollection that liquor gives, her tormented face, her anxious voice, strident with the heat of combat, is unpleasantly, sometimes even odiously, disturbing to him. But Brick's overt sexual adjustment was, and must always remain, a heterosexual one. He will go back to Maggie for the sheer animal comfort of sexual release, even if she did not make him dependent on her for such creature-comforts as only a devoted slave can provide, a devoted slave who is also a devoted master, even if she had not smashed all his liquor-bottles and only she would "drive him in town for more." He is her dependent. As Strindberg said: "They call it love-hatred, and it hails from the pit. . . ."

It seems to me that Luigi Pirandello devoted nearly his whole career as a playwright to establishing the point that I am making in this argument. That "Truth" has a Protean nature, that its face changes in the eyes of each beholder. Another good writer once said: "Truth lies at the bottom of a bottomless well."

[*Added*] In production the whole play points toward and cries out for a non-conventional resolution of its conflicts. The story must be and remained

From left: Michael Steen, Maria, Anna Magnani, Tennessee and
Joanna Albus on the set of the off-Broadway revival of *Streetcar*,
1955. Maria played Blanche.

"Betty Boo" (Mrs. Spiegel), Tennessee, Sam Spiegel, Maria,
Karl Sundstrom, Josanne, Richard White (who played Stanley
Kowalski) and an unidentified man on the *Streetcar* set

the story of a strong, determined creature (Life! Maggie!) taking hold of and gaining supremacy over and converting to her own purposes a broken, irresolute man whose weakness was imposed on him by the lies of the world he grew up in. ("The wisdom of life is deeper and wider than the wisdom of men"—Gorky.) In manuscript this basic meaning may appear susceptible to some varying interpretation, but in production the whole play builds unmistakably to this single truth.

I don't think it reduces either Brick or Maggie for both to stay faithful to their true original character-line in the play. On the contrary, I think it confirms the truth of their characters and the truth of the play, and that's the distinction and value of the work.

———

"YOU CAN imagine the horror of the American immigration authorities to discover that I had been born in Leningrad. The Russian quota, of course, had been closed since 1905 or something." Notwithstanding, Redgrave, Kazan, and Gielgud all spoke up for Maria, and, to Tennessee's delight, her permit to work in America as "an artist of outstanding merit and ability" was granted.

Maria played Blanche in a revival of *A Streetcar Named Desire* at the Actors' Playhouse, New York City. The first performance was on March 3, 1955. Brooks Atkinson wrote in the *New York Times*:

> Maria Brit-Neva already has some exciting ideas about the doomed heroine. She uses unexpected humor to reveal the gallant soul beneath the cracking veneer; the absent-minded way she drapes a curtain about her as if it were an ermine wrap is a startling forewarning of madness; the serenity of the final and complete escape from sanity, hitherto the weakest scene in the play, now comes as close to tragedy as anything by an American playwright since O'Neill.

———

[*On letterhead The Robert Clay, Miami, Florida, sent to 323 East 58th Street, New York City*]

1431 Duncan
Key West, Fla.

April 27, 1955

Dearest Maria:

Choppers [Carson McCullers] just now hauled her freight out of here but the Froggies are still here sitting! Key West was not for Choppers. She was

here sitting for about two weeks, in Havana sitting for about five days, all
the time swilling my liquor and gobbling my pinkie tablets in such a way
that I reeled with apprehension. I was about to run out of pinkies. Two a
night for Choppers, content with no less! Fortunately I was able to buy some
without prescription in Havana. I had hoped Chops would start bobbing
with creative activity. After two days dictating a short play [*The Square Root
of Wonderful*] to me, she scuttled up [to] her ivory tower and bolted the
door! Said she could not be rushed into writing, had to think and dream
a long time first. Since we pursue opposite methods, she thought she'd better
go home and germinate there till she got the whole thing in her chops and
then start writing. So off went Choppers this morning on the nine-forty-five
plane to Miami. Marion [Vaccaro] is to meet her at the airport and put her
on an afternoon plane to New York, where Johnny [Nicholson] is to meet
her and put her on an evening bus to Nyack. I hope he will drive her all
the way in his car. I am worried over Choppers. I feel that she is dreaming
herself away. I was very unkind. Did not quit work to go to the airport
with her but let the Horse put her on the plane to Miami, but I paid her
expenses going and coming. It is much easier to give money than love.
Choppers needs love but I am not the Baa-Baa Black Sheep with three bags
full for Choppers. I don't even have any for the Master or the Dame or the
Little Boy Down the Lane. I care only, very much, about the studio
mornings at the Olivetti. Perhaps in this way I can give more love to more
people, at least I sometimes hope so. Of course there is a chance, maybe a
good one, that Choppers will continue to work on the play, which was a
very, very good one (she started [it] here) and keep her promise about
it. Will you call her in Nyack? She needs every little bit of attention
or affection, real or make believe, that anybody can give or pretend to
give her.

The trouble is that life makes many demands, and these decimal offerings
of the heart are never sufficient, not, at any rate, to someone like Choppers
who asks for all but expects to get nothing. I think that her poor mother
is dying of cancer. Her sister has been at home with her for the past two
days. The first day her mother was able to answer the phone, but yesterday
when we called again, she didn't. Choppers has had so much tragedy in her
life that it scares you almost into feeling indifferent to her, as if she were
hopelessly damned and you couldn't afford to think about it: the way I feel
for my sister.

I hope you are still playing Blanche as well as you can with your whole
heart and complete understanding and no intrusive annoyances from the
management, because when I think about her, Blanche seems like the youth

of our hearts which has to be put away for worldly considerations: poetry, music, the early soft feelings that we can't afford to live with under a naked light bulb which is now.

I think we're returning in about ten days. I will call you when the date is set. Spieglie Wieglie [Sam Spiegel] has been on the blower a lot, but is leaving this week for Europe. He says that he and Martin Jurow can work out a work-permit for you if Audrey doesn't. Keep on Jurow about it. He can easily do it and Audrey is on the West Coast for several weeks now. I think you should be able to get steady work on TV.

Love, 10

———

"PINKIE tablets were Seconal. From his youth, Tennessee told me, he was so desperately shy that he used to take a pill before he could face the outside world."

Johnny Nicholson had a restaurant, Nicholson's Café, on East 58th Street in New York, which was all the rage; Tennessee's apartment was above it.

Carson McCullers's play, *The Square Root of Wonderful,* was produced at the National Theatre in New York City on October 30, 1957. It was not a success.

Tennessee left for Europe with Frank, and lent Maria his apartment.

"He told Audrey Wood that I was to have as much money as I wanted. Audrey gleefully invited me up to her office: at last she had a stick for my back. She asked how much I would like.

"I said, 'A dollar a day.'

"Audrey went deadly quiet. 'But you must have more than that.'

" 'A dollar a day.'

"But one could manage perfectly well on a dollar a day. Gore Vidal was very kind to us all, finding little bits of work, small parts. I was out to most evening meals. Irene Selznick gave me old clothes of hers, wonderful clothes. And if the worst came to the worst, there were jobs demonstrating puppets at Altman's towards Christmas. Then there was Klein's Bargain Basement, a marvellous place where they sold discontinued lines from Bergdorf or Saks, all at a dollar ninety-five. We'd pick among the clothes like scavenging vultures, while speakers positioned high above us boomed out, 'DROP THAT HANDBAG! DROP THOSE PANTIES!' One woman there was caught shoplifting every day of the week. The management in despair finally begged her to take her patronage elsewhere. 'So why shop elsewhere?' she said. 'You don't get such good bargains!'

"Tennessee was most impressed and proud of my resourcefulness, pointing out my Saks one-offs to people. 'Guess what that cost her? One dollar ninety-five!' " I was livid.

———

[On letterhead Hotel Excelsior, Rome, sent to 323 East 58th Street]

American Express

June 12, 1955

Darling Maria:

Forgive me for putting off writing you, it wasn't because I wasn't thinking about you. Rome lacks your presence, as do most places where you have been and gone.

We are right now camping at the Excelsior but have found the most fabulous apartment, for less than we paid for that two-story furnace last year, and we'll move into it in six days. (My typewriter's on the blink, the space bar is broken and the Horse finds many excuses to not have it fixed.) The new apartment is in Trastevere, right across the river from last year's location, but surrounded by a lovely little piazza, a beautiful giardino, and the Palazzo Corsini in which Queen Christina of Sweden lived twenty years and died. It has four lovely rooms, a huge bath and kitchen, and will be cool since there is exposure on all sides: a perfect room for me to work in.

Anna is determined to play *Orpheus* but is *not* studying English, I think she is just too lazy. Her English, however, is better than it was in the States, for some reason; I will have to be severe with her about it, for even Anna couldn't get away with the part if she doesn't speak freely. She sincerely admires your acting, but says you are best in very dramatic scenes. Of course this is true. She is an excellent and completely honest judge of acting. She also feels that you would be at your best in high comedy, where you could use to advantage your unusual sense of humor. Sophisticated high comedy, in other words. I think so, too. Either that or highly charged drama such as the final scenes of *Streetcar*. You have not yet learned to play quiet scenes quietly. (Gently.) There is still a little too much snap, snap, off with his head, or hers, the hell with croquet!

There is to be a film of *War and Peace* here in Italy and Mario Chiari, Luchino's friend and designer, has a job with it. I told him at once you ought to be given a part and will press the matter if there is any chance to. Will advise you if anything comes of this. Meanwhile, work hard, I think John [Perry]'s letter makes it clear that London is stout as far as your acting is concerned. The day I sailed I told Audrey to give you a cheque when you need one, so don't hesitate to let her know if you run short of funds.

Please try to preserve the big fern. I've never had anything so graceful and lovely in a place of mine.

Much love, "Wee" Tennessee

———

"CARSON MCCULLERS suddenly appeared and said that Tennessee had lent her the apartment and that I must move out. I explained that as a foreigner I had nowhere else to go. She, an American, must have had alternatives—besides which, Tennessee had lent the flat to me. Audrey settled the matter characteristically by saying that her client, Carson, should have the flat. I went to stay with Tatiana [Schvetzoff]."

———

[*On letterhead Hotel Excelsior, Rome, about June 20, 1955, sent to 323 East 58th Street*]

12 Via Corsini
Rome

Maria darling:

You keep saying "Do write" but don't mention the letter I sent you about a week ago. Did you get it?

I think you and Carson are *both* in the wrong. You are not considering enough the shock of her mother's death who is the last person who was close to her in the world. I think she is panicky with loneliness, at this moment, and staying in the apartment for a while probably gives her some tangible evidence of being cared for. Laughing at Choppers is too easy, but when you remember the poetry of her work, you feel differently about her, appreciate her isolation and her longings, and you forgive her selfishness.

She is being selfish about the apartment, on the other hand, and I am writing her and mailing at the same dispatch this letter and appeal to limit her stay in the apartment to the shortest period that is psychologically essential to her. I think she simply could not bear to stay, for a while, in the house where her mother died. She does feel deeply, though she is now constantly on the run-away from her feelings, and the liquor has a lot to do with that, and the pinkies, too. I think I understand a good deal about her, she has suffered so much that she has had to put on a hard suit of armor.

Tennessee and Carson McCullers at La Florida in Havana, Cuba

If you are gentle with her, and show her some affection, there will be no problem. I am sure she will release the apartment very quickly.

So Bigelow is back! DON'T LET HIM OR ANYONE ELSE OUT OF YOUR SIGHT IN APARTMENT. Naturally I prefer you to occupy apartment as soon as possible as you will care for my beloved fern and are conscientious about getting things done and cared for. I do wish you would have the bedroom chaise covered for us, I like the green velvet idea, anyhow a color that will go well with the gold and deep red which are now the dominant colors. As it now appears, it is an eye-sore.—I am flying to Athens on Wednesday, then around the Greek isles and may pop up to Istanbul as Gadg said it was delightfully evil. We are in new apartment. Cool, and quiet. Work going badly, very. Have to finish the film-script for Gadg and really don't know what more to do with the thing. Catch-as-Catch-Can [Kazan] just says re-write, re-write, and I don't know what the hell for or about. I ran into Mita on the street last night, sitting with some boring member [of the] Roman nobility. We stopped at her table. She did not ask us to sit down but the Horse said, May we join you? She complied in a tone of some surprise. I got claustrophobia and fled in a taxi to fetch a pinkie from the apartment having just discovered that the pocket supply was missing. When I got back, she had gone and the Horse was sitting there drinking double vodkas and sucking his huge Horse teeth with a very grim look. You know how he is about the Roman nobility, and how they are about the Horse.

I am back at the swimming club and Pepino is still on the run. Had a row with a Roman censor there yesterday, a dour lady who is secretary to the head of the censors, who said she had turned down *Tattoo* for Visconti because it was "insulting to Italians." I said "To censors the human heart is a dirty thing" and that "censors are the death of the arts," and so forth, and she fled and there was a terrible hush, with sibilant whispers, all about the pool. I may be stout!—However, I am flying to Athens on Wednesday and shall bathe in the Aegean and think of Lord Byron so raptly that I may develop a limp, if not write a canto.

Now I must stop and write Choppers. "Play it cool," as they say, and I think you will be re-instated earlier than you suspect.

Love, Tenn.

[*Added in handwriting*] This is a *very* dull letter. It reflects my spirit this hot Sunday. I must keep on the move until something revives me.

[*On the back of a postcard of the Parthenon, Athens, postmarked June 25, 1955*]

> Today, here, sitting
> Tonight, Istanbul, sitting.
> Horse & Dog, Rome, sitting.
> Glad you are 58th Street, sitting!
> Love—10

IN CHEKHOV'S *The Three Sisters,* the disagreeable sister-in-law, Natasha, complains to Olga about Olga's old nanny, saying, "She does nothing: she just sits!" Olga replies, "Well, let her just sit." Maria and Tennessee used to have endless jokes about people "sitting."

Maria was re-installed in Tennessee's Fifty-eighth Street apartment, sitting.

1955

[On letterhead Hotel Excelsior, Rome, sent to 323 East 58th Street, New York]

12 Via Corsini

July 1, 1955

Dearest Maria:

The big heat has descended on Rome but this apartment turns out to be a really cool place and so we don't suffer from it.

I took a remarkably brief trip through Athens and Istanbul, all by air, in turbo-prop planes which are the finest flying I've done yet, no vibration, wonderful take-offs and landings and incredibly short times in the air. *Hated*—the Turks. Dirty, ugly, hard as rocks and nails, and profoundly, monumentally cynical about the hopeless inequality of their social conditions. In Italy they do nothing about it, in Spain they don't want to do anything about it, in Turkey they don't even *notice* it. Somehow I got no kick about being in Europe and seeing Asia at the same time. I just said to myself, There's Asia, and retired to the bar for another screw-driver. I was driven to vodka because Scotch was two dollars a shot. Athens was nicer, but unendurably hot. My room was air-conditioned, they had the air-conditioner but it was set in too large a window and there were inches of open space all around it, promptly letting out the cool air as fast as it came in. I tried stuffing the spaces with towels, the chambermaid snatched them out and—I didn't stay long. . . .

Evenings are devoted to Anna, and greater love (or is it endurance?) hath no man. Today she departed for the sea, Circeo, for a five-day respite, hers and mine! She has taken off *stones* of fat! Those old satchels under the eyes are still there, but she's practically a pin-up in shape. And her English is better, though still not good enough for a Broadway debut. She promised to study hard, with her English records at Circeo. I believe she wants to do the play [*Orpheus Descending*] sincerely, especially if it is possible to get Marlon. Is Marlon in New York? I don't think he is going to answer my letters, so would you try to worm out of him some idea of his intentions so I can let poor Anna know? She also has plans and commitments that she has to think of, though she is willing for Marlon to say when. He never answered her letter, and she claims that the romantic side of her interest [in] him has been dispelled, but she feels that only he, as a co-star, could give her the necessary confidence to do a play in English.

The Horse is sick. I think my sudden return from Greece and Turkey was a severe shock to him. Well, I am taking off again for Spain to see the bull-fights and may drop down to Tangier to see Bowles who has returned there from Ceylon.

That fancy cow Lilla van Saher was here, and has already left to see Bowles. She wants him to compose music for her play.

Oh! Yesterday I bumped into Jenny Cross on the street. She was charming to me. She said that Monkey Tree is in London, where she will have two plays produced next season (one about monkeys, one about trees, I guess!), but is heading back this way. I'll advise her to make it *one* play, just putting the monkeys in the trees!—very simple, and livelier, I should think. I cannot be kind about other people who are writing plays, especially since my work is going so badly this summer.—Long letter from Choppers, all about her great new love for "Saint" and his for her and the play they're doing *together.*

A passing reference to her mother's passing. Absolutely no mention of the apartment, thank heavens! It looks like you're Flynn till we return anyhow.

How is the horrible Henry Hewes? Give him a good kick for me, and tell him he knows what he can do with his vote at the Critics Circle.

I'm so glad that Jane and Tony [Smith] are back. Will you please pick out a nice gift for the coming twins and let Audrey or Lefkowitz know that I authorized it? Send it from us three, you, me, Frankie. I think maybe two little silver cups or spoons or cereal bowls or something of that nature, Oh, *dear!*—I *do* hope they're not *Siamese . . .* If they are, just *one* cup and *one* spoon, dear!

Must hustle my bustle to Amexco before she closes for the afternoon; then to that dreary old pool—when will something really new and different take place in my life? Not till the "Reaper" comes, dear? Not till five after five?

Much love, Tenn

―――――

"Lilla van Saher was a Hungarian émigrée, a would-be producer and novelist, who idolized and pestered Tennessee.

"Iris Tree was a poetess, actress and 'great lady,' the daughter of Beerbohm Tree. She had about as much a sense of humor as Julius Lefkowitz, an accountant to whom I had taken Tennessee. Audrey Wood was most displeased at my interference in the matter. The fact that we childishly chanted at her 'Well, is it alrightkowitz about Lefkowitz?' did not appease her."

―――――

1 9 5 5

[On letterhead Hotel (added in handwriting: "Spastic") Colon, Barcelona, sent to 323 East 58th Street, New York]

July 17, 1955

Dearest Maria:

I've just come from the bull-fight, a very good one, so tense at one point that I had to wash down a pinkie with a great gulp of Scotch in my little flask, am now half in and half out of the conscious world. It is pretty good here. All the little black dwarfettes are still scuttling about, and a few hunch-backs, and the gigolo with the great melting eyes and tiny mustache is paying flattering court, all but drinking champagne from my slipper. I made the mistake of going to Sitges last week-end. I had simply forgotten we had been there, and when I recognized it as that place we had been with Oliver last summer, I caught the next train back. The Horse, poor thing, has been continually sick. Soon as he recovered from hepatitis, he came down with dysentery or colitis; when I talked to him on the phone yesterday he told me in a very faint voice that he had bled and fainted on the toilet. I think he works himself into these conditions through sheer nervous tension. When I tell him this, he flies into passions. I do hope he'll go to the analyst next fall, soon as we get back to the States, as he is going to ruin himself this way. I would stay with him but he is so cross that I feel it's better for him for me to stay on the hoof; besides, I am restless this summer. I am supposed to meet Kenneth Tynan here in Spain the 25th but I hate to remain here that long. It does get wearing after a while. I have yet to find a single Spanish dish that I enjoy eating except paella Valenciana, that huge rice dish which usually makes me ill, and the lovely, cool and sweet white melons. I spent every afternoon on the beach, swimming and sunning, and have turned as black as—black as. . . . A huge "vague de chaleur" is sweeping relentlessly up and down and across Europe! Everywhere's burning! I spent a lot of time under my electric fan in bed with the movie mags and whatever pocket re-print I can find on the Ramblas which is possible to read. What news of Tony and Janie? and their twins? Did you see Henry's production of *Three Players* [*of a Summer Game*]? What happened about that son of a bitch Bentley's Russian play? How is Choppers, are her chops full of pinkies, or has she swallowed a few in a fit of "Dame Pique" or "Oh, dash it all!" Give her my love. We must stop making fun of Choppers. Is the air-conditioning working all right, are you on good terms with our landlady, Miss Nicksie [Johnny Nicholson]? Give all the Russians my love. Be nice to Audrey, I think she does her best for you. What has Catch-as-

Catch-Can [Kazan] caught lately besides a great clout from Molly? Is the Dame back from London, and if so, how are atmospheric conditions around the Pierre, on close summer nights?

Spieglie Wieglie took us to dinner, in Rome, my last evening there, along with Ingrid Bergman and [Roberto] Rossellini. Got me drunk and I told him he could do *Orpheus* if he signed Brando, but only on that condition. I guess it's a long shot so I needn't worry. But I like Sam better all the time, and don't really understand Audrey's dread of him as a producer. Betty [Spiegel] saw your mother in London and Sam says she was enchanted by her and didn't notice that she was not perfectly well, so probably she's in better condition now.

Send the Horse some very fine toilet tissue and a quart of blood plasma and some spirits of ammonia: just a thought! (This is my vulgar summer!) My bête noir Leslie Eggleston just phoned from the lobby suggesting that we have dinner, so I must put a period to this pointless letter.

Much love, Tenn

[*Added in handwriting*] P.S. Leaving tomorrow for Valencia—then Tangier or Rome—write Rome.

———

AT ABOUT this date Maria came back to the apartment to find Marlon Brando typing this letter:

Dear Tenn:

I am contemplating making a pass at your girl, but she doesn't look easy and besides I'm beat anyway. I just had a look at the keys of this typewriter and I was glad to see the ashes that had fallen off your cigarette through the keys on to the table. I am satisfied to see that your general obliviousness to externals still rages on, magnificent and un-checked.

Please disregard telegram if you get it. I sent it when your phone was off the hook.

I feel like a bucket of stork shit for having fucked things around so, but I've been walking around in a forest of old toilets these past three days what with having to fill out 27 visas and get passport pictures taken and finger prints for the police dept., blah blah

blah . . . anyhow I won't expect you not to be irked. I'll keep calling and I hope I will catch you . . .

Love, Marlon

The new U.N. motto is
Fuck hate

Bob MacGregor, whom Maria christened "Twitching-Unbewitching," was by this time managing director of New Directions.

——————

[Handwritten up to "that faithful hoof!" Sent from Rome, [?] August 1955, to 323 East 58th Street]

Dearest Maria:

My Olivetti suffered a sympathetic breakdown between here (Rome) and there (Barcelona) so I must ask you to decipher my scrawl as cunningly as I sometimes manage to make out yours. The Horse has trotted out with Miss Olivetti under one hoof, which leaves him only three to prance on through the dazzling noon streets, and I wonder if I will ever see Miss Olivetti again, or will she write two plays for London production, and be pelted with nut-meats from the wings and forget that she ever lived so sad and dutiful and tedious a life with Tennessee. I trust that she will appreciate that I never *blamed her* for my failures.

Please *don't* be cross with poor *MacGregor*. You and I have exactly the same fault of judging people by their attitude toward us. (I loathe Windham because he despises my work, you hate MacGregor because he maintains his loyalty to Dyepot.) *We* are *both* dreadfully wrong. Windham is right to despise my work if he truly despises it (he's only wrong to inflict his despising on my out-of-town-opening nerves)—MacGregor is right to be faithful to Dyepot if that's his true attachment. In our hatreds of people we always betray our own weakness, don't we?—They have just now—

(Horse has returned with Miss Olivetti under that faithful hoof!)

—Picking up where I left off: A letter from Mother and Dinky indicates they have put Rose back in the asylum because she refused to remain with her companion who had slapped her three times for unspecified transgressions. This shocks me beyond endurance. There is right now eight thousand in her trust fund and she will get any minute thirty thousand more from the movie sale, and what could be more dreadful than a state asylum, which is surely not air-conditioned, in the Missouri plains in mid-summer!

I think my dear little sister deserves a crown in heaven, if there are crowns and heaven, for what she's had to suffer these eighteen years since committed. To give Dinkers credit, he recommends that she be transferred at once to a Catholic private asylum in St. Louis where Mother could see her regularly. Mother is apparently in love with the head doctor at the state asylum, Dr. Hoctor, nice alliteration [*sic*] there, and waits upon his decision in all matters concerning Rose. He is probably a good man, but you can imagine what state asylums are like. The trouble is that private ones are sometimes worse. I was very late in getting this news about her as my mail was not forwarded to Spain and I just returned yesterday. More good news: my father has cut off his old maid sister who is eighty years old because she accused him of drinking(!).—He hasn't drawn more than one sober breath since he went back to Tennessee, and hardly more than two before then!—Consequently I must assume her support unless she is to become a public charge. She is a wonderful old girl, truly heroic, so I don't really mind, but aren't people savages really?! As bad as us . . .

But you are sweet to write me so many letters, the only fun I have had this summer has been your letters, I mean the only good humor.

I suppose it's impossible to resist one's own babies, regardless of a consistency of sex in all three, but I do wish Fate had dealt the Smiths at least one male child, I think they had one coming. However!—I am longing to see the lot of them when I get back.

It's beastly of Josanne, I never really trusted that creature, not to return the hard-earned money you loaned her for the trip. Don't let her get away with it! The frogs are the world's most mercenary people.

The death of Margo [July 25]!—such a frightful shock. The Horse told me about it over long-distance. Somehow I don't believe it was a natural death. She was too sturdy. You know what I think? She may have had an abortion. That frequently results in uremic poisoning, if it goes wrong. There was an odd bit about her inhaling fumes from a carpet being cleaned which doesn't ring true at all. The Reaper has been altogether too busy these last few months, he must stay his hand for a while, or move into other pastures. It hurts me to think how often we laughed at dear Margo for her little silliness and paid too little attention to her great heart.

I encountered Oliver Evans in Barcelona. He suddenly appeared out of nowhere, stalked up to me, his face the face of an absolute mad-man, and hissed at me: "I want to pay my respects to the gifted author of 'Hard Candy' "! I rose terrified from my seat and offered him my hand which he

Professor Oliver Evans, 1948

took. His hand was icy! I introduced him to my dinner companion. Then he nodded and swept on. I left for Valencia at once! Paul Bowles wrote me that he [Evans] had been in Tangier, very desperate, complaining of terrible headaches. I still think my story was a compassionate study but I should have realized he would think it was just about him. How we do pay and pay for being thoughtless! And go on paying . . .

I have requested MacGregor to hold back the poetry book [*In the Winter of Cities*] till I return from Europe, there are too many misunderstandings. Also Jay should go over it, he has such a wonderful ear and mine is no good. I like the Sandra poem except that I should say either three or five men and stick to it. You might mention to Bob (if you still speak to him) that I want to keep all the dedications but remove all dates and places of composition at the ends of the poems, which are fairly irrelevant, and also very pretentious. I haven't seen *Cat* book. Sorry it doesn't look good. I'm sure you will have a nice, friendly chat with Lefkowitz [and] he will correct the delays in meeting household bills. I should have underlined friendly, as opposed to snip-snip-snap in the frequent Tartar fashion!

Keep a civil tongue in your head and a tolerant heart. I will [*handwritten*] try to do *likewise*. It *is* very hard to do.

Love—10

TENNESSEE referred to Maria in his *Memoirs* as "the furious Tartar." Maria is true to her race. Tennessee liked Maria's story of her Tartar great-grandmother, who would occasionally, and impulsively, visit the remote corners of her estate:

"One peasant, Kosimai, lived only to glimpse his mistress in her carriage, and he would squat cross-legged by the roadside in anticipation for years on end. When finally the carriage appeared, her little jewelled hand would wave from the window to urge him on, laughing, as he tried to run alongside and kiss it: *'Begi, begi, begi, Kosimai!'* ('Run, run, run, Kosimai!')—until he tumbled, weeping, into the dust, and the carriage vanished. My mother, telling me this story, was horrified: 'It was so awful!' And yet, this same great-grandmother kept a convent, at her own expense, for the foundling children of Tartary."

———

[Sent to 323 East 58th Street, New York City]

Atlantic Hotel
Hamburg

September 4, 1955

Dearest Maria:

Did you get the notarized papers in time? Constant travel very rapid made it hard for me to go through the legal procedure but in Stockholm my Scandinavian agent arranged it for me and I think it was still in the interval you said was allowed. I hope so. Audrey also sent me some papers to notarize but I haven't done it yet. I have been somewhat crazy this summer. Maybe "somewhat" is too modest a statement! The Horse gave me a very bad time in Rome; perhaps I gave him an even worse time. He was always with that cynical street-boy Alvaro. I understand Alvaro and rather like him, though he's an absolute unashamed whore except on the rare occasions when he's a bad chorus-boy in a "rivista" but his influence on Frank is disastrous. The Horse's character, each summer with Alvaro, is hardened and cheapened so that I can't stay with him but must keep flying around on these sad little trips which are always so disappointing, to Athens, Istanbul, the month in Spain (I must admit that wasn't so bad, really!). And now Scandinavia and Hamburg, to be followed by Berlin, Paris, London before we sail the 22nd of this month, losing things wherever I go, being terrified in planes, swallowing pinkies, having dangerous dates with pick-

ups and so forth. It seems to me that now the Horse has decided he never
has to do anything in his life, not even exercises to keep his figure, and that
I can like it or lump it! [*Here thirteen lines of type have been deliberately
cancelled out with handwritten comment:* "x'd this out because it was unfair
to the Horse."]

Stockholm was a mess! Lilla van Saher Riwkin and all the Riwkins
were there, and they used my visit as personal exploitation, that is, of
themselves. They immediately gave a huge party with a guest list of all
the people they wanted to meet, using me as live-bait. Then Madame van
Saher Riwkin proceeded to conduct herself with such pomp and ceremony that it made me ridiculous to the press-people, crying out to them,
You go here, You go there, You photographers stay in a corner till I give
you a signal, etc. etc. You can imagine what an impression it made!
Consequently the press was very satirical. They said I had come with a
"powerful press-agent to Stockholm," described me as "an elegant playboy flicking ashes from a long holder." Fortunately the European premiere of *Cat* in Göteborg was a huge success, although done so badly that
I could hardly sit through it. People cheered at the curtain. Of course the
van Saher–Riwkin crew was along. My Scandinavian agent-impresario,
Lars Schmidt, a really nice and attractive man, did everything possible to
hold them in leash but they got into pictures with me at the theatre and
rushed up to give their names and biographies to the newspaper people
and I came out on the front page of the paper, grimacing desperately
between them!—Lilla is not, in spite of this frantic self-publicizing, a bad
person, but the man [Riwkin, her husband] is a horror. Do you know
what is going on? He is courting Lilla's daughter, Stella, by one of her
earlier marriages, doing it openly, and openly discussing, before me and
Lilla, the idea of divorcing her and marrying the daughter. Poor Lilla is
not herself and I think she was as embarrassed as I was by the Riwkin
"push." Can you imagine? He even had the nerve to try to make me pay,
to put on my hotel-bill, the money for all their passage to Göteborg from
Stockholm, probably feeling that the expense of the big party, which
made such a fool of me in Stockholm and which I would have longed to
avoid, should be evened-up in this way. I said loudly and firmly, in front
of all four of them, I shall only pay for my own train-fare!—I think the
man is a monster, and so is the daughter, openly flirting with her mother's
husband before her—poor Lilla's just a victim. But their goings-on did all
that could be done to make me an absolute ass on the trip. NOW
PLEASE NOT A WORD OF THIS TO ANYBODY IN NEW
YORK, as it will get back to them, and they have a coterie of gossipy

queens in New York who will make a big thing of it to my discredit, and I mustn't hurt Lilla. She read me her play and I think it will be very beautiful when it is finished. I know that I can trust you to keep my confidence about the whole story—I thought it would amuse you or I wouldn't have told it.

Well, now I'm in Hamburg. You remember those incredibly plush, weirdly elegant hotel rooms in Vienna? Nothing compared to this one! It looks like the throne-room of a very pretentious nineteenth-century Balkan monarch!—Vast! With golden damask wall-paper, mulberry and silver velvet upholstered chairs, all big as thrones, huge floor-lamps and three Persian carpets, a chandelier with twelve branches, two triple sconces, a seascape and another painting, sleigh-riders chased by wolves across what must be the steppes of Russia.—I enquired timidly if I couldn't have something a little less pretentious and they said, Oh, it doesn't cost more than the smallest room in the hotel! I'm afraid they didn't get the point. . . .

We live in *fantasy,* don't we? Last night I went to two places where the boys danced together and that was nice, and now I'm going to have a little bite of lunch and a glass of wine and walk about a bit as it's a heavenly day in spite of being a Sunday. Take care of yourself, mein Liebchen. It will be nice to find you in New York when we get back there the end of September.

Love, Tennessee

TENNESSEE and Maria had briefly visited Vienna together while the city was still divided into sectors in the wake of the Second World War. The Russian quarter was guarded by Soviet soldiers, who turned a blind eye when Maria visited the chapel attached to the embassy. Indeed, as she emerged afterwards they would shout out teasingly, *"Horacho po mole-las?"*—"Had a good pray?"

[Telegram sent from Hamburg, dated September 8, 1955]

CABLE ME YOUR DRESS MEASUREMENTS HOTEL ATLANTIC HAMBURG HAVE FOUND LOVELY EVENING COSTUME FOR YOU LOVE TENNESSEE

1 9 5 5

IN THE autumn Tennessee returned to New York and completed the revisions to the screenplay *Baby Doll.* He also worked on *Sweet Bird of Youth.*

"One day we were walking up Fifth Avenue with Tony and Jane Smith, discussing unicorns. As luck would have it, we were passing Tiffany's at the very moment I was chanting a rhyme my nanny had taught me.

> Unicorns do not exist
> They only think they do.
> Unicorns do not exist
> They've better things to do.

"Tennessee gave a yelp of delight and flew into Tiffany's, where, by an even bigger stroke of luck, there was a golden unicorn brooch with diamond hooves for sale. Tennessee bought it for me there and then."

Maria moved to an apartment which she had found near the Central Park Zoo. "It was an astonishing bit of luck; I opened the *New York Times* and there it was. It had a wonderful big room with an open fireplace. I used to hear the wolves howling at night, which I loved. The most central address, and only one hundred dollars a month."

[*From "The Voice of Broadway: Gossip in Gotham" by Dorothy Kilgallen*]

The high spot of Marlon Brando's visit to New York was the session he spent helping British actress Maria Brit-Neva hang her curtains. Maria didn't give Our Boy the big movie star treatment, just handed him the draperies with a casual, "Here, Marlon, hang these!" and he stayed around all afternoon, humming as he played handyman in her new apartment.

A revival of *A Streetcar Named Desire,* with Bankhead as Blanche, directed by Herbert Machiz, was being rehearsed at the Cocoanut Grove Playhouse in Miami.

Maria had reproached Tennessee for what she construed as his disloyalty in dining with "Dyepot."

[*On letterhead The Robert Clay, Miami, Florida; address on envelope 1431 Duncan Street, Key West, postmarked January 10, 1956, sent to 3 East 63rd Street, New York*]

Dear Little Sister Maria:

I hope you don't really feel that I have let you down or betrayed you during this unhappy interval in your life and affairs. If I appeared to in my behavior, I did not in my heart, for I am fully conscious of what you have been going through, but felt utterly helpless to intervene without being false to my own beliefs. I don't think intimate matters between two people can be solved by the intrusion of a third. J. phoned me in Miami. I was writing at the time. I spoke to him far more forcefully than ever before about his responsibility. I said that I thought he needed the psychological therapy of doing something for you even more than you needed it, and I urged him, strongly as possible, to go on with it. Apparently my advice and exhortation fell upon deaf ears, and this is sadder for him, much sadder, I think, than for you, for I spoke to him sincerely. I think he failed himself even more than he failed you. But is there any help for it, unless it comes from his own heart? I don't think so. You are about as well-balanced and mentally and spiritually healthy a person as I know, except that you sometimes hit the wrong target when your fighting spirit is up. I have great faith, however, in that spirit and the essential (though sometimes misguided) goodness of your heart. On certain points we have always been openly at odds. I have never shared your hatred for the one called "Dyepot." Her situation has always struck me as being as vulnerable and unfortunate as your own in regards to Lover Boy. I simply can't be persuaded to share your hatred and intolerance, since I think it springs from something natural for you but unnatural for me. You reproach me for dining with her. I must admit I was disconcerted and discomfited when she appeared for dinner, but remembering that she was with J. even before I met you, I could not find any valid reason in my own relations with her, which have always been friendly as far as I know, to be rude to her and make a scene that would be helpful to no one. So there we are. He tried to ditch her and make another alliance, but he couldn't and went back to Dyepot. So there you are! If I were him, I would want to make some sort of sacrifice, even if only a financial one, to expiate the obvious injury he has done you, but he didn't, and there we are! Ahead of them both, Dyepot and J., lies an endlessly difficult and torturesome series of compromises with very little prospect of a lasting solution. But there you are, that's life for you. You, on the other hand, have only your own free self to contend with. You have "all these treasures locked in your heart" [Blanche in *Streetcar*]. You only have to unlock them. It's been two years now, and it's time you put it behind you and went on from there. You are vigorous and healthy in mind and body. Of course it's possible to hang back in bitterness and disappointment, but is it desirable to? Let's remember the wonderful ones in our lives, Grandfather and Sandra who went on as far as their brave, patient hearts would go, and go on from there. That is also life for you!

I am back in Key West. La Bankhead and Machiz made it clear that I was not wanted. They said I made them "self-conscious" so I have left them to their own devices now. Bankhead was horrid to the Horse. When he arrived, I said, Isn't he good-looking? And she said, "He looks like a horse. It's very nice of you to love such a hideous person." And when I remonstrated mildly over a bit of business in rehearsal, she turned on me with a fury and shouted, "Shut up, idiot!"—so I have retired to Key West, with my "Hideous Horse"! whom I love. However, I still think she will give a very exciting performance, though maybe it will not be clear that Stanley is the one that represents the brutality of the world. On the other hand, maybe her ferocity is a mask behind which something like Blanche exists and can be released in performance. One's enemy is always part of oneself.

If you feel like spending some time in the sun, come down here, or to Havana as my guest. I miss you.

Love, Tenn

Seriously do come down! I will pay the plane-fare, of course, and old Doctor Sun-and-Sea might make you light-hearted again.

———

MARIA went to Miami for the revival of *Streetcar,* which opened at the Cocoanut Grove Playhouse on January 16, 1956. The production was transferred to the New York City Center on February 15, 1956.

"Bankhead and I took a mutual dislike to each other. Tennessee, in a misguided moment, had suggested to Bankhead that I should maybe play Stella, the younger sister. Bankhead gave a yelp of fury and said, 'I'm not going to act with that Cruikshank cartoon!' Tennessee was furious with her, but couldn't resist running back to tell me. I was rather impressed that she knew who Cruikshank was. They were all so awful that Tennessee and I took off for Havana for the rehearsal period, where we drank daiquiris and did impersonations of Tallulah as Blanche.

"Bankhead banned me from the theatre, and Tennessee had to smuggle me in incognito to the opening night and party, hoping that in my wig she would not recognize me. But alas! she did, and made a huge scene."

With the following letter Tennessee enclosed a cutting from the Miami *Herald* of February 9, 1956, with a picture of a woman being helped down a staircase by a man and another woman. The caption to the picture is "Cynthia Sargent is helped to ambulance . . . by the driver, an unidentified woman, right." The unidentified woman was Maria.

––––––

[*On letterhead The Robert Clay, Miami, Florida; address on envelope 1431 Duncan Street, Key West, Florida*]

February 9, 1956

Dearest Maria:

The second lady on the stairs is either you or a practical duplicate, including the coat! How about it?

Your portrait (oil) turned out very good, I think, admired by the Horse and Don Pinder. I'll bring it up with me on Monday. Will spend about a week in New York for business talks with Audrey, Tallu's opening, etc.

Love, Tenn

A portrait
of Maria by
Tennessee

———

W IL.LIA M S had painted Maria's portrait while she was staying with him in Key West. "Tennessee always painted by the pool. The splashes of oil paint are still there, on the paving slabs." Maria was not overenthusiastic about this painting, feeling that there was a touch of Edith Evans in the fact that Tennessee had painted one eye distinctly larger and higher than the other.

The first, work-in-progress version of *Sweet Bird of Youth* was produced at George Keathley's Studio M Playhouse, Coral Gables, Florida, on April 16, 1956. It was directed and designed by Keathley, with Alan Mixon as Phil (Chance) and Margrit Wyler as the Princess.

———

[*On letterhead The Towers, Miami, Florida*]

1431 Duncan Street
Key West

April 20, 1956

Dearest Maria:

I guess you know all about my intense preoccupation with a new play, by this time, so you'll understand my lapse in letter-writing. Have never worked so hard in my life. The result was gratifying as the play was well-received here, and Audrey is planning to produce it early next season in New York. I am still working on it and the little theatre here is putting in new bits from time to time, as I complete them, so that I can see how it is shaping up in production. Frank is driving to Key West this afternoon and I'm flying back tomorrow. Will return to Miami late next week when Kazan comes down to cop a gander at the show. Cheryl "Hard Luck" Crawford is here now. La belle "Quarter Past Eight Foot" [William] Inge was also present for the unveiling but delayed attending till the third performance and now is flown to Havana. It annoyed me that he came down as I was not ready for this kind of inspection. I wasn't sure it was friendly. But Frank always says I am far too suspicious. I guess I am. The Horse says he called you several times in New York but couldn't make contact. I think he is still terribly disturbed over the loss of [Signor] Buffo [their dog]. He has suddenly, for the first time since I've known him, started drinking a lot, and is full of complaints about his health and generally depressed and distrait. We must cheer him up in New York, even if it means buying a new animal for him.

Unfortunately he has his heart set on a big one, such as a German shepherd or chow, and I only like little dogs with funny faces and figures. Actually I would prefer to buy a pair of English bulls, with noses not quite so flat as poor Signor Buffo's, and a less active program of activity for them in the tropics.

I will call you from Key West, and we'll have a nice chat. I have to spend a week with Mother, about the end of April, so I won't get back to East 58th St. till early in May but that will leave a couple of weeks before sailing, and if your Mummy's still there, we'll hop around lively to give her a little fun—Russian cuisine and a cocktail party and the new shows. I told my young cousin Jim Addams to call you. In case he calls . . . he's just out of college and wants a career in theatre: needs a job quick. I think you'll like him, he's a very nice, naive kid.

Love, Tenn

MARIA had nicknamed playwright William Inge "Quarter-Past-Eight Feet," as his feet seemed stuck permanently in this position on a clock face.

"Tennessee came up to New York and announced that his favorite play was *Waiting for Godot,* which he'd seen several times, and that my mother and I must see it. He took us, with the Horse. Tennessee and Mummy slept solidly through it, much to the irritation of Frankie and me.

"On a walk one day, Tennessee was very solicitous of Mummy. Frankie, following behind with me, suddenly hissed in exasperation, 'Look at them. Look at those two!' Tennessee was tenderly leading Mummy by the arm straight into a brick wall.

"Tennessee and my mother had enormous affection for each other. He would always be demanding to see her—'I must have a chat with Madame Britneva.' On one occasion, I came into the room, and they were both sitting in dead silence, staring at each other with eyes glazed. I said briskly, 'I simply don't understand this friendship. You never say anything to each other!' Mummy looked up at me and said with great dignity, 'Tennessee and I understand each other in silence.'

"Tennessee and I went to visit the poet Ezra Pound, whose daughter, Mary, I knew. He was in St. Elizabeths Hospital for the criminally insane in Washington, having made a series of terrible broadcasts during the war. Although these were indefensible, he was by now an old man, and a group of writers was campaigning for his release. He was there in his little cubicle with a group of adoring disciples. He held court by the radiator.

He wore khaki shorts and socks and a very white shirt. He was tremendously virile, pacing the corridors and expounding. The other patients clustered around, drawn by the warmth of the people there, until Pound clapped his hands, shouting 'Go away!' in Italian, and they all fluttered back like little birds into their cages. Tennessee was most excited to meet him, and it was reciprocal. They talked endlessly about J., their mutual publisher. But we left dazed, and compassionate at seeing him: old, over seventy by now, and mad, and in a cell, no matter how awful the things he'd done."

[*Address on envelope c/o Amexco, Rome, sent to 3 East 63rd Street, New York*]

July 3, 1956

Dearest Maria:

It is nice to know that you will be in England this summer, some time, as that is closer than New York and I always feel more secure when you are near the same continent. Your puppy sounds sweet but I'm sorry it isn't wall-eyed or bow-legged, as Frank and I now feel that those are essential virtues of all members of the animal kingdom. Perhaps I am or was prejudiced to begin with as my eyes have a similar disposition, and there is some curvature in my limbs from knee to ankle.

We have the nicest apartment here that we've had yet; it is on the Via [del] Babuino, that street of art-galleries between Piazza di Spagna and Piazza del Popolo. It belonged to a reasonably young man named Harold Levy who moved out, I would guess, to escape from his eighty-five-year-old termagant and shrew of a mother who has a *connecting* apartment. There is a five-foot hallway and door between the two establishments, and we can hear her screaming at her servants who scream right back at her. When she falls silent for more than twenty minutes we can only suspect that they've brained her, and it's hard to be sure that we're sorry.

Anna [Magnani] is here. She has a new twenty-three-year-old lover named Gabriel. I guess he blows the horn satisfactorily. Anna still has the disconcerting habit of pounding her abdomen, so I guess you would call it a two-piece band! Tonight she is going to the American Legion Ball as guest of honor. So we have a night off. She wants to do *Orpheus* this fall but for TWO MONTHS ONLY! We're waiting to see if Hal Wallis is willing to absorb the loss on such a short stage production. Anna's English has not improved but she is thin as Tallulah: almost. Looks very good, I must say.

Finally received a typed copy of *Sweet Bird,* etc. but the typist made such a mess of it that I can't tell much about it, but I suspect it will be at least half a year before it is in shape for a Broadway showing. Will you please ask Jean Stein to send me the Paris address of that young composer, Ned Rorem, that I promised to send a short work or libretto? I think it is ready for him, and perhaps I may go up there a week or two this summer. Please send me this address right away as I'm not sure I can stand Rome much longer.

Much love, Tenn

———

A FEW DAYS after receiving this letter, Maria flew with her friend Jean Stein to have a holiday in Europe. Peter St. Just, to whom Maria had been writing while she was in America, met her at the airport and for the fifth time proposed to her. Maria accepted.

Peter had been unwell, and his mother, Lady St. Just, wanted the wedding to take place as quickly as possible. Maria and Peter were married in Salisbury on July 25, 1956. Madame Britneva was in Canada and was put out that they had not waited for her return. It was decided, however, that a wedding ceremony in the Russian church would take place shortly afterward. Wilbury Park, the St. Just family home in Wiltshire, is of major architectural importance, being the first Palladian house in England, built by William Benson in 1710. It has always remained a private home.

———

[*From the Dowager Lady St. Just to Maria, handwritten, from Wilbury Park, Wiltshire, July 25, 1956*]

Darling Maria

I am giving you my ruby chains, and ring, also Peter's regimental brooch as a token of my love on your wedding-day.

May God be near you both today and always. I believe you will bring love and salvation to Peter, he has suffered cruelly, and his great courage not turning to drink or drugs has amazed the doctors, and filled me with admiration.

Go forward with my love, already you have worked wonders.

My prayers go with you both, blessings and all love.

Florrie

At Wilbury on Maria's wedding day, July 25, 1956. From left: Jean Stein, Giles Baring (who was best man), Lady Rupert Nevill, the Dowager Lady St. Just, Lord John Cholmondeley, Gordon Latta (Maria's uncle), Maria, Peter, Nina Latta (Maria's aunt) and the secretary to the Dowager

Wilbury Park, Newton Tony. It was the first Palladian house in England, built in 1710 as his country seat by William Benson, who was to succeed Sir Christopher Wren as the court architect.

TENNESSEE flew into London for the Russian service.

"While arrangements for the Russian ceremony were being discussed at my aunt and uncle's house, Peter and I were dismissed from the room like naughty children and sent upstairs to have tea in the nursery. Tennessee remained downstairs. The Dowager said pointedly, 'I really do feel that this is a matter for family discussion only.' Tennessee, in all innocence, shot a baleful glance at the Dowager's best friend, Vera Bowen, who was also still in the room, and said, 'Oh, Lady St. Just, I couldn't agree more.'"

After the honeymoon in Switzerland, Peter St. Just and his mother felt that Peter was not equal to the strain of the Russian wedding. The service never took place, and Tennessee returned to America.

The following letter shows Tennessee's intense depression, which he had begun to try to control with pills and alcohol. He never sent it.

[*On letterhead The Towers, Miami, Florida*]

September 7, 1956

Dearest Maria:

The plane trip was seventeen hours and it knocked me out so I could hardly walk from the plane to the air-station. Trying to pull myself together today, but the air-conditioner is not working and I had another sleepless night.

Please write me at once how things are going in London. I am a total wreck, nervously, seeing or calling [Dr.] Gourewitsch tomorrow. Going to ask him about analysts in Zurich. May fly over there soon to begin a course of analysis, unless my present dilemma works itself out before long, as I feel close to a crack-up.

Love, Tenn

GOUREWITSCH was a Russian nerve specialist whom Tennessee and Maria had met in Venice. He attended Sir Osbert Sitwell and Eleanor Roosevelt. Tatiana Schvetzoff, Madame Britneva's childhood friend, was most helpful. Tennessee was impressed, and asked her subsequently to visit Rose and to take her out on occasional weekends.

[*Address on envelope 323 East 58th Street, New York*]

September 25, 1956

Dearest Maria:

I wrote you a long letter soon after I got back here but it's lost, I can't find it. And darling, I'm not able to write you another. Too much has happened. I am flying to the Virgin Islands tonight to try to recover some nervous equilibrium.

I spent Friday and Saturday visiting Rose in the new institution. When I got back late Saturday night I had a wire to call the doctor in St. Louis and was informed that my mother had been put in a psychiatric ward, suffering from paranoia. She thought her colored maid was trying to poison her and the colored chauffeur to murder her, result of her disturbance over the anti-segregation violence in the South, and had not eaten for days and was in a state of hallucination. They say I should not see her now. That it would be too shocking for me. I couldn't suffer another shock now so I'm flying to the Virgin Islands to pull myself together and then coming back to St. Louis to cope with the situation.

I talked to her on the phone in the ward. She said she couldn't tell me what was going on because the phone was not private.

Tatiana and I spent an afternoon in your apartment and everything is stored at Manhattan Storage, so don't worry about that.

How are things between you and His Lordship? I will write you again in a few days from St. Thomas, Virgin Islands, and will doubtless be in a much better condition.

Love, Tenn

[*Added in handwriting*] P.S. Magnani is not doing play [*Orpheus Descending*]. Deal fell through because of her unwillingness to play more than two months.

[*Envelope postmarked Key West, January 3, 1957*]

Dearest Maria:

These last few months in my life are the worst that I can remember, and that's why I haven't kept in touch with you. I was too preoccupied with the necessary business of trying not to crack up, and I am far from sure that I have succeeded. I still keep up, as well as I can, a pretense of being a rational person. I have been absolutely alone during this ordeal. I have not been able

Tennessee in his Key West studio

to write a decent line since last spring and I believe my writing career is finished. My writing career was my life. I failed in everything else in a spectacular way. Last summer I planned to go to Zurich and start analysis but I came back to the States instead because I was committed to put on another play [*Orpheus Descending*]. We're going ahead with the play. It's all cast now, except for some minor character parts. Maureen [Stapleton] is taking the part I meant for Anna and two brilliant young actors [Cliff Robertson and Lois Smith] are signed for the other two leads. However, for the first time I think I may stay away from rehearsals. I am too destroyed at this time to be of any assistance. I will go to the Chicago opening and stay with it till the opening in New York. I am trying desperately hard to hold myself together and maybe pick myself up. Of course I have been through periods somewhat like this before, when the sky cracked and fell and brained me, but this time I seem less able to struggle out of the debris. I'm at a loss to explain it. I suppose it's partly Mother's nervous breakdown and the shock of Rose's sudden deterioration when I put her in the "Institute for Living" which I had hoped would do her so much good. But the unaccountable collapse of my power to work, since work has always been my escape and comfort, is more likely to be the root of the trouble.

Christmas is past. I gave Rose a wonderful Xmas at Carson's house in Nyack which is very close to her present asylum, the best we've found for her. The poor thing thought we'd forgotten her for Xmas but I came up for the New York opening of *Baby Doll*—a harrowing experience!—and the one good thing accomplished was that I could give her a Xmas. I gave her some lovely clothes, $250 worth of them, a regular wardrobe, and she said that she was "in raptures," that she had not expected anything at all. She took a dim view of Carson. Carson immediately said, "Rose, precious, come here and kiss me." Rose said, "No, thank you. I have halitosis." When Carson was ready for bed she invited Rose to come in her room and undress her. Rose said, simply: "No!" I think you would like her. She has now become quite pretty again. Slender and clear-skinned and with her lovely grey-green eyes, and such incredible sweetness, patience, and poise. After all she's been through in the snake-pits, it's really a miracle that she remains an unmistakable lady. At the new place, she has a lot more freedom, walks about the beautiful grounds over-looking the Hudson River, has a parakeet in her room that she has named for Mother, Edwina Estelle. She talks very little, as if she was afraid that she might say something that would sound crazy. But all that evening, five hours, she seemed like a normal person. I am very proud of her! I think she's the greatest person I have ever known.

Rumor has it that you're coming back to New York, early this month. It would be wonderful to have you near if I should go there for rehearsals. Your perfect sense of theatre would probably save the day, since I doubt if I will be able to judge for myself.

Will you forgive me if I wait till you arrive in the States to celebrate Xmas and New Year? Perhaps we could excuse the delay by celebrating Advent.

Give your adorable mother a kiss and hug for me.

Much love, T.

I'm enclosing a little cheque, smaller than I would wish, due to the many expenses coming up lately, as I suspect that you haven't hocked the rubies.

―――

PETER ST. JUST's trustees kept Peter and Maria on a minimal allowance. Maria had the continuing financial responsibility of caring for her mother, whose illness was progressing.

Williams's screenplay was a fusion of two one-act plays that he had written before 1946, *Twenty-seven Wagons Full of Cotton* and *The Long Stay Cut Short.* The Warner Bros. film, directed by Elia Kazan and starring Carroll Baker as the thumb-sucking child bride, Baby Doll, Karl Malden as her husband and Eli Wallach as their vindictive neighbor, was released on December 18, 1956.

Before the premiere, Cardinal Spellman denounced the film from the pulpit of St. Patrick's Cathedral, forbidding his flock to go see it.

―――

[*Handwritten letter postmarked Key West, January 3, 1957*]

Dear Maria:

Auntie fish hopes this will keep you in stuffed tomatoes till you crash into pictures, thus proving that all a girl needs to do about sex is *project* it!

Love—10

[*This letter was written on the back of a sheet of paper torn in half with the following fragment of a poem typed on the back:*]

Dear Maria —
Auntie fish hopes
she will keep you
in stuffed tomatoes
till you crash
into pictures,
thus proving that
all a girl needs

to do about sex is

Project it!

Love —

Gods passeth.

In this way humanity pass.

And no beggar that grouche

is superior to it, for less

the photographers of your ruins and moralists of your ruin,

what fortune had we that was more than geographic,

what virtue have we that is more than fortuitous?

Perhaps we have wanted only a yellow moth in an orchard.

or a girl's mouth, or a boy's,

but the scar of what went in our still private brain-tissue

is neither smaller nor larger

than his, exposed that craved empire.

Take it, son of Italy,

recapture it as your own. an? we not ashamed

nor proud of it. Gods passed this way,

in this way humanity passes...

Tenn. Williams
Key West, Fla

VIA AIR MAIL

The Lady Maria Saint Just
% Mme. Britneva
20 Tennyson Mansions
Queen's Club ~~Gardens~~ Gardens
London W 14 England

A note from Tennessee, 1957

Gods passed [. . .] [*the tear makes the rest of the line illegible*]
In this way humanity passes.

And no beggar that crouches upon the sunny steps called Spanish
is superior to it, nor lesser than it. And we,
the photographers of your ruins and moralists of your ruin,
what fortune had we that was more than geographic,
what virtue have we that is more than fortuitous?

Perhaps we have wanted only a yellow moth in an orchard,
or a girl's mouth, or a boy's,
but the scar of that want in our still private brain-tissue
is neither smaller nor larger
than his, exposed, that craved empire.

Take it, sun of Italy,
recapture it as your own, and be not ashamed
nor proud of it. Gods passed this way,
in this way humanity passes . . .

———

THE FIRST performance of *Orpheus Descending,* the revised version of
Battle of Angels, was at the Martin Beck Theatre in New York on March
21, 1957. It was directed by Harold Clurman and designed by Boris Aronson,
Lucinda Ballard and Feder. Cliff Robertson was Val Xavier, Lois Smith was
Carol Cutrere, and Maureen Stapleton was Lady Torrance. It closed on May
18, 1957.

Tennessee's father, Cornelius, died at Knoxville on March 27. Although
father and son were never very close, Tennessee later admitted that his
father's death had affected him much more than he had expected.

In the spring Tennessee began intense psychotherapy with Dr. Lawrence
S. Kubie, a Freudian analyst, who told him to stop writing. Contrary to all
established etiquette, Tennessee disclosed what Dr. Kubie had been saying
in a series of television conversations with Mike Wallace, to the huge delight
of the New York audience. "As a result of these interviews, Dr. Kubie asked
Tennessee to terminate his sessions with him, as all his patients were leaving
him in flocks."

Tennessee began writing *Suddenly Last Summer.* Maria was expecting her
first baby.

———

1957

[On letterhead The Towers, Miami, Florida]

[Date obscured]

Dearest Maria:

It's wonderful news about the "Little Stranger." I had heard it indirectly, of course, but was not certain until I found your letter waiting here for me in Miami. I've been very bad about writing this fall, mostly because I've been doing so much work, the work has been going well again, for a change, about three or four hours a day, and afterwards I can't type a letter. Too exhausted.

The Dowager must be a demon! I am glad, now, that I "blessed her out," as I did at your aunt's in London. I wish I could do it again. I am sure she is responsible for poor Peter's condition. He is simply the victim of an overpowering mother who wants to make him a helpless dependent. Don't believe that stuff about hereditary influences affecting the child. Insanity on all 4 sides of my family, and look at me! A model of mental stability if ever there was one.

I heard a wonderful joke today about a pregnant woman. She went to the market and bought a skinned rabbit and a bottle of catsup. On the way home she thought it wouldn't hurt her to have a nip at the pub, so she went in and had several stiff ones. On the way out, she slipped and fell, and the skinned rabbit came out of the bag, and the catsup broke over it. Just then a sailor came out of the bar and saw her weeping in the gutter and said to her, "Don't cry, lady. Look at them ears. It never could have been normal!" So do be careful!

Are you planning to come to the States before, or after, the blessed event?

We will be in Key West till about Jan. 15th and it would be nice to have you visit us there if you pop over before the baby. I'm afraid you're going to be Miss Five-by-Five the next time I see you.

Lots to tell you but it's so late the late late show is starting on the TV. I really am very happy for you!

Much love, Tenn

Horse has remained in New York, phoned me yesterday that he and Johnny Nicholson are re-decorating the apartment, re-covering the sofa, new pillows, new frames on the pictures, new carpet, new coffee-table—I'm sure this will keep him up there a month longer, will cost me several thousand, and Johnny will open a new restaurant! Aren't I a bitch?!

TENNESSEE was concerned that his beloved but diminutive Five O'Clock Angel, expecting a baby imminently, would measure five foot by five foot.

On May 23, Maria gave birth to a daughter, who was given the Russian name Pulcheria; Maria thought this preferable to her first nickname, Pearl Harbor, bestowed on her because for many months Pulcheria looked Japanese.

[Telegram sent to Welbeck Street Hospital, London W.1, May 26, 1957]

GIVE THE LITTLE LADY MY LOVE HAVE ALSO BEEN IN HOSPITAL BUT WILL WRITE TOMORROW MUCH LOVE TENNESSEE

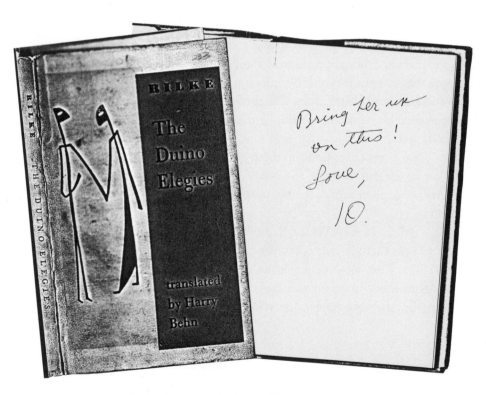

On the birth of Maria's first child, Pulcheria,
Tennessee, as her godfather, sent Maria this book,
with the inscription on the front endpaper.

TENNESSEE was one of Pulcheria's godfathers. He sent Maria a copy of the *Duino Elegies* of Rilke, inscribed:

Bring her up on this!

Love, 10

Tennessee's mental condition was deteriorating at the same time. He committed himself to psychiatric treatment.

[*On letterhead The Towers, Miami, Florida*]

June 7, 1957

Dearest Maria:

I'm between the hospital and the psychiatric clinic in Massachusetts for a few days' respite in the sun by the sea, but unfortunately the summer sun in Miami is so fierce that I am more inclined to stay in my air-conditioned hotel room with TV for company and a rather dead Olivetti. I discovered that the Olivetti has been running mostly on gin, and now that they've found I have a bad liver, what makes the Olivetti run is supposed to be "stout." However, I am cheating a little, not enough to make the Olivetti run but enough to make it hobble along just a little.

I am sure by this time you are out of the maternity ward and are making friends with the new little lady. Of course I had hoped it would be a boy. But maybe a girl, if she turns out to be a pretty little Tartar, will be more fun and company as she grows. Anyhow, I'm sure you're glad that she's made her debut, her first one, and I bet she is already casting a Tartar slit eye on the world and making some private but cogent notes on how to cope with it.

Kenneth Tynan (without Elaine [Dundy, his wife]) was in New York last week. He made no effort to get in touch with me, I ran into him by chance at a chi-chi party. I called him the next day, he was out and I left my number but he didn't call back. Since the failure of *Orpheus* my stock has fallen enormously. My [. . .]

[*The rest of the letter is missing.*]

PETER ST. JUST had become unwell shortly before the birth of
Pulcheria and remained at Wilbury with his mother. He did not visit the
maternity hospital.

[*On letterhead Hotel Comodoro, Havana, Cuba*]

June 17, 1957

Dearest Maria:

We are both entering very strange summers. I am supposed to leave
tomorrow for the plush-lined loony-bin at Stockbridge, Massachusetts and
the start of analysis. Have been having nightmares about it for the past three
nights. If I come out just with ¼ past 8 feet I'll be lucky!

I think of course that His Lordship's behavior is abominable beyond
description. If his alleged sufferings were at all genuine, he would have come
out of them with a bit of humanity or feeling for others I should think,
that's the one usual profit to be reaped from them. Now I think he is just
a cad and a faker.

The picture of you and the baby is so charming. I am sure that she'll make
up to you for all the trouble to get her.

This is just a preliminary letter. I am not in a state of mind to say much
right now, but if things fare well at the Institute, I will write a sequel, more
lengthy.

I love the name Tamara. Give her my love and my godfather's blessing.

I am going to pick out a little something for her if I have a chance to
do some shopping before I'm packed off.

Love, 10

[*Added in handwriting*] Write me here in N.Y. Frank will forward. I don't
know Inst. address.

MARIA went to Paris to see her friend Alexandre Benois, one of the seminal
figures of Diaghilev's Ballets Russes, who had designed the original production of *Petrushka* and many other works. "I asked him if I should call my
baby Tamara. 'Is she a beauty?' he asked. 'Not really.' Benois said, 'Then
don't call her Tamara. Think of Karsavina.'"

[*From Southampton, Long Island*]

August 27, 1957

Dearest Maria:

My analyst and I have been taking a two-week vacation from each other. I'm in Southampton, Long Island, on a beach in the bay. Frank went to Key West and, the answering service tells me, has now removed to Nassau. I can't imagine what the Horse is doing in Nassau; it doesn't sound to me like a place for horses.

He has changed a great deal in the last month or two. DRINKING VERY HEAVILY! A couple of double vodkas before dinner. At night, coming in LOADED!—but sometimes you can't smell liquor on his breath. I am very worried about him. There is practically no real communication between us. I believe he's disturbed over a couple of things: my analysis, for one, and the fact that his disturbing, depressing behavior prompted me to take another apartment, West Side, near the Hudson, on an 18th floor from which I can look over the river and Washington Bridge at night and in which I can entertain my own friends, which I could never do on 58th St.

I still spend the nights with Frank at the old apartment, only using the new one for purposes mentioned above.

As you must know, from your brief experience with it, analysis is very upsetting at first. You are forced to look at and examine things in yourself that you would choose not to. So it's necessary to have a retreat, a peaceful place to retire to. So I took the West Side apartment. At the same time, I feel very guilty about it because I know that Frank interprets it as a threat to our relation.

The Horse left Miss Brinda with me. A cat scratched her eye-ball a month ago and it became ulcerated. Before Frank left for Key West he had apparently cured it, but now, here in Southampton, the ulceration has suddenly returned. I took her to a vet in East Hampton yesterday and he said there is a possibility that she may lose the eye, it may have to be removed. Of course I am terribly distressed over this, she is the sweetest of the three bulls we've had and I have become very attached to her. She's full of penicillin, streptomycin, and cortisone, now, and it may be that the ulceration, which has gone into the inner eye, will clear up so she won't have to lose it.

Jean Stein phoned me that you are thinking of coming back to the States. I hope you will, darling. That is, if you're not happy in London. Of all the people I've known in these nightmare years, I feel you are the one that I can most talk to, with a feeling of sympathy between us.

The "good doctor" has shown me many things about me which I hope will make me less self-centered, gradually, in the future. I can be a better friend some day than I've been up till now.

Love—Tenn.

[*Added in handwriting at the top of the letter*] P.S. Call me collect in N.Y. at the old number if you want to talk. Love to the little "Honourable" who is it! Can't remember those crazy Russian names. I want to give her a natal gift but don't want you to pay duty on it.

———

TENNESSEE and Frankie had by now been companions for eleven years.

In Britain, the daughter of a baron is styled "the Honourable ———." Tennessee gave his goddaughter a silver christening cup, engraved in his own writing, "To Katousha En Avant—Tennessee Williams."

———

[*From 124 East 65th Street(?), New York City, October 30(?), 1957*]

Dearest Maria

I am writing immediately for a change to catch you at the address. Your letter gave me the first real laugh I've had in donkey's years, I mean the boiling the new pram bit. That was up to your standard, the highest, of modern wit. I'm just recovering, not yet recovering, from a bad attack of Asian flu despite two shots against it. I came down with it immediately after the second shot.

The analysis is still going on, and it gets a bit dreary. It can be an awful drag, concentrating so thoroughly, day after day, on all the horrid things about yourself. If only we could turn up something nice, but so far nothing of that sort even worth mentioning, just envy, hate, anger, and so forth. Of course he is attacking my sex life and has succeeded in destroying my interest in all except the Horse, and perhaps the Horse will go next and I will start getting my kicks out of dirty pictures like you know who with the quarter past eight shoes [William Inge]. I give it just one year. Then I start traveling again. Being tied down to New York is almost unendurable.

We have moved to a new apartment in a smarter and safer neighborhood, a little bit bigger than the old one. It's at 124 East 65th, and it has a good-sized kitchen so the Horse can cook and we can eat in. This will be a relief, as we never want to go to the same restaurants.

I am doing a new short-long play off Broadway [*Suddenly Last Summer*], one that grew out of one act. I hate telling you who is directing. Yes, Machiz. But I am having Audrey put a clause in my contract that will prevent him from excluding me from rehearsals as he did with *Streetcar* in Florida.

One of the actresses has just called me. The conversation went on and on and now I am quite worn out. Brinda is well and seated at my feet in my little study. The Horse is very busy with decorating plans, nothing from the old place fits the new one. So he is out all the time with Nicholson, shopping around.

I'll call Tatiana [Schvetzoff]. Give the god-child my love,

Much to you, Tenn.

BOTH *Suddenly Last Summer,* a play in one act, directed by Herbert Machiz with Anne Meacham as Catharine Holly and Hortense Alden as Mrs. Venable, and *Something Unspoken,* also in one act, directed by Herbert Machiz with Patricia Ripley as Cornelia and Hortense Alden as Grace, were produced together under the title *Garden District* at the York Theatre, New York City, on January 7, 1958.

The first London production of *Cat on a Hot Tin Roof,* directed by Peter Hall, with Kim Stanley as Maggie, Paul Massie as Brick, and Leo McKern as Big Daddy, had opened at the Comedy Theatre on January 30, 1958. Tennessee did not go over for the first night.

[*From New York City, April 23, 1958*]

Dearest Maria:

You have been so sweet and faithful about writing me. I am ashamed of not responding more often. I get such a joy out of your letters. But I have been too depressed to return in kind. The old doctor says that I am passing through "purgatory." I thought I had been going through that all my life, but he seems to think it has to get worse before it can get any better. Well, it ain't better yet! I had just about made up my mind to quit the doctor this week, in fact I'd written him a long letter of farewell, but instead of posting it I delivered it by hand and of course he talked me into going on with it again.

Well, that's life for you, as you would put it, my dear.

Ken [Tynan] and Elaine [Dundy] are coming over this evening and I guess they'll bring the charming gifts you mentioned for me and the Horse who is in the pastures of Key West, frolicking, while I stew in my sour juices here in New York.

Chances are I'll fly to Europe in the late spring. I hope by that time "purgatory" will be through with.

Much love—Tenn.

———

TENNESSEE stopped his analysis before leaving for Europe six weeks later. Maria was expecting her second baby.

———

[On letterhead Grand Hotel & San Domenico, Taormina, Sicily]

August 5, 1958

Maria dearest:

Just time for a quick note as I must dash up to the Salvator Mundi Hospital. My old friend Marion Vaccaro is seriously ill there. You remember her from Miami where she is known as "the Banana Queen," having inherited a goodly share of the United Fruit fortune. She had been travelling about Europe with me when she got this very acute ear-infection complicated by fairly constant inebriation.

My dear, aren't you over-doing this maternity bit? However, my congratulations, as ever!

I'm leaving Rome Thursday for Hamburg as the heat there is unendurable, and so is the Horse. I had just taken a very handsome and expensive Roman apartment when this abrupt decision was forced upon me by the two elements I have mentioned. I may pop over to London to see you and the English theatre. Or maybe we could meet somewhere on the Continent. Will you drop me a note right away c/o American Express, Hamburg, letting me know your itinerary, program, schedule, etc. I'm afraid Paul Bowles will be in our New York apartment all of August as we told him he could. But I will check on it through Audrey. If he's not there would love to have you take it.

Much love to you and the little ones and to your mummy,

Tenn

[Added in handwriting] (I am *very* depressed.)

1958

[On postcard of panoramic view of Positano, date stamp illegible]

Maria dearest—

Changed plans, cancelled trip to Hamburg, and spent 10 days here at Posey—now plan to fly to Barcelona for week, then to Paris & London. Not drunk—writing in boat, choppy sea.

Love—Tenn

———

"TENNESSEE was drunk rather less frequently than people sometimes imagine. Quite often he would *pretend* to be drunk, since that released him from having to make conversation and therefore enabled him better to eavesdrop on that of other people. A phrase someone would use, thinking Tennessee wasn't listening, would turn up in a play a few years later.

"Tennessee and I used to swim in a private club pool in Rome. It was plagued by a perfectly revolting child, completely square, like a biscuit. I am a very cautious swimmer, and like to have one toe firmly on the bottom of the pool at all times. This little brute, however, would jump in, nearly on top of me, and splash me.

"One day I looked around the pool and remarked to Tennessee, 'Oh, my goodness! There's that no-neck monster here again!' Tennessee roared with laughter. And then, a year or so later, the 'no-neck monster' resurfaced in *Cat on a Hot Tin Roof*.

"He always seemed slightly out of focus, dreamy—carving imaginary words in the air to himself as other people were talking, building sentences to himself. I'd get impatient. 'Oh, do wake *up*, Tennessee!' Then he'd get indignant. 'I *am* awake!' "

———

[On letterhead Albergo Miramare, Positano]

"Amexco," Rome

August 18, 1958

Dearest Maria:

I think I should be in London for a couple of weeks before opening of *Garden District* so would you please try to reserve a room for me at Claridge's on September 1st. I will be coming alone as the Horse cannot bring the dog into England and must stay with her in Rome or Paris. I may fly up to Paris for a week before I go on to London. I read in an interview with Angus Wilson that he stays in London at an apartment house that contains a swimming pool. Could you check that? If I could get a little service flat with swimming privileges that would be better for me than Claridge's—you know how good swimming is for my nerves when I have a play in rehearsal. I am pleased with the casting. Have not heard directly from anybody involved but saw in the *New York Times* that a very fine American actress, Patricia Neal, is co-starring with Beatrix Lehmann whom I thought marvelous in [Jean Anouilh's] *Waltz of the Toreadors.* However, I feel that I ought to be on hand to supervise this production as I am not happy over the reports I've heard about *Cat,* excepting Kim Stanley.

Am busy re-writing *Orpheus* for Magnani, and adding some bits to *Sweet Bird.* The Horse took poor Miss Brinda to Sicily during a heat wave. I don't know how she survived as she is subject to heat-stroke. When she returned to Rome, to an air-conditioned room at the Excelsior, she retired at once under a bed and only came out now and then to do numbers one and two on the bedroom carpets, a very eloquent protest of her ordeals. We now have a very handsome and very hot apartment in Rome. I couldn't only stand it a few days and fled to Positano. The social life is dull, here, but the swimming is fine. I will leave as soon as I hear that the heat-wave in Rome has let up.

Wonder if you've gone to America? I will call your mother's apartment when I get to Rome to find out your location and plans.

Much love, Tenn

————

THE FIRST London production of *Garden District,* directed by Herbert Machiz, with Neal as Catherine Holly and Lehmann as Mrs. Venable in *Suddenly Last Summer* and Beryl Measor as Cornelia and Lehmann as Grace in *Something Unspoken,* opened at the Arts Theatre on September 16, 1958.

"Tennessee was being interviewed by the press in the foyer in Claridge's when a reporter asked him, with great intensity, 'What is your definition of happiness, Mr. Williams?' Tennessee leaned back, slowly raised his eyes to the ceiling, and said, 'Insensitivity, I guess.'"

————

Anna Magnani and Tennessee during a break in the filming
of *The Rose Tattoo*, 1954

[Handwritten letter, undated, 1958(?)]

Hotel Colon,
Barcelona

Friday: 2 a.m.

Dearest Maria:

Writing you on a page from journal as I'm sleepless and the rooms are
very close together at the Colon, you can hear the man next door breathing.
I want to thank you, darling, for your sweetness and patience with me in
London and apologize for not going back & am really very sick. Have been
all summer, perhaps longer than that. But now it's come to a point and I
can only pray that I will be able to take the trip back by plane to States.
Worst regret is not seeing your baby and your mummy. I was a wreck in
London. This present collapse was coming on. Frank has lost my return trip
ticket to States, must buy a new one. I've begged him to hurry but it's hard
to hurry the Horse. If I mail you the perfume from Lisbon could you get

it through customs OK? Enclosing check for baby's cup. Please engrave it with my motto which is "En avant"—I put it after every entry in my journals, no matter how things have stopped. Courage to go on is a lot in life.

Much love, Tenn.

Will try to get a plane from Lisbon early next week. Don't write me here as letter would come too late.

———

RETURNING from Barcelona to London, Tennessee suffered an attack of sunstroke, and in London Maria had to fend off a number of curious reporters.

———

[*On letterhead Hotel Nacional de Cuba, Havana, postmarked Miami, Florida, November 25, 1958*]

Next address
1431 Duncan Street
Key West

November 1958

Dearest Maria:

As you would say to me DO BE CAREFUL! and I hope you follow the advice better than I do. I was just getting over the after-effects of the flu that I caught in Cannes when Kazan summoned me back from Florida to look at a bunch of old platforms and back-drops that [Jo] Mielziner was designing for *Sweet Bird* [*of Youth*], and now I have caught another terrific cold, am sneezing every few seconds. However I catch the three o'clock plane this p.m. for the Sunshine State again. Yesterday we missed the four o'clock plane as the Horse started too late and we got tied up in Sunday traffic so today we're trying again, like all those rocket shots at the moon at Cape Canaveral.

My "coup de soleil" which you reported to the London press has become quite famous. It was even reported on TV in the States and was subject to many interpretations by sympathetic friends and enemies, if there is any distinction between the two, in New York. Some thought I had been coshed by a gigolo, others that I had gone off my rocker, others that I had collapsed from acute alcoholism, etc. etc.

Cheryl Crawford had another flop last week, starring Judith Anderson, "the Queen of Tragedy," in a play [*Comes a Day*] that had a real live crow sitting onstage in a tree. It looked exactly like Paul Bigelow, kept ducking and nodding and cawing so that the Queen of Tragedy was completely unnerved. The young author, Speed Lamkin, is the brother of Marguerite Lamkin, the one that you said was an unlucky witch when she coached Barbara Bel Geddes for *Cat.* Well, she brought her brother no luck. He threw a great ball to celebrate the opening, then quickly disappeared as the notices began to come out, but the Queen of Tragedy and the crow are still out-cawing each other.

John Osborne's new play, *Epitaph for George Dillon,* is another casualty. The critics are on the rampage this season. I think I will have a plane-ticket to Hong Kong in my pocket when I come up for my turn.

Later, ten days: Thought I'd finished and mailed this to you but it just cropped up among my papers. I trust by this time you are back in good spirits if not in perfect shape. I am in Miami. Spieglie Wieglie is here, having purchased *Suddenly Last Summer,* and Gore Vidal is arriving this afternoon to start working on the film-script. We will collaborate on it but I can't start my bit till after *Sweet Bird* opens. I am already suffering badly from over-work and nerve-strain. I do hope Gore will come through with a good job. We ought to work well together if we can avoid a collision of artistic egos (the real meaning of "temperament").

The Horse and Miss Brinda passed through briefly two days ago on their way to Key West. The back seat of Frank's MG was full of his HI-FI equipment so I guess he's intending to blast our neighbors out of the neighborhood with symphonies far above their conch appreciations.

We have been jokingly calling Spiegel the Eagle. Marion Vaccaro got so loaded last night that she began addressing him as Eagle. "Eagle, how is your drink?" "Take another lamb chop, they're good for eagles," etc. Luckily Sam is a very tolerant and warm-hearted man. I am really very fond of him, I think he rates next to Gadg in my list of normal male friends, and I think I like my normal male friends a bit more than the others. Out of the hay, that is . . .

Dinky Dakin passed through town last week. He wants to put Mother back in a sanitarium. I think his wife has been working on him. She hates Mother. Dakin admitted that she—wife—is "psychologically frigid" and that's why the Williams and Dakin families are now doomed to extinction. Maybe God has his reasons. Of course I told Dakin that I would never permit the old lady to be put away again. She is just old, really, and full of heartbreak and loneliness. Even her old cook, Susie, got married (at fifty) and will only come in three times a week. She has taken in a university student for companionship, as a roomer, but he is out of the house till four every morning so that is not much companionship for her. I'm planning to send her a dog.

It is now set that Brando will play opposite Anna in the film of *Orpheus* and they will film it on Long Island starting early spring.

My love to your mother and much to you, my darling, Tenn.

[Part of a surviving letter from Maria to Tennessee, handwritten, undated]

Darling 10:

Just finished talking to you on the telephone which was a nice little treat that I gave myself. Kept feeling all day that I wanted to speak to you, so I did. Do try to get to London with your Mama in June. Anyway, keep me in touch with where you are.

Spieglie Wieglie gave me and Leslie Caron seats to see *Suddenly Last Summer* last night. Rather an interesting review in today's Sunday *Times* for you. Do you write where you'll be, otherwise we'll miss each other, which would be maddening.

I took Mama to the specialist last week, and he says she's far better—I've been painting up the flat for her, and trying to keep her spirits up. She had tea here today and we talked of you, darling. You know how fond we are of you, so you must not feel lonely and depressed, just pick up the telephone day or night.

Sorry to hear about Gadg, but I'm sure your play is beautiful, as all your things are.

Dear sweet Tennessee, take care of yourself, please. Don't talk too much, cry too much, laugh too much, or be too like a Russian! You are like one, you know. We are always too gay or too something.

God bless you, all love to you, Maria

Why on earth have you got a werewolf hound?

———

IN JANUARY 1959 Tennessee went to Havana, Cuba, with Marion Vaccaro to meet Fidel Castro.

The first performance in New York City of *Sweet Bird of Youth,* produced by Cheryl Crawford, directed by Elia Kazan, with Paul Newman as Chance Wayne and Geraldine Page as the Princess, was at the Martin Beck Theatre on March 10, 1959.

———

"Tennessee and I celebrate in Havana having escaped
from Miami and Tallulah Bankhead, 1956."

Five O'Clock Angel

[*From Tatiana Schvetzoff to Maria, handwritten from New York, March 10, 1959*]

Dearest Maria:

   Imagine Tennessee very kindly gave me a ticket for the opening night, and I was privileged to be a memeber of the distinguished audience. The play is marvellous and had a roaring success. Curtain after curtain at the end, and Tenn, flustered, shy and excited, came on to the stage to take a bow.

   I thought the play is so true to life. It is very raw and crude at times, at times it is funny—comedy-like. The writing is magnificent. It is different from all his [other] plays—it is realistic, not allegoric as his other plays, it is all there to see and hear, not to guess. G. Page is superb and the entire acting magnificent. The opening is similar to *Cat*—a huge satin and velvet bed and the action is around it—G. Page lying in the bed and Newman in his pajamas fussing around. Well, I suppose you will see it in London. . . .

———

"HERMIONE BADDELEY, the actress, was an old friend. She invited Tennessee and myself to watch polo at Cowdray Park, with the Maharajah of Cooch-Behar. A huge Rolls-Royce came to collect us, in the back of which were already installed Hermione and her love, the actor Laurence Harvey. We watched the polo, the dreariness of which was anesthetized only by the constant flow of champagne. Already drunk, Harvey nevertheless persuaded the miserable Maharajah to stop at a pub on our return journey. There, befuddled by vodka, Harvey became quite extraordinarily abusive, especially to me. His bloodshot eyes blazed hatred and spite. The Maharajah, by now bitterly regretting the whole expedition, hustled us back into the Rolls. Enraged, Harvey spouted a tirade of abuse so vile that our host, fearful lest his chauffeur might hear it, shot the partition across with a report of pure desperation.

   "Tennessee loudly announced, 'I cannot have my friend abused in this way. Stop the car!' The car stopped. Tennessee and I settled smugly back into our seats. Thereupon, to our astonishment, we were told that it was we who were expected to leave the car. Dusk had fallen as we began to tramp the twenty-odd miles back to London. We muttered to each other that it was all Liebling's fault, anyway.

   "Then a car appeared. Frantically, we waved it down. By an enormous stroke of luck, it contained Kenneth Tynan, his wife Elaine and their party.

Squeezing ourselves in, we drove straight back with them—to London, and to dinner at the Caprice."

The film version of *Orpheus Descending,* with Anna Magnani, Marlon Brando and Joanne Woodward, directed by Sidney Lumet and retitled *The Fugitive Kind,* was released on April 8, 1960.

Sam Spiegel produced the film version of *Suddenly Last Summer* with Elizabeth Taylor, Katharine Hepburn and Montgomery Clift; it was directed by Joseph L. Mankiewicz. "Gore Vidal did a brilliant screenplay, and wrote in a small part for me, which opened the movie version. I played a young girl in a mental institution being prepared for the first lobotomy operation."

Tennessee had gone to London for the opening of *Orpheus Descending* at the Royal Court Theatre on May 14, 1959. The production was directed by Tony Richardson, with Gary Cockrell as Val and Isa Miranda as Lady Torrance. The play was not a success, and Isa Miranda was a disaster. She had engaged two Italian waiters to sit in the audience. They were the audience most nights. Maria had a small part. At the end of the play, Miranda had to stand at the top of a stairway and say Lady's last line: "The show is over and the monkey is dead." One night, after saying her last line, she fell over the bannisters, and Maria, in a loud stage whisper, said, "The monkey is over and the show is dead." The cast never spoke to Maria again.

———

124 East 65th Street
N.Y.C.

July 8, 1959

Dearest Maria:

Read and laughed myself breathless over your letter!—especially the revision of Lady's last line. When will you take to literature like a duck to water? Sooner the better, I think.

Last night I took a two-hour drive into Pennsylvania to see Diana Barrymore do *Streetcar.* She has gone off the bottle and onto the happy pills and the sleepy pills, in rapid alternation, but she turned in a very good job. She is so thin that ladies behind me exclaimed, "Sick, sick!"—doesn't eat except late at night or so early in the morning that . . . Well, a couple of weeks ago, after more than the usual quota of pills and maybe a few sticks of the weed, she decided to have some scrambled eggs and somehow or other she managed to perform the neatest trick of the week, she fell ass-down, and bare-ass, into the pan of hot fat and got second-degree burns on her ass so bad that she had to go into a hospital and whenever she sat down on the stage last night, she made a face like she had a throbbing hemorrhoid. Nevertheless she has the Barrymore madness and power and her last three scenes were remarkable. When we went backstage, the poor thing looked as if she had been drenched by a fire-hose. Even her hair was soaked through, and she couldn't get off her make-up. However, we managed to get her to a restaurant and persuade her to eat something for the first time in several days—two poached eggs on white bread, of which she made a great disgusting mush, cutting and scrambling it all up together: she practically had to be "spoon-fed." What happens to actresses in my plays?! . . . I seem to push them over, I mean around that well-known corner, maybe because I'm around it too, and not pushing but calling?

How are things with the Eagle known as Spiegel? I have heard tell that Monty [Clift] is back on the big and little bottles, both. And that Spiegel delivered an ultimatum, show up sober or go! Could you get onto the set or see some of the rushes [of *Suddenly Last Summer*] for me? I feel that I let Spiegel down rather disgracefully, he had counted on me to work on the script and I'm not sure that his failure to provide me with the yacht is really an adequate excuse for my failing to work. It's true I was pretty exhausted, but I do feel guilty because I am fond of the Eagle, really very fond of him, and have the greatest respect for him, too. But a time comes when we fail everybody, we have failed ourselves so badly that we are good for no one, ourselves or others. After that? We recover, at least a little. At least we do go on, don't we?

I think they are making a really beautiful picture of *Orpheus.* They just finished the location scenes in upstate New York, a town that looked like Mississippi. Magnani is obsessed with her age, she thinks that her neck is gone and they are putting tapes on the back of the neck to pull it up and together. She regards this as a terrible insult and yet she rages whenever she sees a neck-line in the rushes. Yesterday I sent her a lovely silk parasol. She probably thought I meant it as an oblique suggestion to cast a shadow over the neck and will probably break it over my head when we arrive to take her out to dinner ce soir. She seems to forget that she never got by on her youth or beauty in pictures! Brando has taken off pounds like magic, he showed up fat for rehearsals, fat and coarse-looking, but soon as he started working, the fat melted away and the wonderful face came back, and Maureen [Stapleton] as Vee is turning in an almost sure-fire Oscar-winning performance as supporting player of the year.

Frank and I fly to Tokyo on August 20. We will do the whole Orient, making a stay of several months and coming back around the world, through Europe and London, so expect to see us about four months from now. I hope it will do me good: something needs to, now.

Give little Mama my love, and Spiegel.

Much love, Tenn

———

"DIANA BARRYMORE had a romantic infatuation with Tennessee and once even suggested marrying him and having his child. Tennessee was gentle with her and felt sorry for her." She died in January 1960.

Clift was an old friend of Tennessee's. "I visited Monty on a number of occasions when he was living with Libby Holman, the famous blues singer. There was something curiously intangible, inconclusive about Monty. But at least he wasn't as cracking a bore as James Dean, whom I met on a number of occasions with Tennessee. Dean simply sat there glumly, thinking about himself."

Tennessee and Frank went on a trip around the world for three months, returning to spend the winter in Key West. Tennessee worked on *The Night of the Iguana* and revised his comedy *Period of Adjustment*. Later, when Elia Kazan declined to direct *Period of Adjustment,* the press tried to suggest that the two men had had an irreconcilable argument. In fact, the production clashed with Kazan's directing the movie *Splendor in the Grass*.

———

[*Handwritten letter on letterhead Dupont Plaza Hotel, Miami, Florida, postmarked April 17, 1960*]

1431 Duncan Street
Key West, Fla.

April 1960

Dearest little Maria:

You never wrote me that long funny letter you promised me on the phone months ago. As for me, I haven't written either for the usual reason, depression, fatigue, etc. Since Xmas I've been almost constantly in Key West; every now and then Audrey commands me to appear in New York for a few days—just long enough to catch another bad cold—then I fly back.

Right now, I'm conferring with Louis de Rochemont and Gavin Lambert about the proposed, in fact planned, film of [*The Roman Spring of*] *Mrs. Stone* in Rome next fall. I hope that I can go over for it. De Rochemont is the first real "gent" I've dealt with in the producing end of the film industry. You'd love him. I'll try to get Gavin Lambert to write you into the picture if you're still interested in anything besides marrying and begetting infants.

Gore has had a huge smash hit with his new play [*The Best Man*]; Windham has written a book about me published in England [*The Hero Continues*]. Rather flattering, although I don't think he meant it to be so.

Well, darling, it doesn't have to be long or even funny but let me hear from you.

I don't dare to ask you about your adorable little mummy. I'm a terrible coward, you know.

Love, 10

———

GAVIN LAMBERT did write in a small part for Maria in the film of *The Roman Spring of Mrs Stone*.

———

[*Telegram sent from New Orleans, May 28, 1960*]

SORRY SO SORRY BUT UNDERSTAND MATE LAWYERS TELEPHONE WHEN YOU FEEL INCLINED SEE YOU IN PARIS LOVE TO MY LADYSHIP

1431 Duncan Street
Key West, Fla.
August 10, 1960

Maria darling:

After studying your financial prospects I have come to the conclusion that we should try to see more of each other in the near future. And about the big house [Wilbury Park]: is there an attic in it for a distinguished American lunatic? I have a fright wig and will travel. Would only require one domestic, a bonne-à-toute-faire in his teens, preferably with ballet training, who can double as "dresser" when I get into my Chantecleer costume at daybreak to crow on the roof. Of course there must be a safe means of access to the roof from the attic as a broken hip at my age is no laughing matter. I don't like a mansard roof: too steep, especially when ice-coated. I like a rather flattish roof with a single turret and a spiral staircase with railing to get me up it. In fair weather I crow five times at daybreak: in foul weather, I may crow only once. Of course for my Thursday "At Homes" I will require your whole staff in the downstairs drawing-room, properly liveried, and trained to receive the janitor's boy as if he were Mr. Armstrong-Jones; and not to betray the slightest surprise if he *is*, for the grapevine has it that this charming commoner who is introducing humor to British royalty is sometimes inclined to appear in various guises, especially during the holiday seasons.

So much for funsville.

You must be prepared to support a Horse, two dogs, a screaming parrot, and "the living playwright," especially if you can't keep the Tynans in England till after my next couple of plays.

Oliver Evans is arriving in Miami today with a lady-companion of 65, and is expected here tomorrow. I am trying to figure out some good excuse to anticipate their arrival by a strategic departure, for I have no assurance that those great baby-blue lamps of Oliver's don't still bug out like Atlas missiles at the glimpse of a sailor in well-fitting whites or blues or that his myopia has been cured as successfully as his deafness so that he doesn't have to approach within six inches to pay his respects to their charm. Key West is "hot" in summer in more than one way, in fact it is "hot" at all seasons now. Our social life has necessarily become as circumspect as a little bunch of spinsters at a summer resort in New England. However, we have a most beautiful new patio, a TV set, improved bathing beaches, and the water is cool after sundown.

The Horse is on pills and aged Cuban rum which he drinks out of ice-tea glasses filled to the brim, and is writing poetry, some of it remarkably good. We don't quarrel anymore, it's all very sad, nice, and peaceful, with the Horse pushing forty and me pushing fifty. Where did the years go, so quickly? Even the dogs and the parrot seem to wonder. Dinky Dakin is forty now, too. Saw him last week in New York and he is also on tranquilizers, now, which makes all four members of the family on them. Also he is about to be booted out of the Air Force, his wife is suffering from "psychological frigidity," and they are planning to adopt a child to cure her of it. (I hope I managed to talk him out of *that*!) Why does Peter have the corner on fertility? I like having a god-child but I would love to have a niece or a nephew despite the genetic liabilities indicated at present.

I am trying out a new play in Miami the 20th of this month which is the only *long* one I've done that I like since *Cat*. It is called *Night of the Iguana* but has no other connection, except a Mexican background, to the short story called that. Actors Studio players are doing it under a brilliant young director, Frank Corsaro. I know you would like it but there is no certainty that a Miami audience will.

So much for Gloomsville.

Anna wired Frankie that she is "molto basso in morale." I don't know why that makes me laugh a little but it does. We are planning to return to Rome in November and probably to settle there for at least a year if I can get hold of a "villino" with a swimming pool: otherwise maybe Taormina—I think it is the swimming that keeps me going the bit that I go.

There is a little but effective part, Mrs. Jamison-Walker, in the film-script of *Mrs. Stone* which I think you could give more distinction than it is worth. It is comedy. I am not yet satisfied with the script and now that *Iguana* is temporarily frozen (in rehearsal) I am knocking out a few scenes to give it [*Mrs. Stone*] the "lunatic touch," for which I am justly famous.

Donnie [Windham] and Sandy [Campbell] will be in London soon. Give them my love and make no adverse references to the book about me. I feel that Donnie has worked out all his old animosity toward me in this book and that now we may be able to resume our wonderful old friendship which meant more to me than he seems to know. He looks very beautiful with his silver white hair and his fantastically clear blue eyes, and his writing gets better and better. Homage is indicated: envy is put far away.

Write me another of your wildly amusing letters.

Much love, 10

———

AFTER his death, Maria found among Tennessee's papers the following draft of the previous letter. Comparison between the two versions shows how carefully Tennessee wrote, even when writing a letter to a friend.

Maria darling:

I have studied the lawyers' papers and the financial statements very carefully and have come to the conclusion that we ought to see more of each other in the future. About the house: does it have a good sized attic suitable for a distinguished American lunatic? I have fright wig and will travel: will only require one good looking bonne-à-toute-faire in his teens, preferably with ballet training: whether or not I am to have the downstairs drawing-room for comedy rehearsal I leave up to you, my dear: I am sure we will come to an amicable arrangement. Of course I will expect your complete staff to be at my disposal when I have my Thursday evening "At homes" and they must be trained to receive a butcher's apprentice or bootblack as if he were Mr. Armstrong-Jones, which he might very well be, if there's any truth in a grapevine, trans-Atlantic. Also the neighbors must be warned to pay no embarrassing attention when I appear on the roof at daybreak in my Chantecleer costume, and of course there must be something less hazardous than a rope-ladder to get me up there, because at my age a broken hipbone is no laughing matter. I don't like the mansard roof and I don't like gables. I like a single turret, dead in the center of an otherwise flat roof, and I like a winding staircase with railing and rubber matting. In fair weather I crow five times: in rain or sleet only twice: of course in heavy fog there must be adequate illumination on roof, turret and staircase. In addition to usual menage—the dogs, the parrot, the Horse—it is possible but not positive that I may be accompanied by Mr. Paul Swan whose recitals at Carnegie Hall are nearly as well known as mine. I want the attic exclusively for myself: the rest must be somehow accommodated downstairs. And I don't want to know the arrangements: just that they're made without fuss. Au revoir.

So much for funsville. Now for Sobersville, even after martinis. I'm very pleased and proud of you, darling. I was never otherwise but I'm more so now. Without any dishonesty ever you have realized the life that was meant for you: two children, and security for yourself and them. I'm not a gypsy with a crystal ball but I think you are going to be happy and I think even if you're not happy, you will still be you, and to be you is lucky. Peter was very unlucky when he wouldn't or couldn't accept your care which he needed. If he comes, offer it to him again. I'm finishing this letter after our phone conversation. The terms are not especially good but the terms seldom are. Go to Counsel, but I suspect that they will advise you to accept them. And then go on with your career as an actress. I believe there is a fairly effective little part for you in *Mrs. Stone,* and I think you'll make it better than it is. As I said on the phone, just now, we don't want lives without worry.

Love, T.

[Letter not sent, on letterhead The Towers, Miami, Florida, December (?) 1960]

Dearest Maria:

On top of the internal bleeding, I now have a touch [of] pneumonia! A witchdoctor just shot me full of Demerol to which I am allergic, it nearly drives me wild. He didn't tell me what it was till after the injection. Tomorrow I go to Mercy Hospital. Oh, mercy!

And all those plans for travel. A few more weeks and I would have made it to London, at least. I'm sure you would have made me die laughing.

Anyhow I had planned to stop work in the sixties. I am so far out of fashion, now, that I am almost back in. Withering attacks from all critical directions, they even hold me responsible for the corruption of other play-wrights.

I think I should enjoy resting now for ten years on my withered laurels. I am sick of my work myself. Besides I'm too tired to continue.

A bit incoherent, sorry, the effects of the damn injection.

I know you must think it strange that I didn't get you the part of Mrs. Jamison-Walker but I really have no influence anymore. Call Louis [de Rochemont] at the Ritz (How dare you talk to me like this at the Ritz!—Remember Valentina?) and tell him you must have the part of Julia. Your influence is much more than mine. It is a very funny little part, Gavin [Lambert] has a terrific sense of humor and all the funny scenes are very well done and much progress made on Vivien [Leigh]'s. See Vivien, I think she likes you. But why do you want to do little screen-parts when you have two adorable children and apparently they're not even going to shoot the exteriors in Rome.

[*Letter not sent*]

1431 Duncan Street
Key West

Xmas day, 1960

Dearest Maria:

Excuse me for disregarding the Christmas season. I have over-played my hand lately and it wound up with the month of bleeding and then an attack of pneumonia which put me in a Miami hospital, what sounded like the terminal ward, with groans, coughs, gasping, nuns saying prayers at dark hours and the Reaper whisking someone out on a rolling table. In the morning of the single night I stayed there, they wanted to put me in an oxygen tent. I immediately snatched up the phone, woke the Horse up at the Towers, and said, You come right over here to the Mercy Hospital and check me right out and get me on a plane to Key West. But the Horse and the doctor insisted that I stay for X-rays and treatments. I was too weak to resist and I'm glad of it now. They stuck a needle up an inferior orifice of my body and injected three huge hemorrhoids and the bleeding stopped like magic and hasn't returned since. The X-rays showed a condition called "diverticulitis" or "diverticulosis" for which I take, every evening, a teaspoon of Vaseline mixed with apple-sauce, rather pleasant tasting, and I feel fine now, in fact you might expect to see me passing through London early next month on my way to some warm, sunny retreat like Marrakech. Gielgud has been there, I know. Would you please ask him if there is any swimming, and if it's really as lovely as I've always heard it was?

I'll probably have to travel alone, since we now have two dogs, one a big black wolf, the other a bitch bull-dog that a journalist described as the ugliest bull-dog bitch in the world, and we also have a parrot in a huge cage, and anyway the Horse needs a little respite, a little rest from me now, I have gotten more and more difficult to put up with, I don't think even you could put up with me as I am now. I've kept forcing myself to work when any sane person would know that I ought to stop for a while and try to be human again. The recent work isn't worth burning the candle at both ends for it, maybe not even at one end. I think I am finally losing my critical faculty and don't know any more if the work is good or awful.

Period of Adjustment, for instance. I thought it was an unimportant but charming little play that would be a hit. But Miss Dolly Drop is booking it right and left with a vengeance. Audrey and Liebling had invested $3,500 each in it and were certain it would be a smash but I should have known better when Kazan suddenly dropped it and sent me a turkey feather months before it started rehearsals. It came on and went like a hit in Philadelphia, audiences laughed their heads off, but then we went on to New Haven and there the heavy frost fell on more than the pumpkins. I had the Margaret Sullavan suite, which was Paris green, I crept about like that man who'd slaughtered 5,000,000 Jews in Nazi Germany, I drank a quart of liquor a day: and then the bleeding started. . . . Only Thornton Wilder and his sweet old maid sister were nice to us there. We got five good notices out of seven in New York but the good ones were [not] really good enough to off-set the two bad ones, and *The New Yorker* came out with the bitchiest, most nastily personal notice I've received or remember receiving, worse than Tynan's notice of *Sweet Bird.*

I figure that I have had my day in the Broadway theatre, and just hope the money holds out as long as I do and the capital, the investments, are enough to keep Rose out of a snake-pit and the Horse in the Key West cottage, with his menagerie on fairly full rations. Mother's OK, in fact she's in a better financial shape than I am, and Dinky Dakin is getting promoted to a major the first of the year. Did I tell you he adopted a little five-month-old child, a little girl with East Indian blood, who is said to be a great beauty, and his lazy and "psychologically frigid" wife has him mixing the formulas and sitting up nights with her at the air-base compound? Poor little Dakin was advised by a psychiatrist that an adopted child would cure his wife of her built-in Frigidaire, or deep-freeze compartment, but a girl that has her wedding-picture taken with rimless glasses on does not seem likely to thaw out anywhere but in an oven on the Equator, in July.

Are Donnie and Sandy and Gore still there? Give them, if they are, my shop-worn love and let me know where I can write Donnie thanks for the lovely book of short stories. And *write* me! Including the Gielgud report on Marrakech, please.

Loving best wishes to you, Tenn.

––––––

"MISS DOLLY DROP" was an expression Maria had first encountered when she was working for H. M. Tennent in London. "Dolly Drop, we decided, was a lady wearing a hat with a very large brim, who sat conspicuously in the middle of the stalls, obscuring the view of several rows. When she slithered into the theatre, it signified that the show was on the skids."

Period of Adjustment was written in 1957–58. Although it had been performed (as a "work in progress") at the Cocoanut Grove Playhouse in Miami on December 29, 1958, directed by Tennessee himself and Owen Phillips, it was not produced in New York until November 10, 1960, at the Helen Hayes Theatre, where it closed in March 1961 after 132 performances.

Tennessee was bewildered, on wandering one afternoon into Gerald Road, to confront a purple-faced nanny, muttering beneath her breath, "They're the dirtiest little children I've ever had in my life. *Twenty-three* pairs of knickers I've washed today!"

"Where is my goddaughter?" he asked her, lovingly.

"Her Ladyship has locked them out in the backyard—and a jolly good thing, too!"

Tennessee wandered on up to the drawing-room, where the window was open. He later described how he'd heard Pulcheria giving orders to Natasha in a very grown-up voice: "Now, Natasha—one, two, three! Pee-pee in the pants, to get rid of the new nanny! And don't do too much. Save some for the clean pair!"

Tennessee later said that he had slept through the 1960s—his "stoned age." They were years of few letters, although he kept in constant touch with Maria by phone.

––––––

Maria's daughters, Pulcheria (Katya) and Natasha Grenfell,
with their dog, Froggy Footman, London, 1966

Pulcheria with her godfather, Tennessee, London, 1964

Pulcheria, Froggy Footman, Maria and Natasha at Wilbury, 1972

Froggy Footman, Maria, Tennessee and Pulcheria, London, 1971

My darling Maria:

I wrote you a two-page letter the day after I got here, Key West, but when I returned to the studio to pick it up for mailing, it had mysteriously vanished and the most diligent search has not recovered it, so I'm writing another, after the day's work is done. It won't be as funny as the first one, for the relatively gay spirit in which I came back has disappeared like the letter.

Nothing in the vacation trip was half as wonderful as the few days with you and the little girls and Mamacita seated in the dining room and asking "How are the sweets running?" And the little party and getting to know dear "Bunting" and our fun together.

I don't think I can sweat out another summer in Key West, as I did the last one, and I am seriously considering a return to Europe early next month, or the end of this one. Do you think it would be possible for me to take a room or two in that apartment building with the swimming pool where Charles [Bowden, producer of *The Night of the Iguana*] is staying, for a little stay before flying down to Barcelona, Positano, or Tangiers?

I've done about all I can on this last long play [*Iguana*] for Broadway, and I need to rest in some charming place on the sea before I go through its production which starts rehearsing the middle of October and opens in New York a few days after Xmas.

It would be wonderful if you or Bunting could come along with me! I'm very fond of the Banana Queen but she creates more problems than she solves as a travelling companion, and I have too many problems of my own these days to safely take on others'. I can only hope that mine can be understood and endured by a few understanding and enduring friends now.

This week-end the Horse and I are driving up to Miami to inspect the new bay-shore house in the Cocoanut Grove, and get it ready for Rose in case I am able to bring her down there. I saw her when I flew back and she seemed to be in excellent condition, and she looked lovely and ten years younger than when I last saw her. The Banana Queen drove up with me to "the Lodge" but got quite drunk on the way and kept repeating things over and over. In the restaurant, Rose said to her: "Why don't you have a drink, dear?" And this got a laugh even out of the Queen of Bananas.

I received a nice letter from [writer] Peter Wildeblood. He says his TV series won't start till February but you are having the play [*Iguana*] typed up for me now. Perhaps you should hold my copy till I come back through London, or, if some unexpected contingency keeps me on this side of the drink, let Audrey bring it back. She is due in London for the opening of *Oh Dad, Poor Dad* [*Mama's Hung You in the Closet and I'm Feeling So Sad*, by Arthur Kopit], which I think is the 22nd of June. I just might be able to fly over in time to catch it.

The Horse has just ordered a colossal new Frigidaire for the house and we have just taken measurements of the kitchen and the kitchen doors which indicate that it will have to sit in the patio or on the lawn as a "status symbol" unless the pantry is removed or a section of it sawed off the wall, or even possibly both. The life here could only be described by Lewis Carroll, but I am swimming twice a day so that I can "play it cool." We have six dogs of which only two are house-broken or even paper-broken. The parrot laughs maniacally when she isn't screaming like a southern spinster being raped by a negro. The Horse falls asleep on the living room floor and when I get up, at daybreak, the TV is still blaring and glaring. A huge rat lives under the house and she has gnawed a hole into the pantry and cleans up the left-overs on the patio dinner-table and is so fearsome-looking that the big black wolf-dog we bought in Rome just stands off looking at him respectfully although he, the dog, has inflicted bites on some pretty tough friends here which required five or six stitches, when they came near him when he was having his horse meat.

Well, darling, a rat under the house is a pretty good symbol for all of our lives, now, I mean my own, and the lives of all whom I love.

We just have to catch it or stand it, I guess.

Much love ever, 10.

———

THE HONORABLE Guy Strutt, nicknamed "Bunting," is a close friend of Maria's.

Rose never lived in the house in Cocoanut Grove that Tennessee bought for her, although much later he moved her to a house near his in Key West.

———

[*On letterhead Hotel Miramare, Rhodes, Greece, undated, 1961(?)*]

Grand Bretagne Hotel
Athens

Dearest Maria:
A very quick note this must be as we are about to fly back to Athens after a week in Rhodes which is the most charming island next to Alcatraz

in all the world. We stayed at a hotel on the sea which looked very much like a model prison-farm. It even had the neat little bricked-in geranium and petunia patches, and concrete ramps leading up to the cell-blocks. It was full of middle-class Germans that shouted "Quiet" if you spoke above a whisper at 11 p.m. and got up at six a.m. and started beating their children and then beating them again to make them stop howling: unsuccessfully. The one happy thing to report is that we managed to ditch the Banana Queen's gigolo in Rome, after he had taken her for several hundred dollars, at least. But getting rid of him was cheap at any price. There is one lovely little hotel there, called the Hotel Des Roses. Every time we tried to get in there Marion would be so drunk that the reception desk would pretend not to understand, French, English, or Italian, or even sign-language. Verily, this has not been a vacation-trip but the seven stations of the cross!—Verily I say unto you, and I kid you not about that. Still, I am devoted to Marion. She is so lonely and so funny and sweet sometimes. It's a pity to see her drinking herself to death but then I suppose she must say the same thing about me, quien sabe. We make an odd pair in public.

I still hope to pass through London on the way back to the States which must be very soon now. I think it's useless trying to book me into any reputable hotel under Tennessee Williams as the English press has made such a fool of me so consistently these past few years, but you might try Thomas L. Williams. I could shave my moustache or put on my fright wig. Not much change required there, just brushing the crowning glory against the grain. I am so longing to see you and your Mamushka. And the play before I go back to God knows what. I'm afraid not to Frankie. The Horse has done just about all in his power to shatter me and humiliate me, so I must find the courage to forget and put away a sick thing. But to be fair, it isn't easy to live thirteen years with a character walking a tight rope over and a thin one over lunacy. But the time has come to "cool it" and I trust that I can.

We've been so unlucky in love, you and I, but at least you have two beautiful little girls to compensate for it. Call me at the Grand Bretagne when you get this. I need you and the dignity of London and some laughs together before I go back to my last Broadway production. I mean it: at least I hope it.

Much love, T. (no pen or pencil)

———

AFTER tryouts in Rochester, Detroit and Chicago, *The Night of the Iguana* was first performed at the Royale Theatre, New York City, on December

28, 1961, directed by Frank Corsaro, with Bette Davis as Maxine Faulk, Margaret Leighton as Hannah Jelkes, Patrick O'Neal as the Rev. T. Lawrence Shannon, and Alan Webb as Nonno. Tennessee did not watch the performance but paced up and down outside the theatre.

———

[*From Tennessee to Bette Davis, paper headed Sheraton Hotel, Chicago, undated*]

Dear Bette:

I was over-joyed when Chuck told me last night you have decided to revert to the blue shirt in Scene One. It is much more in character for Maxine and it does so much more to establish the locale and the atmosphere. Maxine was the wife of a great game-fisherman, the Costa Verde is a place for people that like to "rough it." Everything about her should have the openness and freedom of the sea. I can imagine she even smells like the sea. Time doesn't exist for her except in changes of weather and season. Death, life, it's all one to Maxine, she's a living definition of nature: lusty, rapacious, guileless, unsentimental. I think this creation of Maxine will be enormously helped when all the "externals" have been set right. One of these "externals" that isn't right, yet, is the wig. I like the color of it, but it is too perfectly arranged, too carefully "coiffed." It ought to be like she had gone swimming without a cap and rubbed her hair dry with a coarse towel and not bothered to brush or comb it. When she says "I never dress in September," I think she means just that. Her clothes shouldn't look as though they had just come from the laundry; there's nothing "starchy" about her, nothing that smells of naphtha. She moves with the ease of clouds and tides, her attitudes are free and relaxed. There's a touch of primitive poetry in her: hence, the shouting and the echo. These two "echo" bits are moments when a touch of this primitive poetry can be pointed up more. The poetry here is simple, folk poetry—natural, undevised, but lyric. About a week ago I submitted a little re-write for Act One but it's disappeared. I remember one lovely line from it which I think should be salvaged: "Old Fred used to say, Find your place and sit tight, and sooner or later a sea-gull will fly right over your head and drop a pot of gold on you." This is pure Maxine as well as pure Fred, and it could be cued by Shannon's line "And me do what?" and come right before the first entrance of the Germans.

Since this was written before we "locked the show," I think we can put it in without violating the agreement, that is, if Pat [O'Neal] will accept it.

If there is any one thing for all the cast to remember it is the primary aim of the play: the making of "poetic reality" in which everything occurs with the ease and the spontaneity of occurrences in life, no matter how long and carefully the play has been planned and written with that objective in mind.

There is so much that's wonderful in your characterization that it seems a crime to risk its total effect by neglecting the final touches.

Yours devotedly, Tennessee

———

M A D A M E   B R I T N E V A ' S   translation of *The Cherry Orchard* was produced at the Lyric Theatre, London, on December 14, 1961, directed by John Gielgud, who also played Gaev.

The film version of *Summer and Smoke* with Geraldine Page as Alma and Laurence Harvey as John was released on November 15, 1961.

The film of *The Roman Spring of Mrs. Stone,* directed by José Quintero, with Vivien Leigh as Mrs. Stone and Warren Beatty as Paolo, was released on November 24, 1961.

———

[*Undated letter, early 1962, found among Tennessee's papers but never sent*]

Dearest Maria:

It is always so good to hear your voice and to get your wonderfully sweet, funny letters. It brings me back to life and to something closer to sanity.

Almost everybody is either going round the bend or has already gone round it, that is, in our little circle of friends on the Key.

They put Mother away again for a month, for instance, but she is back home again now and sent me a postcard saying: "There is no place like home." I think Rose is still top girl on the totem pole in the rational competition. She sits there, guarding her goodies, attending the weekly dances and she has three beaux, quite a come-down from Mother's but she seems unembarrassed by the discrepancy in number. She has a rather sly smile about it. Quality, not quantity, perhaps, is her objective.

I am feeling almost unbelievably well, in a physical way, compared to last spring when I thought the Reaper had me next on his list.

I leave tomorrow for New York to see Shelley Winters take over for Bette Davis. Miss Davis is really quite ill. In fact there is a rumor that she has a life-expectancy of from three months to a year, but I discount all such rumors from personal experience.

Paul Bowles has found a lovely house for me in Tangiers, only two minutes' walking time from the beach. I will try to make that scene and if it's a good one, I hope you will come down with the off-springs and Peter.

I don't for a minute believe that all is over between Ken and Elaine [Tynan]. They really love each other very much. They must just learn to live with the primary fact of life, which is not a monogamous thing on the animal level.

Call me in New York. I will be there when you get this letter. I love you.

"Well, Ma'am, stay healthy, my sweet, extraordinary actress"—a quote from Chekhov's letters to Olga Knipper [whom he married], in the wonderful translation of them by Lillian Hellman. I quoted it in my last letter to Maggie Leighton, too.

Love, Tennessee

[*Added in handwriting*] Love the ties.

Tennessee
and Jane Bowles
crossing the
Atlantic

THE FILM version of *Sweet Bird of Youth,* directed by Richard Brooks, with Paul Newman and Geraldine Page, was released on February 20, 1962. On March 9, Tennessee appeared on the cover of *Time* magazine.

At the beginning of 1962 Tennessee was working on *The Milk Train Doesn't Stop Here Anymore,* which was first produced at the Festival of Two Worlds, Spoleto, Italy, on July 11, with Hermione Baddeley as Mrs. Goforth.

In 1962 Tennessee gives the first hint of Frank Merlo's illness.

Address (future) unknown

April 15, 1962

Dearest Maria:

It is wonderful of you to think of me now and then: I do wish you'd send me one of your illustrated letters. Sorry I was so sleepy when you called. We have a couple of male guests from New Orleans. I brought them back with me from the Mardi Gras. I only meant to bring one but the other followed. Perhaps the first called for reinforcements and the call was heeded. They are both from Gulfport, Miss., originally, where my mother spent her honeymoon with Cornelius. They call themselves "swamp-bitches." They are really very nice kids and provide a bit of fun and frolic which is needed here badly. When they want to they can camp up a storm and then all at once the hair-pins fly back in the hair and they could pass for a couple of young country gents: that is, they are geared for any social emergency that comes up. I was afraid the Horse would resent them, but they are getting along fine together.

The Horse is going through all kinds of laboratory tests to determine the cause of his weight loss and highly nervous condition. Perhaps it is just the cumulative effect of passing 14 years of his life in my company. I have wished, for a long, long time, that he would find some occupation but he seems to have a block there. I doubt if we can go to Europe together this spring. He seems to improve when we're travelling separately. If I make the trip, as planned, I'll probably have some other companion with me, since I can't travel alone.

LATER——I am continuing this letter to you after a lapse of two weeks or more. I am now alone in New York, having received one of Audrey's summons[es]. Bette Davis quit the show [*The Night of the Iguana*] and Shelley Winters went in. It is hard to say which was worse but at least La

Davis drew cash and La Winters seems only to sell the upper gallery. To make matters worse, La Leighton (Maggie the kitten) is threatening to give her notice which would mean the demise of the play. All is chaos. La Winters has a fifth of Jack Daniel's Tennessee sour mash whiskey in her dressing-room and nips all through the show. She never enters on cue, sometimes she will cue Maggie on or off the stage a page before an exit or entrance is required by the script. Then, two days ago, in a very chic restaurant, our leading man, Patrick O'Neal, threw a table laden with cocktails, coffee and canapes at Audrey Wood and the director. I had just left and was on the street flagging a cab when I heard a huge commotion behind. Waiters came charging out of the restaurant (which is the one patronized by all the top brass at MCA) and shouted, Catch him, stop that lunatic. At first I thought they meant me and was about to take to my heels when I saw poor Patrick racing down the street like a dark horse in the Derby. I went inside and the big front table was upside down and Audrey stood white as paper under her little pill-box hat and the little director was dripping with coffee and cocktails and picking canapes off himself and Audrey. Audrey was playing it for Greek tragedy, saying, "OH, don't let Liebling know this, promise you won't tell Liebling, I don't know what he would do!"—However, I think you will suspect as I do that it contained some elements of Mack Sennett, the old slapstick comedy days.

About plans now: I don't know what to do. I mean this summer. I don't feel well enough, nervously, to travel alone, but to have Frank with me, in his present mood, would be as bad if not worse. I have offered to buy Frank his own house in Key West as I feel that if we didn't have to share the same roof we might become friends again. He says flatly no. I think he wants me to get out of the house, it is the only home I have known. Perhaps if I can drum up the energy for a summer abroad, things will right themselves in both our minds. I am fond [of him], there is still some kind of attachment. But it would be nice to know if it was a good or a bad one, I can't tell anymore.

That's all the good news for right now. I'll be back in Key West in two or three days. Please let me hear from you, I loved your last letter.

Much love, 10
[*There is a face drawn in 0.*]

If I came to London and advised you a week or two in advance, say in late May, would you be able to get a booking for me in that new apartment building that has the swimming pool? There is the prospect of renting a house in Tangiers for June and July, described as a very charming little house just two minutes' walk from the beach. Give my love to your mummy and my god-child and her sibling rival.

———

TENNESSEE travelled to Europe without Frank, but with Charlie Nightingale, a poet, the first of several travelling companions. Maria gave them all nicknames.

"They were always called 'travelling companions.' Tennessee was too exhausted to travel alone and needed someone to pack, to carry suitcases, typewriter and scripts. He never let a manuscript out of his sight—not since the occasion when he was with Audrey Wood on a plane, having just written *Streetcar*. He'd fallen asleep. To her horror, Audrey suddenly saw this precious script—the only copy—slithering away down the aisle of the plane."

———

[*From 4, rue Pizzaro, Tangier, Morocco, postmarked July 24, 1962*]

Dearest Maria:

I hope you understand why I had to run back to the beach in Tangiers. I arrived in Europe so sick that I nearly flew straight back, and have been struggling against a terrific state of depression and physical depletion ever since.

I really didn't want you to see me like this, because I know that you have had enough painful experiences lately. Let me come to London and then you will see me in a better condition, God willing.

No jokes in this letter, darling. I am just hanging on.

Hermione Baddeley was marvelous in the Spoleto try-out [of *Milk Train*] but there's still a lot to be done on the script and I can only pray that I will be able to do it. If I can, we hope to tour it through the provinces of England. It's a tour-de-force, but Baddeley makes it amazingly believable and the American boy, [Paul] Roebling, was perfect, too.

The Banana Queen has been released from the hospital, but they found nothing wrong with her. She wants to fly here, but I must advise her not to as I don't want her to see me till I am better than I am right now.

Don't worry about me, honey. The young poet travelling with me is all that a poet should be: kind, gentle, and understanding, even when I have washed down a crazy pill with a double martini.

Please have a good summer, and count your blessings: the children, the better relations with Peter and his mother, and your indomitable and very beautiful spirit.

All my love, Tenn

Of course I send my love to your mother. I do hope she's "got the sweet running." If not I will get them running when I get there, marrons glacés, fresh from Fortnum's, and chocolates and all other goodies she likes including fine tea. And we'll all have some good fun together. Peter Wildeblood is here till day after tomorrow and we had a wonderful day on the beach.

Please remember me to Ken [Tynan] and Elaine [Dundy], I hope they're still together.

———

DURING the autumn Frank's condition grew steadily worse and was finally diagnosed as lung cancer.

The Milk Train Doesn't Stop Here Anymore was produced at the Morosco Theatre, New York City, on January 16, 1963, with Hermione Baddeley as Mrs. Goforth.

———

[*From 1431 Duncan Street, Key West*]

April 5, 1963

Dearest Little Sister Maria:

I have been thinking of you so much lately but haven't had the energy to write or call.

I put on one play too many and it did me in.

Right now I am "in retreat"—Key West. Licking my wounds, which include a mysterious infection of the salivary glands in my face (which was round enough without being swollen) so that I look like a jack o'lantern without the grin.

Frankie is down here, too, and despite the rather negative prognosis, he is full of energy and spirit and when I saw him at dinner last night, a fabulous pasta which he cooked with his culinary genius, he coughed only once and was jumping and charging about with all his old vitality. He has his own "pad" while he is waiting to take over the house when Charlie Nightingale and I go back abroad, later this month or early next. It isn't a perfect arrangement but nothing in life is. I hope I can fly to London for a week before I settle for the summer somewhere like Taormina or Athens or the island of Rhodes which I found so lovely two years ago.

Hermione Baddeley and Kenneth Tynan, London, 1957

Gore Vidal and Maria at the Tynans', Mount Street, London, 1957

We may leave in a week for New York. If you send me your phone number to the N.Y. address I'll call you.

My love to you all, 10

———

IN THE summer of 1963 Tennessee went to England again with Nightmare Charlie. In London, Tennessee confessed to Maria that he felt bad about leaving Frank behind and that he missed him. Maria spoke on the telephone to Frank, who told her: "I miss him too."

Maria then persuaded Tennessee to return at once to New York. For a while he and Frank lived in the New York apartment together, until Frank's condition deteriorated. He was admitted to Memorial Hospital for Cancer and Allied Diseases in New York.

Tennessee travelled between New York, visiting Frank, and Abington, Virginia, for rehearsals of a new production of *The Milk Train Doesn't Stop Here Anymore.*

———

August 5, 1963

Dearest Maria

Just after getting back I wrote you from Key West but the letter remains down there, I hope I get this one off. I wanted to thank you for making the stay in London such fun.

I wish I had some good report to give you about Frank, but I can only say I am glad you are not here to see him, the wasting away is so dreadful after the wonderful vitality of the past years, and it would hurt you as it does me.

I have sent Nightmare Charlie (who is still having nightmares) down to Key West so that Frank and I could be alone in the apartment. We do very little. Read and watch television.

Is it true that Dr. Ward was really assassinated? By the govt.? There is a rumor to that effect going around here.

None of your gifts have been delivered as yet, but they will be. Tatiana [Schvetzoff] is never at home, I don't know how to get in touch with Jean Stein, and Nightmare just sits and composes his nightmares when he is here. The last time he had one I woke up with his hands on my throat. I said, very coolly, Cut the shit or I'll bust the bed-lamp on your head. I really think they're a subconscious way of expressing his repressed violence, don't you?

I have written to Magnani to enquire about a small villa with a swimming pool in Rome, as I don't think I can stay in the States when the present situation has run its inevitable course: and I will go over alone.

Must seal this letter at once as Frank is returning from the barber's. He doesn't eat but he still goes out a little.

Love as always, Tenn

If you know where Jean Stein is, would you drop her a note saying I have something for her and would she call me at BU 8-7986. This is not laziness, believe me, it's just that anything, everything is too much for me right now. Things *have* to get better, don't they?

––––––

DR. STEPHEN WARD was involved in the call-girl scandal in England which led to the resignation of John Profumo and eventually to the fall of the Conservative government.

––––––

[*From New York City*]

September 23, 1963

Dearest Maria:

The little Horse left us two nights ago, after two weeks of suffering which he bore so bravely, as very few could. I had been with him during the day at the hospital. He kept climbing back and forth between his bed and his chair. I tried to make him stay still but he said: "I feel too restless." He was taking oxygen but didn't like it and kept removing the tubes from his nose. I think he left us just short of the time when his condition would have become too awful. All the system was breaking down and his spirit, even his spirit, might have broken if he had had to sustain it any longer. He died proudly and stoically; they tell me it happened in a matter of minutes, before the floor-doctor had time to reach him, but there was a nurse in his room who had just given him his nightly medication. They say he just gasped and lay back on the pillow and was gone. I am just beginning, now, to feel the desolation of losing my dear little Horse.

I must go away somewhere. Perhaps I can go to England for the London production of *Milk Train* or to Mexico for the shooting of *Iguana*. I am not yet ready to go back to Key West which is so full of recollections and

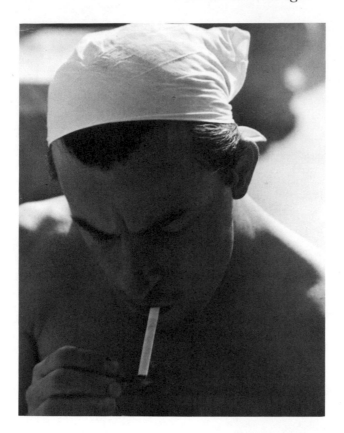

Frank Merlo,
1953

A portrait of Frank
by Tennessee.
On the back of a
photograph of
Frank, Tennessee
had written:
"When your candle
burns low, you've
got to believe
that the last light
shows you something
besides the progress
of darkness."

associations. Mexico may be best because of the swimming that may be able to pull me together a bit after this awful experience, the effects of which I am only beginning to feel.

I think our Russian church-service worked to the extent that he never lost his dignity and pride.

This morning the family are having their Catholic Mass for him. Tomorrow there is to be a big service to which his many friends in New York will come. I saw him yesterday, lying in state at the family wake, and he looked like a saint, and like himself, too.

Much love, Tenn.

[*Added in handwriting*] (Please call me collect.)

———

A F T E R Frank's death Tennessee went to Mexico for the filming of *The Night of the Iguana*, directed by John Huston, with Ava Gardner as Maxine, Deborah Kerr as Hannah and Richard Burton as Shannon.

"Tennessee and Frank had been truly devoted to each other. Tennessee has described Frank as the only real love of his life. This was absolutely so. After Frank's death, Tennessee felt a profound and increasing regret. He'd heard it was heart failure that was the great killer, but he felt that it was loneliness. He gradually suffered a complete breakdown, which was exacerbated by the treatment prescribed by a Dr. [Max] Jacobson, who was subsequently barred from practice.

"Jacobson taught his patients to inject themselves with a concoction of his own invention. Tennessee used to walk around with capsules and a syringe. I was very concerned by Tennessee's condition, and so I stole a capsule and had it analyzed by my own doctor's laboratory in London. The analysis confirmed that the capsule contained 'speed,' mixed with other dangerous drugs. I would throw away his pills and capsules whenever I could."

Williams's latest revision of *The Milk Train Doesn't Stop Here Anymore*, directed by Tony Richardson, with Tallulah Bankhead as Mrs. Goforth, opened at the Brooks Atkinson Theatre, New York City, on January 1, 1964. The production closed three nights later.

———

1431 Duncan Street
Key West

February 26, 1964

Dearest Maria:

This has been a year of mistakes for me, as well as tragedy. It was a terrible mistake to come back to Key West, with all the old associations haunting the place. I want to escape to Europe in the next few weeks, and I am wondering if I could spend a month or two in those London flats you mentioned that have a swimming pool. I mean, till it is warm enough to go to Italy, Spain, or Greece. I plan to come alone, and I think the plan is unalterable. It became increasingly apparent that "N.C." [Nightmare Charlie] was mostly "N" as far as I was concerned, and perhaps I was "N" for him, too. There comes a time to burn bridges as you go.

I feel that I have kept on hanging on to old things too long and must make a clean break if I am ever to make one.

"The Banana Queen" is in New Jersey, recuperating from a face-lifting operation. I must say that I approve of the measure, that is, if it has worked, as she looked a good ten years older than her actual age, due to John Barleycorn's reciprocal devotion. She wants to come to Greece in early summer. I want to spend the spring in London, PROVIDED you can get me a flat with a pool to swim in, CAN YOU?

Please call me collect, CYpress 6-6942, Key West, as soon as you've found out about it. I can't stand hotel life, have had too much of it, lately.

I have much to tell you about Lady [Tony] Richardson. What a one that one was! She screwed me six ways from next Sunday and since we had the same agent, I was helpless. However, I don't suppose the play would have worked even if she had not been so irresponsible as she was.

I must learn how to rest for a while now. PLEASE DO CALL ME!

Love to all your loved ones, especially your Mummy and Fatty [Natasha] and my God-child [Pulcheria].

Much love, 10

———

MARIA's mother, Mary Britneva, died on Friday, November 13, 1964.

———

[*Telegram sent November 14, 1964*]

DEAREST MARIA SORRY I CANT BE WITH YOU AS MY HEART IS YOU MUST NOT GRIEVE OVER YOUR LITTLE MOTHERS RELEASE FROM SUFFERING MUCH LOVE TENNESSEE

Maria with her mother, Mary Britneva, and her brother, Vladimir

145 West 55th Street

January 20, 1965

Maria dear:

I hope you are feeling a bit better now. I did want so much to do the piece about Mme. Britneva but I found there was just not enough personal recollections that could be used, and my energy is still very low after so many months of depression. Some day I will be able to write about that marvellous lady in a way worthy of her, but it can't be now. I explained this to Tatiana [Schvetzoff] and she understood it and promised she would explain it to you.

A few nights ago I spent about twenty minutes with Gore before he flew to London. You've probably seen him by now. He's having a fabulous success with his novel *Julian*. It has been on the best-seller list for about a year.

I am going into rehearsal in a couple of weeks with a couple of very odd plays [*The Mutilated* and *The Gnädiges Fräulein*]. I don't suppose the critics or public will know what to make of them, and I can't say that I do either. But it is better to be occupied with something than with nothing. [When financial backing could not be found for 1964–65, the production of *Slapstick Tragedy,* as the double bill was called, was postponed until the following season.]

I saw both Gielgud and John Perry, separately, not long ago. Gielgud is giving a brilliant performance, I think the best I've ever seen him give, in Edward Albee's new play [*Tiny Alice*]. I had a drink with him in his dressing-room after the show and he was in fine spirits and looking remarkably young. The English don't seem to grow older. Perry had not changed, either. He was with a couple of attractive young men so I guess he's enjoying the States.

My house in Key West was broken into recently so I am renting it to protect it while I have to stay in New York. The winters here are abominable. When spring comes, I hope to feel in a mood and condition to travel.

Elaine Dundy is here and says that you are going back on the stage, that there was a photograph of you and the little girls in the paper making the announcement. I would love to see it, and I hope it will come about. You need to be doing something creative and diverting now. There is no doubt in my mind that one or both of the little girls will have a theatrical career, it is in the stars and the cards and in the Russian tea-leaves.

With much love, 10

145 West 55th Street

March 12, 1965

Dearest Maria:

I'm writing to inform or warn you that I am flying to London on the 23rd of this month, three days before my unfortunate birthday, to attend the transfer to the West End of *Night of the Iguana* which I have heard was received well in the suburbs because of a fabulous performance by Sian Phillips, wife of Peter O'Toole. Of course I will call you soon as I get there and have had forty winks at the Savoy hotel that I am booked into. The company is paying my flight expenses and I guess hotel, too. It comes, this trip, at a good time for me, as I am beginning to work my way out of my long state of depression which immobilized me all but completely.

I hope I will be persona grata with you, despite the terrible ticking off you gave me in your recent letter. I made several attempts to write about dear Mme. Britneva but found that all I could say was: "She was a tiny little woman who was a very great lady. She had the gift of grace. She had the gift of kind humor. Perhaps of all the ladies I have known in my life, only she and my mother's mother had that rare quality of being above the circumstances that are brutally imposed upon us when we grow old. But Mme. Britneva was a sage as well as a saint. In her small, elegant person was 'the wisdom that passeth human understanding' which is a good thing to pass. She could make a Russian dinner in a kitchen seem like a banquet, and all that she said had grace, warmth, and wise perception in it. At first her hands began to tremble a little as if they had a constant restlessness in them. When I saw her again a year later, they seemed still more restless, but still she continued her profession, which was translating Russian writers such as Chekhov into English as well as if that was their original language. She had that thing most valuable to a person, a wisdom and grace that are a pair of white sails to bear them bravely away, and, finally, it is this nobility of spirit that makes a human life an experience deserving of our loving respect and esteem."

You see, that was really all I could say and it wasn't enough and I was not at all sure, I was very doubtful, that Mme. Britneva would have wanted that sort of sincere but rhetorical eulogy written about her by someone, an American playwright not much valued in London, to whom she was a beautiful enigma. I wonder if it wouldn't be possible to put together a memorial volume, including her book about her emigration to England, your own portrait of her and her gallant struggles, and loving recollections and impressions from we others who had a chance to know her a little.

The ghastly winter here is beginning to break. I still live alone except for a cousin who occupies the upper floor of the duplex apartment. I go to an analyst every week-day and he calls me on Saturdays and Sundays to see if I am getting through the week-end and if I have taken my vitamins, anti-depressants, and not too much booze. Every week-end my cousin drives me out to see Rose. The last time she was in a state of euphoria, she seemed to imagine she was a queen, for all the way to the restaurant for dinner, she kept smiling, bowing and waving, to left and right, at everybody we passed along the highway. She has a boy-friend at the "Lodge." I asked her how he was and she smiled brightly and said "Emaciated!" Then I asked her if she'd seen Jo Healy, the girl who looks out for her when I am not in New York, and [she] said, "Oh, no, they told me she's dead," also with a bright smile. When we got back to the Lodge, she asked us up to see her parakeet named Ella, and as I entered the room, I said to the bird, "How are you, beautiful?" And Rose said to it, "Say good evening, Rose." She had suddenly decided to identify with it, since I had called it beautiful. Call me, please, before I take off for London.

Love, Tenn.

"ROSE, for mysterious reasons, absolutely loathed poor Jo Healy, who ranks to this day among her dislikes. When Tennessee was feeling very mischievous, he would give me a deep dig in the ribs and suggest, gently, 'Rose? Shall we go and visit Jo Healy now?' Rose's immediate reaction was always an emphatic 'No!' "

On March 30, 1965, to mark the twentieth anniversary of Tennessee's first great success in the theatre, *The Glass Menagerie* was revived at the Paper Mill Playhouse, Millburn, New Jersey, with Maureen Stapleton as Amanda. The production was transferred to the Brooks Atkinson Theatre in New York City on May 4, 1965.

The double bill *Slapstick Tragedy* opened at the Longacre Theatre in New York City on February 22, 1966. It was produced by Charles Bowden and directed by Alan Schneider, with Margaret Leighton as Trinket and Kate Reid as Celeste in *The Mutilated* and Leighton as the Fräulein, Reid as Molly and Zoe Caldwell as Molly in *The Gnädiges Fräulein*. The production closed after seven performances.

1966

[*Address on envelope 15 West 72nd Street, New York City*]

April 15, 1966

Dearest Maria:

How sweet of you to write me, even from the Dowager's [Wilbury Park] where I doubt there is much else to do! I think it is wonderful that she is coming around. It is hard to be severe with old ladies. I keep getting letters from my mother and forget to open them because almost invariably they contain a printed prayer that she thinks appropriate to my pagan way of life which has actually become so conventional that it would bore even a mother.

I have been to a fine dental surgeon about my facial swelling. He took X-rays and today he told me that the swelling is probably caused by an impacted wisdom tooth—clearly visible in the X-rays—which is "decalcifying." I am not altogether happy about this diagnosis because if it were the whole truth, I should think he would want to pull the tooth right out instead of telling me to go to Sicily—where I'm going next week—and forget about it. He gave me the name of a dental surgeon in London who he says is the dental surgeon "to the Crown," and to whom I must fly if there is a sudden emergency—such as my face exploding in all four directions, I suppose. I always beg doctors to tell me the complete truth but for some reason I never feel that they do.

We leave here a week from today for Rome and then Taormina. The water will still be cold but preferable to the YMCA pool. We're taking Frankie's little Boston terrier Gigi along. She is an absolute genius compared to the long succession of English bull-dogs that preceded her. She wears a jewelled collar and is much the smartest and most sophisticated animal in this skyscraper apartment. She is even beginning to understand the English language.

I am not surprised about Richard and Elizabeth [Harris], but it's very sad for him. He needs someone or something so badly.

[Lester] Persky is hopping off to London again in a few days. I know you will want to be there to receive him. His back gets worse, not better, and he is wearing a corset. Could you arrange for him to meet the Queen? I suppose you would first have to explain to her exactly why he walks about clutching his derriere as if he had just had a violent love-affair with a donkey.

Have a good trip. It would be wonderful if our paths could cross somewhere.

Devotedly, your blue fish, 10

———

MARIA often teasingly remarked that Tennessee looked like a fish.

Tennessee's travelling companion at this time was Henry O'Lowe. "I know nothing about him."

Tennessee had finished a film treatment of *The Milk Train Doesn't Stop Here Anymore*. The film, released in 1968, was produced by Lester Persky and directed by Joseph Losey and starred Richard Burton (too old for his role) as Chris Flanders and Elizabeth Taylor (too young for hers) as Mrs. Goforth.

———

15 West 72nd Street, apt. 338

October 5, 1966

Dearest Maria:

You know about my problem about letter-writing, the letters have always to be written after the day's work, and I nearly always work till exhausted. I went months without writing Mother till I received such an anxious post-card from her that I put work aside one morning and got off a long letter to her. She said she was so worried about me that she was coming to New York alone (at 82) to check on my condition, and Rose's. There's nothing that upsets Rose more than a visit from Mother, since Rose doesn't want to or isn't able to accept the fact that people have to grow older. Once when she saw Grandfather in Key West, she looked horrified and said, "Who is this old imposter?" Fortunately Grandfather was too deaf to hear her.

As for the phone, I am terrified of phone-calls, I always feel that I won't be able to talk, especially across an ocean.

It looks like I will soon be returning to London in connection with the film-play *Boom!* I must stay here until October 20th as Maureen Stapleton is appearing in a two-week revival of *Rose Tattoo* at City Center. She took off about 40 pounds, and right now is thinner than when she originally appeared in the play. It is enormously important to her to be seen with a plausible figure again.

Since I last saw you I have completed an almost full-length play [*The Two-Character Play*] that Audrey likes. It has only two characters and we feel it ought to be done first in England because it needs two marvelous actors, and stars of that quality seem to be more prevalent in London than here.

Life is pretty dull except for the poker nights twice a week. I have become quite good at poker because of my fishy eyes which betray no emotion whether I have a royal flush or nothing in my hand. Last night I was the big winner, over forty bucks in coin of the realm.

How sad it is to have nothing else to tell you!

Much love, 10

T H I S is Tennessee's first mention of *The Two Character Play,* which contains a play-within-a-play about himself and Rose. As subsequent letters indicate, he was obsessed by this play for many years. The revision was called *Out Cry,* but so important a play was it for him that he always referred to it as *OUT CRY*—of all his plays, the only title that he *always* typed in capital letters. Others he occasionally typed in capital letters.

The Two-Character Play was first offered to the Edinburgh International Festival for 1967 but was rejected. It was first produced in London at the Hampstead Theatre Club on December 11, 1967, directed by James Roose-Evans, with Peter Wyngarde as Felice and Mary Ure as Clare.

Peter Wyngarde recalls: "It is the most harrowing part I have ever done. To convey the madness within the madness, like Chinese boxes, and yet to appear to be saner than Clare: we both came out after the show with hoops of steel around our heads. Because it is so near the bone, it's a terribly depressing piece to play in, which is unusual; ordinarily, one comes out of acting in a play, any play, invigorated. And yet, halfway through it takes over. It is unquestionably a great piece, especially since the *Out Cry* revisions. It is impossible to be bad in it . . . well, almost impossible.

"Tennessee was at all the rehearsals, with his wretched companion of the time bullying him. But Tennessee was gone [drunk or stoned], out of it, completely. He could offer nothing approaching directorial advice.

"I never saw Maria and Tennessee together, although I met her separately. But I knew this: that she was a good influence on him at a terrible time. The death of his friend Frank Merlo had overwhelmed him."

In 1967 Tennessee also wrote *Kingdom of Earth,* which for its New York production was called *Seven Descents of Myrtle.* The first performance was on March 27, 1968, at the Ethel Barrymore Theatre, produced by David Merrick, directed by José Quintero, with Estelle Parsons as Myrtle, Harry Guardino as Chicken and Brian Bedford as Lot. Tennessee had hoped that Maureen Stapleton would play Myrtle, but Merrick chose Parsons instead because of her recent enormous success in the film *Bonnie and Clyde.* The production closed after twenty-nine performances.

During the summer of 1968 Tennessee continued to revise *The Two-Character Play* and also wrote the first draft of *In the Bar of a Tokyo Hotel*.

"Tennessee came over to England and was in the most awful condition. I was finally able to persuade him to see a nerve specialist. The only reason Tennessee went to see him was because he had been my mother's specialist as well. We went to the hospital and Tennessee was in such a state that I had physically to sit on a chair barricading the door. The doctor was keeping us waiting, and Tennessee was running up and down the room like a lion in a cage. Eventually he went in and was in there for about an hour, alone. And then I took him back to the hotel and the next day he left for America.

"I knew that Audrey [Wood] was very concerned, so I wrote a quick note to her saying that I had taken Tennessee to a hospital, and the doctor definitely thought that he should go into a clinic, as soon as possible. Knowing of Tennessee's paranoia, I gave the note secretly to Harry O'Lowe, telling him to post it in New York. True to form, O'Lowe immediately showed it to Tennessee, who then accused me of ganging up with the Widow Wood against him. 'She wishes I was dead,' he said. Which was complete nonsense. 'Don't you know what she did to Liebling after his heart attack? She had a little locket made in the shape of a heart, which she hung round her neck, and inside it were all his heart pills. She would look at him and say, "You don't look so well, Liebling. Would you like one of your pills, dear?" So the poor man was constantly reminded of his condition, which made it even worse. AND SHE KNOWS I'VE GOT A BAD HEART TOO!'"

[*Typewritten letter from Audrey to Maria, dated July 16, 1968*]

Dear Maria:

Your cable received. Tennessee is still not in a hospital, but residing at the Plaza Hotel.

Your presents have been delivered and he is pleased with them.

I wish I could say I was as pleased with his present physical and mental status. He still is not taking care of himself. Certainly I will be in touch if and when he ever does stay in a hospital.

Affectionately, Audrey Wood

Dictated by Miss Wood and signed in her absence.

AT THE end of June 1968, Tennessee wrote a letter to his brother, Dakin, which contained the now notorious sentence "If anything of a violent nature happens to me, ending my life abruptly, it will not be a case of suicide, as it would be made to appear." Dakin was worried, as Tennessee apparently had disappeared. The story was in the newspapers, and two days later Tennessee reassured his brother that he was still alive. But Tennessee began to wonder whether he should not admit himself to his sister's asylum, Stony Lodge.

[Telegram from Key West dated July 10, 1968]

DEAREST MARIA, SO HAPPY TO RECEIVE YOUR LOVELY LETTER. I AM RETURNING TO NEW YORK TOMORROW TO ENTER A HOSPITAL AND WILL CONSULT BEST NEUROLOGIST AVAILABLE. EVERYTHING YOU ADVISED IS QUITE APPROPRIATE. MY LOVE TO YOU AND THE CHILDREN. WHEN DID YOU LEARN TO TYPE A LETTER. AT LEAST YOU SHOULD SIGN IT WITH AN INK SIGNATURE BUT THAT IS A SMALL MATTER THAT I WILL NOT HOLD AGAINST YOU. ALL MY LOVE TENNESSEE

"TENNESSEE'S continuing decline left him more and more dependent on doctors. He felt that his strength as a writer was ebbing away from him, which made him more desperate. But somehow he survived 1969. He was awarded that year's gold medal for drama by the National Institute of Arts and Letters."

The year had begun with Dakin persuading Tennessee to become a Roman Catholic.

On May 11, 1969, *In the Bar of a Tokyo Hotel* was first produced at the East Side Playhouse, New York City, directed by Herbert Machiz, with Anne Meacham as Miriam and Donald Madden as Mark. The production closed after 25 performances.

In June Tennessee went to Japan with Anne Meacham for a production of *A Streetcar Named Desire*. It was a year of restlessness—travelling from New York to St. Louis, from New York to San Francisco to Tokyo and back, to Miami, New Orleans and Key West.

After Tennessee burned himself at Key West, Dakin persuaded him to go to the Renard Psychiatric Division of Barnes Hospital in St. Louis on October 1. Tennessee underwent a total withdrawal from all drugs, only just surviving the "cold turkey" treatment, and stayed in the hospital for three months.

Despite continued requests from Maria, Audrey Wood refused to tell her where Tennessee was.

———

[*Typewritten letter to Tennessee from Maria, London, dated November 17, 1969*]

My darling Tennessee—

It is such a long time since I heard anything from you, but I know that you are in hospital. I am pleased from one point of view, because at least they should be getting you off those damn pinkies. On the other hand, I am very worried. It is so very difficult to contact you. I wrote you a very long letter three months ago to Key West—I really don't know where to send this letter. Can't you try and write me a note, and let me know how you're getting on. You know with your fat little banana fingers it only takes a minute.

You know, darling Tennessee, you are my family, and [the] very deep love and affection and respect I bear you has never diminished over the years. If you are in trouble and unhappy, you must feel that you are not alone. I will happily come to the ends of the earth to see you and give you any comfort. I know you are going through a very bad time emotionally, and knowing how much your work means to you, you mustn't despair if it is going slowly at the moment. Think how much you have written. How much pleasure and encouragement you have given to thinkers and creative people all over the world. Some people like, and some people don't like what you write. But it can never be dismissed as something which is not of enormous importance, especially to our generation. I feel sure, my darling Tenn, that you will come out of this black patch. You are always in my prayers, and also in my thoughts, and also in your god-daughter's. Pulcheria is a beautiful, sensitive child, and as sly as ten flies in summer. Natasha is a beautiful child, and as sly as twenty flies in summer. And as for Froggy Footman, well, you know what it is with footmen, in their livery; they are always asleep when they should be passing round the coffee after dinner. He spends a lot of time in the butler's pantry with his feet up—all four of them—and as for catching forty winks, Froggy's winks add up to 240 a day, every day!

Can you imagine, I've been to Russia? And got back alive. I've written an article which will appear in *Queen* magazine, and I'll send you a copy of it, plus a photograph of me in furs looking like an orangutan—this is a form of monkey with really Russian spelling.

I do hope, darling Tenn, you will get this letter. Do let me know and I will write you one as often as you want—every day. In the meantime, God bless you, and call me collect any time. Think how many times I've called you collect.

Love, Maria

ON JANUARY 8, 1970, *Camino Real* was revived at the Vivian Beaumont Theatre, New York City, directed by Milton Katselas, with Al Pacino as Kilroy, Jessica Tandy as Marguerite Gautier, and Jean-Pierre Aumont as Casanova.

[*Envelope postmarked Key West*]

March 16, 1970

Dearest Maria:

As an extremely long delayed afterthought brother Dakin forwarded to me a letter that you had written me while I was in the "bin." It was wonderful to receive it as I had stupidly feared that you had dismissed me from mind and heart.

I have just returned to Key West from Miami where I went to visit what I fear is the death-bed of my old and dear friend Marion Vaccaro. I have been up to visit her in hospital several times. She keeps having partial recoveries and then relapses and has spent most of her six weeks in hospital in what is called "the Intensive Care Unit," a chamber of horrors in which all the patients are connected with mechanical devices that record their breathing and heart-beat and are usually fitted with tubes to their kidneys, etc. On this last visit I found her with tubes down her nostrils, conscious but unable to speak, only able to cling to my hand. With the free hand she kept gesturing toward the door, meaning that I should take her out. While I was there an electric device over her bed suddenly sounded off shrilly and doctors and nurses rushed to her bed-side as she was having a cardiac spasm. I won't go into further details: enough to say it was a shattering experience, although the dear lady still survives. I sometimes wonder if it is right to keep people surviving in that condition.

Doctors should know when a condition is quite hopeless and then let the patient go.

I went to a neurologist myself for a check-up. He said that the three convulsions which I had suffered in the bin had not damaged my brain, that my "cogitation was totally un-impaired" and that despite the coronary which I had also suffered in the bin, I was likely to follow the family tradition of longevity. I was not displeased by this. I lost the fear of death in the bin, but I have come to value and to enjoy life very much and would not be reluctant to go on with it if possible. I am taking care of myself for the first time since the death of "the Horse." I take only one drink of hard liquor a day, just before dinner, and between times allow myself only occasional little glasses of inexpensive California wine. I have cut out all the pills except the ones prescribed for me by my regular doctor in New York, a marvelous anti-depressant pill called "Synequan." I swim thirty lengths of my long pool here in Key West every day and usually devote the evenings to bridge or poker. Do you remember Harry O'Lowe? Well, he was so objectionable to me when I returned from the bin that I finally had to send him packing. I am paying him three hundred dollars a week to stay out of Key West, it will be be instantly discontinued if he sets a great Irish foot back on the island. Don't you think that is proof of a return to sanity? I now have two companions in the house. One is a benign sort of con-man whom I call "Gentleman John." Unfortunately he is inclined to play a somewhat tricky game of bridge. But the other house-guest is a friend since 1942. He is an aristocrat, of southern plantation heritage, Andrew Lyndon III, and I will probably take him to Europe with me in June. In late June I have an engagement to read verse at some poetry society in London. Meanwhile I am working very hard every morning, and am trying to entice Margaret Leighton, who lately received a New York critics' citation for having given, in *Night of the Iguana,* the best dramatic perform-ance of the decade, into acting in a play [*The Two-Character Play*] of mine again. (I believe that I am the only one who knows that Maggie is quite starkers!)

I am enclosing some newspaper clippings about brother Dakin's political career in Illinois. The last time I phoned Mother I said: "Is Dakin still in politics?" She cried out, "Oh, son, haven't you heard of the scandal? It's been on TV, I can't speak of it on the phone!"

I shall remain here in Key West all spring so please do let me hear from you. The address is 1431 Duncan St.

Much love, 10

[Part of a surviving letter from Maria to Tennessee, written aboard a British Airways flight to Nairobi]

Darling Tenn—

"Go get de lord, go get de lord, de lady's on de phone!" (Peter, on safari, placing a call to me from his hotel in Nairobi.) Now de lady's on de plane.

I cannot tell you [how] happy I was to hear your beloved voice on the telephone, and to receive your letter. I have been so concerned about you, and Dinky Dakin obviously didn't forward my mail, or any news from you or your whereabouts. Now you seem much more like your old self. You have dropped the Mad Hatter's hat, from my favorite *Alice,* forever I hope. We all tend to have his hat on from time to time, don't we? We can start a lovely new game together, just deciding quietly among our friends who is wearing the hat and who isn't. What a delicious idea! [Maria here drew a few illustrations in suggestion.]

I'm sure we can think of many people who've been in the hat SITTING for years and years, and don't even know they have it on. . . .

[Postmarked May 8, 1970]

1431 Duncan Street
Key West, Fla.

May 6, 1970

Dearest Maria:

You see I have worn my typewriter ribbon quite thin with my fat little fingers.

It was such a relief to finally receive that immediate letter you promised me over the blower 30 years and several months ago.

Yes, Dinky Dakin has the mad-hatter's hat over every bit of his face but his gap-toothed grin. When Mother was down here for an unbearably protracted visit she said that Dakin's father-in-law in Big Springs, Texas, was not well enough this year to have him and his adopted no-neck monster down there for the summer and they were planning to stay in my house instead for that season. A dead silence fell at the table when she made this announcement—until I said "An angel seems to be passing over the house."

When finally Mother's visit had exceeded all bounds, I called her one morning and said, "Mother, your plane to Miami is taking off in one hour, we'll come to pick you up in 45 minutes." When we got there we had to pack for her. She left her cane, formerly Grandfather's, at the hotel-desk— also a nine-foot feather boa. Refused to board the plane without them. The proprietor of the hotel rushed them to the airport in a cab, so great was his apprehension that she might return.

She surfaced on Biscayne Bay a few days later but was luckily mistaken for a sea-monster of some unknown species—so I am still at large.

I still hope to make it to London in early June and am longing to meet Vanessa [Redgrave], she is one of my two or three favorite actresses and she might be right for the role in my last long play [*The Two-Character Play*]. I am getting bored with the hesitations of Maggie [Leighton] and her insistence on some director I've never heard of named Peter Dew or New. Are all English directors called Peter? As for the play, it is special, difficult, yes, but I have worked on it longer and harder than anything else I have written and now finally dare to hope that it will wind up my theatrical career with the lyricism that I began with in *Menagerie*.

Have you read Gore's brilliantly written piece in this month's *Esquire*? He makes repeated references to me, saying I have "gone a bit mad," implying that I am a Communist which is a system totally unpalatable to me—I am still just an old-fashioned anarchist—abhorring anything bureaucratic—and yet I have a feeling that Gore realizes that I am one of the few friends he has in the world and that he grudgingly half likes me still, though I shudder to think how he probably talks about me to you. As a writer, particularly as an essayist, he has made enormous progress with maturity. If I get to Europe let's visit him in his house on the Tiber and straighten him out a bit.

I still speak a bit tentatively of my trip to Europe as my cardiac condition persists and I only get a few hours' sleep a night. I am resolutely off the hard liquor and strong pills that landed me in the snake-pit last September. I do drink one cocktail at six-thirty and a couple of glasses of wine during lunch and dinner. A person with my tension has to have something to keep him in his skin but must avoid things that may blow him out of his skull.

I swim about thirty lengths of my 35-foot pool every day and am looking forward to those lovely clear, cool waters of Sicily.

Yesterday we went out in a cockle-shell of a boat headed for the Dry Tortugas, a group of historical little islands about four hours away. But a third of the way there the vessel sprang a leak and began to go under. The captain and first-mate were a pair of pot-heads, so high on the grass that we had almost foundered before they discovered a valve in the bilges which was pouring in water like a wide-open fire-hydrant—and we were just about to sing "Nearer My God to Thee"!

It is morning and time to go back to bed.

Much love, 10

TENNESSEE went to London for the poetry festival readings organized by the Institute of Contemporary Arts.

"He arrived and had a nap. The poetry reading was in the evening. He came and picked me up an hour beforehand, and on the way to the reading very casually asked me if, by chance, I had any of his poems. I said, rather snappily, 'Yes, of course I have. I've got *In the Winter of Cities*.' 'Well, can we go back and pick it up?' he said. The taxi turned round. On the way back to the ICA, Tennessee, lazily thumbing through the pages of his book, was asking, 'What about this one? . . . Shall I read this one?'

"We arrived a short time before the readings were due to begin, and realized to our horror that Stephen Spender, W. H. Auden, Pier Paolo Pasolini, Thom Gunn, Wole Soyinka and Allen Tate had been rehearsing all day, setting complicated lighting cues, microphones and speakers. And Tennessee was still wondering what to read.

"When the moment came, Tennessee shuffled onto the stage, insisting like a fool that I go on with him. There was a cry of dismay from Charles Osborne, who was organizing the event. Tennessee went on alone, read his poems, and then drew out of his pocket the prose poem 'What's Next on the Agenda, Mr. Williams?' "

WHAT'S NEXT ON THE AGENDA, MR. WILLIAMS?

I. *Apostrophe to Myself*

Not every morning that you awaken to morning could it be indisputably proven of you that you had awakened quite well to that morning, no, not with some mornings those tattle-tale stitches of a considerable discomfort along the left arm and in the left side of the chest, and also some mornings, as well as often at night, now, those premature contractions of a heart-valve, giving you the sensation, hardly agreeable enough to be called nostalgic, which you felt as a child when the roller-coaster at Forest Park Highlands dropped down the big dip after the long skyward climb, no, it could not be accepted without question that you awakened quite well to all mornings lately with these little insinuations of mortality pinned to your pillow, slipped under your door, projected on the dim ceiling of the bedroom, no, Tennessee. No more mementos are needed to remind you not to forget a damaged ventricle of your heart, the black souvenir of your season in Friggins Division of Barnacle Hospital in the city of St. Pollution on the gobble-nobber of waters . . .

Oh, but you know, don't you know, there are, oh, so many places such a long way from that place,

And on the work-table in your studio on that Key to which you now hold a key

(a gold key presented to you by the mayor of the Keys, on the otherwise rueful occasion of your fifty-ninth birthday this season)

a glistening globe of the world competes for attention these days with your aging Olivetti, and why not, old voyageur?

You've circled the true globe once, companioned then by a friend called Little Horse

(now seven years lost)

and would love to circle the globe once more, uncompanioned, perhaps, but still reasonably ambulatory,

putting down, now, at more places including those blistering places in India where migrants starve on the way to other luckless places,

in questionable honor of such as you, Tennessee, who have yet to offer a rice-bowl to those mendicant brothers, a sin of omission for which there may still be time to perform at least a token act of contrition, and perhaps to receive in return a thin-fingered gesture of much-needed benediction.

(Why not entertain it, that vision, why not entertain whatever is comforting to you, and ignore, if you can, the not altogether unwarranted suspicion that there is a Fatal Sister under your skin who is mighty quick with the needle,

Yes, man, you feel those stitches, by morning, as well as by night, but not yet again, not so far, not for the charm of a third time, the very deep toe-curling stabs of a black-cloaked assassin's stiletto, that fierce opponent of your fierce will to continue,

no, not that again, not so far,

that long, long moment of air-starvation and anguish that triggers your fingers' quick reach

for the bottles of tiny, precisely fragmented and bevelled, bits of white China rabbit,

present at night close beside your single bed and by day in your jacket pocket, no, not that again, not so far, but what is the whisper of the guru in the moon if it isn't the word "soon"?

IV. *Now*

Release has enormous occasions such as now, and I want to wash the slate clean and then scrawl on it in luminous chalk "EN AVANT!," the command with which I concluded all entries in my old journals of days and nights gained and lost, because I still have a long play to finish, one more, and I am erecting the Jane Bowles Summer House in my front rose garden, and . . .

What's left for me to say but the Brahmin's and Ginsberg's word "Om." Of "Om" I've discovered the meaning through my sleepless night reading of *Siddhartha,* yes, old friend Gore, I really do read, even the Bible and *Myra Breckinridge,* in separate volumes of course, and the meaning of "Om" is the one who is perfect or a state of perfection. I say it and understand it but can't live by it, that perfection which is a surrender of separate being. I'm afraid that I'm too incorrigibly Western for it and have been in show-business much longer than you have, Allen.

And as for you patient listeners tonight, I've presumed too long on your patience, and so good night and may you have good morrows, not inside but outside of Friggins Division of Barnacle Hospital in the city of St. Pollution on the gobble-nobber of waters and, one more and, in case you don't know the meaning of gobble-nobber, a black musician, an authority on the idioms of his race and vocation, told me a long time ago that it meant a boat-load of mothers, which, as you've probably guessed, is a definition omitting a couple of syllables and a hyphen, yes, a term of extreme opprobrium among such effetely snobbish peoples as yours and mine. . . .

"IT STOLE the show. The young audience gave Tennessee a standing ovation."

Charles Osborne recalled the occasion in his memoirs, *Giving It Away*:

I wrote to him asking him to come and read his poems at the 1970 Poetry International, for a fee of £50. He rang me from Key West, touched that I should have remembered his poems. "No one else does," he said. "Do you really want me to come?"

He came, and was the star of the show. However, he took some looking after, from the moment he rang me from Ireland, having got off the plane at Shannon by mistake.

[Part of a surviving letter from Maria dated August 1, 1970]

My dearly beloved Tenn—

Obviously Audrey has a pair of wire clippers connected to the New York telephone exchange from her office to the Plaza. Because the second you said, "Well, now for Audrey," there was a crackling sound of burning flesh and a hissing sound. I got a short, sharp electric shock, and I imagine the operator is a small pile of ashes. I just hope you're alright. Nobody would put the line back to you. I had to send a wire.

How happy I am that Oliver [Evans] is with you and I was able to organize something constructive for both of you. He is a marvellous companion, full of humor and culture, and is devoted to you. Now DON'T YOU DARE quarrel with him. I shall be livid with you if you do. . . .

[Postmarked Key West]

August 14, 1970

Dearest Maria:

I woke after three hours' sleep at three a.m. and it is still dark out of the studio and I have squandered my energy, such as it is, on writing verse. But I want to get off a bulletin to you before I go back to bed.

Schenker and Kook have both signed cheques, according to Audrey, but I have not yet signed a contract and none has been submitted to me. I have privately set a dead-line for all this legal haggling to be done with, the dead-line is midnight, West Coast time, Sept. 9th, the day before Oliver and I set sail for the Far East on the S.S. *President Cleveland.* I have, also privately, told Chuck Bowden, a very creative producer who put on *Night of the Iguana* with Maggie in the early sixties—a "gent" who has true feeling for theatre and sincere friendship toward me—that if nothing has been consummated by that deadline, I am going to give him the play. The problem is that he is hard up financially while Kook and Schenker are loaded with the hard-stuff.

I knocked Audrey's little hat off her head this p.m. by informing her that I wanted you to receive 15% of my royalties on this play (if any) and for that tricky lawyer of mine (Alan Schwartz) to get cracking on the "agreement." I feel that you have done far more to advance the production of this play than the Lady Mandarin [Audrey Wood] or anyone else and I want you to continue to do what you can to interest English artists in its behalf. I'm going to send you the latest typed version since it contains an important (less predictable) ending.

Things have been hectic here in Key West to which Oliver accompanied me. We were greeted by a placard hung from a beam in the living room which read: "WELCOME HOME, MOTHER GOD DAMN AND SISTER OLIVE!"—the gardener's style of humor. Oliver's red nose immediately started twitching and things went from bad to worse between them. There was a howling confrontation between the two in my rental car on the way down-town, the gardener calling Oliver "a frustrated old pink pansy" and Oliver shouting him down as "a half-witted illiterate, revoltingly coarse and common."

Of course Oliver was right in his resentment but the scene was shocking. The gardener jumped out of the car and has moved back to his little pad. Oliver and I and the menagerie (dog, cat, and iguana) are the sole residents right now, but an agreeable little "trick" of Oliver's is being imported late today from New Orleans. And of course there's always Leoncia—Black Majesty—who sits like a huge Froggy Footman in the fifty-thousand-dollar kitchen, alternately fuming and grinning. . . .

I hope I find your address at the Harrisons': otherwise I'll send this to 9 Gerald with a "Please Forward." You can best reach us at the Royal Orleans Hotel, as we have to go back to New Orleans in less than a week for more medical check-ups. We have the same doctor, the greatest cardiologist in America, and he has put us both on probation. The verdict on Oliver's case is that he did suffer a small "warning" stroke in Rome: on me that I have a damaged heart-valve: on both of us that we have high cholesterol counts. The doctor told me that if I followed his instructions I'd be relatively well in a year—if not—*well!* Oliver got much the same ultimatum but he still indulges himself in some high-cholesterol food, and I continue to drink a bit more than I ought to.

Here is our approximate schedule (and addresses)—

Arrive Hotel Royal Orleans, New Orleans on or about August 20th. Arrive Hotel Hollywood-Roosevelt, Hollywood, Calif., on Sept. 5th. Sail on S.S. *President Cleveland* out of Los Angeles on Sept. 10th. Arrive at Hotel Oriental, Bangkok on or about the end of September, that is, if we fly safely over Vietnam.

Will keep you posted of any changes in this itinerary and schedule.

We talk about you constantly with great love.

Tennessee

[*Added by hand*] Kisses for Pulheria (phonetical spelling), Natasha, and Froggy, and a novena for His Lordship in absentia.

LEONCIA MCGEE had been Tennessee's housekeeper since he and Frank Merlo first moved to Key West. She and Maria corresponded.

"Frankie had left some money to Leoncia in his will, which was immediately contested by his family. Tennessee reassured Leoncia that he would look after her and leave her adequately provided for. Sadly, he forgot to do so. Tennessee told me that Leoncia was the only person whom he totally trusted in Key West. He would leave his scripts in the house which he had bought her, rather than in his own, knowing that there they would be safe."

[*On letterhead American President Lines, on board S.S.* President Cleveland]

Hotel Peninsula, Hong Kong, Oct. 1,
Oriental Hotel, Bangkok, circa Oct. 5,
or c/o Tourists Mail, American Embassy, Bangkok
Keep in touch!!

September 24, 1970

Dearest Maria:

Here is a very brief communiqué from the Far Eastern front.

Geraldine Page and Rip Torn (her husband) have agreed to appear in the play [*The Two-Character Play*]. Schenker and Kook are stout. There is no producer nor financing and Audrey is in one of her Old Testament furies so no support can be expected from that quarter.

The ship is nosing into Yokohama harbor through a fog as impenetrable, visually, as the future.

A rather disturbing thing has happened to me. A sudden, mysterious lump has developed just under my left nipple so that the left side of my torso, from the waist up, is rather like a nymphette's. The New Orleans doctors advised me to cancel this voyage but I refused to. They said that "breast carcinoma" was rare among men but that rare things sometimes occur, which is a truism that hardly needed to be spelled out to someone with my history of chronic astonishment. Well, there will have to be surgery and Oliver knows of an excellent surgeon in Bangkok, he is a graduate of John Hopkins Medical School in the States and has operated on the king of Thailand.

Please do go on with your activities in behalf of an English production of the play which could be simultaneous with, just following, even preceding an American production. All going well, when I leave Bangkok, I'll fly by easy stages to Rome and London and could linger there if an English production was in the works. I could stay through the first days of rehearsal to put in the cuts, etc.—then go on to the States for the American version, all this contingent upon whether Golda Meir succeeds or fails in her efforts to ignite the fuse for the last blow-up. . . .

So far Oliver's nose has not reddened or twitched except with sun-burn and when smelling good. My God, how that man can eat! He orders practically the complete menu at every meal, must have a colony of tape-worms to feed.

Love, love, love, Tennessee

[*Maria to Tennessee, in a surviving letter, typewritten, dated September 28, 1970*]

Darling 10—

I have just spoken to Dr. Goldman, who is a partner of Dr. Mitchell, and they couldn't be more horrified or distressed by your idea of having an operation in Bangkok. Surgery takes a long time to heal in the tropics, and this doctor should not undertake such an operation under any circumstances. Come either to London best of all, where there are the top medical people, or Boston they say.

This is far too serious to muck around with.

Much love, from a very angry Maria.

If you think Audrey is as X as two sticks, you should see my face. Really, darling, NOBODY has operations in the East unless they have been bitten by a crocodile and have to have legs OFF—LISTEN TO ME.

[*On letterhead The Peninsula, Hong Kong*]

September 29, 1970

Dearest Maria:

It appears for all practical purposes, and some of an entirely spiritual nature, you are now representing me, not Audrey Wood. She will continue to collect her ten percent and I don't begrudge it, but you are now my functioning representative and from now on whatever you place for me, for publication or production, I want you to receive fifteen percent.

If this sort of an arrangement can be drawn up contractually by an English lawyer, I wish you'd have it done and I will ratify it on my way home by way of Rome or London, unless I am unexpectedly tripped up by some immobilizing misadventure.

I am here in Hong Kong waiting for Oliver, the insatiable sight-seer (wrong spelling) who still wants to see a couple more places in Japan. However, he's said he'll join me day after tomorrow and meanwhile I will enjoy the days of rest in my large air-conditioned room at the famous "Peninsula." Tony Smith used to say that I was really a Chinaman and I think he was right about it, I feel completely at home here and the Chinese seem to recognize me as home-coming kin.

When I went through customs last night, the Chinese girl said to me: "Have you any file alms?" (She meant "fire-arms.")

"No, dear, I can't stand the sight of them."

She chalked an immediate clearance on my unopened luggage as we laughed together.

It is hot and muggy outside. I don't expect to leave my quarters except for meals till Oliver gets here. But the city looks enchanting from the air, so many lovely lights reflected in the water all about. I think the exactly right instinct has taken me to the Orient now.

In the next few days I am going to mail off to you a number of manuscripts which I would like you to have professionally typed up for me in London. A play in two scenes, a short story, and a funny and touching recollection of my father to counter-act Mother's grossly unsympathetic portrait of him in "her book." [Added in handwriting] Send the bill to Bob Simon c/o Julius Lefkowitz, Inc., 1350 Ave. of the Americas, New York (10019) N.Y.

The family fortunes have picked up. Dakin's wife's father was recently lost to the Reaper, and Mike Steen, who keeps in touch with Dakin, says that just after losing his father-in-law, Dakin acquired an air-conditioned Cadillac limousine.

I expect he will be running for President in '72 on some ticket of his own invention, [added in handwriting] and with the usual response of the electorate.

Neither Dakin nor Mother have written a line to me since the reading of "What's Next on the Agenda, Mr. Williams?" at the poetry thing in London. The ms. is being published in the *Mediterranean Review* (published in Spain) [Winter 1971] and a copy of it is in that bunch of mss. I gave Oliver, on which he raised ten grand for this Far Eastern adventure.

He is as happy as a clam on ice, although, in his mad rushings here and there, he will suddenly cry out: "Another stroke!" His eyes pop out and he beats his hands together like a middle-aged hippie on a way-out "trip," but he is OK in a few minutes and goes rushing on, up and down-hill at a speed I can't keep up with. After one of these imaginary strokes, in which he declared his left hand had gone numb on him again, I said: "If I were you, baby, I would forget that left hand"—to which he retorted "Luckily you are not me and I am not you!" It is hard for me to remember that Pop-eyes has absolutely no humor about *himself,* just about everything *else,* especially me. But we are having a wonderful time together, at least I know that *I* am.

I don't think much about the impending surgery in Bangkok. I will only submit to the excision of the lump itself, not to any more radical procedure which they would want to perform if the tissue is malignant. I'll just have a bit of opium in my tea in the morning and let things go their way, with the knowledge that I have had a good run for my money.

KEEP IN TOUCH!——Much love always, 10

[*Added in handwriting*] P.S. Of course I'd be delighted for [Paul] Scofield to do the play with the National Theatre or any other, whenever he is free to.

———

"NATURALLY, I never took the fifteen percent. I'm not an agent, nor have ever considered myself capable of being one. I sent back the package telling him not to be such a fool."

———

[*Copy of telegram sent by Maria to Williams at the Hotel Peninsula, Hong Kong*]

LETTERS SENT BANGKOK. BEG YOU NOT TO CONSIDER ANY SURGERY HOWEVER MILD UNTIL LONDON PLEASE PLEASE. VERY WORRIED DON'T TAKE UNSEEN RISKS SO FAR AWAY. UNKNOWN DOCTORS INEXPERIENCED MEDICATION NURSING NOT ADVISABLE TROPICS. LOVE MARIA.

[*Telegram sent by Tennessee to Maria in London*]

WILL FLY LONDON IF CONDITION SERIOUS MEANWHILE HAVING FINE TIME MUCH LOVE TENNESSEE

[*On letterhead Hotel Peninsula, Hong Kong*]

Tourists' Mail
American Embassy
Bangkok, Thailand

October 3, 1970

Maria dearest:

I could and should kick myself for having alarmed you about what is a very innocuous enlargement of a lymph gland. The doctors both in New Orleans and a very fine one in Tokyo assured me that it did not have the characteristics of a malignancy, I was only disturbed because the enlargement had appeared so suddenly, but I once had, and still have, a harmless cyst on the back of my neck, have had it for about fifteen years and it hasn't grown any and has in fact decreased in size.

Nobody, nobody who loves life as much as I do, after my seven long years in limbo, is about to kick off now with the new, deeply sensuous pleasure that I take in every moment of living. I would fight like a tiger for my life, now, having totally recovered from my submission to an unconscious death-wish that obsessed me, possessed me since the loss of the Horse who gave me life while he lived.

Every day I discover new richness in the fact of being alive and in travelling and in knowing and loving people such as you and Oliver and even many of the strange new people on this side of the world.

So don't worry at all about me. You will be the first and only person to know if there is anything at all seriously wrong, and as I said, I will fly to Rome and to London if I am advised by the king's surgeon in Bangkok that anything more serious than a biopsy is indicated.

I did suffer a serious misfortune yesterday. As you will observe from the enclosed photo [not yet found], I grew a beard on the voyage, a Lenin-type beard, but it grew in too grayish and yesterday I went to some goddam Chinese barber in the hotel and said I want my beard dyed to match my hair and he proceeded to dye it black as a Chinaman's, my dear.

Oliver says I look so fierce that he can hardly stand to look at me. Today I've been applying peroxide to it. The only effect is that the skin around mustache and beard's peeling off. As I observed to Vivien Leigh's mother when she told me that she was a cosmetician, "I have several cosmetic problems. What can you do about them?" She very wittily remarked that if I were seventy she could make me look sixty-nine!

I am really and truly very, very touched by your concern for me. It has been a long time since I felt anyone gave a damn. But you have too much to worry about with poor Peter's strange behavior and that awful dowager. I'd like to have another go at her, some day.

I am going to send you a big bolt of Thai silk from Bangkok and expect you to greet me wearing a lovely gown made of it. I am going back to the States by way of Europe after the Bangkok stay, probably when Oliver has to return for his next teaching term. Actually I am not at all sure that Oliver should expose himself to the turbulence of a California college campus again and I hope I can persuade him to settle in Key West with me.

With all my love, 10

The Oriental Hotel
[Bangkok, Thailand]

October 12, 1970

Dearest Ninotcha:

This is a charming hotel right on the river. I am occupying a suite that Noël Coward occupied and in which Somerset Maugham had typhoid fever. But the city is flooding, the bath-water almost brown and one can only drink bottled water.

I am just recovering from a terrible day and night which began with an experiment with opium which Professor Evans obtained from a very shifty character who hangs out in front of a neighboring flea-bag. Oliver gave me one slice of it, but I, of course, was a novice. I phoned him yesterday morning and said, "Now just how much of this stuff do I dissolve in my tea?" He said: "Half of it." Well, I cut off half of it and drank it down with my tea and about half an hour later I could hardly stand on my feet and started vomiting and kept on vomiting all day, couldn't even hold water in my stomach. From time to time Oliver checked on my condition. He said I should not have taken that much of it and when I protested that I took exactly the amount he'd told me to take, he said, "Oh, I didn't mean that literally, you're only supposed to take a fraction of that the first time." Well, late in the afternoon, since I was too weak to stand up, I got the hotel manager to call in a little Thai doctor and explained what I had done. He was wonderful. Gave me immediate relief with medications to coat my stomach and absorb the poison. Took my blood-pressure, it was terribly high, one hundred and eighty. Then Professor Evans, having been in a state of euphoria all day from a fraction of the stuff I'd taken, comes to the door with a party of Thais and a bunch of classified ads about apartments and houses for us to rent here. I said: "Have you looked into plots in the graveyard?" and returned grandly to bed.

I'll tell you something about the Professor. He is so involved, from a whole life-time of living alone, with himself and his own problems and concerns that he is hardly able to focus on the problems of anyone else. He couldn't be a more delightful companion when you are well and able to frisk about with him, but when you fall out of pace, he trots right off without you and it's a wee bit scarey so far away from all known people and places. And I am not the bravest and most self-reliant of God's creatures.

We were met here by a little harem of his former catamites. They're like a simpering, grimacing litter of little kittens, all in their early twenties but looking no more than fourteen. He has a couple of them at a time and offers me one of the extras but that is just not where I am now, it's embarrassing and degrading and I can't believe that Oliver doesn't feel it, too. It is shocking to realize how lonely he must have been here to have accepted the companionship of these little hustlers that he can hardly speak to or understand, and he is fantastically jealous of them even when he pushes one at me. I just can't enjoy a totally physical thing anymore, there has to be some sort of sympathetic communication with it. I know that in his heart Oliver must feel, or is going to feel, the same way. If he would only start working but he doesn't seem to care to.

Please don't interpret this as turning against him. I haven't and won't. But I am afraid now that our original intention of taking a place here is no solution for me.

The little Thai doctor was a graduate of a London medical school and has his own clinic. He examined the lump on my chest. He said that it ought to be removed as soon as possible, that although it was enclosed in a "sac" and was an apparently benign tumor, not hard and not adhesive to the skin (which it is just under), if it were permitted to remain it might turn malignant and invade other tissues, which is substantially what the other doctors have told me. He advised me to go home at once, since he said that prompt action was essential. He also said that in its present state it could be removed with just a local anaesthetic. I have yet to see the doctor that Oliver says is "the king's surgeon." I am going to try to see him today and then make some immediate decision.

Fortunately I've discovered that I can still tolerate plane-travel. I flew from Tokyo to Hong Kong and then from Hong Kong to Bangkok without any bad effects. Of course the long, long flight from here to Rome would have to be broken by stop-offs in a couple of places. Perhaps I could fly my large bags ahead and just stop off for three consecutive nights in Singapore, New Delhi, and Istanbul enroute to Rome. I feel that I would much prefer the minor surgery in Rome than in London as it would inevitably get into the papers if I had it done in London and since the excision of the lump is minor surgery, I don't need a big-name surgeon for it, just a good, competent man with good hospital equipment. And it would be nice to convalesce in Rome. If I decide on this program, please don't tell Gore. I will travel incognito and would want nobody but you to know. Reporters take such a morbid interest in any illness or trouble that I get into.

I am going to the embassy today to pick up my mail and you will hear from me again early this week.

With much love, 10

PLEASE NO MENTION TO OLIVER of my comments on him. He would have a stroke! I practically have to remove my shoes in his presence like in a Japanese restaurant.

[*On letterhead Amarin Hotel, Bangkok, Thailand*]

October 19, 1970

Dearest Maria:

The doctor said that the laboratory report was that the tissue was benign and I can only hope he's telling me the truth. He did say that he would give me a full written report when he removed the stitches this Thursday. He really is an awfully nice man. I asked him to dinner and he smiled and said, "I would love to have dinner with you when you are not a patient."

He said that this thing which is called something like gynecomastia (that's probably spelt wrong) is usually associated, in men, with a bad liver condition. I've known for some time that my liver's in a bad shape. It naturally would be after all those years of abuse. I had worn my nerves out in the middle fifties (I mean of the century) and just couldn't operate without booze.

Now I'm a lot more prudent but may be locking the stable door after the horse is gone.

Oliver has been very difficult the last couple of days. Stopped seeing me or speaking to me. It's all because of those boys. Oliver was mad about one named Oot (which means pig). Well, when we got back here poor Oot, who was dropped on the head as an infant and was too retarded to go past two years at school, had also deteriorated a bit in appearance and the Professor no longer finds him attractive. He has switched his attentions to Oot's first cousin, Nippon, a very bright and sweet kid who is enormously helpful. But Oot's heart is broken. He looked up to Oliver as a father and last night when I took both of the boys to dinner—Oliver refusing to answer his door or the phone—Oot kept crying. He is too retarded to understand anything but the fact that he is being discarded. I am seeing Oliver at lunch and am going to give him a good talking to. He suspects me of having designs upon Nippon while the fact is that I was simply too weak after surgery to function without some assistance and Nippon placed himself at my service. I got through to Oliver finally on the phone and assured him that I hadn't the slightest romantic interest in either of the two boys, that I simply loved them as people and that I was shocked by his callous treatment of this retarded boy whom he had made such a profession of loving. I think the situation can be temporarily straightened out but not for a long term. I am having some silk suits made and as soon as the tailor has completed them, I am flying to Singapore and there I am going to catch a boat to somewhere like Beirut: then fly to Rome. Luckily an old friend, Andrew Lyndon, a real southern gent but a bit of an alcoholic, is coming to Europe this month and I have written him to join me in Rome. I don't like to leave Oliver here but I suspect that he will be relieved to get rid of me as it will allay his suspicions.

LATER—Oliver has calmed down and is out looking at apartments. I have not yet told him about my altered plans. I love Oliver like a brother, and I don't mean like Dinky, but to maintain a good relationship it is best that I travel on. Besides I have developed a great fondness for sea voyages. It's wonderful to feel the ocean under you at night, I even enjoy storms at sea.

As you'll observe from this stationery, we've changed hotels. This one is comfortable and convenient but has no charm and practically the whole staff is hustling. All in all, this is just about the most decadent place I have ever been and I mean including Tangiers. The decadence is not native to the people but has infected them through Western imperialism.

My mailing address is still c/o Tourists' Mail, American Embassy, Bangkok, Thailand.

Received letters today from Mother and Dinky. He had the consummate effrontery to accuse me of having ruined his career as a lawyer by obliging him to give so much attention to my business affairs. He enclosed a press-clipping in which he announces he is going to run again, and also that he is publishing an article in *Harper's* about how he saved his brother.

It took me several hours to compose a suitable answer.

I have the lovely pictures of you and the little girls on my writing desk.

Much love, 10

Tourists' Mail
American Embassy
Bangkok

November 9, 1970

My dearest Maria:

I probably have some letter from you in the mail which was forwarded to Singapore and hasn't followed me back yet. I had been intending to fly to Bombay, spend a couple of weeks in India, and then ship out around the Cape of Good Hope and up to Europe so that I could go home by way of London. But then Audrey Wood sent me a copy of the *Atlantic Monthly* (a venerable and usually respectable literary monthly in the States) which contained the worst piece of character assassination that's ever been tried on me for size, an article called "Tennessee Williams Survives." [*Added in handwriting*] By a man named [Tom] Buckley—who was introduced to me in Key West last spring by a very sneaky, invidious writer named David Loovis who had me over to meet him, saying he was in Key West to recover from an illness. The man was all charm, so was his wife, I never dreamed that I was being set up for an axe-job. I invited them to my house for dinner and bridge the next evening. He claims in the disgusting piece that he had a concealed tape-recorder with him. The article is full of the most humiliating, in fact devastating misquotations, libel by insinuation and distortion, that you could dream of! I just couldn't start home after this. So I've returned to Bangkok. Oliver and I have taken apartments here. However tourists are not permitted to remain more than a month in Thailand now, so in three weeks I have to get out. What I would like to do, now that I have discovered that plane-flights are not too difficult for me, is fly back by way of London, show you my re-writes on the "2-characters," have new scripts typed, and confer with you about what legal steps I should take about this piece in the *Atlantic*. It is too awful to be simply ignored. I think I have an excellent case for libel. The man has me saying the most preposterous things, he misquotes from my work in a way that makes me seem not merely demented but downright illiterate, he says I cut my mother out of my will, he goes into the most tastelessly clinical details about my sister, he says that I brag about my masculinity although I am a homosexual and that I boast about being "one of the two or three richest writers in America"—in short, I am portrayed as an ass and an absolute vulgarian. I am now determined to face this yellow journalist and the *Atlantic Monthly* in a libel court-suit but I have to get the best obtainable counsel as if I should lose the case—in fact, if I failed to contest the article—I'd never have a whore's chance of another play-production in the States, and possibly not in England either.

Christ! As if I hadn't been through enough this past year!—I needn't say that Audrey was in on the conspiracy. She is quoted in the article as saying that I was paranoiac and that she and I had a love-hate relationship for 30 years. Well, she can cut out the love act, now!—I've had exactly two communications from her since I left the States. One was to send me ballots to vote on nominees to the National Academy which is an institution that I can't bear and the other was this disgusting "exposé." Of course Oliver is appalled. Do please get hold of the article, it's in the October or November issue of the *Atlantic* and it is your advice about this I most want. I have a feeling that, with good counsel, I could hardly fail to win the case and perhaps a pot of loot.

A lot more to tell you but I've had a bad night in the new apartment and need some rest.

All my love, 10

[*Added in handwriting*] Kisses for Pulcheria & Natasha

———

MARIA read the article and advised Tennessee not to contest it, as it would inevitably cause more publicity and nothing would be achieved.

———

[*On letterhead Pattaya Palace Hotel, Pattaya Beach Resort, Thailand*]

Tourists' Mail
American Embassy
Bangkok
(till December 5)

November 22, 1970

Dearest Maria:

We are spending a few days at this enchanting beach-resort two hours' drive from Bangkok. The view from my top floor picture-window is the loveliest I've seen since that from the balcony of the Hotel Miramare in Positano and the sea-wind is so cool that for the first time in seven months I don't sleep with an air-conditioner.

We came down with two members of Oliver's little harem, nice kids but of course mercenary and Pop Eyes will not acknowledge the fact that there is inflation all over the world and still rewards them for remarkable services with the same that he did seven years ago. So the more attractive one, naturally billeted with Pop Eyes, flew the coop yesterday morning and Pop Eyes had to have a morphine shot for a head-ache and his left hand went numb again. If there were more than two ends to the candle he would leave none unburning. Now he wants me to buy these concubines' passage to the States as he has already squandered six of the ten G's I raised for his holiday. I have no intention of doing this, since his alternating ecstasies and rages with the kids would finish him off in a few months. As it is, I doubt his ability to resume teaching yet, I suspect he will need to rest for another half year—have invited him to Key West. Of course he also gets livid with me but I have learned how to cool it.

We had a very amusing evening not long ago in Bangkok when we were invited to dinner by a prince of the royal family. He received us in a sleeveless lady's negligée and got out his jewel box and began tossing rubies, diamonds, emeralds about the room like pocket marbles. I stuck a couple in a pocket and His Highness was very upset about it as he thought I intended to keep them. He took Oliver aside and begged him to get them back from me as they had been jacket-buttons worn by his grandfather, the great King Chulalongkorn. I pretended I didn't understand what all the agitation was about, but I finally relinquished the rubies. However the Prince was still so upset that he dined separately and sulked like a child.

I am carefully plotting my libel suit against the *Atlantic Monthly*. I don't think they have a Chinaman's chance of substantiating any of this rubbish and the circumstances under which my privacy was invaded are indefensible, ethically.

Awfully unhappy that I can't follow my original plan to go home by way of Rome and London but I do feel that I have to go through this trial first: If I didn't get cleared of this mess, it would be practically impossible for me to have another play produced in the States and possibly not even in England. Tastelessly presented as it is, I don't mind about being called a homosexual but I won't have it charged against me that I refused to see Frank while he was dying—I was with him constantly including the day of his death—that I cut my mother out of my will—that I had a secretary who "arranged assignations for me" and that the ridiculously mutilated "quote" from my poem about my stay in the snake-pit is my writing.

There is now a plane-flight directly from Miami to London—so after a week's rest in Key West, I'll fly over to consult you and your lawyer about my legal position re: article.—I'm feeling quite well at present.

All love, 10

[*Added in handwriting*] Sailing out of Hong Kong Dec. 12th on S.S. *President Wilson* for L.A.—fly from there to Key West, arriving end of December. It will be wonderful not to hear "White Christmas" except on a ukelele in Honolulu, where the ship stops for Xmas Eve.

[*On letterhead The Hongkong Hotel, Kowloon, Hong Kong*]

December 2, 1970

Dearest Maria:

I am here sitting in Hong Kong on the world's most magnificent harbor waiting for the Professor and some member of his little seraglio to join me before the ship sails on the 10th. The Professor ran through his ten G's taking his seraglio to posh restaurants and wining and dining them—caviar and Baked Alaskas and vintage wines, my dear! So now I have to pay his passage and the passage of one of the catamites back to the States. When I left we had settled upon the intelligent one who could be of some use to him but for all I know he will show up with the one who was dropped on his head as a baby and is a low-grade moron.

In a few days you will be receiving my gift from the Orient. Not Thai silk but a lovely matching pin and ring from the best jewellers in Bangkok. Enclosed will be the sale slip for customs but it is listed at half the actual price so that you won't have to pay so much duty on it. Oliver who is an aficionado of gems in the Orient told me that the stuff is authentic and a good buy and I think you'll like it. Soon as I get a new cheque book I'll send a cheque covering the duty which they estimated would be about thirty dollars.

I have done an awful lot of work on the play [*The Two-Character Play*], mostly trying to get a tighter form for the second part. They do go on too much in the performance section and the effect is formless. Please do keep in touch with Maggie [Leighton] and [Paul] Scofield from time to time to keep them on the hook, that is, if they're really on it. Audrey claims that she has been in touch with Scofield and he has told her that he will be available in fall of '71—such a long way off for someone with my bad liver and a ticker that is still sometimes a bit irregular.

However I am now definitely convinced that the lump on the left breast was *not* malignant, it has a bit of postoperative induration but there is very little external sign of it, the doctor did a good job.

It's going to be awfully lonely in Key West. I may try out the play somewhere at a regional or university theatre just to get the script in final shape—would use professional actors and director but keep the try-out as inconspicuous as possible.

[*Added in handwriting*] Would be lovely if you could fly over (my expense) for this shake-down production. It's a cold world without you.

I have read over the piece in the *Atlantic* and I don't think I'll bother to sue, it would be such a strain and bore. I'll simply arrange to have another interview to expose the lies of the first and repair my image as a serious person. I think that is important, for my family and myself and future work in the theatre.

We sail on the tenth on the *President Wilson* (American President Lines). I'd love to hear from you during the voyage. We put in at Honolulu on Xmas Eve so why don't you write me a cheery bit of a letter c/o the ship at that port of call.

With all my heart, Tennessee

THE JEWELRY arrived, bearing the name of the shop: "Sincere Jewelry."

Tennessee's reply to the article, "An Open Response to Tom Buckley," was published in the *Atlantic* in January 1971. In it he wrote: "You say you entered with a tape recorder. . . . It appears to be given to the most dangerous misquotations, distortions and libel by venomous implication."

The Two-Character Play, now retitled *Out Cry,* opened on July 8, 1971, at the Ivanhoe Theatre in Chicago, directed by George Keathley, with Eileen Herlie as Clare and Donald Madden as Felice. Tennessee referred to his preferred version of the play as "the Bangkok version."

"For the family holiday in St. Moritz, Peter had bought himself a particularly nasty cardboard suitcase, about which I complained bitterly, and which, rather proudly, he filled with his ski clothes. Arriving at the hotel, he triumphantly opened his case in order to take out his dinner jacket and found, nestling in the top, a pale mauve nylon chiffon evening dress. The identical suitcases found their rightful owners the following day. That could only have happened in Switzerland."

[*Envelope postmarked Key West, Florida, January 15, 1971*]

My darling Maria:

I was so afraid that you would go skiing in St. Moritz, just to be chic, and break something like Laughlin always kept doing when he got his quarter past eight feet on skis. I was so proud of you when I read your letter, written a-top a mountain you got up on a funicular, that you had consigned the skis to the rest of your little commune, and, Christ, how funny, poor Peter arriving with a suitcase full of bad drag. You know, I really am awfully fond of Peter, have been since the last time I saw him in London surrounded by all those pill-bottles and giving me a Librium when I asked for a Milltown and so apologetic about it. Maybe you are a little hard on him sometimes. Try to keep him up on the go!—The Dowager never gave poor Peter a chance, like Miss Edwina never gave any of her children one.

This is my first day back in Key West. My Canadian pen-pal, the high-school English teacher from Montreal, has been an angel. I never thought I'd see Gigi again, since she'd had a serious heart attack and was on digitalis when I left for the Far East, but at the door there she was dancing and prancing and THINNER!—and the cat, The Gentleman Caller, whose ribs were sticking out when I left, is now fat and purring with ordinary contentment.

My dear, I am quite-quite sick! Am coughing all night like Frankie and yet—I don't know, I just don't feel I ought to worry about it. In a week or two I will know if I'm going to go on or stop, now.

About the play.

Maggie Leighton called me from London with the hardly credible news that Paul Scofield was indeed seriously interested in the play [*The Two-Character Play*] and planned to appear in it "sometime late next fall" in the National Theatre, and she said that she feared that this would let her out since she doesn't belong to the National Theatre.

NOW, DARLING, DO PLEASE GET THESE TWO GREAT ARTISTS TOGETHER AND CONVINCE THEM THAT THIS PLAY NEEDS THEM—TOGETHER! Every line's written for Maggie, and—unconsciously—for Scofield, too.

Somehow we must circumvent the machinations of the Widow Wood / —never up to no good! She wrote me two letters while I was in Asia. In one she stated that Scofield was available for the play in the fall of '71. In the second letter, brought aboard ship at Honolulu, she laughingly informed me that Scofield was out, tied up all through this year. The Widow wants this play written over, after my decease, by some half-ass commercial hack and put on *only then*!—I am resolved to thwart her by having a finalized script performed at least somewhere in the boon-docks with no publicity outside of the locale—so that the true script can be established.

Oh, I do wish you were here to deal with this situation!—as only you could.

My gentleman friend from Georgia—the alcoholic—arrives today. He's a luv but he goes at the booze like it was half an hour before the return of Prohibition.

The pen pal seems likely to be able to cope. Freak-out [O'Lowe] is in town, serving as a barman at the big gay bar. I couldn't care less except I feel sorry for him.

It's going to be difficult to get hold of a good typist here but I am starting on that project today and I should get the Bangkok version of the play off to you soon.

I feel that there are now so many different versions that out of this plenty there can arrive something that would work. I just want to be permitted to OK the final script. Jesus, you'd think I was writing the St. James [*sic*] edition of the Bible, if not *Myra Breckinridge*!

Many loves, all to you,* 10

[*Added in handwriting*] (*and Miss Rose)

[*Added in handwriting*] 5 days later—The cold has dried up. Scripts have been typed. Mailing copy in next couple days.

———

"O'L o w e , known as 'O'Lowe Must Go,' was encouraging Tennessee to drink: such is the nature of alcoholism. The kind Canadian pen-pal, David Lobdell, looked after Gigi in Tennessee's absence. Gigi had been Frankie's dog, and Tennessee cherished her."

David Lobdell wrote to Maria in 1985 after Tennessee's death.

———

Montreal, Quebec, Canada

Dear Madame:

I have never had the pleasure of meeting you, but I recall Mr. Williams speaking very highly of you during my brief sojourn in Key West in the winter of 1970–71. He was very grateful for the fact that you continued to take an interest in his affairs at a time when most of his friends and acquaintances were forsaking him.

. . . You asked me why my correspondence with Tennessee Williams ended so abruptly, after it had been sustained for so long in a spirit of such mutual concern and understanding. . . . For the moment, suffice it to say that my abrupt departure from Key West in the winter of 1971, following a seven-month sojourn in T.'s little "conch" house (most of which was spent alone while he was travelling in the Orient), had nothing to do with any alteration in my feelings for him but was dictated rather by the urgent need to put a certain distance between myself and the tribe of parasitical retainers with whom he had seen fit to surround himself. I was far too young and naive at the time to be able to hold my own with those diabolical creatures and simply found it easier to quit the scene, before I was drawn irretrievably into their machinations. . . .

[*Handwritten note from Tennessee to Maria's husband, Peter St. Just, who was suffering from depression, undated, on paper headed The Berkeley, London*]

Dear Peter—

My friend Henry Faulkner [a painter] and I have discovered a most extraordinary clinic in Kentucky. I do wish you'd try it sometime—the methods are more natural and the results finally more effective.

Sorry to have missed you, and hope this finds you feeling better.

Warmest regards, Tennessee

1431 Duncan Street
Key West

February 7, 1971

Dearest Maria:

I heard on the evening newscast that the postal strike has finally ended but there is a huge back-log of undelivered mail so it may be quite a while before you get this. I received a letter from you which was post-marked Selma, Alabama. Contained some lovely photos of you and Pulcheria. She sits beautifully on a horse! Is she training it to jump over the Dowager?

I had rather a nasty accident a couple of weeks ago. Stepped into a fish-pool over five feet deep just at the bottom of an outside staircase in an unlighted patio. Cracked a rib. Called four doctors, none of them responded. A few days later began to ache terribly. Finally got a Cuban doctor to X-ray my back and discovered the rib fracture. I am now in a tight elastic bandage and running a low fever.

A New Orleans newspaper announced that I was too ill to attend Mardi Gras, the glad tidings were picked up by a St. Louis paper, and Dinky Dakin immediately came flapping down here like a buzzard. He arrived in Key West after midnight, climbed over the back fence. I saw him through the sliding glass doors of the kitchen where I was preparing some Ovaltine and sent my new secretary out to intercept him and get him off the premises till noon the next day. He hung around for a week. I began to feel rather sorry for him, he has had so many misadventures. His wife's father died. Left nothing, not even life-insurance, and Dakin admits that he married under the misapprehension that the old fellow had a cool million. Now his mother-in-law has come to live with him, he says she looks like a bull-dog and "runs a very tight ship." I said, "Well, Dakin, I suppose this could happen to a worse person but I wonder who."

He is running again for the Senate, has composed and taped several singing "campaign commercials" which he kept bellowing at us, even in restaurants. Yesterday I finally packed him off—my fever's running lower. . . .

I am tentatively booked on the S.S. *Canberra* out of Port Everglades, Florida, on May 10th for Lisbon, from which I'll fly to Rome for several weeks before the play [*The Two-Character Play*, now retitled *Out Cry*] starts rehearsing the middle of June in Chicago. The Widow Wood called me a couple of days ago enquiring if I had a copy of my agreement with you. She wanted to get it out of my hands. I told her I couldn't find it and she said she would get it from you. For God's sake, don't send her the original, get it photo-stated. It is absolutely valid, there is nothing she can do about it as long as the original remains in your hands or your attorney's. I hope that we are going to get Eileen Herlie and Donald Madden for the Chicago try-out—and that you'll fly over for the opening.

Everything is a bit tentative or conditional in my life right now. I feel so goddam "wasted" that I wonder if I will make it to Chicago, and it is awful to realize that this American representative will do everything in her considerable power to prevent me from ever seeing this last long play. However I'm not yet running up the white rag.

Wire me when mail starts normal delivery and I'll dispatch the scripts for Maggie and Scofield.

Much love, Tenn.

———

"WE WERE once walking up Fifth Avenue past a celebrated glassware shop, in front of which was an illuminated pool. We stopped, and Tennessee, to my astonishment, stepped right over a six-inch curb, plunging one foot deep into the water. We squelched on up the Avenue to the Plaza. Tennessee refused to enter the hotel in the state he was in and so led me instead into the little Plaza Cinema, to dry himself off. Patrons leaned forward angrily as he waved one foot in the air: 'Would you mind putting your foot down? We can't see the screen!' 'I'm terribly sorry,' he replied insouciantly. 'I'm trying to dry it.'"

The Dowager Lady St. Just died on April 5, 1971. Peter and Maria took over Wilbury Park and lived there and at Gerald Road in London's Belgravia.

———

The Plaza
Fifth Avenue at 59th Street
New York

April 15, 1971

Dearest Maria:

My gardener read his transcription of your wire over long distance but since it had been read over the phone in Key West and both he and Key West Western Union are almost totally illiterate the wire as read to me did not make sense. All that I got, or surmised, out of it was that the poor Dowager has departed and of course I am very, very concerned for Peter since there was such a deep attachment there. Mothers of her generation are usually wrong but always convinced that they are completely right and whatever things they do are without intent and so we love and forgive them and when they go, it is an awful shock to us.*

I think that Peter may find himself more at peace after the unavoidable period of distress, and I do hope I'm right as there is so much quality in him which has been kept under [inserted in handwriting] maternal wraps, relatively speaking.

We sail tomorrow (16th) on the S.S. *Rafaello* (Italian Lines) to Naples. The voyage takes a week so we would be arriving on April 23rd. We'll spend a night at the Excelsior, Naples, and then take a *rapido* for Rome, spend a few days at the Parco dei Principi (because it has a pool) and then catch that lovely night-express to Taormina. I hope that you can somehow manage to get away for a while and meet us in Rome, or Sicily.

Saw Don [Windham] and Sandy [Campbell] last night at a party after the world-premiere of Charles Henri Ford's underground film *Johnny Minotaur*. My little secretary was petrified by the film and even more by the party as he was sure they were dropping acid in the wine. He was still more alarmed on the cab-ride home from the Village as there was a dark man with whiskers sitting next to the driver who kept glancing back at us. I told him to get ready to jump out at the first stop light! This is my first sustained encounter with "a holy Russian idiot" and, of course, I love it. . . .

Yesterday we heard the musical score for the opera being made of *Summer and Smoke* by a fine composer, Lee Hoiby. It has its premiere [June 19] at the opening of a city auditorium in St. Paul this summer and the vibes are good.

I will wire you precise time of Naples landing—you'll get the wire before the letter, of course.

Must now go buy traveller's cheques.

Much love, 10

[*Added in handwriting*] *Tried to phone you in country—no answer.

TENNESSEE's private secretary was quickly nicknamed "Miss Mary" and "Mary Poppins."

Tennessee invited Maria down to Rome for her birthday. He and Gore Vidal gave her a birthday party at Gore's flat.

"We went on to dinner, where they both presented me with beautiful gifts. Tennessee gave me a brooch of Pegasus; Gore had gone to Bulgari and bought a swan. Now, Gore's pet name for Tennessee was "the Bird." Typically, Tennessee decided that Gore's brooch was in fact a goose and took deep offense. Nothing either Gore or I could say would convince him that the brooch was so obviously a swan, and not a veiled insult to him. He grumbled to me continuously after that: 'I thought it was very spiteful of Gore.' "

[*Telegram from Taormina, Sicily, dated May 6, 1971*]

CANNOT CHANGE RESERVATION WILL BE AT SONESTA TOWER [London] THROUGH MAY 13 DESPERATELY ANXIOUS DISCUSS CHICAGO WITH YOU PLEASE ARRANGE ONE EVENING LOVE TENNESSEE

[*A surviving letter from Maria to Tennessee, dated May 31, on BOAC paper, en route to Bermuda*]

My dearly beloved 10—

. . . I've been having the most hilarious time at Wilbury. (I must say I felt very sorry for the Dowager when I received the household bills, she's been robbed right left and centre by a seething mob of insolent apes for years and years, systematically and without respect. I bought myself a very military trouser suit, with lots of zips and buttons, which I call my firing-suit. BANG BANG BANG, and out like stout go the following. I fear the chef, who's epileptic (shades of Hop Skip and a Limp) has had a twist and a turn—he's out. The butler is stout, and as for the pantry-boy who is in his late sixties, he cannot find his way to the pantry, he's in such a state of alcoholic shock after my peptalk. His wife, the housemaid-cum-lady's-maid, spends her entire time putting all my dirty clothes back into the drawers instead of washing them. She had the stupidity to ask me which was going to be Natasha's permanent bedroom. So with a Russian wolf-grin [drawing] I said, "Yours, Mrs. Mitford, yours." So she went spinning out of the room, backing away from the wolf-grin like a top. I've had to get all this organised in two days. The only people of any loyalty are called Toogood, and they are staying.

We return to London on the 9th June. Then I shall get Paul [Scofield] and Maggie [Leighton] face to face—or back to back—three steps, FIRE, and see who wins, and what the real score is. I feel Paul is very reluctant to do the play with Maggie, in fact he said so, but who is there, je me demande?

. . . Now, don't be nervous about [*Out Cry*]. It is beautiful—have confidence. You have written a poem of extreme, staggering sensitivity and elegance—and strength—DON'T overstate, keep the subtlety and love between the brother and sister, the panic, fear, and the understanding—don't let all sorts of common touches and vulgarities such as we discussed creep in, to get shock effects. It is pure. The panic needs no more elaboration. Keep it clean, and then it has impact and force. . . .

———

MARIA returned from Bermuda to find two letters awaiting her.

———

Key West

May 23, 1971

Dearest Maria:

I hear that Audrey is bearing down on England aboard the *QE II* which is the most alarming threat to the island since the approach of the Spanish Armada and I hope that the English fleet has been alerted.

It is Sunday and Mary Poppins is reading the—guess what?—comics. . . . He insisted on reading me one called "Peanuts" but I have escaped to the studio. He has been very active however in a constructive way about the compound. Fixed the door of my studio—which had been broken into during my absence—pulled up all the weeds, and has prepared all the meals. Work continues on his book about "Tricky Closet" and the peace people— he read it all aloud, from start to finish, to some lunch guests yesterday and there was a noticeable reaction.

I have thought a good deal about your fear that I am corrupting him and I really don't think that I am, since I am probably the only person who has cared for the boy besides his mother and grandparents and I can't say that his mental horizons are immense but they have slightly broadened since he came to stay with me. I make it a rule for him to listen to the newscasts and I have even gotten him to read Solzhenitsyn and perhaps in a month or two he will start the Mother Goose book, it takes a little while, I'm afraid, to get him off comics.

He took hundreds of photos in Europe and dispatched a lot of them to his "Mom." The captions were brilliant, such as "Me at Pope's house, in Rome," "Mountain with snow," "Me on cop's bike in London," "Tennessee with God-daughter and lady" . . .

I am sure that he would accept a reduction in salary if things go wrong in Chicago.

George Keathley is coming down here to assist me in cutting and preparing the script for rehearsal. He says that there is a remarkable advance sale.

Dearest love to Pulcheria and Natasha and Froggy and of course to you always and please do come to Chicago! Kiss Bun [Guy Strutt] for me and tell him I love him!

Love, 10

[*Postmarked Key West, May 24, 1971*]

Monday

Dear Maria:

I'm sending this separately because I can't put it in the same envelope with the frivolous stuff in the other.

I have had repeated anxiety dreams about Oliver, so a little while after I wrote the other letter, I called him in Northridge, California, and a woman answered the phone and identified herself as his aunt and said he was sleeping and that he was ill but that she would wake him to talk to me because he'd been trying to get in touch with me and couldn't.

Well, he came on the phone and he told me that he was recuperating from an operation for a malignant brain-tumor. Jesus!

He said he had sent me four cables to Italy, but none of them reached me because of the mail-strike, I guess.

He sounded lucid, his memory seemed to be intact, but there was no sign of the operation except that his speech was sometimes hesitant and a bit slurred. He said he is totally paralyzed, now, on the left side but can get around the block on a cane, dragging a leg. He was hopeful about the prognosis, said that the growth was "encapsulated" and on the surface of the brain so that they did not have to cut in. However he is receiving cobalt treatment which is not too reassuring, as it is the strongest form of radiation and I don't think it is administered unless there is still some malignancy. I have not yet gotten in touch with the head of his English department who will be able to give me the real out-look for Oliver.

Oliver says he has not been able to pay for the operation and I suppose must have financial assistance. He also wants one of his Bangkok boys over here to "give him massages," etc. I assured him I would be glad to put up the money, and that I would come to California as soon as the play has opened in Chicago, and if he wants to—and he says he does—I would fly back to Bangkok with him.

Toward the end of the talk his voice trailed off a little so I have the impression he is quite weak still.

I knew you'd want to know about this. He says that Audrey knew about it. I don't know why she gave me no word, I would have flown immediately out there.

He really has been quite heroic, I think, and cannot be let down at this point.

Oh, God, what things do happen to people! Usually to the wrong ones.

Call me collect—(305) 294-1801—we must not alarm Oliver with excessive attention at this point but make it clear that he's not alone.

I'm writing him a long letter today—after I've talked to his department head—and will do what I can to cheer him up. (He did *not* sound depressed.)

Love, 10

———

MARIA went to Chicago for the previews and opening of *Out Cry* on July 8, 1971. This and *Camino Real* were Tennessee's two favorite plays.

"In Paris, I'd taken Tennessee to the Russian gypsy nightclub, Novy. Tennessee had loved hearing one particular song there. Lugubriously Russian, it ran: 'Coachman, don't whip the horses / There's nowhere for me to hurry to / There's no one for me to love anymore.' Racked by nerves before the previews, Tennessee asked me one night to sing this gloomy little ballad to him again. Eileen Herlie drew me aside a day or so later.

She said pleadingly, 'For God's sake, Maria, please don't sing any more Russian songs to Tennessee. I've now got to put them into the show—*in Russian!*' "

Jane Smith recalls: "We were walking along in Chicago, all of us, and I fell back a little, and ahead I watched Tennessee and Maria walking together. And it struck me so forcefully that this was a couple. Not just because they were the same size. But there was a harmony of spirit there, and love, and respect—and laughter. I don't know when I've heard laughter like that. He loved and respected her candor. She told him what she thought about anything and everything: she would let him have it unedited, and he would value it. Her loyalty to him was as fierce as a tigress's, and he knew he could count on it.

"Audrey Wood, who had appeared to Tennessee to have lost her enthusiasm for his work, and who he felt had very little faith in this particularly poetic script, came to the first preview. The audience consisted mostly of young people and university students. They were fascinated by the play, went mad with delight, and, yelling, gave it a standing ovation.

"At dinner afterwards, Audrey seemed to withdraw from the mood of jubilation that we all felt. Tennessee remarked to me, 'Did you notice how Audrey was?'

"After a subsequent, less successful performance, we were all in Donald Madden's dressing room. Audrey somehow looked smug. Tennessee completely lost his temper. He shouted abuse and screamed hysterically at her; he accused her of stifling his work and wanting him not to succeed. He said that she wanted him to die and that he was going to outlive her. And then he fired her.

"Audrey was extremely dignified but seemed to crumple physically. I felt very sorry for her and tried feebly to interrupt this flow of abuse—it was such a terrible public insult—but he was like a madman. We walked back alone to the hotel together, and I expressed my disapproval of his truly outrageous behavior. We came into the bar of the hotel, and I noticed Audrey sitting in the corner with some friends. I suggested to Tennessee that we go up and say something, but he flatly refused, and tugged me out of the bar.

"I always thought that there would be a reconciliation, but Tennessee was adamant and severed every connection. He even left their joint lawyer, Alan Schwartz, which was a great mistake."

Questioned about the incident eight years afterwards, Audrey Wood said: "I don't think [Paul Bigelow] is accurate in saying I had quarreled with

Maria Britneva, or that she had quarreled with me. There was, to my knowledge, no quarrel. I have known Maria for many years. I am not aware of any contretemps with Maria. I think she simply favored Tennessee, and he remains one of her oldest friends."

"In retrospect, it seems that Tennessee had for some time felt that Audrey was not promoting him properly, that he felt that her representation had coincided with an unsuccessful period in his work. It is almost as though he were forcing an excuse for a showdown."

The Chicago production was not the success that Williams had hoped for this deeply cherished play, and there was no New York transfer.

————

[*Envelope postmarked July 23, 1971*]

Hotel Ambassador
Chicago

Friday a.m.

Dearest Maria:

I finally overtook Jansen who owns the Ivanhoe [Theatre] in his restaurant after rehearsals and gave him such a row that everybody in the restaurant stopped eating and the bar-men froze in action, cocktail mixers lifted! It was one of my really apocalyptic rages the sort usually reserved for "the Widow" [Wood]. I told him that my outrage was inexpressible!—that he would be so cheap as to put no daily ads in the entertainment pages, that I had come there expecting to be treated at least as respectably as a cockroach in his kitchen, etc. etc.—Well, this morning there appears a daily ad in the Chicago *Tribune*—with one of our better quotes, "A Masterpiece in the making"—so I am once again vindicated in my conviction that in the presence of pigs it's best to have and to use a big stick.

I enclose a picture of a familiar creature. A lady sent it to me but it exposes only her chin—perhaps she looks better that way. How sad the Froggy looks over his two birthday candles!

Yesterday a sweet letter from Claudia [Cassidy, drama critic of the Chicago *Tribune*] which I'll have duplicated and sent to you. She says she is still haunted by the play and its "unsparing magic."

I told Herlie to quit singing everything but the gypsy song.

Madden gets better and is really now taking the play away from the burly Scot.

Hastily and with all my love, 10

Maria had sent a photograph of her pug, Froggy Footman, on the important occasion of his second birthday.

———

[Part of a surviving handwritten letter from Maria to Tennessee, undated]

My darling 10:

I do miss you so very much and worry about you. Are you alright? Please don't disappear to the East or Tahiti yet awhile. Why not come and stay at Wilbury? Let me know your address, etc. If you do decide to go to coast, bring Oliver back with you to see the play.

Get on to Kazan. He is a good, valuable friend, and his opinion is well worth considering. Also, I feel he might like to direct the play. He would do such an exciting job.

Give my love to Eileen Herlie, please. Pulcheria and Natasha look adorable in the outfits you sent them. I am writing to Rose and to your mother, by the way. I do miss you. We had such fun together.

Well, no jokes. No singing in taxi-cabs: "Everyone knows she's a rambling rose." DON'T QUARREL WITH ANYONE! Take care of yourself, God bless you, darling. WRITE WRITE WRITE,

Maria,

———

IN CHICAGO in July 1971, Tennessee gave a rough manuscript to Maria for safekeeping.

———

SOME MEMOIRS OF A CON-MAN

(Tennessee deleted his original title, "Some Scattered Idioms.")

I was informed this past spring, by a prominent denizen of the jungles of Academe, that I have in recent years turned into what he calls "a public figure," a creature which he meant as distinct from a creative writer still at work.

I am not happy about that allegation, and I cry out against it.

I am about to have installed in my Key West studio—for the benefit of this critic and also, if possible, at his expense—a closed-circuit TV camera which will show me living and working seven mornings a week under a sky-light the length of my long work-table—with two typewriters, one of them electric for those ineffable mornings when the touch is still quick and sure and one, well, the nice familiar old blue Olivetti portable that goes about the world with me, a machine more inclined to pauses than in its youth but still knocking out several pages whenever I choose it.

I know, of course, that I have offered, however unwillingly, some provocation of the charge, the suspicion, that I am no longer so committed to serious work as I was, say, ten years ago.

Here in Chicago this summer of '71, the business folk connected with the theatre (where my latest and possibly last long play is to be unveiled in a couple of days) have exploited me as a public figure through an unprecedented series of back-to-back interviews for newspapers and radios and TV in order to spare them[selves] the expense of taking out the ordinary ads which precede the opening of any type of public entertainment. As a consequence I have made a continual fool of myself. In public. (Not just in private.) Of course, I don't much mind making a fool of myself either publicly or privately but I don't exactly see how it is about to enhance the critics' or the public's pre-conception of what they are about to see at the Ivanhoe this Thursday. . . .

I am sure you must have already suspected that this is a windy introduction to some other animadversions of a cranky old gent. Right on!

Imagine you see here a row of starry little asterisks preceding—

A year ago last spring an ostensibly respectable journalist who came on much like a gentleman, with excellent credentials, invaded my home-town, Key West, at a time when I was only a few months out of a psychiatric ward in which I had suffered a couple of coronaries and three brain convulsions in the course of one apocalyptic morning but which, being a crocodile, I managed to survive.

Go-betweens told me that he was a sincere admirer of my work and wished to write a serious critique, and so I arranged to meet him at the apartment of one of these go-betweens. Only those who have the experience of break-down and consequent confinement can understand fully how much you want, when you have been released, to spill your guts to anybody who can or will listen to you.

Now at this time I was limiting myself to just two drinks of hard liquor a day and just one pill. The pill, prescribed for me by a fine doctor in New York, was an anti-depressant called Synequan. The trouble was not with it, but with my practice of combining it with my second hard drink of the day, washing it down with a pretty strong martini.

I prefer to mix my own martinis, but being a guest, a younger writer inclined to violate the privacy of older writers in novels more sensational than literary. He was the chief go-between, and I have no proof that he actually slugged the drink with which I washed down the Synequan that evening, but I strongly suspect it, and sometimes my suspicions are not just paranoia. I do know that all at once my head floated up to the ceiling and right through it and into outer space, and I could hear myself chattering like a magpie but didn't know what I was saying. The younger writer was sitting there smirking, and I couldn't help but notice him smirking there in his quiet corner like a spider with web, waiting.

The older gentleman-journalist did not confess or expose his tape-recorder. I had no warning of it.

The subject got around to precocious sexuality. This I do remember quite clearly, we were talking about the extravagancies of the early adolescent experience in sex. In the context of this discussion, I told a story of how, long ago, I had experienced an instant orgasm when I circled the bare shoulders of a childhood sweetheart with my bare arm on the dark upper deck of a Mississippi excursion-steamer.

This anecdote did not get through to the concealed tape-recorder. Perhaps the apparatus was too small for accuracy. At any rate, what was reported was that I had an orgasm when a college room-mate "scratched my back."

This college room-mate was undoubtedly included in the general discussion on adolescent sexuality. I was indeed, at eighteen, quite infatuated with a college room-mate who had very large and luminous green eyes, but certainly this was a mostly sublimated attachment, and never did it go to the point of "instant orgasm."

Still, what if it had? Would it have been so remarkably different from the adolescent experience of many boys, then and now?

No. But it made good copy and so it was played up for exactly that: good, tasteless copy for which I've such a penchant. Or is the word panache?

However, I didn't much mind this stuff about my early love-life, distinguished for its inhibitions, variabilities and intensities, all three, and with hardly a moment that I can honestly say I regret. What I did mind was the word-portrait of a vulgarian, a man who boasted of imaginary riches, who spoke scathingly of an eminent actress for publication, and, most dreadfully of all, a man who had abandoned his dearest friend on that friend's death-bed and a man who had cut off his eighty-eight-year-old mother from his last will and testament, condemning her, by implication, to the poorhouse. Well, it so happens that I was in constant attendance during the agonizing end of my dearest friend's life, and it so happened that my mother, having received half of my father's not inconsiderable savings and half of my biggest financial success, *The Glass Menagerie,* had never been mentioned in my will, since Miss Edwina is not only a lady but a lady of considerable means as well as indomitable spirit.

At this point, I can hear the interior out-cry of some editor, "Hold, enough!," and applaud his sense of measure, but nevertheless . . .

What has most annoyed me about the various published inaccuracies on the subject of that stranger who bears my professional name is the propagation of a certain myth, which is the myth that "during my lean years"— which were all of my years from late childhood until the mid-thirties of my way through life—I was the pampered creature of subsidies, grants and gratuities. I did, indeed, receive a grant of a thousand dollars from the Rockefeller Foundation in 1939 and at another crucial time they hit me with five hundred more, and in appreciation of this endowment I have done all my banking, since I had something to bank, at the Rockefellers' Chase Manhattan and its subsidiaries. Those fifteen hundred dollars from the Rockefeller pocket did not noticeably deplete the Rockefeller fortune, but they added much to mine, on occasions when most direfully needed. They got me to Manhattan for the first time in 1939. And got me into the theatre, which remains my most congenial home.

Now let me, without much attention to chronological sequence, proceed with a skimpy itemization of those early years after I left home and before the Rockefellers took favorable notice of me and for six years after they did.

Item One: On a bitterly cold Friday which was not Good, in January 1942, I was unexpectedly evicted from a fickle friend's apartment in the warehouse district of the West Village of Manhattan. This friend was, nervously speaking, a basket-case: I mean he was very nervous. He was also an abstract painter. He had taken to bed with some malaise of nervous origin but he still desired company, and each evening he would dispatch me out upon the streets of Greenwich Village to fetch home carefully specified kinds of visitors. I was willing to oblige as Barkuss, and so was another friend whom we called "the pilot fish," and the nervous young painter was kept agreeably diverted most evenings of that season. But one night, "the pilot fish" and I fetched home some guests of a roguish nature, and the following morning the painter found several prized articles missing. After making an inventory, he sadly decided to dispense with my company and services: I was kicked out, and I had the ticket but not the cash to pick up my laundry at the Chinaman's, and no "bread" to score an evening meal.

Two days later, for the first and last time in my life, I made a direct appeal for personal and economic assistance. A phone-call was made to the dramatists' branch of a union devoted to the care and feeding of writers. I was loaned—yes, loaned—the sum of precisely ten dollars to keep me off the slippery streets until the spring thaw set in, a season later.

A dear friend of mine once remarked: "The wealthy have such a touching faith in the efficacy of small sums."

But in my own addled fashion, I am a rather ingenious, as well as ingenuous, creature, and in those days I had a certain pathetic appeal to certain individuals, and when the ten dollars were exhausted, I dropped in for dinner at the Madison Avenue pent-house of a very successful composer of "pop" music, and I not only stayed for dinner, but for the next four months, when the spring thaw did set in. Then, after that, it was summer and I had another friend [Paul Bigelow], much less prosperous but equally good-hearted. Knowing the problems of my situation in Manhattan, he wrote me from Macon, Georgia, inviting me to spend the summer with him.

Well, I arrived in that deep southern town, and I found that he was occupying a room in the attic, and that I was to be billeted in the other half of it.

It was the middle of summer and it was the middle of Georgia. My room in the attic had two windows the size and shape of transoms.

Let's say it was a very wet summer, despite the fact that there was practically no rainfall.

My friend had a revolving electric fan and was unable to sleep without it. I had no cooling appliance, and I spent long hours at night glaring across the breathless hall between those attic rooms at my friend lying in bed with that revolving Westinghouse fan ruffling his hair as he chuckled over cartoons in the *New Yorker*.

In the dog days of August, another tenant arrived in this Georgia attic, a somewhat retarded youth who worked at the A & P. This tenant sweated enough to die of dehydration and he never, literally never, bathed or changed his socks and I mean to tell you that the odor which emanated from this nice country kid began to permeate the attic like O'Neill's sense of doom. And if I wanted to elaborate on this item, I would add that late in August a pole-cat moved into the attic one night and moved out before day-break to escape that odor of doom, since it wasn't his own.

Item: Another winter in the early forties of this century and in the Old Quarter of New Orleans. Everything that I owned of a negotiable nature had gone to a loan-shark's on Rampart Street—my portable typewriter, my portable phonograph and all clothes except for a soiled flannel shirt, a pair of riding-breeches and boots which were souvenirs of that class in "equitation" which I had been permitted to take instead of ROTC at the University of Missouri years before.

Rose Williams, 1928

My social position had declined with my fortune and most of my "Quarter" friends pretended not to notice me on the streets.

I thought I had better "split," and so I did; in my cavalry outfit, I set out for Florida, hitching rides, with much the same romantic notions of that state that were held by Ratso in *Midnight Cowboy.*

Although it was wet and chilly on the road, I began to feel quite warm. It was the warmth of a rising fever. When I reached Tampa, I barely had the strength to climb the stairs of a Ritz Men Only. I had expected to pick up a fifty-dollar cheque at general delivery in Tampa—somebody had taken out a cut-rate option on three one-act plays—but what I picked up there was a note which informed me briskly that the unofficial option had been dropped. And there I was stranded, with a fever of 102 and spitting blood.

In my life there have been two Roses: one is my sister, Rose Isabel, and the other was Rose Otte Dakin, my maternal grandmother. She had a mysterious way of sensing when my fortune was at the opposite of zenith and at such times she would stitch into the pages of a letter some five-dollar bills which were really a prodigal gift since they were all that she earned as a piano and violin teacher.

One of these letters provided me with the means of surviving my Tampa catastrophe and going on to where I don't remember, but it was not to a suite at the Plaza.

Item: A period of employment at the southern branch of the U.S. Engineers, also in the early forties. On the graveyard shift, those hours between eleven p.m. and seven a.m., there were just two of us in the office, myself and a young man prematurely discharged from an asylum. Our job was to receive and acknowledge coded messages which would sometimes come in at night on the teletype. My co-worker was a silent creature, but he would glance at me now and then with homicidally suspicious eyes. We were almost equally incompetent, but you may remember the awful shortage of man-power in those years: our boss kept begging us not to force him to fire us, and this continued for three months till one night some really important message came through over the telephone and we blew it sky-high and then our boss finally let me go and kept on the certified looney. A touch of humanity and of wisdom, too.

Item: Several years earlier, I was employed as a squab-picker on a squab-ranch on the periphery of L.A. This was not winter, but early spring, and although this job was not very lucrative, it had its compensations. Several times a week a group of young fellows would gather in the killing-sheds. The squabs were killed by slitting their throats and holding them over a bucket to bleed to death. (I managed squeamishly to avoid this part of the business.) For each squab that we picked, each of us would drop a single feather into a milk-bottle bearing his name, and we were paid according to the number of feathers in our bottles. There was some wonderful rapping among us squab-pickers, and I remember, never to forget, a homely bit of philosophy that was voiced by one of the kids. He said, "You know, if you stand on one corner on this coast long enough, a goddamn sea-gull is gonna fly over you sooner or later and shit a pot of gold on you."

I have quoted this line a couple of times, once in a play and once in a film; I have yet to hear it delivered from the stage or screen, but I still think it is a lovely line.

While I was in employment, a great piece of luck hit me, and not from a sea-gull.

I received a telegram from the Group Theatre in New York informing me that I had received a special award of one hundred dollars for a group of one-acts called *American Blues*.

The wire was signed by Harold Clurman, Irwin Shaw and the late Molly Day Thacher (Kazan).

A hundred bucks in those days was a pretty big slice of bread, and on the strength of it, another squab-picker and I bought second-hand bikes and drove from L.A. County down across the Mexican border. In a Tijuana cantina, we met with some financial reverses and on our way back up the coast we had to sleep under the stars. In a canyon outside Laguna Beach we came upon a chicken-ranch that needed ranchers while the elderly proprietors went upon vacation to Canada. (I don't know why I was so committed to poultry in those days!) We received no salary but were given occupancy of a nice little cabin at the end of the chicken-run.

That summer was the healthiest and happiest, the most golden summer of my life. In the journal I kept in those days I call that summer Nave Nave Mahana which is the title of my favorite Tahitian painting by Gauguin and which means something like enchantment.

That summer I kept falling in love, I seemed to fall in love almost every time I went out, for my southern blood has always magnified a flirtation to an important romance.

(Conrad would say "Youth.")

But disaster struck us in the lovely month of August, or more precisely it struck the chickens. We came out of our cabin one morning to discover about a third of the chicken flock lying on their backs and sides with their legs rigidly extended, yes, dead, in rigor mortis, and the survivors of this flash epidemic were wandering dizzily about as if sun-and-thunder struck.

My friend was so dismayed and alarmed by this catastrophe that he split the scene without warning in a beat-up old Ford that he had lately acquired, and I was then alone with the plague-stricken poultry, and that was the longest time in my life that I went without food and it was about ten days without food except for an avocado stolen, now and then, from a grove nearby, since the diseased but surviving poultry did not appear fit for eating and I hadn't a dime left on me, not even postage for a letter home to "Grand."

I discovered that after three days you stop feeling hungry, you just drift into a strangely peaceful condition which is ideal for meditation. After a fortnight in that condition, mostly horizontal, I heard my friend's scatter-bolt sputtering with exhaustion toward the cabin and he entered as casually grinning as if he had left ten minutes before. It was like a vision. . . .

During his absence he had played his clarinet in a night-spot near L.A., had received a week's salary, and the sum was sufficient to get us into the San Bernardino Mountains for a time of recuperation from our respective ordeals.

I was receiving letters that summer from various agents on Broadway who had seen my name in theatre columns as winner of that Group Theatre award. One agent said she was not interested in serious plays, but was looking for a good "vehicle." I wrote her that the only vehicle I had to offer was a second-hand bike. But another lady, Audrey Wood, expressed a more serious interest, and at the advice of Molly Kazan, I chose Miss Wood to represent me, which she did for thirty-some years later. [The typescript reads "which she's still doing thirty-some years later," altered in handwriting.]

Although it's a bit of a detour, it may amuse you to know how I first encountered Miss Wood in the offices she shared with the historical William Liebling, way, way up in the RCA Building at 30 Rockefeller Center.

I had arrived by Greyhound at daybreak, had not rested or shaved, looked pretty seedy when I presented myself at the imposing offices of Liebling-Wood, Inc.

The little front office was full of girls seeking chorus jobs in a musical that Mr. Liebling was casting, they were milling about, chattering like birds on a loco-weed high, when Mr. Liebling came charging out of his inner sanctum and shouted, "OK, girls, line up now!," and everybody lined up except me. I remained on a chair in a corner. A number of girls were selected for auditions, the others gently discouraged, and everyone left except me, and then he noticed me and said, "Nothing for you today." I said, "I don't want anything today except to meet Miss Wood." "Out to lunch," he informed me.

And dead on that cue she entered the outer office, a very small and dainty woman with red hair, a porcelain complexion and a look of cool perspicacity in her eyes which remains there today.

I figured that this little lady was Miss Wood and I was not mistaken. I got up and introduced myself to her and she said something like, "Well, well, you've finally made it," to which I replied, "Not yet." And we went on from there, through various kinds of weather, until this present year of Our Lord and the Pentagon and this gig at the Ivanhoe Theatre in Chicago.

Audrey Wood and Tennessee (with an unidentified man), 1954

Last spring my publishers informed me that the coming fall they were going to begin publication of a series of volumes to be called my "Collected Works."

I was filled with alarm at this news which I received the day before sailing for Europe. I got at once on the phone. The publishers were not in, but I reached a secretary and I said: "I hear you are about to publish my Collected Works and I think you should know my works are not collected, that a good many of them are distributed among trunks and boxes in warehouses, in the archives of university libraries, and in the filing-cases and closets of my home in Key West, so it will be years before you can publish anything that can honestly be called my Collected Works. So if you want to bring out a collection of my produced and published plays, please do, that's fine, since most of my work is now out of print in many parts of the world, owing to your troubles with distribution. Now, for these proposed volumes, if you want an omnibus title, I suggest that you call them 'The Pigeon Drop.' "

"What is 'The Pigeon Drop'?" asked the secretary.

"The pigeon drop," I told her, "is one of the oldest confidence games. It is the game in which somebody fills out an envelope with waste-paper, picks out a half-witted 'mark' and tells this mark that the envelope is full of paper money, and that if this mark would like half of it, he should run to his bank and draw out such-and-such sum of the green stuff and put it in a large envelope, hand it over to the con-men and receive in return an envelope containing half of the green stuff in the pigeon dropper's envelope."

This sounds like a preposterous trick to get away with, but it was revived successfully in the French Quarter of New Orleans a few months ago. These two very sharp young ladies had observed an older lady who was not so sharp, and they approached her with the pigeon drop, the envelope filled with waste-paper and gave her the pitch about having found this envelope full of hundred-dollar bills and they really and truly did persuade the old creature to trot over to her bank and draw out her life-savings and put them in an envelope which she exchanged for the pigeon drop.

Well, the secretary was not amused. Neither were the publishers.

When I was one day out at sea, I was summoned from the dinner-table by a phone-call from the shore. It was my publishers assuring me that they would discard that alarming title "Collected Works" but they were not going to substitute "The Pigeon Drop" for it. They said that they really did not consider me to be a literary con-merchant and that they proposed to publish my plays under the title "The Theatre of Tennessee Williams." I told them that I did not care for that title either but that I preferred it to "The Collected Works of ———."

Any suggestions for alternative titles are welcome. Several of my travelling-companions think I ought to stick to "The Pigeon Drop" but I wonder if that degree of self-deprecation is wise.

I suspect too many people might agree with it.

Beverly Hills Hotel
Beverly Hills, Calif.

August 4, 1971

Maria dearest:

We are here sitting in a suite that makes the one at the Ambassador East look like a waiting room at the Salvation Army. I say we are here sitting, but actually sweet Miss Mary has just set out for Disneyland and God knows when she will surface from that kiddies' heaven.

We were at Oliver's last night. He gave a dinner party and his improvement is truly phenomenal. He is flying out this week for Bangkok and the boys. He is just a little perturbed over a "love-letter" he received from his favorite, Oot, which began as follows: "Glad about operation. Please send one hundred dollars." Actually, of course, it is madness for Oliver to fly back there alone at this steaming time of year, but then the Professor was ever wont to follow a somewhat irrational course through life. I believe he expects me to finance this junket. There have been numerous hints as to inadequate funds. For instance, he got himself a fifty-dollar wig which he put on for dinner last night. It was a mod-type of wig and nobody could keep a straight face. The Professor removed it crossly, gave me a piercing look, and said that to get a proper wig would cost two thousand.

I will consult [Julius] Lefkowitz about my ability to invest again in Oliver's travels but I suspect the office will inform me that I can barely afford my own and Miss Mary's. We are not quite decided where to go for a rest. I think it will probably be Tahiti and the Samoan Islands; must decide today. You'd better write me c/o William Fitelson [Floria Lasky's husband], 580 Fifth Ave., till I have settled somewhere.

At last, the night before leaving Chicago, I saw a truly beautiful performance of *OUT CRY*. All the comedy came through and although Herlie looked like she had pre-empted the space for the Empire State Building, and was in exceptionally good (strong) voice, several people came up to me afterwards and said they considered it my best play. It is far from that, since one does not write his best play at sixty, but out of the Chicago gig I feel there has come, at long last, a closely knit and effective piece of theatre which would be a knock-out in the hands of Leighton and Scofield and a real director. [*Inserted in handwriting*] (Like one of the English Peters)

I am as delighted with the Fitelson office as you are with Lord Goodman. So far he has not been able to get the Widow to show a contract with me and he suspects there may not be one. What I want to do is to stay with IFA [International Famous Agency] so that there will be no dislocation of royalties, but to disengage myself completely and permanently from the Widow who, for the past ten years, has had my worst interests at heart.

Françoise Sagan has translated *Sweet Bird* for Paris.

It is opening there, she told me in a very sweet letter, on October first, and I hope you'll attend it with me, it will have two big stars and should be a gala occasion, that is, until the notices come out.

Now I must get to work but I will keep in touch. Tell Pulcheria I am travelling with her beautiful good luck picture. [*Inserted in handwriting*] And the folding icon.

Fondest love, Tennessee

[*Added in handwriting*] Am having latest acting version of *OUT CRY* typed up here and will dispatch copies to you—by Air Pakistani, perhaps.—I was not sure Gadg survived the veteran shrimp evening till his Chicago girlfriend told me he is going on the David Frost talk-show.— Hope he doesn't talk too much about his abduction to West Orange [New Jersey].

''THE 'SHRIMP EVENING'! That was an occasion when I was over in New York and Tennessee kept promising Jane and Tony Smith that he would dine with them. But he kept on stalling. We telephoned Gadg and persuaded him to come up from the country to have dinner with us, at the restaurant of his choice. Dutifully he appeared, only to be whisked away in a hired car to West Orange and dinner with the Smiths.

"Jane had produced a raspberry soup with shrimps in it, which had by this time been frozen and reheated three times. We were all terribly ill. Gadg and Tennessee talked to each other the entire dinner, and never addressed a word to either Jane or Tony or me."

Maria went with Tennessee to the opening, at the Atelier Theatre in Paris, of *Sweet Bird of Youth* as translated by Françoise Sagan, starring Edwige Feuillère. Sagan had arranged rooms for them in a lovely hotel overlooking the Père Lachaise cemetery. Tennessee misconstrued this as a macabre joke on her part and was determined to change hotels. Paris was then full because of the Prix de l'Arc de Triomphe at Longchamp, but eventually they managed to find rooms at the Lancaster.

"Françoise Sagan was very concerned, knowing how vague Tennessee was. However, she had tried to impress upon him that the only person he should hug and kiss and congratulate on her performance was Edwige

Feuillère, and that, most importantly, he must *ignore* one of the leading men, because he was giving a disastrous performance and was hated by the rest of the cast. Tennessee and I got bored during the play and spent the second act in a strip joint near the Moulin Rouge. Tennessee always said he hated the second act anyway. We returned to the theatre for the last act. There was tumultuous applause at the end.

"Afterwards, in the Green Room, Tennessee caught Françoise's eye and remembered he had to say something to someone. He rushed up to the offending actor, flung his arms around *him,* and shouted *'Vous êtes magnifique!'* He completely ignored Feuillère, who went into a deep sulk. Sagan yelled at me with rage. *'Mais, qu'est-ce qu'il fait? Est-ce qu'il est fou?'* But Tennessee was delighted with himself."

Tennessee and Oliver Evans came to Wilbury.

"He and Evans spent endless hours sitting on the terrace, talking about literature. It was wonderful to see the pair of them sitting as obliviously contented as that—like a Chekhov play.

"The Spanish butler, Raymond, had recently come to us from the Duke of Marlborough's seat, Blenheim Palace. He was married to the housemaid, Emmy, who was unaccountably in perpetual floods of tears. Tennessee asked an exasperated Raymond why this should be.

" ' 'Cos she fool! She say her dead sister come here to Wilbury Park to haunt her. Why her sister haunt Wilbury Park? If she come haunting to England, she haunt Blenheim Palace!'

"Tennessee remarked wryly, 'I'd no idea ghosts were such snobs!' "

––––––––

[*Envelope postmarked Key West, September 6, 1971*]

Dearest Maria:

The situation here is impossible. I have adopted a child without having any gift or inclination for paternity. It is tragi-comic and I don't know the solution. He confessed to me, recently, that when his parents broke up, they put him into a home in Tampa called "Mary, Help a Christian." He ran away from it. He had a knack for mechanics and electricity and got a good job with a telephone company and as night-clerk in this gay motel in Coconut Grove where I met him. It was ill-met by moonlight, fair Titania. The disparity of ages is nothing compared to the disparity of interests. Today was Sunday and there were six pages of colored comics that had to be read aloud like a religious service in a preacher's house. He is becoming obese, all below the waist, about the hips and the legs so that he has an hermaphroditic appearance. And yet I feel a moral responsibility. I am ashamed of my impatience. He has two friends, a pair of queens, one of whom plays the part of a character named "Scruffy" in an early morning TV show for children. They came to dinner tonight and the dinner was an hilarious catastrophe. He prepared a meat-loaf and mashed potatoes. He took the sizzling hot platter of meat-loaf out of the oven and screamed and dropped it on the floor. He didn't read the instructions for the "instant mashed." The mix was supposed to be poured in boiling water gradually and whipped but he emptied it into the pot before he set it on the stove and the result was a dreadful sort of gruel that he poured on the plates and which splashed over the table. I had to go straight to bed although it was not yet dark. He came into the bedroom and said "Poor baby" and I don't know if he meant me or him but I said "Poor baby your ass." His buddies made a precipitate departure, they said they had to get to a pizzeria before it closed, and he went to bed weeping noisily so that I had to take an extra pill to get to sleep. I don't know how this situation is going to work out, I only know that it will be an expensive solution. But I think he was better off in the telephone business. His write-up in *Esquire* was almost worse than mine.

About more practical matters. I wrote Floria the kind of letter you suggested, demanding copies of any contracts still in effect and telling her I was returning to New York and would stay there till the agency question is resolved.

As for Maggie, I think if she prefers to appear in a creaky old melodrama which was a vehicle for the Lunts thirty-five years ago, then she has lost her vocation in spite of her great talent. I am afraid that she has committed herself to the world of Binkie, probably through lack of faith in herself. What a pity for her and for me, too. Please don't mention my feelings about it, just give her my love and best wishes, sincerely.

Perhaps I have had so much dreadful personal publicity that I am being excommunicated from the theatre. But I won't stop working.

After a while in New York, when things have been set straight if they can be, I will fly to London and then to the Hotel Minzah in Tangier, which has a pool, or the Mamoulian in Marrakesh where there is swimming, too.

I certainly can't sit here much longer.

Much love, 10

[A sad face is drawn inside the 0]

The library at Wilbury Park

The South Hall, Wilbury Park

1431 Duncan Street
Key West, Fla.

October 22, 1971

Dearest Maria:

I thought you might like to see Miss Mary's new stationery, well, here it is, the cabalistic inscriptions at the left were designed by this talented young lady herself. Sometimes she reminds me of that Dickens character called the "Infant Phenomenon" [Ninetta Crummles in *Nicholas Nickleby*].

I have not bothered to have the latest version of *OUT CRY* re-typed, as I read over the published version of *THE TWO-CHARACTER PLAY* and it seemed to have a simplicity and freshness that is now lost. Have you read the book-version? It was published privately while I was in hospital, meaning you know what. If you haven't a copy, I'll have New Directions send you one so you can compare it yourself.

I have such lovely memories of our European junket. Please let me know how things are going domestically. Is Golders Green still the new constituency?

The peace and quiet of Key West makes the bovine meadows of Wilbury Park seem tumultuous, so I think I will leave soon for New Orleans, take a little furnished apartment in the Quarter and sit there. Meanwhile my new agent, Bill Barnes, is promoting a production of a long short play called *Confessional* for off-Broadway.

Pulcheria's good luck fantasy is beautifully framed, Miss Mary has photographed it and you'll soon get the photo.—I forgot to call Gore before I left Rome but will write him, perhaps right now.

I am well except for insomnia, haven't had a good night's rest since Wilbury. Or a good day's, either.

With much love, 10

———

"TENNESSEE slept and slept at Wilbury, like Rip Van Winkle. He would wander into the South Hall at about six in the evening, saying, 'Why don't we all go into a pub in Sall-is-berry, and have lunch?' He loved pubs, and a pub lunch was his idea of heaven. It's my idea of hell.

"On one occasion, I recall, we had a group of Russians staying. Tennessee was asleep, and one man started to sing a Russian song, playing a guitar softly. Suddenly, Tennessee appeared in the doorway, his face rapt. He stared at the Russian. 'You must be a prince!' he said, in quiet wonderment.

" 'As a matter of fact,' the man replied, 'I am.' "

Maria found this poem written into her diary.

NEAR THE SILENCE

Near the silence and the snow
steep the climb and very slow,
Strange, each footstep, not to fall
each catch of breath an anxious call
But were they ever quite so fair,
the skies, or quite so fine the air?

Tennessee, Oct. '71

Begun in 1967, *Confessional* had first been produced at the Maine Theatre Arts Festival in July 1971, directed by William Hunt. Tennessee expanded the play into *Small Craft Warnings* for its New York premiere the following year.

———

909 St. Louis Street
New Orleans, La.

November 23, 1971

Dearest Maria:

Your hilarious letter, forwarded from Key West, was very encouraging to me. And I am sorry that I can't be funny right now, but it is 4:30 a.m. and I've slept not a wink. [*Inserted in handwriting*] Love!

I guess you would call me a dying duck in a thunderstorm or a pregnant fox in a forest fire but I can't help feeling depressed. I don't sleep more than one or two hours a night, I seem to be having a nervous crisis and I am not sure what it's about. The situation and the prospects aren't bad. We have taken a charming little house in the French Quarter of New Orleans, a living and dining room with twenty-foot ceiling, two double bedrooms, with two baths, a lovely patio with a fish-pool and a little swimming pool, and the Quarter is fantastic as ever.

It may be that I am distressed over the tragic condition of Oliver. We met in Houston, Texas, last week-end, to catch a production of *Camino Real,* which he is teaching. I was shocked by the physical deterioration. He had to be assisted up and down aisles of the theatre, supported by each arm.

"Please forgive me," he said, "I've had my brain removed." He is now back at the California college. God knows how he makes it. But he told me he was about to have another "brain-scanning" and that if the malignancy was still active, he intended to kill himself. I called our mutual doctor here in New Orleans and he said to me: "They didn't get it all out." Oliver is still very lucid but obviously his time is short. I feel that I ought to take him back to Bangkok, the only place where he is at home now. Certainly he can't be allowed to go alone. He is so terribly touching and so brave. I can't leave the States till January as I have an off-Broadway play production [*Confessional*] coming up then but I think I'll fly to Bangkok with him immediately after. Don't you think I ought to? We have always been so close. As for *OUT CRY* and *TWO-CHARACTER PLAY,* I don't want to press it. I know that it will be done and the time no longer seems important to me.

I am going to leave you these plays in a codicil to my will which I will make out as soon as I'm able to get up to New York. That will be as soon as the doctor gets me sleeping again.

[*Added in handwriting*] Harold Pinter wrote me a very sweet, short letter, asking me to call him when I'm in London again.

If Scofield wrote me, I don't know where.

P.S. Have been in N.Y. a week—*sleeping as at Wilbury!* Will write again this week but want to get this right off. Quack! Quack! (no claps of thunder).

[*Handwritten Christmas card, dated December 18, 1971*]

Dear heart:

I am drunk, or should I say stoned? We are beautifully settled in a French Quarter building in New Orleans. The holiday festivities are in full swing. Oliver is in Rome (c/o American Express). He'd love a word from you. He's travelling with a very bright distinguished old lady—Ardis Something. You might entice them to the dairy farm but please (excuse the warning) don't let him suspect you've heard any negative report from me.

Sorry I must express Xmas greetings with a cheque, but there's all that water between us.

Much love, Tenn.

Paying Mom a surprise visit next week-end. She may drop dead. Me too.

909 St. Louis Street
New Orleans, La.

December 30, 1971

Dearest Maria:

Something is singing in the patio, I don't know if it's a goldfish or a mocking-bird, but it is warning me that it's time to return to the sack from which I got up at four a.m. to continue work on my memoirs.

I don't want to retire again without briefing you on the situation down here.

I spent Xmas holidays in St. Louis. For this occasion Mother released herself from her "retirement home" in the city and resumed residence in the suburbs. Dakin joined us. I was very distressed by Mother's report on this "retirement home" so I went to inspect it. It was very much like a first class hotel. The public rooms were lovely, there were elegant old ladies sitting about making no outward disturbance, and her personal quarters were charming. She had declared to me that "the place is run by the blacks for the blacks"—and I did not see a single face colored by anything but that touch of jaundice that sometimes touches the face of an old Caucasian.

When I left, three days ago, she was still adamantly refusing to return to the retirement home. "They are dropping like flies there," she said. "One day it's a cerebral hemorrhage, the next it's a coronary, the next it's some kind of plague which isn't mentioned and I am never going back there— why, the Black Panthers are right around the corner and they parade past the entrance all day on the look-out for us!" Then she would burst into song to convince Dakin and me that she was too happy for words to be home. . . .

By last phone-check she is still home and determined to stay. She has a servant-companion who is almost her age and as black as your hat, and yet whenever Susie starts home, Mother peeks out the terrible triple-locked door and says, "Oh, Susie, wait, there are three blacks at the bus-stop!"

Susie says: "Now, Mizz Williams, they look lighter than me," and goes on out and Mother never expects to see her alive the next day.

All in all, it was an enchanting visit. . . .

Dakin still running for the U.S. Senate—is now visiting me in New Orleans. We put him up in the attic but he comes down. I'm giving my first party for him in the new house on New Year's. Then he goes on down to Key West to get a sun-tan which he thinks will enhance his TV appearances in that hot race for the Senate in Illinois.

By way of a Xmas greeting, Oliver sent me a nude male photo from Paris. As for our trip to Bangkok, if this does, indeed, materialize we will go by way of England and perhaps Moscow to pick up those royalties there, if the consulate can confirm their existence.

I am hanging around the States till early March which is when these three young producers are going to expose *Confessional* off-Broadway. I plan to stay through rehearsals and pre-views and then split by jumbo jet just before the notices come out. I don't know how this is going to fit in with Oliver's schedule and anyhow it all seems as dreamy as the gold-fish song in the patio right now and I close with

Much love, 10

I remember your uncle clearly and fondly and I feel that people like that stay with us.

———

MARIA's mother's brother, Uncle Freddy Bucknall, had died in Helsinki.

———

[*Address on envelope 909 St. Louis Street, New Orleans, La.*]

In transit

January 22, 1972

Maria darling:

I've just received word from Jo Healy that Rose is seriously ill. Vomiting and losing weight: very ambiguous reports from hospital. Of course it's unbearable that physical suffering should be added now to her dreadful experience in life.

No, I'm not going to Russia with Oliver.

I plan to settle somewhere abroad but I haven't decided at this point where that place will be.

Perhaps a villina in Southern Italy or Sicily would do.

This is a bed-time note without much hope of sleep.

Much love, 10

[*Added in handwriting*] Je suis très russe ce soir.

[*Postmarked Key West, February 5, 1972*]

February ?, 1972

Love, I literally hadn't a moment to write you while I was in New York. I was kept constantly going—casting the play [now titled *Small Craft*

Warnings], conferring, party-going, etc., the whole exhausting bit. Toward the end, a big bash was given for me by one Lester Persky—whom you may recall with delight—at his pent-house on the East River. Well, I got terrifically high on "Jamaica grass" and took off my coat and went out on the terrace with a young Dutch actor. Next day, in flew the flu which I am still with—in Key West. Also with Dotson Rader and a very rude young actor—he said, "Here I am, a yet-to-be actor with a has-been playwright!" Well, I put him down. I said, "Baby, there are yet-to-be and never-to-be actors but there is no such thing as a has-been playwright since once you have written plays you are always after a playwright if you live to one hundred."

He is still sulking in bed, alone, and poor Dotson is upstairs sleeping off a hang-over. I got up bright and early to get this memo to you.

I have been reading reports of the dreadful difficulties in England due to the coal-strike and have been continually worrying about you and the girls and His Lordship.

I hope you have all survived—not like dying ducks in thunderstorms about it.

I have to re-appear in New York for start of rehearsals and TV talk-show on Feb. 18. Don't know where I'll stay—but hope to be a little bit out of the bad air of the city.—Are you really coming over?—The cast is *brilliant!*—the director a dud.

All my love, Tenn.

ON APRIL 2, *Small Craft Warnings* opened at the Truck and Warehouse Theatre, New York City. William Hunt was replaced as director by Richard Altman. The production was the first real success that Tennessee had had since *Night of the Iguana* in 1961.

Tennessee bought a house in New Orleans at 1014 Dumaine Street, one of the beautiful old houses in the French Quarter, with the slave house still in the back garden. "It was divided into two apartments, of which he let one. His own apartment had three rooms, a kitchen and bathroom, up a staircase, with a beautiful balcony. There was a swimming pool at the back which was never used. It badly needed restoration and management.

"Tennessee loved New Orleans, and delighted in showing it to me: the various different nightclubs, the cakewalk dancers . . ."

Five O'Clock Angel

[Postmarked Beverly Hills, Calif., April 14, 1972]

Dearest Maria:

I had a car waiting just outside the theatre and soon as the curtain fell I was whisked to the airport just in time to catch a night plane to Miami. The returns are trickling in. The *New York Times* was a good review—but qualified. The other important papers—except a morning tabloid—are about the same. This week the magazines will have at us. The critics in New York are no longer inclined to make allowances for my advanced age nor for the dues I have paid. They keep saying "This is not up to Williams' best such as *Streetcar* and *Cat.*"— Well, for Chrissake how could it be? If it were a major play such as *OUT CRY* it would not have opened at the Truck and Warehouse in the Bowery, would it?

Poppins drove down here to Key West with Gigi who is much slimmer, thanks to diuretic tablets that made her pee off quarts or gallons of fluid. As for Poppins, he had dyed his hair again, this time jet black, and had it cut in a style that makes him look like a vamp of the silent screen. I just don't care anymore how he looks—but I was a bit distressed to learn that he had fallen through the upstairs floor of our little house in New Orleans and landed in the kitchen and is on antibiotics because of abrasions he suffered.

Darling, I wish you would give me a truly, unsparingly accurate assessment of Paul [Scofield]'s intentions regarding *OUT CRY,* since I have to make so many plans. It is obvious that the Professor's college wants him out. He was intending to teach a summer term but they have placed him on a schedule that would break a well man and the Professor is hardly in that category. I think it is morally wrong to desert him—but I feel that I could bring him to England this spring if there were going to be a spring production of *OUT CRY.* I don't think a sweltering summer in Bangkok would do him much more good than trying to hold classes eight hours a day. I mean the poor boy has forgotten his age. He thought he was 53 but then he remembered the year of his birth and came to the conclusion that he was 56 and I happen to know that the Professor is only two years younger than I which makes him 59. Do you get the picture?

This week-end I am flying out to the Coast as I have been invited to present the award for best screen-writer at the annual Oscar ceremony out there. Then I will be able to check on Oliver's present condition.

I have some lovely house-guests besides my golden-eyed black Angora kitten, [Black] Sabbath, and Gigi. Dave Dellinger is here with his beautiful fifteen-year-old daughter, Michelle. He is the grand old man of the anti-war movement and a great humanitarian with a fine intellect. Then there is the daughter's girl friend, also beautiful, but wearing an Afro hair-do and steel rimmed specs.

In New York I saw a lot of Chuck Bowden. I think he made a mistake in bugging Scofield on the phone. I understand Paul's problems—maybe more than he does mine—and I know he must serve his vocation however he feels it is best.

I wish you'd write me at once, c/o Oliver, English Dept., San Fernando State College, Northridge, California. I will be out there only about five days—on this trip—and that's why I ask you to write me at once if you can.

How lovely it would be to be in England this spring, you, Paul, Chuck and I, bringing my last important play to life under the best conditions! I feel that Angela Lansbury, although a very large lady, is such a great actress that she could be believable and powerful in the play, especially in the first and third acts.

With my love, 10

[*Added in handwriting*] Miss Rose is in full flower.

[*On letterhead The Beverly Hills Hotel, Beverly Hills, Calif., postmarked Beverly Hills, April 19, 1972*]

Hotel Elysée
60 E. 54th Street, N.Y.C.

April 18, 1972

Maria dear:

This being the morning of our departure—for New York and more TV appearances to swell attendance at the Truck & Warehouse—I must limit myself to a token response to your hilarious account of your stay with The Laird. [The family went on holiday to Scotland as guests of Colin MacPherson.] He sounds lovely to me.

I am reading Gore's book [and play *An Evening with Richard Nixon*]—it's already been published and is now having previews on Broadway, I will see it this week—and it is quite marvellous, it keeps me howling with glee, it makes such annihilating exposures of our chiefs of state, including the sacred Kennedy.

I do wish Gore still liked me—I am always so fond of that man.

I long to get back to the peace and quiet of Poppins, Gigi, Black Sabbath (my Angora kitten) and the old family retainer "Black Majesty" [Leoncia McGee] who appears and sits giving orders and watching colored TV for her pay/

Well, my dear, that's life for you. I mean it's not death. Yet.

I saw "the Old One" (J.G.) [Gielgud] at a party given by the Michael Yorks last week. He is about to appear in a new film of *Lost Horizon* and is extremely bitter about the script. "Sentimental crap," he pronounced it. As I left I said to him, "John, you're such a beautiful man" and he replied, "You noticed that too late."

Sorry I alarmed you about my health. I didn't have a "stroke." The doctor who gave me the shot to get me on the TV talk-show immediately after a jet flight put in something like "speed"—the results were rather funny. I asked [Dick] Cavett, the TV host, if anyone ever dropped dead on his show and he said, "Yes, one did. Change the subject."—I'm feeling quite all right now and I hope it will not be too long before I see you and your loved ones.

With much love, 10

[*From Leoncia McGee to Maria, undated*]

Dear Mrs Maria

I know take this pleasure in anser your letter But sorry I took so long in anser your letter I have bin sick But going much better know Do hope all is well with you Mr Tom was here in Key West but hes gon back to N.Y. His mother and Brother was here two That Viola [Veidt] she worry Mr Tom to Death about money, it is so hot here had no rain Mr Tom told me that you liked me, I also like you too You trete me Just like Mrs Marion Vaccaro Frank [the gardener] sends his love to you Mrs Viola she want to take over Mr Tom house. Give my love to your family for me Do hope to see you again Love your Leoncie McGee

1431 Duncan Street
Key West

Maria darling:

Before commencing my morning's work in the mad-house I want to set down a few rational remarks to you and Chuck [Bowden] and our friends in the English theatre.

You know that my heart has always been with those who have shown kindness, affection and understanding to me as consistently as you and Chuck have and that is what always comes first. The fact that a new person, Billy Barnes, has also shown exceptional consideration of me as a person as well as a writer has touched me a great deal, too. My object is to contrive a rapprochement—rapport—between you all and Billy. After all, Billy doesn't know you nor does he even have more than an acquaintance with Chuck. [Barnes, in fact, was always extremely kind and courteous to Maria.] I want Billy to come with me to England as soon as possible for I know that you'd see in him the same qualities that I do. [*Inserted in handwriting*] He really *is* a southern *gentleman*. On the home front, I shall try to my damnedest to get him closer to Chuck.

Now there's one thing I think Paul [Scofield] should find it possible to do for me at this point.

This thing is that I think he should give some attention during the months preceding his film to the preliminary arrangements of the production, such as the choice of a director, a theatre, the final casting of Clare, etc. Then let him do the film and say on paper, in the way of a commitment which would appear completely resolved to a firm like IFA (of which Billy is, of course, a rather intransigent member) that within one or two and a half months after the completion of the film (*The Tempest*) he will start rehearsals on *OUT CRY*. [The film Tennessee refers to as *The Tempest* was released as *Scorpio*.] Forgive me for putting *OUT CRY* in caps but that's how an old playwright thinks when he has his back to the wall. . . .

Doesn't this strike you as a reasonable request? I mean after all, time is not waiting for any of us—indefinitely—and time cannot be omitted from any rational arrangement of human affairs.

I am so longing to get to London for a while and be among friends. It seems to me that in America I am surrounded only by frantic dependents and by such amorphous neutral creatures as Poppins and by—oh, hell, no complaints, they're a waste of this beautiful stationery. I know you get the picture. Now I must go to work.

Please in your own subtle way try to get Paul to sign an agreement. You see, in the American theatre, Maria, ladies and gentlemen hardly exist anymore and the word of honor is not in the American dictionary nor even the present vocabulary, my dear, and that has a lot to do with my intention to buy a little farm with goats in Sicily. [*Inserted in handwriting*] and engage an attractive youngish wop gardener, to prevent abuse of the goats. I prefer baa-baa to oink-oink-oink.

Much love 10

Hotel Elysée
60 East 54th Street
New York City

Dearest Maria:

Just got here last night and I'm still fairly pooped and the situation is one of great confusion. I left Poppins in New Orleans decorating my new apartment and you should see how she's done it! At the air-port in New York, Bill Barnes was waiting for me with a limousine. I was touched by that. It's been a long time since anyone has done that for me in the States. He has collated the play [*Out Cry*] for publication and I'm going to put in very important revisions while I'm here. It is still going on, thank God. I am going to send you a copy because I think you'll dig it.

Well, love, we're just about the last of the impossible romanticists and we've got to stick together but keep a watch on each other.

Did you know that Scofield is in America to do a film? Your letter doesn't answer my question, will he or will he not commit himself on paper to do *OUT CRY* in two and a half months after the completion of his film of *The Tempest*?

I would reckon that you had to dodge that question because poor Paul— although he obviously sincerely likes the play—doubts that it could be a success, at least not very commercially. Of course I know that it could. But we have to convince him of our conviction about that.

Bill Barnes and I are going to visit him on his set where he is taking *third* billing after Burt Lancaster and some other inferior actor [Alain Delon]. Christ! What an act of humility! Bill and I are going to have to ask him to put it on paper that he will really and truly do *OUT CRY* within two and a half months after completing *Tempest*. I suspect that I am going to attend Oliver to Bangkok, stay there a few weeks, and then go about the world to England or Italy.

Baby, you and Oliver and Bill Barnes are the only friends I have left. No. No. Chuck, too. I think the program is to cool it till I've completed the round the world trip and then let's get cracking at a London production.

Poppins stout. Continues to get pay-checks but must soon get back into the telephone business. She couldn't even pack for me. I mean I had half an hour to get to the air-port in New Orleans and she'd packed not a thing—poor Gigi looked so desperate when I left, her little face a real tragic mask. I think she knows what she's left with.

Look. I'll call you. But please let's remember the facts and practicalities of theatre and not fuck up.

I am completely alone which has always been the nightmare of my life.

Much love, Tennessee

———

SCOFIELD was not doing a film in America. It was becoming evident that machinations were afoot against the Bowden-plus-Scofield project.

———

New Orleans tomorrow
(1014 Dumaine, Apt. B)

Dear little girl:

I am writing as usual at daybreak. Received your card. "Il n'y a que la vérité qui blesse."

Then I have given many blessings? Is that the message?

Well, through you, I have met dear Jacqueline [Fogt, a school friend of Maria], [playwright] John Cromwell, and most of all, your mother, who has created heaven if it did not exist before. Yes. Am drunk. Why not?

"Blesse" really means wound.

Never mind wounds; to feel them proves a continuing existence.

Yesterday—having flown from Key West for the event—I saw Magnani in her (final?) TV appearance, *1870*—her art was untouched by her approaching death, her impeccable truth and intensity never greater—even Kazan wept in the small screening room . . .

Afterwards, dinner with Chuck Bowden, Paula (Chuck's wife) and Beatrice Straight, an aging actress. I said: "I have never regarded age as a disfigurement"—which pleased her.

More chit-chat. Two days ago a homicidal Puerto Rican kicked in the front door of my house in Key West and struck me repeatedly with a board studded with rusty nails. Slashed my chest and arms and was about to deliver the coup-de-grace to the face when—miraculously—police arrived—I survive.

Why?

I supposed I prefer to.—Mother now seals her letters with little printed stamps "Edwin Williams"—not Edwina, but Edwin—wheel come full circle?—I called Gatesworth Manor at once and said: "May I speak to

Edwina Williams?"—The switchboard operator giggled and said, "Do you mean Edwin Williams?" I got her on the phone and discreetly enquired about the missing vowel and she said, "Oh, son, I am inundated with so many appeals!"

When life turns into an old tired joke we just remember *Old Times* by Harold Pinter . . .

Or—no, not David Storey.

Remember how every afternoon at two, Anna would phone and that great, rich voice would shout: "What is the program?"

And at eight a.m. the Horse and I would enter her apartment and on the table would be Johnny Walker's Red Label whiskey, a bowl of pretzels, a bowl of peanuts—and she would be shouting, shouting back of closed doors. I would walk out on the terrace and watch prima sera turn dark blue until she came charging out preceded slightly by an exhausted young lover . . .

And at midnight we drove all about the places in Rome where homeless cats congregate and she would scatter food for them.

Thousands at the dock-side when we sailed for the States, from Naples, on the *Andrea Doria* (ill-fated) shouting, weeping "Nonarella, Nonarella, Nonarella!"—And she came out on the deck and waved till the ship was out of the harbor.

She drove up to Spoleto to see Hermione Baddeley in *Milk Train*—we shared a box. She kept exclaiming "Magnifica, magnifica!"—I thought she meant the play but she meant Hermione . . .

Never valued anything but La Vérité, blessed or killed by it.

Who is Sophia Loren? Who is Carlo Ponti? Who is [David] Merrick? Il n'y a rien que le travail!

Love, 10

ON JUNE 6, 1972, *Small Craft Warnings* was transferred to the New Theatre, where Tennessee played the part of Doc. He greatly enjoyed his debut as an actor. The other actors enjoyed it less, as Tennessee ad-libbed constantly. Maria disapproved. "I felt that writers were writers and actors were actors. He was taking a job away from an actor and demeaning himself in the process."

Hotel Elysée
60 E. 54th Street
N.Y.C.

June 9, 1972

Dearest Maria:

You couldn't believe the things that have been going on in my life if it was anyone else's. For the past three days I have been appearing in my own play at the new uptown theatre in an important role AND—surviving and getting big hands.

Also after each performance—holding rap-sessions—called symposiums—with the audience. Do you think I ought to commit myself at once to a nice sanitarium?—Well, I really had no choice. The actor—just at the moment we were moving into the new house—left town to do a 4-day film bit and they were going to put into the part—they had no understudy—a stage manager who is a swish. I shouted, "Goddam it, no, I will play it myself!" And they took me up on it and I flew back from the coast. Well. A star is born. We have played to packed houses. And no cabbages thrown. I guess I have to admit that I am a ham and that I loved it: appearing again tonight.

Now I know you are mad at me because I called you in London. I think Peter answered the phone—after a good long wait I was told that you were not available and that there was no time when you would be. Maria, there is *much* to tell you.

I was thrown for a kangaroo leap when Chuck Bowden called me on the coast to tell me that he was not going to do *OUT CRY* because it was totally negative. I thought he meant the play. Was annihilated. Then it became apparent, as he went on, that he was talking about his professional relations with Bill Barnes—he was furious because Scofield—he said—had been in New York for a week and he, Chuck, had not been informed. WELL!—Since Billy had been instructed to go no where near Scofield I can hardly see the *rationale* of Chuck's complaint about *that*.

I called Chuck when I got here but he had gone to Chicago to be with the Lunts who are ill.

Dear, the play is now in your possession—I have signed the codicil leaving you the two-in-one property of *OUT CRY* and *TWO CHARACTERS*. I still regard you as my primary support during this rather confused period in my life. You will share with me in the play when produced whether you like it or not. I can be very, very firm about some things when determined.

I CANNOT AND WILL NOT BELIEVE THAT YOU WANT TO ABANDON ME TO—WHAT FATE?

Please call me collect as soon as you get this, PL 3-1066, ext. 902.

I'm sure you know how desperately I need to know that you remain friendly . . .

With all my love, Tennessee

———

SCOFIELD had not been in New York: this was a fabrication.

"*Out Cry* concerns a brother and sister, trapped in the desperation and failure of middle age, and with no future. Tennessee was allowing Bill Barnes to ruin the play by casting a *young* client of his own [Michael York]. I was so appalled by Tennessee's weakness in not standing by Chuck, myself, and for that matter Paul Scofield, that I returned all the rights to Tennessee, saying that I wanted to have nothing whatsoever to do with it." Her letter to him has survived.

———

[*Handwritten, undated*]

GIVE UNTO CAESAR THAT WHICH IS CAESAR'S. Darling Tennessee. OUT CRY—or *Two-Character*—is your play, you wrote it. So if and when there was a moment you wanted me to co-produce it with a professional producer, and now you have changed your mind—I give it back to you—and all rights, moral, or in writing, have no meaning. Our friendship is far more important to me than anything else—so that's that, don't worry: I would never really hold anything of yours you did not want me to have. Isn't that what friendship is all about?

I enclose the letter [from] Floria [Lasky, Tennessee's lawyer] and Arnold Goodman [Maria's lawyer]'s answer. I will let the Scofields know the deal is off. And good luck with the New York production. God bless you, darling. Take care of yourself (please).

Love, Maria

Chuck [Bowden] is a wonderful friend to you, and don't forget it.

P.S. I don't want any codicils or anything. No jingle of 30 pieces of silver between us. No pay-off. Just love.

[On letterhead Hotel Elysée, 60 East 54th Street, New York, undated]

P.S. I'm enclosing the first draft of a rather confused poem I wrote this morning. Save it for me and I'll try to finish it whenever I get to England.

Speaking of poems, I accidentally left with your copy of *Duino Elegies*—it's in the Key West book-case and will get back to you some day.

EYES NEAR BLIND

I

Blind eyes are peaceful eyes
at least they look that way
as if they'd accepted the terms of their dark and quiet stay

Oh, but eyes near blind
are full of soundless but reverberant cries
of light, more light!
In flight
from king's seat and crime's mimicry
his panic whistles him down
precipitate corridors, suddenly so much darker than they had
seemed

So limitless, vaulted,
      with turnings before not known
this hall down which he staggers from his throne,

Ancestral carvings swept past, sarcophagi encountered,
stone blocked, iron barred,
till suddenly there's a crypt with its prie-dieu and candle-lit altar

He stops for prayer
as the lecherous queen, with disordered dress and hair,
demands that the Prince be summoned to her closet . . . .
(She dares not think for what reason, but images flash there
of thighs milk-white when a boy and groin where manhood grew.)
O dark, thou has thy mother much confused!

II

Blind eyes are peaceful eyes but eyes near blind
thunder with frustrate groping for
more light when light continually dims

Over the rain forest
and the still-water beach, hearing so distinctly
the false frivolities
of the marimba band at the cantina on the island
hearing even
each different inflection of breath

All watches of the night and of the day are now completed
by the blind
they wear an honorable medal of surcease
Oh, but eyes near blind
cannot appeal for peace . . .

Light will not, cannot rise
I think I hear their shouted prayer, their cry
O Father of fire, with fire put out my eyes!

T.W.

A very nice letter (the second) from Mr. Vivian Matalon at the Hampstead Theatre Club, re-affirming his wish to produce *Small Craft Warnings* there—I shall ask him "When?"

———

VIVIAN MATALON directed the first London production of *Small Craft Warnings,* which opened at the Hampstead Theatre Club on January 29, 1973.

———

General Delivery
East Hampton, Long Island

June 13, 1972

Dearest Maria:
    After a wild midnight ride in a rented car, driven by a California "surfer" high on "grass," I have come to a motel called "Driftwood" near the top

of Long Island and directly on the Atlantic and with an Olympic sized pool. But weather gray as stone this morning. And a disaster (potential) to report. When the luggage was unloaded, my manuscript case was missing. Frantic calls to hotel. No trace of it but possibility it is locked in the check-room. Nightmares about the loss. Woke at daybreak and called Bill Barnes. Now sitting waiting for him to call back if the ms. case has been recovered or not. Terrified the hotel staff decided to confiscate it and hold it for ransom. It held all my uncompleted stuff with no copies. So!

I will continue this after I get a report on the situation from Barnes. Fortunately Edward Albee lives a few miles from here and called twice yesterday to extend hospitality . . .

LATER.—Barnes recovered ms. case from hotel and it is now with me, flown up by plane. We have discovered an hotel with much more charm and a lovely view over the northern point of the island and will move there soon as its pool is filled, perhaps tomorrow. This evening having dinner with Albee and his friend, a Jesus freak who paints but won't show his paintings. Riding horses this p.m.

Address being so indefinite at the moment, best write me c/o General Delivery, Easthampton, Long Island. *Tout va bien.* Going out now to purchase a woolly sweater as it is quite chilly here, there are grouse and deer, it must be rather like Scotland, though not so craggy: Albee and I the only mad Lairds.

Albee has two dogs big as ponies and three cats and the Jesus freak is silent as a deaf-mute but has a beautiful face.

Love,

Hotel Elysée
60 East 54th Street
New York 22, N.Y.

July 6, 1972

Dearest Maria:

I don't know whether or not you wrote me at general delivery in Easthampton, Long Island. My trip there was simultaneous with the attack of hurricane Agnes. I only stayed three days and soon as I returned I took seriously ill and had to be hospitalized for surgery—was in the hospital ten days and am mending, now, but still very debilitated and shaky. I am leaving this weekend for New Orleans and the exhilarating re-union with Poppins who is in my apartment there taking care of Gigi.

I shall have to rest there a while before I resume my travels. I hope that

I can see you this summer when I am well. Vivian Matalon wants me in England for two weeks in July but that seems a bit early for me.

Now, darling, I have to take a hot bath and go back to bed. Please let me hear from you. I have a great deal to tell you soon as I am able.

Much love, Tennessee

[*Added in handwriting*] Hope all is well with you.

1014 Dumaine Street, Apt. B
New Orleans, La.

July 15, 1972

Dearest Maria:

I am sorry to have caused you any anxiety about my hospital experience. It was not so serious and I am definitely on the mend—have resumed swimming at the Athletic Club here in New Orleans and am in no further discomfort.

The household, however, is somewhat shadowed by tragedy. Poor Victor's mother (demented for years) died a couple of weeks ago in an institution. He didn't let me know till I'd been back two days and asked him why he had such a long face. However he has taken up a new hobby which is working with something called "Lucite." It is a liquid material that solidifies into milky white objects. He makes animals out of it. On my bedside table I found a fox, a rabbit and a rat of various shades of Lucite. Aside from color they were remarkably similar in appearance for three such different creatures.

It is quite, quite hot in New Orleans now and I am thinking of taking a trip to the hills of East Tennessee. . . .

As for "the play," I think it's the least of our problems and worries. You know I will handle our interests with the cogency of an old pro. I was happy and thrilled to get that lovely card from you and Paul [Scofield] in Switzerland. You've made a pair of good friends in Paul and Joy [his wife]. Did I tell you that in Purdue (an important university) I put together a new version of *The Two-Character Play* and had it read aloud in a big auditorium where I was supposed to deliver a lecture which I hadn't prepared—it held the house completely and afterwards we received an ovation. It would not surprise me if it should work out that there'll be *two* productions: one of the Bangkok *OUT CRY* in England, another of *Two Characters* over here, perhaps almost simultaneously. What a triumph over a long period of adversity!

Also this year there is going to be a 25th Anniversary revival of *Streetcar,* opening in Los Angeles and then going on tour, with two or three important actors.

Dakin's wife, mother-in-law and his adopted daughters have gone back to Texas . . . perhaps indefinitely. I should think so. And he is still running for the U.S. Senate in Illinois.

Persistence seems to be a family characteristic, among others.

I am sure that by now Peter is out of his depression and addressing the House of Lords. And the girls are having a lovely summer vacation at Wilbury.

Much love, 10

———

TENNESSEE received an honorary degree from Purdue University in Lafayette, Indiana. As part of the ceremony Olive Deering and her brother, Alfred Ryder, performed a reading of *The Two-Character Play.*

A Streetcar Named Desire was revived at the Ahmanson Theater in Los Angeles on March 28, 1973, with Faye Dunaway as Blanche and Jon Voight as Stanley.

———

Hotel Elysée
60 East 54th Street
New York

July 30, 1972

Maria dear:

What a helluva summer! As I observed to a luncheon companion, if we can get through August, we can survive a nuclear blast, we will have it made.

The only let-up in the heat is provided by the freeze from England, and you know what I'm talking about.

You are the last person I'd mistake for a fair weather friend.

I blame it all on Chuck Bowden. He has sold you a very bad bill of goods and you've bought it hook, line and sinker, to compound one cliché with another.

Well . . .

No matter about that. I have been called back from an apartment—unfurnished still because after three months Morgan-Manhattan Storage has still not released the stuff ordered—and from weather that was 92 in the moonlight—back from there to the Victorian Suite in this shrine to Tallulah

Bankhead to resume my acting career [in *Small Craft Warnings*]. The man playing Doc has once more dropped out of the part and the stage manager—a nice Mississippi fag but with such a lisp that he sounds like a river boat's coming into the landing—had been put in the part. I am taking over again for two weeks—when the leading lady [Helena Carroll] departs for Dublin and the Abbey Players. Then we either get the star we needed or we close after a respectable run of 4 and a half months. I plan—if I survive—to leave for Italy as soon as the tourist rush is over.

Did I tell you that a famous transvestite, Candy Darling of the Andy Warhol films, is now in the cast? She is quite brilliant in it, playing the part of a "compulsive groper" named Violet.

I am also writing my "memoirs" for Doubleday—so you'd better stay on my good side if there is one. I have already made some *guarded* references to you. . . .

I enjoy writing the stuff, I am knocking it out at an average of about 16 pages a day and—although I may have to emigrate permanently from the States when it is published—I feel there's a cool million in it!

It's about time I struck it rich with something. . . .

This evening Miss Rose is driving in for dinner. I'm taking her to a new restaurant on Park Avenue which is patronized mostly by senior citizens and where there is a dance-floor and an orchestra which plays popular music of the thirties and forties—she will be delighted and probably out-sing the vocalist.

A couple of days ago I tripped over a potted plant on somebody's pent-house terrace and am still covered with little abrasions—there are some who say that I was more potted than the plant, but that's the sort of story you'd get from Windham and Campbell. I am just an old gent who doesn't see well after sun-down. . . .

Love enduring! Tennessee

———

TENNESSEE'S *Memoirs* were published by Doubleday in 1975. Tennessee later complained that the publisher had wanted too many cuts and had wanted him to concentrate too much on his sensational sex life.

"I thought it ridiculous of Tennessee to publish the *Memoirs*. He gave me some galleys to read: I read them all, and put them in the wastepaper basket. When he asked for them, I told him that they were where they belonged."

In August Tennessee was an honorary judge at the Venice Film Festival. Maria joined him in Venice in order to meet Bill Barnes and Michael York and his wife, Pat. Also at the festival was the film director Paul Morrissey.

"Tony Smith, Tennessee and I were once at a cafe in downtown New York. A party of young people from Andy Warhol's Factory passed by and recognized Tony, but not immediately, to his relief, Tennessee. Eventually, of course, they realized who Tennessee was and invited us to see a film by Morrissey. I thought it was the most disgusting thing I'd ever seen, and refused to sit beside Tennessee and Andy Warhol. I sat behind. Tennessee said he could not enjoy any of the film, as he could feel my disapproval piercing his shoulder blades.

"In Venice, Tennessee had sat, night and day, in dark glasses. He often wore them, on account of his shyness. I finally became suspicious and asked him to take them off. He didn't want to; but when he did, I was appalled by his eyes: inflamed, red, and gummed-up. Perhaps it was the enormous amount of swimming he did, in pools that were frequently overchlorinated. I immediately called a doctor, who, when he finally appeared, said, 'And you, a writer, allow your eyes to get into this condition?' "

After Venice, Maria joined Peter on his yacht off the coast of Scotland.

[*Handwritten letter*]

Excelsior Palace Hotel
Lido, Venezia

August 26, 1972

Dearest Maria—

I simply can't take the pace of life here for more than two or three days longer without a collapse.

Billy [Barnes]'s party (the Paul Morrissey film crowd) are hysterical with rage at their treatment by the officials of the Biennale (festival). They have been shifted from room to room—yesterday Morrissey and Joe Dallesandro were exiled to the Danieli in Venice—Joe returns to the States tomorrow before his film [Morrissey's *Heat*] has been shown.

Sylvia Miles is furious at her lack of publicity—the only photographers who pursue her are the "paparazzi"—and it is more she who pursues them.

Billy is catching it from all sides—but remains cool.

The hotel personnel are insufferably insolent and I called the waiters at lunch yesterday a bunch of "stronze"—that favorite epithet of Magnani's.

My old nerves won't take the frenzied atmosphere here.

I shall probably fly back to the States, via London, in the next two or three days—since I am unable to sleep.

It all went to pieces after you and the Yorks left.

I hope you've found all well in Glasgow and Wilbury.

Much love—Tenn.

[*On letterhead Hotel Elysée, 60 East 54th Street, New York, postmarked New York, September 18, 1972*]

1014 Dumaine Street
New Orleans

Well, girl, life goes on, habitually, and I understand that you're back on the Lido, *en famille*! Lovely. Billy has delivered some Venetian *bijoux* for you in London to transport you with delight when you return.

My play *Small Craft* is being closed on me today.

I was informed that our lease on the theatre had expired and we were going to be replaced by a pair of jerks imitating Gertie Lawrence and Nelly Coward in a nostalgic tribute to their—whatever they did. For the past two performances I have been in such a rage that general terror prevails. Night before last I threw a glass off the stage: and also my reading glasses, just threw them right off. Luckily a friend seated in the front row retrieved the glasses. The audience (packed house) were delighted. And later when I sat down at a table with the bar-tender—I am playing the part of "Doc" who has lost his license but continues to practice clandestinely and who has just returned from delivering a baby, born dead, and the mother expiring from a hemorrhage as well—the bar-tender enquires of me: "Well, Doc, how did things go at Treasure Island?" (a trailer camp). My reply: "Better than how they'll go here at the New Theatre if they replace us with Nelly Coward, Monk!"—Well, today there is to be a conference to discuss a tour for this play. That slob Shelley Winters graced us with her presence last night and despite her chronic inebriation, she could recognize a big fat part for her in the play and it may turn out that we'll re-open on the West Coast with her. Oh—and I also delivered a diatribe against the management in my opening monologue. "A synonym for a manager in the theatre," I bellowed out to the audience, "is a con-man—and all playwrights are shits with their back to the wall. . . ."

You'll think I'm starkers, but, honey, I've had it in aces and spades for 10 years, no one to care for me here till lately Billy.

Say a little Russian prayer for me, love!

10

Hotel Elysée
60 East 54th Street
New York, N.Y. 10022

September 27, 1972

Dearest Maria:

A short note before bed.

Pat and Michael York are here. He has read twice for [Peter] Glenville and Miss Priss hasn't made up her mind. I refer to La Glenville. No. I realize he is doing the necessary thing, I'm just being bitchy because I feel so tired.

Anyway, tomorrow he will—Michael—read a third time with a remarkable (not well-known) young actress [Cara Duff-MacCormick], and this time for me. I don't think La Glenville really thinks a playwright should attend the readings of actors but I trust I have put him straight on that point.

Actually, there is nobody in America but Tony Perkins who could play Felice—with the possible exception of Richard Chamberlain who is busy with films. I can think of no one who could play the dual Felice, the actor-manager and the youth in the play [with]in the play—except Michael—and although I have personal reservations about Michael, I mean I don't feel quite sure I like him as much as I do Pat—he has an actor's aura of narcissism about him—I do think he will turn in a commanding performance such as no American actor could.

I guess tomorrow is "D" day. Either we pull it off—or I return to the writing of my memoirs. . . .

Love, 10

[*Added in handwriting*] Pat showed me some photos she took of us in Venice. You look lovely in them. I look OK from the shoulders up—but the rest (seated in a boat) makes it finally quite clear that I am a very *un*-stylish[ly] *stout*.

I've decided to go to Taormina to swim off as much as I can of that belly—which almost equals Lord Goodman's—without his brains.

[*On letterhead Hotel Elysée, 60 East 54th Street, New York*]

In transit again

September 30, 1972

Maria dearest:

A news bulletin: I am returning for a few weeks to Europe. Flying to Rome Tuesday evening: then after a day or two there, taking the marvellous night-express to Taormina, the one that crosses over the Straits of Messina by ferry-boat and by ten a.m. you are in Taormina.

It looks as if everything is now set for *OUT CRY* here. I bearded the lion in his den, [David] Merrick, and he likes the play, is crazy about the phenomenal young actress, whose name is Cara Duff-MacCormick—shades of Mrs. Patrick Campbell!—and about Glenville and has come around, now, to approving of Michael York, too. (At first thought him too British.) We are all now "coming to contract," as they put it in show-biz, and I know you'll be happy about this.

After pulling myself together (after these crises) on the beach at Taormina, I'll return by way of London—unless you join me a while in Sicily. Write c/o American Express, Taormina. As travelling companion I will have one Robert Carroll who is the most gifted young writer I know of in the States. Twenty-five and a vet of Vietnam (three years there) and altogether a gent and a find of the first order.

Will try to call you before leaving.

A bientôt with love, Tenn

[*On letterhead Hotel Elysée, 60 East 54th Street, New York, postmarked New York*]

Key West, Fla.

October 3, 1972

Dearest Maria:

In yesterday's letter I said that I was going to Italy to rest but now I am going to Key West to work instead. What changed my mind is a return of that eye-condition that you noticed in Venice, only worse. This morning I had real satchels under the eyes. I called my eye-doctor. He said, "I think you're retaining fluid."—If that's the truth, then what I am facing is a dropsical condition, a condition in which I wouldn't like to travel about Europe.

My new young friend—universally approved and liked by all who know me and wish me well here in New York—is glad to go to Key West with me, and I have phoned the house-tenant there, Dr. Lazarus, that I am coming, to have the pool filled with fresh water, and have enquired about my cat, Black Sabbath, whom he assures me is fine. I look forward to the peace of the patio and the studio and the pool-side, and I trust that when we are ready to open *OUT CRY* in January, you will be here to stand with us, since the play is yours, too.

Actually, I am hoping to ease the doctor out of the house in a few days, although I like him. I think that my friend and I want privacy to work in, for the few weeks we'll be there. He and Victor are still on the pay-roll, rightly. Victor has found his vocation, at last, in taking care of the New Orleans rental property and he did not sound at all disappointed when I told him on the phone that I was going abroad.

Actually, I think I wish that you could be here all during rehearsals. I think they are going to take place about November 15th (starting date) in Canada to help Michael [York] with taxes—for some reason.

So wouldn't it be nice if you could join me in Key West and then go to Canada with me and stay through rehearsals and opening?

I can't think of anything that would please me and help me more.

Much love, Tennessee

[*Postmarked Key West, October 17, 1972*]

Dearest Maria:

I am back in the little compound at Key West for a certain length of while, depending upon how quickly the plans for the *OUT CRY* production mature. When I left New York last Friday, everything had been verbally agreed upon but that legally indispensable signature [Merrick's] had not yet been set to the papers.

One Dr. Lazarus had been occupying the premises here while I was away and his iniquities are too many to mention. He had run up a phone bill of $243, which he had refused to pay despite the fact that he had been living there without rent and consequently my phone has been cut off from incoming calls. I had to drop a cheque for the full amount in the night-depository of the phone company to get service resumed today. I had only required of him that he take care of my cat: he did not bother to buy her cat-food although I had assured him the expense would be reimbursed: she has turned back into a wild creature, now, living on birds and lizards and hides behind the sofa when she is in the house. In order to get rid of him—I had given him four days notice that I was returning—I had to put him up as my guest at a motel for the week-end. When I stopped by there this evening to see that he had not over-stayed the week-end, I was told he had run up a large phone and bar bill there which they are billing to me.

All this is boring: but that is one Lazarus that Jesus would not raise from the dead, my dear. . . .

When I get bored with it here—there is no social life for me whatsoever in this town—I think I will fly out of the International Airport in Miami for Rome and then on to Marrakech or southern Sicily. I will be in better shape to travel as this place is quite restful—and still beautiful, despite the melancholy associations with temps perdus—or possibly because of them.

These random thoughts are only to send you my love.

Tenn.

[*On letterhead Hotel Elysée, 60 East 54th Street, New York, postmarked New York, November 12, 1972*]

1431 Duncan Street
Key West, Fla.
(phone: (305) 294-1801)

November 10, 1972

Dearest Maria:

I couldn't wire you this evening as I'd promised because it was not yet decided where to go. Now it appears that the play [*Out Cry*], according to Billy, will go to rehearsal in Canada late this month. He says there is an 85% certainty of this change of date: if it holds, we would have four weeks rehearsal in Canada. Then open at the Eisenhower Theatre in Kennedy Center or Memorial, whatever they call it, in Washington D.C. Then two weeks in Philadelphia and then into New York.—Am I dreaming?

So I will wire you this morning to see me later please. I have a very good feeling about the play, Michael and Cara Duff-MacCormick whom Merrick describes—and I agree—as a young Laurette Taylor. She is a lady from Virginia. I think that you will love her as you do Michael. I just now concluded my memoirs with the single line: "What a very strange year, between beginning and ending!" I am going back to Key West to rest and work and swim to get in some sort of condition. With my friend Robert Carroll. This evening we saw Françoise Sagan off on her return to Paris. She is lovelier than ever: and surrounded by very handsome young—what's the polite word for it? Deviates, I suppose.—One of them was a ravishing young Frenchman with a wild head of hair and one of them was a young "Black" who is probably the handsomest male I've seen ever: he took down my address and phone. And being totally incorrigible, I suspect that I will entertain him as royally as befits him and I can.—That is, if he calls before this week-end.

That formidable bitch Jo Healy is in hospital and she goes under the knife today for a possible "colostomy" which is an abdominal anus. They discovered today that she has an intestinal growth that may make it imperative.—

When she informed me of the misadventure by phone, I said to her: "Oh, no!"—She insists that I be at the hospital at eight this morning and says that Windham will be there, too. A strange encounter! He tells her that he is willing to accept it despite my "insults" to him.

After attending Jo's surgery and Donnie's alleged forgiveness, I must rent a car and visit Miss Rose, who is not at all well. She has recurrent spells of not being able to retain food and is going to undergo hospital examination.

This being the situation, I'd best remain in the States: Mother is also ailing, and Dinky has taken to riding a motorcycle about Illinois to improve his political prospects. Which can *only* be *improved,* even on a motorbike. . . . He sent me a big write-up with a photo of himself wearing a motorbike helmet adorned with the American flag and the name Dakin.—I doubt that he suspects that what he is really running for is the title or office of America's biggest eccentric.—Possibly that could be a successful campaign, in view of Tricky Dick's triumph this week.

Two impending honors: Early in December I am getting an honorary "Doctor of Letters" degree [University of Hartford] and am selected this year for outstanding playwright's award by something I'd never heard of called "The National Theatre Society."—Both occasions are early next month. Well, I have a tux and can still travel—Stateside, anyway.

In forty minutes the day begins officially with a "wake-up" call so I'd better prepare myself for it.

If Key West restores me enough, I will fly out of Miami to London to see you all—and escort Pat and Michael [York] here on a jumbo jet.

I am longing to see you.

With much love to you all, 10

Key West

November 16, 1972

Maria dearest:

The terrible *crise* involving getting Michael [York] into the States legally has taken its toll and I am still feeling unsettled.

Lovely as it is, the little compound in Key West does not have its once pacifying effect.

Actually I do not believe that there was a bit of intrigue in David Merrick, I am afraid the poor man simply could not conceive of anyone wishing to enter a country unlawfully and to pretend he wasn't there while rehearsing for three weeks.

Anyway, it has all worked out: we are due to start rehearsals legally on December the 17th.

What I would like to do, in a week or so, is to fly to London and stop at the Berkeley, the hotel with the pool, and pull myself together.

My young writer friend, the Enfant Terrible, is a typical artist, almost always "up-tight" over something and the something is often me. So I think I'll permit him to be up-tight alone for a while—and join me when I return to New York.—Of course this plan may be revised: it's hard to travel alone.

And I wonder if you would welcome my coming to London at this time: please advise.

Here's an amusing bit of news for you. Poppins—occupying my New Orleans apartment—is having an affair with a Methodist minister who has taken leave of his parochial duties to serve as a cook in a "gay" French Quarter restaurant.—This might work out the whole Poppins situation, and turn into a considerable financial savings for me, as well as an ideal alliance for Poppins.

I have had to change my Key West phone-number as persons unknown had run up a bill close to a thousand dollars on the old one.

The new phone number, and I confide it only to you and Barnes, is (305) 294-6769.

If I do go to London, I want to have a thorough medical check-up: there must surely be some physiological reason for my insomnia: and I must be in good shape for the play.

Much love, Tenn.

[*Added in handwriting*] Saw Françoise Sagan in New York, just before I left. She is lovely as ever.

Hotel Elysée
60 East 54th Street
New York

December 4, 1972

Dearest Maria:

I have tried to reach you by phone but that idiot maid of yours says "Out." [*Inserted in handwriting*] Only word in English she seems to know.

I really don't know the next step which is a symptom of nervous exhaustion or chronic apprehension.

The hounds seem to be on the traces of all seasons lately.

I suspect that I will have to forgo the visit to England and retire to New

Orleans for a while and the pacifying lethargies of "Mary Poppins" and Gigi. Also the Doubleday editor wants to start working with me immediately on my memoirs which look like telephone books of a big city, the boroughs Manhattan and Brooklyn.

I can't come to England in time for the seventh, as on that date I am receiving something called "the National Theatre Award"—and just yesterday I was presented with the honorary degree of Doctor of Literature. Today I am resting between the two gigs.

My young writer friend the Enfant Terrible has been mysteriously difficult these last few days. I think his three years in Vietnam and all that "grass" he smokes is making him "un peu dérangé"—a little period of separation seems to be in order since I must not be bugged while *Out Cry* is going on.

I plan to fly to Europe the day before the New York opening and to settle on a little farm and raise those goats and geese to avoid these "four more years."

[*Added in handwriting*] Wiring you today.

Much love, 10

Later: This letter didn't get off as I've been laid up—or down—with the flu for several days, receiving no phone calls and living on fruit juices.

Longing to escape from New York but am obliged to remain till the "National Theatre Award" ceremony tomorrow: then flying to New Orleans for what I hope will be a relatively pleasant recuperation: I think I've exhausted my nerves with all this New York activity.

I won't come back till after the first week of rehearsal or later. If Glenville leaves the script alone, I won't have to worry. I will certainly try to stay cool—the Enfant just passed through the living room rolling a joint of "grass"—then passed through again already stoned. . . .

I don't know how to cope with this sort of thing.

"Quack, quack," said the dying duck in the thunderstorm. . . .

————

MARIA, Peter and the children went for a holiday in Thailand, prompted by Tennessee's glowing reports.

"Natasha immediately got sunstroke, entirely through arrogant disobedience, and was sick all over the dining room. The waiters were unaccountably delighted. Peter took to his bed with a tummy upset. Pulcheria sulked, as we stared gloomily at Wats.

"We visited King Bhumibol's aunt, Her Royal Highness Princess

Chumpa, who spent whole evenings with Peter singing old Harrovian songs. Her husband had also been at Harrow. The servants crawled in and out on their haunches, since they were not allowed to have their heads higher than that of Her Royal Highness, who was all of four foot nine. She took me shopping for orchids, accompanied by two maids who shuffled alongside holding parasols over us. Although her palace was filled with the most beautiful and ornate antique Thai beds, Princess Chumpa showed us a plank of wood. This, she proudly declared, was where she slept.

"Pulcheria and I were so fed up that we spent the remainder of the holiday buying endless cages full of birds in the markets, which we then let loose."

———

[*Letter sent to Pattaya Palace Hotel, Pattaya, Thailand*]

Hotel Elysée
60 East 54th Street
New York

? 1972

Dearest Maria:

If I can get this letter off tomorrow it may reach you at the Pattaya Palace. How wise you are to go to that lovely beach resort outside Bangkok. Oliver spent all last summer there. His boy-friend Oot is there, hustling.

Look up Ed Headley right away if this reaches you in time. He's a charming American who runs the one good restaurant in Pattaya. It's lovely at night, on the water, with that rare thing in Thailand, really good food.

When you go into Bangkok, eat at the President Hotel: they even serve venison and the management is charming.

Glenville called me today with a very elated report on the first "run through." York and the girl gave great performances and are perfectly matched. He said the play had the quality and form of a poem and runs just the right time.

I think I've told you I'm coming to London January 24th for the previews of *Small Craft Warnings* at the Hampstead Theatre Club—staged by Matalon. It has received a good notice in a review of American theatre in a London magazine called *Plays and Players*.

I can only stay a few days as *OUT CRY* will still be touring before the B'dway premiere. Billy hopes you'll fly back with me: I doubt you'll be free to but hope so.

Jane and Tony [Smith] left me a lovely bouquet of white roses and I've written them a thank you.

I've been sequestered, most of the time since return to New York, by very bad flu.

Have seen only three rehearsals.

While in London want to stay at Berkeley the new hotel with an indoor swimming pool— according to Pat York.

A bientôt, j'espère.

Love, Tennessee

[*Added in handwriting*] I plan to fly to London again the day before *OUT CRY* opens. Find a sanctuary in Sicily and work for English theatre, if permitted. The press here is relentlessly hostile, I fear. I have had too much bad personal write-ups.

[*Postmarked Philadelphia*]

Philadelphia next
Hotel Barclay

January 19, 1973

Darling,

You must be home now from Thailand which you persist in calling Siam, confusing yourself with Gertie Lawrence [who played Anna in the stage production of *The King and I*] and Sexy Rexy [Rex Harrison, who played the King in the film *Anna and the King of Siam*]. It sounds like a wretched vacation. I'd say that Thailand is only for the natives—and for queer visitors with "yellow fever," as Oliver put it, and young monks in saffron robes.

Our *first* night [of *Out Cry*] in New Haven was disastrous but surprisingly we got an intelligent and respectful notice and tonight the actors pulled themselves together and turned in a lovely performance. The house was completely held and business was up from opening night.

You'll be happy to know that I have kept my cool through it all: have suffered some little nervous twinges of angina in the left chest but have uttered not a quack, quack, just concentrated all remaining force on the professional duties. Sunday we leave for Philadelphia to face, I trust, a more sophisticated type of audience. Then Washington for three weeks where we'll have a subscription audience of capital "fat cats"—we really won't hit the right audience till we come to New York.—I will fly to London while we're in "Philly"—I think on the 24th, stay till *Small Craft* opens [January 29]—and then fly back, I hope with you.

If all is looking well by the time of the New York premiere, I will stay for it: but then I intend to emigrate for an indefinite period. Get that peaceful little farm in Sicily with goats and geese and do whatever work is worth doing in the London theatre.—Civilization has really collapsed here under the reign of Nixon.

A funny thing happened last night here, the opening: as little Cara Duff-MacCormick, a stunning actress, made her entrance, her contact lenses popped out and she had to perform in Braille.

Michael is terrific. Glenville is giving me the first first-rate production I've had in about twelve years: these aging English spinsters are a formidable presence!

The Enfant Terrible is being an angel in this difficult time but I think he'd be better off doing his beautiful writing in Key West till it's time to fly abroad, March.

A bientôt, much love: 10

Please book me into the Berkeley, the new hotel with the swimming pool, on the 24th.

Recently Oliver visited New Orleans, stayed in my apartment—lost all traveller's cheques and Poppins had to pay his fare back to the Coast. It's rather alarming, how confused he seems now.

————

MARIA went to Washington to join Tennessee, and then to New York for the opening of *Out Cry* at the Lyceum Theatre in New York City on March 1, 1973. The play was directed by Peter Glenville, with Michael York as Felice and Cara Duff-MacCormick as Clare.

"It was evident that *Out Cry* needed more work from Tennessee. That was later rectified. Most of all, the fact that it was played by two very young and attractive people robbed it of its pathos and its desperation. It remains, however, the most beautiful and poetic play, and the most revealing portrait of the extraordinary spiritual and emotional closeness between Tennessee and his sister, Rose. When, years later, I went to see Rose to break the news of her brother's death, I saw on her dressing table a postcard written from Rome, which was Tennessee's last communication to her. It said, 'Dear Rose, I will be seeing you soon. Love, Rose.' Unconsciously signing himself Rose, he had finally made the two halves whole."

————

Vassilis Voglis, Maria, Maureen Stapleton, Tennessee and
Bill Barnes at Vassilis's flat in New York

Beverly Hills Hotel
Los Angeles

March 5, 1973

Dearest Maria:

I am sure you must know by this time that the sky fell on Chicken Little
in the form of devastating notices in the weeklics.

I had a couple of nightmares about it in Key West and then suddenly
regarded it as fait accompli and I honestly think Bill Barnes was more upset
than I was when he informed me that Merrick had closed the show.

Fortunately we had a week of radiant weather in Key West. I am now
in New Orleans and preparing to fly to L.A. for the next gig which is the
silver anniversary production of *Streetcar*—then a flight to Honolulu and
a Pacific & Orient cargo-passenger ship to Hong Kong.

Soon as he was removed from the pressures of show-biz, the enfant
terrible became angelic again. He is now waiting for me at the Beverly Hills
Hotel, I fly out the day after tomorrow.

It's rather nice to be confronted by nothing more definite than a long
ocean trip.

Laughlin wrote me a truly beautiful letter about the play and his eagerness to publish it soon as I get the script ready. He is really a man of such refined sensitivity [changed from "intellect"] and culture. [*Added in handwriting*] And *kind.*

Barnes wants me to go to another publisher for my book of short stories [*Eight Mortal Ladies Possessed*] but I really don't want to leave J. Don't you think I'm right?

One has to stop leaving people whom one loves. Or finally what are we left with?

I can't tell you what it meant to me to have you with me during those steps to the guillotine which really wasn't a guillotine at all, since you can't chop the head off a man already decapitated, can you?

Nonsense, Constance, on with it!

I will keep you posted. I fly to Hawaii the 27th and sail the 28th.

Such a sweet letter from Tatiana [Schvetzoff]. One of the loveliest things about you is your devotion to THAT WONDERFUL WOMAN.

Poppins just walked in with a huge collection of Oriental dishware and a wooden sculpture of two tigers in combat with an elephant—all purchased from a junkie on the street, I presume, from the rent-receipts. I took up a plate to examine the pattern and dropped it to smithereens on the floor with an expression such as one observed on the faces of those reading that blown-up notice in the Eisenhower Theatre in Washington. Then Billy rang up—and I was still too stunned to speak!

I mean how can you get Fujiyama and a complete fishing village on a plate, complete with snow-caps and boats and fishing-rods and flights of birds, all in prison gray on dirty white? Impossible. But there it was, and I dropped it—and sent him out to get me a bottle of wine, the only conceivable restorative at this moment.

See how astonishment on thy mother's face doth sit and the shattered plate on the floor—even Gigi seems stunned!

Occasionally one comes across a sensitive girl. I must quickly seal this letter before Poppins returns with the wine. . . .

Much love from the headless admirer, Tenn

———

"A SINGLE rave notice of *Out Cry* by Claudia Cassidy of the Chicago *Tribune* had been blown up and posted in the foyer of the theatre. Tennessee and I were most amused to see people reeling backward in astonishment from it, saying, 'Well, what play was she writing about, for God's sake?' "

———

[*Handwritten letter from Maria to Tennessee, undated*]

Dearest 10:

I nearly jumped out of my skin when I received your letter saying *OUT CRY* was off.

I was a bit suspicious, however, as I had heard not one word from Billy nor anyone in New York since my departure. I think Merrick is a [drawing of a farmyard animal]. He obviously did it ½-heartedly, just to get *Red Devil*—I wouldn't give it to him. [Merrick eventually produced *The Red Devil Battery Sign.*]

OUT CRY is such a strange, classic play, so beautiful. It could only be done by the best in the best possible circumstances. It should, as Chuck and I wanted, have been presented as a bonne bouche for a limited season, with Paul [Scofield], and everyone would have flocked. Also the Bangkok version is a better play, as we know.

Of course, J. would understand the play and love it. You really can't keep giving people things and taking them away all the time. I don't mind, because I love you and understand, and I think Chuck has behaved marvellously. But after all, J. has always been your publisher. Why should you suddenly go to another publisher for your short stories? It's utterly disgraceful even to consider such disloyalty. Disloyalty's the thing I hate most in life, except for deliberate cruelty, as my old friend Blanche would say. "Deliberate cruelty is unforgivable." So you can hardly wonder I'm not over-fond of the Enfant Terrible calling Tatiana an old witch, and saying you needed a trained nurse to look after you. Not someone like him. Get him! as Tony [Smith] said. I think I shall get Tony to go to the hospital in Scotland. Have just returned this evening. Tony would make all those damn Scots sit up in their kilts and bagpipes.

I'm terribly worried about his [Tony's] drinking. Jane seems totally terrorised by him, I fear, and unable to cope with those blue poached eggs he has for eyes, with the whites showing all the way around.

I felt so sad and disappointed about *OUT CRY*, but obviously Merrick was not going to nurse it along, or maybe the other notices killed it dead, the daily ones I saw were rather good. Of course poor Billy will feel very responsible as this was very much his idea, this production.

. . . No, darling, J. is not kind. He has many other qualities, but kindness has no place there. The great mistake he made was thinking I loved him for his money. Poor man, how sad he is such a coward—and when I gave him the letter back he wrote to Mummy when we became engaged, he said,

"You are the only person that has ever made me believe in God." Just because I didn't need, want, or even like his dough.

Lord Goodman took me to a big gala at Covent Garden. We sat in a box (he has an especially large chair the management provides for him). The Queen was there in yellow chiffon and a tiara-boom-de-ay, looking delicious. The ballet was ghastly, another version of *Sleeping Beauty* with awful clothes and sets. I adore Lord Goodman. He is kind, and so funny. I always feel I'm going out with someone from *Alice in Wonderland* when I am with him. DON'T even consider leaving your publisher—DON'T go around like a dying duck in a thunderstorm—See Amazement On Thy Mother Sits—SPEAK TO HER, HAMLET!!—take care of yourself, no one else is about to, that's for sure—as I am out of town.

God bless you, write,

Love, Maria

[*On letterhead On Board S.S.* Oronsay, *postmarked Yokohama, Japan*]

Yokohama

April 4, 1973

Dearest girl:

We are defecting from the Cherry Blossom (Geriatric) Cruise at the first port of call, Yokohama, and continuing the next day by air to Hong Kong in order to intercept my dear friend Norman Wingrove (radio newscaster there) before he leaves for holiday in England. I will give him your address as I feel certain that you will find him irresistibly charming: a real gent. After a couple of days there—this will madden you, perhaps—we are flying to Bangkok where we'll settle down to work at a cottage-with-pool on the beach at Pattaya. L'Enfant's malaise disappeared immediately he quit shore at L.A. and he's turned quite angelic again and is working assiduously on his novel called *Old Children.* Darling, I have no fixed date of return to the States. I feel that I am totally washed up there and must start a fresh career in some English-speaking place like Australia or England. A ghastly write-up (sponsored, insisted upon, almost, by Bill Barnes) has appeared in *Playboy* [by C. Robert Jennings, April 1973] and I feel that it has completed the annihilation of my character in the States, can only hope it isn't read in London or Sydney. Do you know that Billy left L.A. the day before my birthday without even a greeting card? I am beginning to wonder if he is under Audrey's thumb, secretly. But that sounds paranoiac, a mood that will probably pass.—You have no idea how dreary this passage has been. Passengers all over eighty—crones, my dear—foul food served by detestable East Indians. We have been virtually immured in our cubby-hole cabin. On the wine-list were three Burgundies and two Bordeaux—rien de plus—and the pièce de resistance at each meal is a flaming hot curry that scalds what's left of my innards. Nevertheless, I feel fairly well and terra firma will never seem more welcome.—I am most concerned how things are going with you, domestically, emotionally, and so forth. The venom, the vindictiveness, the betrayals and callousness of this world incline one at times almost to anticipation of the oblivion to come. This is not the honk of a dying duck in a thunderstorm, honey, but the howl of an enraged beast at bay!

Thank God for a few, very few, such as you.

Mailing address c/o Ed Headley—the restaurant at Pattaya, Thailand.

Much love, dear heart, Tennessee

President Hotel
Bangkok

April 12, 1973

Dearest Maria:

We're in your favorite capital of the world!!

The program is to proceed to Pattaya in a few days and take a cottage with pool and stay there till I've finished the memoirs. [*Added in handwriting*] And the Enfant his novel *Old Children*.

Then descend upon "the continent down under"—Sydney, Australia— where I will attempt to launch a new theatrical career in an English-speaking country.

There has been unbroken silence from Barnes but the P.R. man from West Coast *Streetcar* wrote me a lovely letter—*Streetcar* there out-grossed any show in the country the second week, he said, and he attributes it to my "spectacular appearance."

For the Australian gig, I'm preparing three one-act plays and writing myself into the first one as an "aging playwright" attending a reading with an "aged director."

If I meet with discouragement in kangaroo-country, we'll proceed by air to Italy and try to get hold of "a farm to raise geese and goats."

The Enfant says he wrote you a letter promising to send you a full-grown "gibbon" from Pattaya—don't be unduly alarmed. They're not allowed out of Siam. Would you be interested in a wallaby instead? That's a miniature kangaroo.

Please let me hear from you.

"All's well that doesn't end. . . ." (?)

Much love, 10

[*Two pages of typescript*]

c/o World Travel Service, New Road, Bangkok, Thailand
(American Express representative)

Material: April 18, 1973

For the second time in my life, and unquestionably the last one, I took and survived a direct flight from Bangkok to Istanbul, but for the first time I find Istanbul very beautiful and intriguing. It's the difference, I suppose, between stopping at the Hilton, as before, and at the Park, as now.

Our double looks over the Bosphorus, the Golden Horn, you know: sea fog but ships and birds faintly visible through it.

We went to bed immediately after checking in, about two p.m., and slept through the alarm clock going off at seven-thirty. But I woke at nine-thirty and it was worth it. A lovely old-fashioned dining-room, also looking over the "Horn," an old pianist on a platform at the far end of the big room, playing old tunes. An old waiter full of old jokes: cats coming in and stalking confidently among the tables for hand-outs from the diners and not being chased away, beautiful spangled cats, black, yellow and white.

I was still too tired to eat more than a bit of the excellent food: and we went back to bed right after dinner: woke at six a.m. and there was quick room-service.

But I am still suffering from jet-lag and the writing will show it.

This will have been my second time around the world and although I've not liked sight-seeing since my first trip abroad with Grandfather in 1928, I have always felt places strongly. They get into me without any effort.

In an hour we return to the air-port for a flight to Rome, which remains a must on my trips abroad despite the sadness of change that I find there lately: the suffocating traffic, the noise, the strikes, the up-tightness of the Romans, such a shock after the lovely times there in the late forties and fifties. Still, the city is "the rose-red city, half as old as time."

No, I am not about to write you a travelogue today, that's hardly what you want from me.

We're headed back to New York. Having seen the West Coast Silver Anniversary of *Streetcar,* I have now decided I must pay my respects to the one in New York [April 26] with Rosemary Harris, directed by Ellis Rabb.

I suspect the critics will be hard put to disparage the production (at Lincoln Center, the Vivian Beaumont) but I have a strong premonition that they will find fault with the play. But I know it will be really me, not the play itself, which will move them to bare their claws, if their claws need baring when I come up again.

Yesterday, probably drunk, I mused to myself: "*Streetcar* is the American Play of the Twentieth Century or I've lost my mind. Or never had one to lose." How's that for the arrogance of an old man?

I even went on to "muse" that "*Streetcar* and *Cat* are the TWO best American plays of the century—so far . . ."

And do you know I believe it?

But it's nearly all over now, the great time of creative power. I want to go on writing for the theatre but in other English-speaking theatres than Broadway or even off-Broadway.

For a while, during the whirl-wind round-the-world trip, I entertained the thought of trying a come-back in Australia, but then it seemed too far. In Hong Kong my dear friend Norman Wingrove—who was departing for London the same day we were flying to Bangkok—suggested to me that I work in the regional theatre of England, such as the Bristol Old Vic or even in the Hampstead Theatre Club or the Royal Court again.

A great deal rests with the Enfant.

Things hit a rather awful climax between us in Bangkok. He wanted a separate room, and then a different hotel. I said: "You find me intolerable." He said: "I find you repulsive."—And I said, going into my Blanche bit, "Not as repulsive as you'll be a year from now."

It was then that we agreed to part company when we got home—I mean stateside.

I honestly don't know if the quarrel was that important, if either of us meant a thing that we said.

He charms me as much, as deeply, as ever. But I know that the life-style which he wants, and probably requires, is not quite one that I could survive anymore. You see, I had my rough times early and for a long, long time. I can't go back to them now. I can't settle down even for a month in a steaming hot hell-hole like Pattaya in the hottest season of the year in an ugly bungalow.

We spent a day looking at them there, and I think my refusal to accept one, knowing damned well I could hardly be expected to live

[The typescript ends here, at the bottom of the second page.]

[*On letterhead Hotel Elysée, 60 East 54th Street, New York*]

Key West

April 25, 1973

Maria, love:

A long letter from you was among the mail Billy brought me yesterday, the day after the round-the-world whirl, fastest ever made except by a witch on a broom, stopping nowhere except a few days on a boat between Honolulu and Yokohama, all the rest by air, just visiting hotel rooms in places for a night only.

It was absolute hell but I feel that I have been cleared of "customs" at all of those frontiers.

I have just completed a long, good morning's work and am writing only to tell you that "The Strangest Kind of Romance" has come to a close. He [the Enfant Terrible] has his continuing ticket to San Francisco. I'm staying here only through the New York *Streetcar* which opens on Thursday, then alone to Key West—for even man must rest. . . .

It's very lucky, you know. Along with your letter was one from Floria Lasky saying that there was a new tax-law by which "The Rose Isabel Williams Foundation" (of which J. is a trustee) has to immediately make a "grant" or be subject to taxes that would wipe it out. And the Enfant is a writer and a good one and eligible for this grant.—"Sometimes there's God so quickly."—He'd torn up every pay-check I gave him for a month and has nothing in pocket but some Italian lire and Thai bahts.

You'll doubt my word for this, but it was the only one since Frank that I cared about. And yet I am glad it's finished.

I'll write a true letter soon as I get my head together again.

A very beautiful letter from Jane [Smith], enclosing St. Francis' "Canticle to the Sun" both in English and [in] Italian. The letter was also written in both languages.—Beautiful but spooky.—

Baby, the Scots couldn't take Tony [Smith], with or without his boxes. (I mean the black ones he sculpts.)—I'm afraid only dear Jane can bear that beautiful cross. . . .

Love, 10

———

JANE SMITH recalls: "Tennessee respected Tony's art but didn't understand it. He preferred impressionist paintings."

———

Key West [crossed out]
Hotel Elysée
60 E. 54th Street
N.Y.C.

May 8, 1973

Maria love:

You don't recover from a failure like *OUT CRY* and I am still very depressed.

I feel like my writing career is washed up. I go on writing but it means nothing to me.

The revivals of *Streetcar* received lavish praise but it's no real comfort as my only real joy in writing is continuing with it.

The round-the-world trip was a preposterous disaster. When I got back, Mother was desperately ill. I had to spend a week in St. Louis with her. She had quit eating—probably thinks the food's poisoned: begs me to take her to the south of France. She puts up a wonderful front. Very brave.

I can't go through it.

I run back to Key West.

Physically I seem to be in mysteriously good shape but I am in a dying duck mood which I've got to get out of.

Billy wants me to take a house on Long Island for the summer but I doubt that would work. New York suburban. I think I ought to go to Aix-en-Provence and take a cure. I love Provence and the Carlton Hotel in Cannes.

The Russian cultural attaché has invited me to attend a world congress of writers in Moscow but I don't feel in the mood for it.

Maybe after the congress—I could go there independently.—I hate "meetings" and "agendas." And conducted tours.

I will have talked to you on the phone before you get this dying duck letter.

Any news of the Yorks? And how is your domestic situation?

Things will *surely* get better! God is with us still.

Much love, Tenn

[*Added in handwriting*] So this is "dying duck" letter—just returned N.Y. Feel better here. Could you persuade Zeffirelli or Gore to find me a place in Amalfi?

———

MARIA had realized immediately when she met the Enfant Terrible that it was a disastrous and destructive liaison, which sapped Tennessee's energy and time and would lead to nothing but torment for him.

———

Hotel Sirenuse
Positano

May 26, 1973

Well, dearest Maria, it appears that you are right but if you knew how wretched I am about the whole thing and how desperate the situation is, you'd wish you were wrong, I hope.

You know, he has kept alternating between great sweetness to me—mostly in New York where I have the protection of Billy and others—and down-right beastliness of behavior which makes it all but impossible for me to go out with him in public. He goes out of his way to be rude to everyone. Yesterday we were invited to lunch at Zeffirelli's and he ignored the whole company—just lay there chain-smoking. Franco whispered to me, "Maria a ragione" [Maria is right]. Well, you have a pretty good batting average at perception and this time you batted one thousand.

The trouble is that he plays on my sympathies and on my acute loneliness. You really don't seem to know how awful it is to be alone at my age—and "gay." He makes himself so pathetic at times and I remember his years in Vietnam, his background as the ninth child of a West Virginia coal-miner, out of all touch with his family and with no friends to keep up with.

Still I am just not well enough to bear it. So what do I do?

I have already, through [the painter] Vassilis [Voglis]—the Greek friend of John Cromwell—taken a large apartment in a palazzo near the beach. I was to move in tomorrow but now the proprietors are putting me off, saying that the present tenants aren't ready to move out for five or six more days—their car has broken down, etc., etc. And last night as we entered the hotel dining room, the maître [d'] addressed him as "Signorina"—quite impertinently. We went straight out and had a horrible dinner at a little restaurant down the street. I have a room to myself but still he coughs and bangs around half the night in his room adjoining and I get very little sleep.

I had offered him his choice of Tangiers or Positano—it was his choice to come here and now he hates the place and speaks of himself (to people)

"Tennessee during
our last visit to
Positano, 1973"

From left:
Eli Wallach,
Natasha, Maria,
Anne Jackson,
Gore Vidal and
Howard Auslin
at Franco
Zeffirelli's house
in Positano,
1980

as my "hired companion" and brags about the fact that he was a street-hustler in New York.—A bit more of this will kill me! I am not well enough and I can't work in this condition.

There is no sign of a substitute person, either through Franco or John [Cromwell] and I can't keep packing and moving about alone.

Well, you get the picture, very thunderstorm with a lot of quack-quack in it . . .

Why don't we meet somewhere like Cipriano? I have some nice clothes and can make myself acceptable in any society. It is some society that I need right now, and some respectable living conditions.

Would you be an angel and call me here or write me special delivery through Cromwell? I feel that I have called on your assistance too much in my life but there is scarcely a soul beside you who seems to be concerned with my circumstances.

I am prepared to send the boy home, he has over a thousand banked in New York and so he would not be stranded. It is like kicking out a bad child but I think at this point a bit of self-preservation has to take precedence.

Franco is preparing to do *Camille* with Liza Minnelli. I told him that no matter how well he did it, it would inevitably be compared to Garbo's classic *Camille.* He pretends to despise Garbo. He has given me the present script to read and it is painful—of course I shan't tell him so—very stilted and the part of Camille simply common.

With all love, 10

Did Pulcheria get my wire dispatched from Rome and was her birthday pleasant? How I wish that I had followed the original plan and flown to London—I should have known you would have gotten me in somewhere. But Billy said it was risky and booked me into the Lancaster in Paris.

[*On letterhead Le Sirenuse, Positano, Italy*]

Palazzo Murat
Positano, Italy

May 31, 1973

Dearest Maria:

This is the last day at the hotel: this afternoon we're moving into a large apartment in the Palazzo Murat—that will be the address and do please use it, I am desperately lonely and fighting off depression against unfavorable odds.

John Cromwell and Vassilis Voglis have been wonderful to me. We've been to dinner twice at their house and they arranged for the apartment. They all know and understand the problem with the Enfant Terrible. He is a typical schizoid, I fear. Capable almost exclusively of sympathy with himself. I hate saying this, and am not saying this to please you. I know you don't understand how I became involved, which is natural. The first few months were no indication of what was to come. But soon as trouble arrived in the form of the play [*Out Cry*], the sweetness, true or affected, disappeared and he became a spoiled brat.

He [Zeffirelli] gave me a copy of his film [script] *La Dame aux camélias*. It is a beautiful script but I am very disturbed by his apparent determination to put Liza Minnelli in the role of Camille. She imitates her mother, has a bizarre face with little chin and much nose and teeth—and she is described in the script as "the most ravishing beauty in Paris."—I have invited him to dinner at the new apartment when he returns from Rome and I hope I can persuade him to think of someone like Geneviève Bujold instead. She got an Oscar—really deserved—for *Anne of a Thousand Days*—she read twice for the girl in *OUT CRY*. (Glenville refused to let me hear the readings.) I found her even more beautiful than on screen when I met her at Billy's.

I have not yet opened my great box of memoirs which has been around the world with me. I will open it tomorrow when I am settled. I have an interesting new title for it: *Flee, Flee This Sad Hotel*—it is a quote from Rimbaud.

Hotel is a metaphor for life.

Yesterday the Enfant Terrible was talking persistently about a wish to kill himself, all through our solitary dinner. I finally got fed up and said, "Oh, you mustn't do that, it would please too many people!"

Billy is coming abroad this summer and I hope we can all meet at Cipriani when Venice is warm and Positano is hot. I don't mean "all"—I meant you and Billy and I.

How was Pulcheria's birthday? Did she get the wire I sent from Rome on my way here and the trousers you were to buy for her?

Everything is going to work out rather quickly *chez moi*.— Since he [the Enfant] has over a thousand in a New York bank and his novel is practically finished, the resolution—however triste—is not, at least, an economic disaster for him.

And yet I know it's true when he says: "Baby, I've got nobody but you in the world."—But wasn't that his choice?

Quelques mots, je te prie!

Much love ever, Tenn sans pen

Palazzo Murat
Positano

June 7, 1973

Dearest Maria:

It was so good talking to you last night at Carlino's new hotel [San Pietro in Positano]—we had not been able to get the call through on the phone here at the apartment. I was worried to hear of your eye trouble, having had so much myself over the years. I trust that it has now cleared up OK.

Carlino's new hotel is not "Sad." It is quite a fantasy with huge terraces and view down to Capri. He has two cute little penguins as pets in a little pool built for them. They know that the sea is underneath and whenever the outside elevator door opens they come scrambling toward it hoping for a descent to the beach. We dined with Carlino's lady friend Lilianta who owns the Hotel Poseidon and a Bavarian contessa and it was a lovely evening.

There seems to be a break down of communications with Billy which is very troubling to me. Nearly a week ago he called me—I told him that a large section of my memoirs was not in the box when I opened it and he promised to send it at once along with an earlier draft of a short long play [*The Latter Days of a Celebrated Soubrette*] I hope to produce next season off-Broadway or possibly at a London "theatre club"—the Easthampton has a fine new director, Matalon having been deposed. I met the new director at Chuck Bowden's not long ago.—I suppose Billy is a bit bored with an old and hapless client but I had grown to count on him and am naturally distressed to have no word from him except the short call which only concerned a South African production of *Small Craft Warnings.*—To work well I need a feeling of interest beside my own. Nevertheless I have completed editing all the memoirs that were in the box and I feel that the play, which will include a curtain-raiser, is going to be touching.

"You know who" [the Enfant] got a good ticking off this morning. When I entered the kitchen the kitchen table was swarming with ants because a jar of honey and a bowl of sugar had been left open on it—has been sulking all day, tant pis.—I've found a very good cook. She is an unmarried mother of a three year old girl and is rather sad about it but she prepares a good dinner for us and can serve nicely when we have company. Yesterday I permitted him to do the shopping—she had given him a list. Well, he got everything wrong, including a sack of peas it would have taken her an hour to shell instead of the can she'd requested.—She was unnerved and the dinner turned out badly which was most unfortunate since I was entertaining John Cromwell and Vassilis.

Franco seems to be away. Probably in Rome about the *Camille* picture.—I think you might feel a little isolated there. Why don't you take a nice room in the hotel section of this building? It has very few steps to the beach. We could lunch out every day and have dinner in.—There has been sirocco the past few days with rough sea and the fine red sand of the Sahara makes the air heavy—but weather changes quickly here. This weekend, Sunday I think, I'm going to take the boat to Naples for a couple of days to have some things photo-statted, my watch repaired and some prescriptions filled.—You need a change now and then if you take a place for the season.

Did any notice of Jane Bowles' death [May 4] ever appear in the London papers? What a pig Paul is to have left it unannounced for so long. I'm afraid all that kif has dehumanized him a bit. Let's have a few *legible* words from you!

With much love, Tenn

Billy said he wanted me to join him in London about June 24th to meet Claire Bloom which [*sic*] is having a big success there in Ibsen's *Doll's House*. She is eager to do an English revival of *Streetcar*—I've heard good reports of her work but have never seen her.

Perhaps you could come here for a week and we could fly up to London together. I enclose a brochure of the palazzo—only a bit romanticized.

From present indications the Enfant will be returning economy class to the States in about a week—meanwhile we observe a polite formality to avoid violent discord.

———

A REVISED version of *The Gnädiges Fräulein* was *The Latter Days of a Celebrated Soubrette*.

In June 1973 Maria went to Positano and stayed with Franco Zeffirelli in his villa.

"Tennessee had given the Enfant Terrible his ticket back to New York, with some money, and in the meantime Tom Field, another travelling companion, had arrived from England. However, the Enfant Terrible refused to leave, and hung around Positano in order to embarrass Tennessee."

———

[*From Tangier, Morocco*]

July 30, 1973

Dearest Maria:

I have two or three unmailed letters to you in this single room. I thought they were too down-beat. No good laughs this summer, and no one really to talk to but Paul Bowles who prefers not to talk since it distracts him from his pipe of kif.

The insomnia's been worse than ever before, I sleep about two hours a night and then get up to work on a thermos of black coffee. And *The Red Devil Battery Sign*, a very fierce play which I soften with "presentational values" and *mariachis* dividing each short, fierce scene with lovely Mexican songs that I remember.

Tom is a very sick boy. He tells me—and has scars on the back of his neck to prove it—that he was operated on a year ago for something called Hodgkin's disease, a malignancy of the lymph nodes. Since lymph nodes protect you from infections, and he has had this operation, followed by radiation, he is continually subject to any germ about—and when we went to Gibraltar a few days ago for some supplies from the chemist, he got a bug that affected his stomach and intestines so badly that he eats nothing but soup and his pretty face is haggard.

I've done a fool thing, paid over a thousand dollars to rent a charming villa on "The New Mountain." And now I doubt that Tom is well enough to help me manage it. I doubt he will even be able to drive the rented car to the beach. I think under these circumstances he'd better fly back to London—he is continually sighing for his mom and his "flatmates"—and I'd better have Billy B. join me here for a few days while the script is typed up: then fly with him to Madrid, spend a few days in the lovely old Palace Hotel, visit the Prado and feast on Goya and Velázquez, see the Yorks if they are willing to see me—then fly home, too.

If this program is followed, maybe you could join us there in Madrid. I have that lovely color photo of you, Pulcheria and Natasha in a Venetian gondola and I look at it frequently to help me through this lonely summer.

Much love, 10

[*Added in handwriting*] I'll call you when I've moved.

[*On letterhead Hotel Elysée, 60 East 54th Street, New York, postmarked New York, September 12, 1973*]

Dearest Maria:

This is the ninth consecutive day of a record-breaking heat wave on "the eastern seaboard" of the States. I got away, fortunately, for Labor Day week-end (four days) at Montauk, Long Island, but had to return here last night to find the heat unabated.

I am worried sick about Oliver. Of course I do agree with you that he plays upon my sympathies and that it was sort of unfeeling to press upon me the "photo-biography" which was the last thing I need in this world. Oliver's feeling for me has always been ambivalent, and often quite hostile, and even if I wanted a book of photos myself, I am not sure I would wish to be exposed to his "text" upon the subject of photos. However—

So much must be accepted in the honor of old friendships. . . . And I know that I am at least as difficult as the Professor.

I think the Duchessa probably thinks of me far more.—Has she jetted back to that leprosarium in the Himalayas? I think God has called her there.

I am trying to "get it together" after that dreadful summer, which is still going on.

Air pollution here is approaching "danger level," New Orleans threatened by hurricane Delia—and I may fly to the North Pole.

I say "Christ!"—with reverence: may he bless you and yours.

Love, 10

[*Added in handwriting*] P.S. Heat at last broken. Miss Rose had dinner at the Plaza with me and a very nice TV producer and the following dialogue occurred:
Producer—They say that I look like your brother.
Rose—No.
Producer—I have a sister named Rose. Isn't your name Rose?
Rose (very quick)—No, my name is Evelyn Develyn Dakin!
(Exeunt omnes.)

———

"TENNESSEE adored to take Rose out, and she behaved perfectly, but she had some very strong ideas. On one shopping expedition Tennessee became more and more exasperated as he offered her beautiful dress after beautiful dress.

" 'No thank you, I don't desire it.'

" 'But Rose! This one is exquisite on you!'

" 'No thank you, I don't desire it.'

"And that was that."

"Simonetta was the elder daughter of Nina, Duchessa Colona di Cesaro, and had by now inherited her mother's title. She went to India to look after lepers, got scratched, was rushed back to Switzerland, and never looked after lepers again."

———

[*On letterhead Hotel Elysée, 60 East 54th Street, New York, postmarked U.S. Postal Service, September 21, 1973*]

In transit

September 19, 1973

Dearest Maria:

Isn't it horrible, just after your call I discovered among the boxes shipped down from Manhattan photograph after photograph of poor dear Anna [Magnani]. I've never been so close to a great actress except Laurette Taylor. They say that heart disease is the biggest killer, but I think it is loneliness.

Do please visit me in the States but wait till I have a chance to settle down somewhere.

Merrick has bought *Red Devil* but has not yet announced it, scheduled it, or actively set it up for production and I have misgivings. . . . But haven't I always?

I woke at two a.m. after two hours sleep, did a bit of work, and am much too tired and depressed to write a longer letter.

Much love, Tennessee

[*Added in handwriting*] Please say a prayer and have a novena for Anna. I shall drop in the shrine of St. Jude today and light a candle for her.

Next day—Having swum 26 lengths feel better & my mind is functioning enough for it to occur to me that you might have the Merricks over some evening and perhaps use a bit of Russian Tartar intrigue to fathom David's true intent—and impress him with the moral necessity I have of there being a definite announcement in press. It would give me necessary assurance to continue work on the play.

Mrs. [David] Merrick is a lovely person & spoke of you very warmly when I lunched with them at Pinewood Studios.

Love again Tenn

———

"THE THEN Mrs. David Merrick was a charming woman who, like me, had been a ballet dancer. We had a lot in common."

Anna Magnani died of cancer in Rome on September 26, 1973, aged sixty-five. Tennessee sent twenty dozen roses for her coffin. Later, he gave Maria some notes written over the years for a piece about Magnani:

It is impossible to have what is properly known as an interview with Anna Magnani, that is, for an American visitor to Rome. She does not seem to speak nor to understand a single phrase of English. When she is addressed in that language a look appears on her magnificently expressive face that puts an instant close to the attempt at conversation. It is a look of near panic. Anna Magnani has evidently had some unpleasant experience at one time or another with the American breed of journalists and writers. She regards them now in the way that a child does a dog that is likely to play too roughly. She likes them. She is not at all unfriendly. Wary is the word for Anna!

I succeeded in seeing her in Rome only after assuring her director and closest friend, Roberto Rossellini, that I was not going to interview her, that I was not even an American journalist but was merely someone who had been terribly profoundly moved by her art. This was not an evasion of the truth nor in any sense an exaggeration of it. It is not often that I have been terribly profoundly moved by acting on the screen. By Chaplin and by Garbo in this country: only by them. In France by the new young actor Gérard Philipe: only by him. In Italian films I have been stirred deeply by a number of films, not all of which were the work of Rossellini and Magnani, but of their performers it is certainly only Magnani who sinks the claws in the heart.

———

[*On letterhead The Beverly Hills Hotel, Beverly Hills, Calif.*]

Hotel Elysée
60 East 54th Street
N.Y.C.

September 27, 1973

Dearest Maria:

I am out here on the Coast to pay hommage to Eva Marie Saint as Miss Alma in *Summer and Smoke*—also to encounter a pen-pal who has written me several intriguing letters enclosing color photos & who is a novice playwright who studied under the late William Inge. My God, how many old friends are turning to "the late"—lately.

A propos of that subject, Bowden and I organized a beautiful requiem mass for Magnani in the Lady Chapel of St. Patrick's Cathedral. It was well-attended. Maureen Stapleton and Natalia Murray were there and about a score of strangers and the altar banked with flowers. After the formal service and communion, I stood up front and made a little reminiscent speech about all those midnight tours that the Horse and I made with Magnani, with her packages of food for the stray cats of Rome—Forum, Coliseum, Villa Borghese—it was a nightly ritual with her, you know, she made no secret of her preference for animals over humans. At the end I said: "I trust that the apparition of a hungry Roman cat is seated among us today at this celebration of the passing of a great spirit, our dear Anna."

There was a huge obituary with two photos of Anna, one a "still" from *Rose Tattoo*—and the next day there was a photo of the big crowd outside the church in Rome and an account of the ceremony. Like an appearance of the Pope!

Last night—W. H. Auden died in Vienna. I called Isherwood at once, he was very shaken. He called this morning to invite me to dinner day after tomorrow. Pen Pal is driving me out to Oliver's for dinner tonight: I'm stuck here without "wheels." Billy B. [Barnes] has a rental car but is constantly scooting about on private errands . . .

I think maybe I'll rest a while in Key West after seeing the transfer of *Streetcar* to Broadway middle of this week.

I sent a long wire to Lucca and I called Gerald Road but got no answer—suspected you'd gone to Rome with Franco. Right? I hope so.

Miss Fuckaway [Faye Dunaway] is on the coast, too, and I think she'll be my date for opening tomorrow night—Arthur Williams is having a swim with me this p.m.—this is turning into something like a social calendar of no consequence in London—sooo . . . . . .

God help us all—Much love, Tennessee

1431 Duncan Street
Key West, Fla.

October ?, 1973

Dearest Maria:

God knows that fearful events are taking place on your side of the pond. Why don't you clue me in with a bulletin now and then?

I've had a couple of quiet weeks here in Key West with Poppins. He's really changing much for the better, has the air and deportment of a responsible young man and has learned to cook quite well.

New Directions has brought out a lovely book of *OUT CRY* as I revised it after [Peter] Glenville's abortion.

A really beautiful jacket and perfect proof reading and printing

At the moment I have no plans except to enter the kitchen and eat a cold breast of fried chicken—life is full of little pleasures like that, and so we hang on.

I miss you.

Much love, 10

Sorry to have delayed this letter. The Texas appearance proved to be a terrific experience: 5,000 students in audience for reading and got a great reception. Somebody gave me a lovely silver (Italian) crucifix, another gave me a translucent blue Mexican amulet with a ram designed on it for Aries. Then the next day we toured the archives where all of my old short stories and poems are collected: family pictures that date back to Dad at age four.—Now I'm briefly back at the Elysée to attend a Drama Desk luncheon today. After the *Cat* revival in Massachusetts, I'm going to Providence, Rhode Island, to try-out the double-bill (*Vieux Carré*) which I wrote last summer. Merrick and I have not yet agreed on the director for *Red Devil Battery Sign* but I think he will finally abandon the idea of Kazan and let me have Katselas who is still young and vital. He did great revivals (better than the original productions) of *Camino Real* and *Rose Tattoo* and directed *Butterflies Are Free* [by Leonard Gershe] which ran two years on Broadway.

Early this morning Pat and Michael York called and we are meeting tomorrow evening at [Bill] Barnes' for drinks. They think you are sad about something but don't know what. Please let me know. Of course Pat enquired about the Enfant Terrible and seemed relieved when I told her that I hear about him through mutual friends but never see him. He has a job addressing Christmas cards!—Imagine!—And he has cut his novel in half and submitted it again to IFA. There are so many lost kids in the world but who can find them if they can't find themselves?

I hope to spend Christmas in New Orleans and possibly get Mother to fly down for it.

[*In handwriting*] Ciao, Cara!

About *OUT CRY*—I have just been told that Scofield may do it this spring but that it would be disastrous to mention this possibility yet. I know you see him socially but please don't speak of it to him. Let's leave it to silent prayer. The play remains half yours. He would do the version that he prefers—but for God's sake, no word about it.

———

MILTON KATSELAS had directed the 1966 revival of *Rose Tattoo* at the New York City Center and the 1970 revival of *Camino Real* at Lincoln Center. *Butterflies Are Free* was directed by him when it opened on October 21, 1969, at the Booth Theatre. It was one of the fifty longest-running comedies on Broadway.

Maria went to America for the twenty-fifth anniversary celebration of the Actors Studio.

After this, Maria and Tennessee went together to New Orleans, where Tennessee bought her a beautiful pair of antique garnet-and-gold earrings.

"Oliver was there, by now in an old people's home for semi-invalids. He was extremely bad-tempered, and consequently kept Tennessee and me in fits of laughter, which made him crosser still. His nose twitched the entire time. Tennessee bought him an entirely new wardrobe. Nothing fitted, and he was deeply ungrateful, but insisted on wearing the oversized jackets in order to demonstrate how hideous they were."

———

[*Address on envelope Hollywood-Roosevelt Hotel, Hollywood, Calif., postmarked U.S. Postal Service, December 21, 1973*]

Address when settled in Mexico

December 21, 1973

Dearest Maria:

Whenever the energy crisis in England is mentioned I wonder whether you have got it under control or are you chopping wood in the park at Wilbury. Seriously, it does sound pretty dreadful, but the British have always rallied to such crises better than anyone else with the possible exception of Russians.

Mother was greatly relieved when I called off the family Xmas reunion in Key West. So was Dinky. I think he had already planned it that way. He is intending to go to the Keys with an old war buddy, as he calls them, without any encumbrance immediately after the holidays. Says he has some marvellous "write-ups" to send me, one with a photo, and that he is practically a shoo-in for the senatorial primary in Illinois this time.

I had a legitimate excuse not to fly to Key West, which is a long, complicated flight from New Orleans: then back here and to the Coast. I had a check-up at the famous Ochsner Clinic and the doctor said I should not travel more than necessary and that my plan to rest on the Mexican beach was precisely what he would recommend. I fly to Los Angeles tomorrow and will see Oliver and Ardis [Blackburn] off on their mad tour of the Orient after a lovely Christmas celebration with them.

The lovely Christmas decoration you gave us (the festive candelabra) was just delivered today and it was lighted on the dinner table this evening for my first and quite successful attempt at southern fried chicken, quick grits, black-eyed peas and that salad you taught me to prepare—with the addition of cottage cheese. I guess when I retire from show-business it will be to the kitchen—if anywhere . . .

I am very disturbed over the behavior of Kazan and Merrick: I think it is a secret detente between them. I would be much happier working with Katselas on the Coast than waiting for the Messrs. K. & M. to get their act together. It seems that I am supposed to make all the concessions, as usual, and wait upon their magisterial decisions but that is not the name of the game as I read it. I have received no further word from Kazan, not even an Xmas greeting—nor Merrick either. And I did not find that 25th anniversary gig as reassuring as you pretended to find it. But of course I am not good humored.

Today we selected a new wall-to-wall carpeting for the front room of the apartment, a Regency red that will be very striking with the brass and the white walls. And a heating apparatus (convertible air-conditioning) is to be installed tomorrow—quite timely as there is a record cold wind striking the South.

Billy told me over the phone that you had an hilarious confrontation with Miss Wood at Sardi's after "The Iceman Goeth and Goeth." Please tell me about it!—Did you send the review of Hop, Skip and a Limp's dramatic triumph to Oliver for Xmas? How he would love it!

Love and "God Bless," Tennessee

[*Added in handwriting*] Bonne année!

———

MARIA had nicknamed Tennessee's latest travelling companion Hop, Skip and a Limp because he walked like Lord Byron.

"All I remember about meeting Audrey is breezily greeting her after all those years. She seemed surprised, and said that she'd understood that I was never going to speak to her again."

————

[*On letterhead Hotel Elysée, 60 East 54th Street, New York*]

Puerto Rico next weekend

January 5 or 6, 1974

Dear Maria:

I have just now put the finishing touches to the first draft of *This Is (an Entertainment) for Maria St. Just.*

I suspended work on *Red Devil Battery Sign* till the situation clears. In New Orleans last week, I received another letter from Kazan which totally removes him from the project. His program is to re-write his third novel, then write a screen-play for it and film it: then to write a sequel to his film *America, America,* write a screen-play for that and film that, too.

I accepted his defection with impeccable grace—and a sly bit of pleasure.

A couple of sexagenarians are at least one too many for a new play.

This evening I saw a new play [John Hopkins's *Find Your Way Home,* directed] by the man [Edwin Sherin] who is to direct *Streetcar* in London. I had read the script and thought it impossible to produce and to act. The direction was superb and Michael Moriarty was actually sympathetic in the most revolting role I have read.

Perhaps I can't read anymore.

I had a lovely time in New Orleans (after holidays in Puerto Vallarta, Mexico). The proprietress, Señora Violetta, had a complete mariachi band (nine of them), entertain at lunch for me. Stayed a week, then back to New Orleans. The new carpet was in and looked lovely. Rummaged through many old boxes of scripts and correspondence. Found a priceless letter from my father. Quote: "Dakin does not seem happy with his new job but I think he was lucky to get it."

Also a letter from Rose in which she said that my son had come for dinner, a splendid creature.

Gave Poppins a microwave oven for Xmas. Being an electric freak, he cooked continually. Invented a new name for Gigi—"The Junk Yard Dog."

Saw the Professor and his 82 year old lady friend [Ardis] off on their whirl-wind tour of the Orient. They gave a going-away dinner all during which the Professor's trousers gradually slipped off and when I left, they had fallen about his ankles—and the head of the English department with in-laws were present.

I thought it the ultimate chic.

I appreciated your good wishes for 1974, which I hardly expect to survive.

I've always detested New Year's, but I wish you the best as always.

Much love, Tenn

1431 Duncan Street
Key West, Florida

January 26, 1974

Dearest Maria:

I have just now completed *This Is* which is now sub-titled "The Bal Musette Plays On." I can't find "Bal Musette" in either an English or French dictionary but I mean those little mechanical music-boxes that used to, or still, play in Paris cafes in Montmartre. Is that the right name for them?

Meanwhile, *Red Devil* has been with a typist at IFA for two weeks. Billy helped me collate at my last week-end in New York. He really does deserve over-time. Will have to give him a piece of it if it is ever produced.—When I called ten days ago to enquire when I could expect a copy of the manuscript, his young friend David answered the phone and said that Billy was flying to Rio and would call me from the air-port. Exactly three minutes later the phone rang and it was Billy, all breathless, confirming that he is taking a Rio vacation.

I find it somewhat disconcerting to have no copy of script in my hands. What do you thinks going on? *Entre nous?* Besides our life-long friendship?

There is a confusion of gigs coming up in late February. I am supposed to be in St. Louis to receive something mysteriously called "The Library Award." Billy said I would receive transportation plus an honorarium of one G. However yesterday a rather pretty young female who works for the St. Louis *Globe-Democrat* (a newspaper) appeared here in Key West to interview me. She said she had heard nothing about the one G honorarium or transportation, that all she knew was that I was to receive this library award and was to deliver a speech one day and attend a big dinner the next given by some people named Messing. I said, "Will it be Messy?"—She gave me a cryptic glance and changed the subject to "Are you willing to discuss homosexuality, Mr. Williams?"—For once I clammed up, replied just "Subject exhausted." Today she re-appeared and stayed for lunch and then went swimming naked in the pool. Wanted me to join her skinny-dipping but I declined, très Blanche, with a reference to certain old fashioned reserves. However you-know-who [the Enfant Terrible] was eager to jump in with her. I don't know what to make of his total volte-face from extreme anti-social behavior to an excess of amiability on all public and private occasions. It may be that he has finished his novel and it is now being typed up in the guest-house and he is already half-way through another about Vietnam.

Poppins and the Junk Yard Dog arrive Tuesday. I'm glad you observed the flowering of his intellect and charm. Mieux tard que jamais. . . .

Loved the description of your surprise encounter with little Audrey. She's just about the only living creature that I genuinely and legitimately dislike, and I suppose she may have endured certain provocations, but, my God, even an elephant would forget them by this time.

After the St. Louis gig there is [Claire] Bloom's Blanche in London and a Paris production of *OUT CRY.* I was supposed to receive a copy of the translation but of course have not.

By the middle of the week I'll be in the New Orleans pad. Please call (504) 586-0295, need counsel.

Much love, Tennessee

[*On letterhead 1431 Duncan Street, Key West*]

Hotel Elysée
60 East 54th Street

February 5, 1974

Dearest Maria:

You were quite right in sensing something wrong when we talked today. I am exhausted by my effort to reconcile the business and amatory depts. of my life and also to complete the work. Leoncia [McGee] is the opposite of a help. Comes to be served lunch. I have to shop for it and prepare it. Then she refuses to eat, saying it's not well cooked. Christ, if she'd only retire!—She's pushing seventy, although she claims to be a year younger than me. So naturally I can't dismiss her, she came with the house, after all, and her medical expenses alone take up her salary, she claims. Also she is the social leader of Black Town and her house and lawn have to be maintained in high style. I had Poppins bring her down one of three wrist-watches which had turned up in the stored goods shipped from New York. Unfortunately he presented her with the Timex, which is a cheap metal watch, instead of the gold Hamilton. She came in breathing fire with it this morning and threw it at him, disdainfully. And now Gigi cannot eat. She spent the afternoon at the vet's who said she mustn't go out as she eats inedible stuff, bark, pebbles, anything—the poor thing is famished but it is limited to a small piece of dietary food a day—and now she can't even hold that on her stomach.

Worst of all, the West Virginia Kid [the Enfant] suddenly decided yesterday to smash up all his possessions including a camera that cost him $260 in Vietnam and is worth $800 in the States: then practically all his clothes.—I have locked his mss. in my studio to save them from destruction, too.—Of course you won't believe this, but his revised book, *Old Children,* is a terrifyingly beautiful accomplishment: yet he wants to destroy it.

We were booked to New Orleans today but I have switched the booking to New York. He is only controllable there at the Elysée. I realize how difficult it is for you to understand why I can't live alone. You've never had to try to and it isn't an experience that can be had vicariously.

I will come abroad only with Billy, of course, and stay at the Berkeley. Let us pray that *Streetcar* is pulled off by Claire. Please don't make any waves. I think Claire is very sweet and should be given all possible help in such a demanding role.—My chief interest is in the Paris production of *OUT CRY,* but I have not yet been allowed to see the translation.

There is a marvelous German baroness who is wintering here in Key West. She is "une belle laide"—looks like Froggy and she promises to give me a marvelous time in Munich this summer, if I make it. "Ah, ze boys, ze lederhosen, ja, ja, München, Wien, I find you gut boy, sweet, beautiful, high class vit education!"

She reminds me so much of poor Marion [Vaccaro], divorced, lonely, her only child on drugs, but never comes on depressed. Roosters crowing.

With much love, Tenn

THE LONDON revival of *A Streetcar Named Desire,* directed by Edwin Sherin with Claire Bloom as Blanche, produced by her then husband, Hillard Elkins, opened at the Piccadilly Theatre on March 14, 1974.

[*Letter postmarked Aix-en-Provence, France*]

March 18, 1974

Dearest Maria:

I want first of all to thank you for making that almost unbearable schedule of activities not only bearable but fun to look back on because of your being present, I mean in residence. Of course I have never been given such a grand party and Claire's Blanche and Hilly [Elkins]'s production are the sort of occasion that a writer about to be sixty-three should be satisfied to end his life with. But I have no idea of ending my life and I hope there are no assassins of royalty lurking about the streets of Aix. You know, this place is about equally divided between idiotically beautiful young kids who attend the colleges here and male and female crones of indescribable decrepitude. It must be centuries of in-breeding that has produced so many deformed natives of the place. You would gallop your legs off running to touch for luck all the hump-backs that are snailing along the streets. I have not yet even seen the thermal establishment (will tomorrow) but I have never tasted such marvelous water. I drink three glasses of it as if it were Chateau Lafite Rothschild. It goes right through you. You pee and pee and pee so I guess it is excellent for the kidneys. I must send some to Froggy. Well, dear child of God, it is 2:20 a.m. and I must return to bed. "You know who" has his own room. He has been on an "upper" called desoxyn all day which has given him the velocity of a thunderbolt. He really has been wonderful at packing and at racing to get the luggage on the plane but watching him has exhausted me.

It will not be an unwashed grape [*Streetcar*] that will kill me but a frightful excess of pity for those even smaller and more addictive than myself.

I am sure that Voltaire (*Candide*) really meant the best of impossible worlds. . . . Never, never come here for the waters but have them shipped to you by the gallons—if you get the picture. I suspect that after a week I'll fly to Casablanca and catch a conveyance—anything but a camel—to Marrakech which I've never seen.

Did I ever tell you about the lady on the Mediterranean cruise which Oliver and I inadvertently took in 1970? She said: "It voss so hot that the camels vouldn't stand up and the dancing boys vouldn't dance and my child had a convulsion!"

All love, Tenn

[*Added in handwriting*] Love to Pat & Michael [York] & Totey [Hermione Baddeley] & Bun [Guy Strutt].

————

"O N M Y great-grandmother's estate in Russia, it was traditional to employ a hunchback in some capacity and to touch the hump for luck: a medieval superstition originating from the court jester, I imagine. My mother and her brothers and sisters would chase poor Verushka, the sewing maid, and touch her so much that she was forever rolling down the stairs. In Barcelona there seemed to be a lot of hunchbacks dressed in black;

Tennessee and I used to try and touch them without their noticing. I eventually forbade Tennessee to do it. He was so clumsy that on one occasion he nearly provoked a street brawl."

From left:
Bill Barnes,
Anna Bloom
(Claire's daughter),
Tennessee,
Claire Bloom,
Maria and
Hilly Elkins
at Wilbury
during the
London run
of *Streetcar*.
Claire played
Blanche.

[Letter postmarked New York]

May 11, 1974

Dearest Maria:

I have just now finished the revised draft of my first novella [*Moise and the World of Reason*] since *The Roman Spring of Mrs. Stone,* it is ten of four a.m., the electric storm in New Orleans is over and so is my two-day gig with Dick Cavett all about the city, and my thoughts return to you and your mysterious silence in response to the letter I wrote you from Aix-en-Provence.

I suspect that you have now finally decided that I am no longer acceptable to the civilized world, the same decision Gore made that evening of your Roman birthday and the contest of gold ornaments which I believe I won despite mine being purchased at the Parco dei Principi and his at Bulgari's.

I know that some people preserve each other in amber instead of continuing letters and meetings but hope this isn't the case. At least send me a bulletin on how things are going over there. Who's [in like] Flynn, who's stout, and so forth. You don't have to sign it. I discovered an old letter of yours here. It was dated August 1947 [1948], and was about Miss Hayes at the Haymarket, and what most surprised me about it was that the penmanship was perfectly legible and every word was correctly spelled.

Tomorrow I'm flying back to New York to see a dress-rehearsal of *The Latter Days of a Celebrated Soubrette,* formerly called *The Gnädiges Fräulein,* starring Miss Anne Meacham who raised all the money for it. Today she called me from back-stage and gave me a hair-raising account of recent developments in the rehearsals. The actors have started improvising with weapons such as knives and a tomahawk and throwing each other about the stage. I expressed dismay at this method, and she said, "Oh, it's wonderful, it allows them to get into the underground violence and terror of the play."

Well, I look forward to it provided the actors stay on their side of the proscenium with their weapons. I don't like the underground violence of my work to jump at me in "the stalls."

After a week in New York I'll try to settle somewhere in the States for the summer. I'm thinking of Montreal where there is a high-rise hotel with a roof-top swimming pool. Harry Rasky described it to me, it's called the Bon Venture. I love to speak my Français des écoles and Montreal is in French Canada like Quebec.

Now the "jolie laide" is about to raid the ice-box or the kitchen cupboard for a pre-dawn snack.

Love, 10

[*Added in handwriting*] Poppins and Gigi are well.

———

H A R R Y   R A S K Y was a Canadian film maker who had made a documentary about Tennessee, called *Tennessee Williams Down South.*

The Latter Days of a Celebrated Soubrette ran for only one performance, at the Central Arts Cabaret Theatre on May 16, 1974.

———

[*On letterhead Hotel Elysée, 60 East 54th Street, New York, postmarked New York, June 26, 1974*]

1014 Dumaine Street, Apt. B
New Orleans, La.

June 23, 1974

Dearest Maria:

At last I have a letter from you to answer, but I'm sorry to say it is dated sometime last November when you were at the Lancaster, before I last saw you. It has been belatedly forwarded to me. But it reminds me poignantly of how much I miss getting new letters from you.

I'm headed back to New Orleans, to sweat it out for the rest of the summer. No matter how hot, the air is better for me than here and I enjoy the peaceful presences of Mary Poppins and Gigi. She is entering her thirteenth year and Boston bulls are usually allotted only fourteen. When I left there a week ago, she was dreadfully forlorn. I'm afraid that Mary leaves her alone too much.

Billy tells me that the director [Frank] Dunlop (of *Scapino,* the new smash here) is seriously interested in doing *This Is* in London. Of course I never count chickens before hatched and sometimes not afterwards, but if it should indeed come about, and you hear of it—call me at the Berkeley and I will answer the phone.

Tatiana [Schvetzoff] and I are both very concerned about the lapse in letters from you.

Much love, 10

Hotel Elysée
60 E. 54th Street
N.Y.C.

August 3, 1974

Dearest Maria:

At last your epistolary hiatus has been broken: wish I had fireworks to set off on the verandah. I was not referring to any "rude letter" from you, since I'd received none since my last sight of you, but to a cable which Victor had phoned to me in a somewhat garbled form: it was to the effect that you would write when you were not too busy. Well, I hope you'll sit under the hair-dryer more often, though actually when people have been friends for so long, an unbroken succession of letters is not that important.

Now that I have gotten a doctor's permit to use oxygen on long plane flights it is quite possible that I may fly over to Europe in a couple of weeks! I'm particularly attracted to Venice toward the end of August. Billy and Hilly (Elkins) hold out enticing prospects of an early production of *This Is (An Entertainment)* in London under Frank Dunlop's direction, but I've learned to believe in productions only when rehearsals are in progress and even then it is sometimes a strain on credulity. You'll be happy to know that Chuck and I are engaged in a theatrical project. It is a version of *Camino Real* with lovely music by a young girl of Slavonic extraction and with dancing. Chuck has obtained a large grant to establish a regional theatre near New York, and we hope that this project will be the opening attraction.

I'm returning to New York day after tomorrow. Rose has been under-going tests for stomach trouble and I have to get the reports. She looks well and is very fond of Tatiana who always joins us when Rose comes to town. The last time Rose said she would like to go to England. I said perhaps it could be arranged for her to meet the Queen. She said, with no hesitation and complete conviction: "I *am* the Queen of England."

I think all those rented limousines have gone to her head a bit. I had noticed that when at the Plaza she had been giving the Windsor salute to strangers about the Oak Room. Well, if one must live in a dream world it is nice to be the queen of it . . .

I have been given notice that my autobiography must be finished in August. So if we meet abroad perhaps you can assist me with the ending: it's a good way to make sure you get a good write-up.

A bientôt, chère amie!

Tennessee

Poppins and Gigi join me in love.

———

MARIA's beloved pug, Froggy Footman, died. Maria was heartbroken.

"Tennessee was always most impressed by Froggy for being so consistently unpleasant, not only to Tennessee but to everybody. One evening I was coming up from the dining room to the drawing room at Gerald Road. Tennessee and Froggy were sitting on the sofa, the latter's eyes popping out with hatred. As I entered the room I heard Tennessee whining pleadingly: 'Oh, Froggy, *please* be nice to me!' "

Tennessee wrote an epitaph, which Maria had carved on Froggy's head-stone at Wilbury Park:

Froggy Footman
is attempting to
escape Tennessee's
clutches, London,
1976.

9, GERALD ROAD,
S. W. I.
736 7821

Frog-you
had the matchless
Taste
To find me of
a lesser race

Mischa you lived
in the sun
of love whose
time is never run
T.W.

Tennessee's epitaphs for Froggy Footman, who
died in 1974, and Mishka, who died in 1980

Frog, you had the matchless taste
To find me of a lesser race.

Tennessee Williams

Tennessee wrote a draft of a poem to comfort Maria:

Froggy has not gone away
Our memories have made him stay
Breast of chicken does he eat
Near our hearts, not at our feet

Ours I say, though true it is
He was yours, you were his

Funny dear! not gone far,
God placed him on so near a star.

We cannot see it, more than we
Can the secret artery the heart,

The spirit that is not body bound is . . .

———

[*Handwritten letter*]

Hotel Elysée
60 East 54th Street
New York

September 23, 1974

Dearest Maria—

For past three weeks have been in state of depression for reasons you can surmise. I've thought of you often—wrote 3 letters too dreary to mail. I am back in N.Y. for *Cat* transfer to B'dway.

In a week should be at liberty to take flight. I'll probably go to London for a few days—then down to somewhere like Marrakesh.

Merrick has bought his way back into the production of "R.D.B.S." [*Red Devil Battery Sign*] Scares me. Rehearsals don't begin till February. Time to recover, perhaps. If Froggy's gone, just remember he had a happy life— which some of us might envy.

Can't discuss my plans over phone here, but will call soon from Billy [Barnes]'s or [Charles] Bowden's.

A bientôt, j'espère!

> Much love as always, Tenn.

Later—I have now decided to return to New Orleans, and as I said to you on the phone, I hope you can get away. Merrick & Elkins have finally come to an agreement. From New Orleans we could fly to Guadalajara, Mexico, to audition some "mariachis" for the play—perhaps with the director, Ed Sherin.

ON JULY 10, 1974, *Cat on a Hot Tin Roof* had been revived at the American Shakespeare Theatre in Stratford, Connecticut. The production was transferred to the ANTA Theatre in New York City on September 24. It was directed by Michael Kahn, with Elizabeth Ashley as Maggie, Keir Dullea as Brick, and Fred Gwynne as Big Daddy.

Chuck Bowden and his wife, Paula, interviewed in 1987 about Maria and Tennessee's relationship, gave an account of evenings in New York in their company.

"Maria would arrive, and suddenly Tennessee would start to entertain, and be with those friends who were deeply his friends—not the fly-by-nights who, when Maria wasn't around, he was apt to be with. She brought a family feeling, a continuity. Tennessee's life would then become 'family'—very jolly and very happy. Maria would call us, and the Smiths, and Maureen Stapleton, and say, 'We're going to have dinner tonight, we're going to cook it ourselves, come on over.' Tennessee starts inviting more people to dinner. Suddenly Maria realizes something. 'What are we to cook with, Tennessee? We can't cook in this little closet here in the Hotel Elysée!'

"So, off they go to Bloomingdale's, where Tennessee buys a microwave, which the two of them bring back. Across the street from the Elysée is a Gristede's grocery store. Maria says, 'Right. Now we are going shopping.' 'Yes,' says Tennessee, 'we are going to make Russian cutlets.' Maria picks certain things off the shelves and puts them in the basket; Tennessee keeps putting them back when she isn't looking—'You don't need all of that, you don't need all of that,' he says.

"They get back to the hotel, and Maria says, 'All right, connect the oven. We'll get ready.' Tennessee connects the oven—and blows every light in the hotel. 'You call downstairs,' he says. 'I'm not going to tell them.' So

Maria has to get the lights back on again, and the oven properly connected, while Tennessee hides in the bedroom with the door closed.

"By this time, the guests are arriving, and Maria is very gracious to all of us. She serves white wine, because Maureen is on the wagon. So is Tennessee—so they both have a quart of white wine. And there's some kind of aspidistra, about the only thing growing in the room (there were never flowers except when Maria came), and that aspidistra is as drunk as a lord: Maria keeps pouring Tennessee's wine into the plant and then disappearing into the kitchen, saying, 'We'll be ready to serve shortly.'

"The door closes, and we hear the most terrible eruption. 'What are you *doing,* Tennessee? Don't put your hands in that . . . don't do that . . . no, just add another egg—you haven't got enough eggs, it won't hold together!'

"Then the door opens, and Maria emerges graciously. 'Everyone got enough wine? Yes? Enough wine?' And she crosses the room with a glass of wine she has just taken from Tennessee, when he wasn't looking, and pours it onto the aspidistra. . . .

"That was their relationship—deep, deep, loving friendship, the strongest emotion of them all. Somebody said to me one day, 'When you hear the name Maria in relation to Tennessee, what's the first word that occurs to you?'

" 'Laughter,' I replied. That was what it was, as far as Tennessee was concerned."

Maria had recounted to Tennessee that Tatiana Schvetzoff had recently entered an elevator compartment and told the operator, "I am sixteen." A drunk, also in the compartment, bellowed, "Sixteen? I thought you were ninety!" Tennessee had howled with mirth.

Tennessee had given Maria a small gold heart, inscribed in his writing, "Dearest Maria, A tiny replica of your heart, Love, 10."

———

[*Part of a surviving letter from Maria to Tennessee, written on board a British Airways airplane, the letterhead reading: "Written between* ——— *and* ———*." Maria has filled it in: "Heaven" and "Hell."*]

Dearest and most precious Tennessee—

Well, I am sitting. I am so happy with my heart, the one you gave me, not my own. It is just beautiful. I have already seen Rachel Roberts. We are both, mercifully, far away from each other. She's just told me triumphantly that she's found some drip in first class who will give us a drink.

Tenn, I'm really so excited by the marvellous work you are producing right NOW. It really is so exciting to read, all of it. Now don't do any more re-writing, the *Red Devil* or *This Is*. Wait for rehearsals. Actors and director. I'll get cracking on Monday morning. No stone will be left unturned in the English theatre, I promise you, to get *This Is* on—you see, they will get it in Europe, as it's our sort of stuff. All that is happening in Greece and all over the place has a bearing on it, and it has such a marvellous humour and placelessness, it can be anywhere—and all your other plays, except *Camino,* are so American that they are difficult to do and frighten people off in England. In fact, nobody has ever really done them properly, as we know.

I feel so deeply what you are going through as an artist. I remember when I was acting the frustration of not being able most of the time even to audition for parts; no one minds trying and being turned down, but not being allowed to try—God! You so long to hear your words spoken, and the beautiful things that you write coming to life. I don't know how you stand it. It's so unfair to be subjected to money-talks—pushed around by people who are really only interested in making a quick dime, be it *Oh! Calcutta* or what—just to make some of the hard stuff. At least in England the background of culture and hundreds of years of theatre, and real love of theatre, does not make it so commercial. People will produce things because they love them, not because they think it will be a success and make money. That helps—but it is not enough in itself—whereas in your country, alas, that is paramount to all and sundry, except the poor artists.

What a lovely lovely time I had with you, and how happy I am that we did get to the doctor, did see Merrick, did see Ed [Sherin], did see Elkins, did clear up quite a lot of misunderstandings. I feel so passionately indignant at the way you get pushed around with productions, on one moment, off the next. Your energies must go into your work. Other people should fight these battles for you. Billy [Barnes] does seem to try his best, but his arms are tied by his proffessssion. I know the spelling is wrong, but there's life for you, my dear. I just can't spell.

Luckily the Countess does not have to pick up a quill, otherwise I feel sure she'd use it as a dart, into the Count. She certainly wouldn't be able to spell or write with it, I fear.

No time! I was also happy to see Tatiana, "16! I thought you were ninety," looking so well and taking such care of Rose. I always thought it would be a delicious combination. Tatiana's so intense, and Rose not in the picture. Tatiana getting worked up and saying, "Tom is not in the house!" and Rose smiling her touching and gentle smile and saying, "Tom is next door. I've just seen him." And you are in Key West sitting. Tatiana, her eyes popping out of her head, her hand raised in despair, telling me the whole thing. "Doctor Williams," said Rose. And Tatiana saying, "I try to tell her, but she will not listen, little Mary!" It is all wonderful for Tatiana to have such an interest, because Rose will become more and more like her child, and Rose will feel the loving warmth, something she only gets from you. Alas, what a tragic figure she is. She breaks my heart when I think of her, her life totally cut down, savagely, with a knife.

London, *This Is,* Tuesday. Jeremy Brett of the Greenwich Theatre has nipped over for a glass of my best white wine and taken the script home to read. He's an excellent theatre person. Apart from being a good actor, he is on the board of the Greenwich Theatre. They started doing the new Osborne play this morning. He is very good on scripts, and very with-it, so we'll see what his reaction is.

Thank you, darling Tenn, for having me to stay with you. I feel much cheered up. It was heaven staying with you. God bless you, take care of yourself, loving thoughts as always.

Maria

1041 Dumaine, Apt. B
New Orleans, La.

December 17, 1974

Dearest Maria:

With you flown back to England, things have returned to their old state of dispirited lassitude.

I remember how to make Russian cutlets and have served them twice to guests at the New Orleans pad.

I wish you'd send me the other recipe, the mince-meat stuffing for peppers and tomatoes.

Tonight Poppins prepared his own stuffed peppers in the microwave oven and I made sauteed egg-plant slices and the cucumber, tomato salad with yoghurt.

Ole Joan Good and her book-keeper were guests for supper and afterwards we had a good poker game. Although she once worked as a pro at a gambling joint, I came out the big winner (ten bucks). Poppins was the big loser. He lost five dollars and it threw him into such a depression that he was speechless—possibly a relief.

Tatiana called today to tell me they'd found my reading glasses at Dr. Tichenor's office. I had just had a new pair made here at Maison Blanche Optometrist. Well, now I have a spare pair.

I've been thinking about your plan to put *This Is* in the Greenwich Theatre. God knows I need some action to keep me going, to provide an incentive, but, honey, I started work on that play the time we went to Paris to see *Douce Oiseau de la Jeunesse* [*Sweet Bird of Youth*], and I can't reconcile myself to a run of three weeks. Why don't we try it on at the Royal Court, or push Billy into his original plan of having it done by Frank Dunlop at a West End house? I could come over, stay at the Berkeley and week-end at Wilbury if His Lordship is not in residence there with bird gun.

Dr. Tichenor prescribed a nice, conservative upper for me called Dexsmyl. I take it, half of one tablet, when I get up in the morning. It gives me a lift that carries me through the day. And at night I've got sleeping pills that assure me four or five hours sleep.

I have this evening thought of a new title for my memoirs. Came about this way. Poppins and I were walking down a street in the Quarter, he like a zombie because he'd lost the five bucks, when I stumbled on a bit of shattered pavement. I remarked to him, "A blind man must look where he's going." Do you think that would be a good title for the auto-biog?

It seems fitting to me because I have gone through my life like a blind man, stumbling into various holes, here and there.

I have taken off one pound of the ten—or was it twenty?—that Doc Tichenor said I should lose. swimming and street walking.

Gigi is her old self again, completely recovered from her horrendous stay in Key West. I give her constant attention.

I am doing another painting: it is in the awkward stage and I wonder if it will get out of it.

Please let me know how you found things in England.

I sit here like a chess-player, not knowing the next move.

With much love, Tennessee

[*Telegram from Maria at Wilbury to Tennessee in Key West*]

A HAPPY CHRISTMAS AND HAPPY NEW YEAR DARLING TENNESSEE MUCH ROYAL COURT READY PLAY NEWS AFTER CHRISTMAS LOVE MARIA

———

ALONG with pictures of Maria's family, Tennessee kept the children's thank-you letters to him. One example:

Dear Tennessee,

Thank you so much for the present. I don't know how you knew but it's just what I wanted. I hope you have a lovely Christmas, and the New Year brings you much luck and happiness. How is Gigi? I hope well, and Mummy tells me she is very pudgy, just like my dog.

Well thank you very much again for the lovely ivory tooth, and I hope to see you soon, also thank you for having Mummy to stay. I think that is the nicest present of all, because I know she loves it with you more than anything, and it makes her so happy, so it makes me happy.

With all love and kisses, Natasha XXX

P.S. The dogs send a big lick.

———

Tennessee's self-portrait, drawn at Wilbury for Pulcheria's birthday, May 23, 1981. On the back he wrote, "Pour la chatelaine, la plus belle du monde."

Hotel Elysée
60 East 54th Street
New York

January 6, 1975

Dearest Maria:

Probably my holiday activities have been almost nothing compared to yours—but still more than usual for me. The most important event was having Rose and Tatiana here in the adjoining bedroom of the suite for three days. This was the experimental vacation that Rose's doctor at Stony Lodge allowed her to have and I think it was a success. She enjoyed it and I hope it was not too hard on Tatiana. I'm a bit worried about Tatiana. Since returning from her visit to Virginia she has had "vertigo." It attacks her when she moves suddenly. I will call her later this morning to see how she's doing.

It's obvious to me that Rose does not require constant hospital confinement. Her only problem is excessive smoking. If cigarettes are accessible to her, she will light one from another, chain-smoking. I showed her the "surgeon general's" warning which law requires on cigarette packages now—that smoking is dangerous to health—but she pretends she can't read it, although she has no trouble reading a menu in French. Tatiana and I were kept busy hiding cigarettes from her but when Billy gave supper for her at his apartment, she snatched two packages.

Harry Rasky and a Universal Studio executive and Maureen Stapleton are all convening here in New York to finalize plans for an early shooting of the TV special [*Stopped Rocking*] I wrote for Maureen, and hopefully for Burt Lancaster or Max Von Sydow in the male lead. So life is not all play here.

About the middle of the week I am planning to fly down to a little island called Cozumel off the coast of Yucatán, Mexico. I'll wait there till Ed Sherin, director of *Red Devil,* can meet me in Guadalajara to select some mariachis. Ed wants to start rehearsals in late spring and—this is top secret—is willing to discard both our producers if they oppose this earlier date. Hilly [Elkins] and Claire [Bloom] are both in favor of waiting for Anthony Quinn, but if he continues to put off his availability date, he will turn to a geriatric case before he appears in the play—which I suspect will not happen.

Hope you'll soon have a chance to give me a report on operations over there, who is where doing what and how you can stand it.

Much love and best wishes for the Russian New Year,

Tenn

[From a letter from Tatiana Schvetzoff to Maria, handwritten, February 24, 1975]

. . . Tennessee in addition to gold medal also got the key to the City of New York from the city. I was there and so was Rose sitting next to him on the dais. She was very good, she can adjust herself to any situation. It was a lovely affair. Many people—2,500 or more. He went to Mexico. His play will open about Aug. 15. A. Quinn and Bloom lead . . .

Tatiana Schvetzoff, a great friend of Mary Britneva's and a sometime companion to Rose Williams, in Maria's London flat, 1973

Hotel Elysée

April ?, 1975

Dearest Maria:

I'm spending a few restful days in New Orleans with Victor and our new English bull-dog, Madam [Sophia], before returning to casting in New York. Madam looks just like a much-magnified Froggy and is delightful except that she is not house-broken and is cutting her teeth on the furniture.

As for casting, neither of the stars has yet arrived and we're having to cast around them. So far Tony Quinn refuses to begin rehearsals before June 2 although we are scheduled to start May 14 and if he persists in this obstinacy we will lose our Boston booking and only have four weeks in Washington before the New York opening in mid August. I think it is very dicey to play in summer and open before the season has really started, but Ed Sherin's commitments made it necessary.

Old Merrick condescended to drop by the theatre. I exclaimed, "As I live and breathe, it's Mr. Broadway." He gave me a sour look and said, "I thought you said you'd be dead before we went in rehearsal," and I said, "Never listen to a duck in a thunderstorm, I'm going to out-live you." He looked like you'd asked him if he had no money, and quickly disappeared.

In addition to Merrick, we now have three other producers, including a noisy lady.

Do you hear from Gore? I read a marvellous interview that he gave to a scandalous magazine called *OUT*. He is one of the few people who still make sense in the world—and are funny about it.

Peter back in New York.—Where?

Rose and Tatiana are here for the week-end. We dined at Sardi's tonight and then went to Ringling Bros. Circus. Rose was delighted. Stood up and saluted whenever especially impressed.

All of a sudden, finally, something is actually being done about *This Is*. The director, Frank Dunlop, is going to produce it with ACT [American Conservatory Theatre], the best repertory on the [West] Coast. Many ladies are being considered for the lead.

You see, we must get you over here to see that things are going right.

Angela Lansbury told me at a party a couple of nights ago that she thinks she and Scofield could do *OUT CRY*. She is a lovely lady. As she left she said to me, "Take care of your dear self."

Now how does one do that?!

My love to the girls.

Much love to you, Tennessee

———

MERRICK was dragging his feet so much over the production that Maria, losing her temper, had asked him why he was not producing the play—was it because he hadn't any money? Merrick was dumbfounded.

———

Five O'Clock Angel

[*Handwritten on greeting card from unknown address, but probably New Orleans*]

May 4, 1975

Dearest Maria:

One must be practical about jewelry, regardless of sentiment involved. This lovely-looking ring was sold to me on Royal Street (New Orleans) as rubies and cut diamonds in a 14 k. gold setting. I was somewhat disturbed by the discrepancy between value of the stones & the metal—I'd appreciate it, therefore, if you'd have it appraised in London. I will have it delivered to you by the next friend of Bill's going to London, so you will not have to pay duty on it and go through the bother of customs.

Flying back to New York tomorrow. Rehearsals on *Red Devil Sign* supposed to start May 12th but Merrick is in a rage over the set. I fancy this will be a summer of drama, mostly offstage. Ah, to rest!!

Love, love, love, 10

———

"In the event, Tennessee gave me the ring personally. The card was a hand-pressed rose. Tenn was so excited like a child when he gave me the diamond-and-ruby ring."

The Red Devil Battery Sign, produced by David Merrick, directed by Edwin Sherin, designed by Robin Wagner, Ruth Wagner and Marilyn Rennagel, with Claire Bloom as Woman Downtown, Anthony Quinn as King Del Rey and Katy Jurado as Perla, was first performed at the Shubert Theatre in Boston on June 18, 1975. The production was meant to transfer to Broadway, but because of unenthusiastic notices Merrick closed it after ten days—by which time Williams had flown to Rome. Before he left he approved of a plan to revive *Sweet Bird of Youth,* to be directed by Sherin, with Irene Worth and Christopher Walken.

"Tennessee invited me to Boston for the last rehearsals and the opening of *Red Devil Battery Sign.* Anthony Quinn was brilliant, but poor Claire Bloom could not be heard anywhere in the house, and there was talk of replacing her. She was not helped by the direction, and had had a very tough time. Tennessee remained loyal—although we did run into Claire and her agent in the same restaurant in which we were taking Faye Dunaway [who was being considered as a replacement] to dinner. . . ."

———

Hotel Elysée
60 East 54th Street
New York

July 6, 1975

Dearest Maria:

A telegram of a letter! The play has become a *cause célèbre* here. Tony [Quinn] has declared on TV that he will finance it himself if that's necessary to bring it into New York. Bill says that two other top producers want it and that Merrick and colleagues still want it. [*Added in handwriting*] Bull.

Meanwhile, I work on like the "patient eremite" and am leaving town in two days to sort it all out in my head and work under quiet condition by a pool.

Tony also wants to direct—with an assistant.

To me this play has eclipsed everything else but your letter, written at the Rome air-port, which I keep in front of me like a sacred missal. I know that Peter must understand, now, the desperate need that I have for your sustaining friendship.

Madam is enraged by her recent experiences: taking it out fiercely on hotel furniture: has to be confined behind her kennel in the kitchen.

Poppins will leave with her before me, tomorrow I think. I plan to cut out on Wednesday after meetings with Quinn, and an interview for the *Times* in Bill's precautionary presence lest I start talking too much.

Rose and Tatiana, both seemingly well and happy, were here yesterday, staying over night.

With heart full of love and gratitude, Tennessee

———

DESPITE the continual reassurance that Tennessee needed from Maria, and her frequent absences from England, Peter St. Just indeed realized Tennessee's dependence on her and behaved very understandingly.

———

Hotel Elysée

July 29, 1975

Dearest Maria:

Depression is nobody's prerogative, when and if avoidable, and it is not a mood that I tolerate in myself for long. Or perhaps it has become a habit of which I'm no longer conscious and which I usually know how to conceal in company. When alone, the drugstore is a dependable source of evasion.

I am with Tatiana and Rose. We've just lunched at the Woman's Exchange around the corner which always reminds me of an English tea-room. Even the men have a somewhat matronly and refined look.

I saw Tony once more in New York at Billy's for dinner. The flies had come in from the terrace and assumed full proprietorship of the meal which old black Ernest (69 years old) had prepared: since I am on a very strict diet and have lost a good deal of weight, painlessly, I did not contest a crumb with them. Quinn is very keen about doing a film of the play. He says he can only remain right for it a few months longer. I thought he ought to go ahead and make the film and keep it "in the can" till I had re-written the play (which I'm now doing with some illumination after Boston) and open it in New York for a short run. I am shifting the emphasis away from sexuality to the human values and to the dramatic tension.—Billy was somewhat evasive. Quinn walked home a few blocks with me and he seemed to be baffled. I thought he said quite rightly: It is I (Quinn) who have the passion for the project, and nothing's more important.

He wants me to write the film play while I re-write the play.

Billy called me the next day and wanted me to fly to the West Coast to meet the people who say they are going to do *This Is* and I was reluctantly prepared to go when an associate of Frank Dunlop's called to tell me it would be impossible for me, at this time, to meet the actors who would be involved in the play—he seemed relieved when I said that I thought it would then be pointless for me to exhaust myself with a trip to San Francisco.—I guess I'm in the dog-house with Bill. He hasn't returned my calls since. I shall not make any further . . .

Tatiana and I are wondering when to call you at the Wellington [Hospital]. I know the anxiety of waiting for something like this, remember my journey to the "King's Doctor" in Bangkok. Anytime you want to reach me, the number is PL 3-1066 ext. 1002 in case you've forgotten.

Quinn has invited us to visit him in the Alban Hills above Rome—I long for an excursion.

No doubt we'll be talking before you get this, and an earlier letter which I wrote immediately after returning from Rome.

Meanwhile all my love and faith in the best for you,

Tennessee

———

MARIA had a biopsy of a non-malignant tumor, and was at the Wellington Hospital.

———

KEY WEST, FLORIDA

My dearest Maria —

I am deeply distressed for you
by the news of your grandmother's   and it
death. By thinking of my own grandmother, later,
who also died in January a few   near her
years ago, on the day of Epiphany —
I can understand your feelings.
I was also out of the house when I, so
she was stricken ill but (perhaps usely
unfortunately) returned during her tragedy
last moments when I am sure that your
she, who would never admit even   running.
feeling not well, would not have   of you
wanted me there. But I am glad worried,
that you were in England to be final,
close to her during her last   wear
                                         as
            ...o your grandmother's
warm Russian heart, which is
yours! — with love —
            Tennessee.

A letter from Tennessee at the time of Maria's grandmother's death, 1950

Five O'Clock Angel

[*Telegram sent to Wellington Hospital, August 2, 1975*]

ALL PREGNANT COWS WOULD MISCARRY IF THEY SAW ME AT WILBURY STOP WILL
BE AT HOTEL EXCELSIOR NAPLES TOMORROW NIGHT WILL CALL YOU FROM THERE
MUCH LOVE ALWAYS TENNESSEE

[*On letterhead featuring the* Playbill *program of* A Streetcar Named Desire, *1014
Dumaine Street, New Orleans, Louisiana*]

September 9, 1975

Dearest Maria:

Here's another example of Poppins's infinite ingenuity—had a batch of
stationery made out of an old play-bill for the original *Streetcar* prod.

I turned in my re-write of "R.D.B.S." [*Red Devil Battery Sign*] a couple
of days ago and flew down here to continue exams at Ochsner Clinic—a
depressing prospect but advisable.

It was nice hearing from you however briefly. If state of health permits,
Barnes and I should be flying to Vienna late this month or early next, and
I hope it will be to see a production of their English-speaking theatre doing
Battery. It is really way-out, now, in its social criticism and I think it is a
powerful work. Probably the States are not ready for it—but who knows?
I'd like Tony [Quinn] to see it: will send you a copy. Barnes says the
Viennese company would be happy to engage him if he wants another go
at it.

I'm a bit worried about Tatiana—she's had a recurrence of her vertigo—
but her spirits are heroic as ever.

The Professor [Oliver Evans] and Mrs. Blackburn [Ardis] are selling the
Florida house and returning together to California. He says the social
atmosphere of Gainesville and the muggy climate were too much for
him—and he dreams of returning to Bangkok.

You missed a truly brilliant off-off-Broadway revival of *OUT CRY.* I
got a rave notice from the *Times* and other papers. I simply told the director
[Arthur Allen]—a genius—to cut out one third of the script. Well, he cut
out just about that much and it moved like a house afire—we used the
Bangkok version.

I'm sure it has a future before it, sometimes, somewhere, but the conditions must be right.

The director is visiting me here in New Orleans to get the atmosphere for a pair of one acts called *Vieux Carré.*—Has just arrived at the door.

Viola Veidt received from her mother in Switzerland a very funny item about my arrival in New Orleans with the huge female bull-dog Madam Sophia. On the air-line transcript it had carried her name as a first-class passenger with me. The Eastern employees here had somehow concluded that she was Sophia Loren and had turned out in full force—to confront "Ein grossen hunde-damen" [*sic*]—a big dog-lady.

Alors, I must play host.

With all love, Tenn

[*Typed*] Tennessee

V I O L A   V E I D T was the daughter of German actor Conrad Veidt.

On September 16, 1975, *Summer and Smoke* was revived at Roundabout Stage One in New York City, and on December 18, 1975, *The Glass Menagerie* was revived at New York's Circle in the Square, with Maureen Stapleton as Amanda. In between the two revivals Tennessee's *Memoirs* were published and became one of the season's best-sellers. One afternoon before Christmas Williams signed more than eight hundred copies at a Doubleday bookstore, beating the previous record for such events. Maria detested the book, much of which had been written at Wilbury. The opening chapter gives a account of Tennessee's stay there:

> To begin this "thing" on a socially impressive note, let me tell you that one recent fall, before the leaves had fallen, I happened to be weekending at one of the last great country houses in England, an estate so close to Stonehenge that one of the stones was dropped on the lady's estate before it got to that pre-historical scene of druidical worship and, probably due to collapse or revolt of slave labor, it was not picked up but allowed to rest where it fell, and this bit of information has only the slightest and most oblique connection with the material which follows.
>
> It was bedtime, and the lady of the manor, giving me a sharp look, inquired if I didn't want to retire with a good book, since she knew I was a restless sleeper. "Go into the library and pick out something," she advised me, pointing me to a huge, chilly room in the left wing of the Palladian mansion. Since she was already on her way upstairs, I had no recourse but to follow her suggestion. I entered the library

and discovered it to contain almost nothing but very large leather-bound volumes of an ancient vintage almost comparable to that stone which didn't quite make it to Henge. Incidentally, I also discovered a secret doorway, floor to ceiling, rather amateurishly disguised by false book-fronts, and this was not the only touch of deception that I encountered. There was a book in there which was titled *International Who's Who,* or something of the sort. Quite naturally, I snatched it out of its case and turned immediately to the index to see if I had made that scene. . . .

By the end of the year Tennessee was working on the production of *This Is (An Entertainment)* at San Francisco's American Conservatory Theatre.

———

[Part of a letter from Tatiana Schvetzoff to Maria, handwritten, October 10, 1975]

I was happy to hear [Tenn] found you looking well and peppy. I hope that you don't have pain any longer.

The day before I came there was a terrible bust-up with [Enfant Terrible]. Both Tenn, and Billy to whom he went after leaving Elysée. He is now in Key West—Ten gave him $1,000—which he considers nothing. He asked long ago for $100,000. I said nothing to Tenn but my feeling is that he will not rid himself unless he gives him $100,000 or about that. Also I personally feel that the idea of his always going to Key West is not a good one, that still keeps him attached to Tenn. Tenn is in Wash. for opening of *Sweet Bird* and then going to New Orleans for 2–3 weeks. I told Tenn over phone that I hope he will have strength of character to stick to his present condition. He is very weak. I am sure that this whole atmosphere affects his writing.

I and Rose went with him to opening of *Summer.* Over the phone later Tenn told me that this was the only good review others very bad. Not critical of play but of production and setting.

———

DURING rehearsals of *This Is* Tennessee flew to the opening of the *The Red Devil Battery Sign* in Vienna on December 17, 1975, at the English Theatre, a little theatre that performs plays in English. Ruth Brinkmann, joint owner-manager with her husband, Franz Schafrenek, played Woman Downtown, Keith Baxter was King Del Rey, and Maria was Perla.

"I met Tennessee at Vienna airport with a large pair of scissors—a joke which did not go with a swing. The next day at rehearsal Tennessee said softly and sweetly to me, 'Honey, you feel the play needs cutting?' 'Yes,' I replied gleefully. 'Well, I have followed your advice.' He handed me his script. He had cut out my best scene—all five pages of it.

"He did not like the way that rehearsals were going. He took me out to the Vienna Woods, where there isn't a single tree, and gave me the most awful row, as though it were my fault he said that I should have telephoned him in America and warned him.

"He decided that the only way to draw suitable attention to the way he felt was by staging a heart attack in his hotel suite. A large cylinder of oxygen was wheeled in. Tennessee lay on the sofa, in giggles. Keith Baxter and I stood at the back, trying not to laugh. Then, the Schafreneks were hauled in, so that they might hear the dying playwright's last words on how the disastrous production was killing him. They had both come thinking that they were going to be highly praised and were looking forward to an invitation to a good luncheon. Ruth happened to be wearing a Tyrolean costume, with a little hat perched atop her head, sporting a perky pheasant feather. This enormously irritated Tennessee, who kept making terrible grimaces which he thought nobody could see or interpret. Ruth took it very badly and screamed back at Tennessee, her feather fairly bobbing in fury. Franz fell to his knees and apologized for her outburst.

"However, they heeded everything Tennessee said, and the production was an enormous success in Vienna, with rave notices worldwide. We have all of us remained great friends to this day.

"The cast was staying at a pensione in Vienna, and my daughter Natasha flew out to join us there. It was a charming place—its only drawback being that the elderly lift would not budge unless one stamped on its floor. Only then, very reluctantly, would it wheeze into life.

"Tennessee had promised me faithfully that he would not bring the Enfant Terrible to Vienna. He made Tennessee hysterically nervous before first nights and created extremely vicious scenes. However, to everybody's dismay, he arrived a few days after Tennessee.

"On one occasion during rehearsals, when the three of us were driving home after a meal, the Enfant was unbelievably insulting to Tennessee in the taxi. He told him that he was washed up as a playwright, and that he couldn't write anymore. Tennessee was shattered. I told Tennessee to get out of the taxi with me and stay the night at the pensione. We scrambled out of the taxi and into the house. However, the Enfant managed to slither through the front door behind us, screaming abuse at the top of his voice, and trying to hit Tennessee.

"Hearing the noise, Keith Baxter and Natasha came downstairs just as the

Enfant, out of his head, was shouting at me in the hall, 'You're no more and no less than a rich whore!' This did not have the desired effect. Tennessee and I both burst into laughter and collapsed on the radiator. I said, 'Oh, go away, you little twerp!'

"The Enfant Terrible lunged at us with a great cry of frenzy. Natasha was still rooted to the spot at hearing her mother addressed this way. Keith, more quick-thinkingly, bundled Tennessee and me into the lift. And then we remembered. 'Stamp, Tennessee, stamp!' I yelled. And, to Tennessee's greater bewilderment, I began stamping like an Apache.

"And thus, while the Twerp was clawing at us through the lift gates, we made our rickety escape."

———

[*Handwritten on letterhead The Berkeley, London, postmarked New York, January 9, 1976, sent to the English Theatre, Vienna*]

January 1, 1976

Dearest Perla:

Called twice to wish you a happy '76—pensione & theatre—no luck.

I enclose one last joke on the "Brink" [Brinkmann]—it popped out of a paper "favor" on the table last night at a rather dismal "gala dinner"— about 3 tables occupied—today very rainy & nothing much on the telly.

Love always, Tenn

[*On letterhead Hotel El Cortez, San Francisco, California, sent to the English Theatre, Vienna*]

January 13, 1976

Dearest Maria:

Hardly a moment to catch my breath. We face our first paid pre-view [*This Is*] audience tomorrow and I'd say we were about five days behind public exposure. However the press doesn't come till the 20th. One of the two papers belongs to the Hearst chain so a bad review there is almost already written. The leading lady is excellent, the leading man beautiful.

The Vienna notices were the best set of notices I've had since '61 and of course I was especially gratified by the way they singled out you and Keith [Baxter]. Ed Sherin flew over, as my guest, with Bob Colby, the nice one of the four Boston producers. Both are now convinced that the play needed a man Keith's age, not Quinn's. Colby had made a firm offer to produce the play in the States next fall so let's pray Keith's available then. Of course I would prefer to go first to London. I think perhaps the play is too exhausting to present for longer than six months anywhere before it's made as a film.

Barnes just called and he is still insistent that I keep the booking in Australia, next month, and I need about four months rest. Also I find planes over long distances a devastating experience: could make it to Hawaii, but after that—wow!—it becomes like inter-stellar flights, and the old hound dog needs home. But Bill has a way of having his way.

I am continuing this letter late at night, Twerp sleeping. His latest homage to me is a dose of the clap. The streets of Frisco are crawling with hustlers which he finds irresistible as drugs and he doesn't bother to use the protections such as "Sanitube." I think he is someone from outer space. He tells me that he needs only to call a certain phone number in Key West to have anyone zapped out of existence: claims he means not me but the gardener, Frank Fontas. Also says he will never see me again if I resume my *romantic* relations with poor Poppins in New Orleans to which I plan flight soon as this gig opens. I think Gene Persson, who is producing with ACT, plans to take the play to B'dway via L.A. and Toronto. I want Michael York to come from L.A. to see it, I think the two-character male lead suits him. He and Pat were marvelous to me in New York and said they'd come up here for opening. Maggie Smith is also, apparently, in L.A. Excellent as the leading lady is, she has no national "name." If she's as great as I think she will be, I will put up a fight for her retention in the role.

If only you were here! I can't thank you enough for coming to Wien, I couldn't have gotten through it without you, you know. Will you go on acting now? Would you be able to fly to Australia with me and help me translate *Sea Gull* and serve as artistic director there?

I understand La Brinkmann has quit her wolf-howls. I thought they were what she did best. Now, honey, please stop telling Billy the play is too long. To tell this story, the play has to be long. When it is properly cast and produced this will be apparent.

I hope you'll write me at 1014 Dumaine in New Orleans. Kiss Natasha and Keith for me.

Love always, Tenn.

T ENNESSEE's adaptation of Chekhov's *The Sea Gull* was called *The Notebooks of Trigorin.*

This Is (An Entertainment) opened at the American Conservatory Theatre in San Francisco on January 20, 1976. It was directed by Alan Fletcher, with Elizabeth Huddle as the Countess—a part inspired by Maria—and Ray Reinhardt as the Count. Tennessee dedicated the play to Maria.

————

[*1014 Dumaine Street, New Orleans*]

January 29, 1976

Dearest Maria:

There is a note of *tristesse* in your last letter which I received here in New Orleans where I went primarily to get away from "the Twerp" for a few days. I guess it must be that the cold and damp of Vienna seeped into your spirit, and no wonder. Dear heart, it will soon be behind you and I hope that then you'll look back on it with a little more—I was about to say nostalgia but that would not be the *mot* St. Just, I fear. However I've discovered in life (which has been quite a long one for me) that there is a kinder and softer aspect to things as they are further removed into retrospect from immediate endurance. For one thing, you say you enjoyed acting again. Well, that is something, especially since you did it so well and were so favorably reviewed. You're mistaken about Ed Sherin's reaction. He called me up to say that Keith's performance had convinced him that the part was only suitable for a relatively youthful man such as Keith, since it made the tragedy so poignant. Then one of the four Boston producers, Bob Colby—the one that was nice—called me to say he wanted to produce the play as it now is on Broadway. So does Gene Persson who is co-producing *This Is* with ACT in San Francisco. He wants to produce *both* on Broadway. For *Red Devil* he would like his first wife, Shirley Knight, a brilliant actress who is up for the awards after her recent appearance in *Kennedy's Children*. She has true elegance, dramatic power and beauty. If Sherin put people down for being gay, do you think he would have directed three plays recently for this founding father of the uncloseted gay world? He is just a sort of reserved person but I think he's the best director in the States since the palmy days of Kazan.

Honey, don't you think you've been a little bit of a Tartar about La B. [Ruth Brinkmann]? After all, without her and Franz [Schafrenek] I would never have had this opportunity to see the new *Red Devil* and they did give it their all: and I thought she did show remarkable power in delivering her long monologues and in creating some illusion. I have nothing but sympathy for an actress who can deliver the meaning of a role despite being miscast, and such a complex difficult one. And poor dear Franz, putting it on without wings [to the stage] and with his nervous disabilities all but knocking him out.

Obviously the production has had quite an impression on the Teutons, as right now a German TV company is assembling in our patio here to do a talk-show with me.

Please don't think I'm a rat who doesn't appreciate your ordeal of a Vienna winter. But you did have your furs, love, and had I been there I would have bought many violets for them.

I think you would have been pleased with *This Is* in San Francisco. They gave it their most opulent production to date, 57 costumes, countless light cues, beautiful music—and what a talented star! I don't think there's a legit actress in America who could have equalled her. Of course I was shooting re-writes at them daily, they learned them over-night. It was the first time I've had the first draft of a play produced and they were heroic. Of course it is not exactly an establishment play, [and] the two San Francisco papers are reactionary. Our good reviews came from the university papers—but it makes no difference as the play remains in rep until late May and I have now completed a very solid script which they will put in as soon as I return to Frisco on my way to the kangaroo land. I've never felt so surrounded by love and understanding as I did out there.

The Twerp poses a very serious problem. I thought I had persuaded him to return to West Virginia. I did get him to phone all his relatives—mother and all eight siblings—who had thought he was dead since they hadn't heard of him or from him for five years. I could hear them shouting with joy all across the room and he told them he was coming home. Then he chickened out the next day. I have concluded that he is mentally deranged. He is pleasant to only three people, Rose, Tatiana, and Anne Meacham, and he's only nice to Rose because she mistakenly regards him as my son. Of course he is furious that he's not going back to San Francisco and to Australia. Life, life, life—this sounds like bad Chekhov—is so dreadfully sad! One has to be mad to endure it. . . .

I shall write Keith separately. I can never thank him enough for contributing his great talent and his kindness and charm to R.D. [*Red Devil*] under such trying circumstances. I hope he regards it as a rehearsal in Wien.

I mean I hope the experience hasn't turned him off all my works from hence forth.

The crew are now waiting downstairs so I must shave and dress. I will be back in the States sometime in April if I survive the island-hopping. I can't fly that far without rest-stops. Meanwhile, please write me for the first week at the Elysée and then c/o Billy—and give Francolino [Zeffirelli] my affectionate greetings. Don't let him cast you as Mary Magdalene unless he's cut out the part where she is publicly stoned. Tell him that I am just about eligible for Lazarus.

With much love always, Tenn

[*Added in handwriting*] Gore has written an hilarious review [in the *New York Review of Books*] of the *Memoirs* which will sell many copies—it has been creeping gradually up the best-seller list. It's 20 pages long!!

———

MARIA, Peter and their daughters went to Tunisia to be with Zeffirelli and to watch the shooting of *Jesus of Nazareth*. The children worked on the film.

———

[*Handwritten on letterhead Ingleside Inn, Palm Springs, Calif., postmarked San Francisco, March 10, 1976*]

March 5, 1976

Dearest Maria:

I'm writing by pen as it is, as usual when not at Wilbury, long before daybreak when I waken and shuffle to my work desk, and walls have ears and angry mouths here. I haven't known where to write you as I've heard Franco is shooting the Jesus story in Tunisia but not precisely where. Incidentally, is there not a bit for me in the film? Will do anything but drive a nail into the hand or foot of Our Saviour!—Will even play a money-changer flogged screeching from temple, having dropped a shekel in the scramble. Seriously, having extricated myself, I trust, from the Australia gig—I am most anxious to go abroad and am clutching at straws. Have been invited to preside over Cannes Film Festival and may retract my declination of that curious honor if no better excuse to get away is forthcoming.

I have devoted these recent months to preparing second draft of *This Is* while the first was being performed in San Francisco. I am still on West Coast, a fugitive from arctic cold wave so intense it probably presages the new ice age which is soon expected to hit us. I had always heard Palm Springs was a desert paradise but, like Marrakech, its charms are vastly exaggerated. Not even warm.

I must return to San Francisco the 10th to see my latest re-writes being performed. Then I hope to rest in Key West where Madam Sophia waits

Natasha, aged seventeen, and Pulcheria, aged nineteen,
photographed by Franco Zeffirelli

for me. Her whole character was transformed by the transfer from the confining circumstances of New Orleans to the freedom of the grounds in Key West. She has stopped eating furniture, has even made friends with cats.

B.B. [Bill Barnes] is still urging me to go to Australia although I have two doctors to certify I am not well enough to undertake such a long & difficult trip and all the tiresome, exhausting hoopla that would surround it. However I very much fear that I must never view a poem lovely as a kangaroo—in its native habitat.

If this reaches you, would you please send me Keith's address—the best address for me is Hotel Elysée. Also where I can call or write you in Tunisia.

[Unsigned]

[*Handwritten on postcard Ingleside Inn, Palm Springs, Calif., undated*]

Did not have operation on eyes but did acquire a soft contact lens for left eye which has restored vision remarkably after being blind in that eye for about 30 years.

Wish you were here or I was there. Take care.

All love—Tenn.

———

TENNESSEE decided to accept the offer to go to Cannes and invited Maria to join him there.

———

[*Surviving letter from Maria, handwritten*]

My saint's day is April 14. Do you remember *The Three Sisters* starts on Irina's saint's day?

Wilbury

April 12, 1976

Dearest Tenn:

My broken foot will have healed in three weeks, when the plaster comes off, so I should be quite agile for Cannes. We will have fun there. My only stipulation, put in writing, is that the little Twerp is not to be along on that trip—let him take his own trip, of a different nature, I fear. I really cannot stand his physical appearance, which he can't help, or his atrocious manners, and native vulgarity, which he can.

It all adds up to bad news for our friendship, and who needs the strain, and oh God! the boredom of those scenes? Let's have a bit of fun, drinking lots of champagne, and giving top marks to the worst films, swimming and eating in La Reserve in Beaulieu.

What news of poor Oliver? I do worry about darling Tatiana. She and me are a couple, falling around all the time. I'm just writing to her. What a pity she can't take a boat trip to Europe, as she's not allowed to fly. Why don't you scoop her up and take her with you. She can stay at Gerald Road and Wilbury.

Darling, I do hope you are taking care of yourself and dear, tender Rose. How exciting having her in Key West! My love to Leoncie. I must restart my correspondence with her.

All the daffodils and primroses are out here. The beauty of the place is unbelievable, the cows grazing in the park, the birds singing, peace and bliss. Just like a Constable painting. Mishka [Maria's golden retriever] asleep at my feet, and the failure from Harrod's [Kabanos, the dachshund] is a father with two mongrel bitches.

I bought you a beautiful edition of Shakespeare's sonnets for a present. I shall bring it to Cannes, except you'll lose it, like my Rilke. Give my love to Andrew Lyndon. I'm so glad he's with you. He's a lovely man. God bless you and Rose. Happy Easter, darling. Take care of yourself.

Always your loving Maria

[*Postmarked Key West, April 19, 1976, sent to Hotel Sidi Mansour, Monastir, Tunisia*]

1431 Duncan Street
Key West, Fla.

Dearest Maria:

Lord, how long it takes to get through this awful stationery that poor Poppins laid on me some birthdays ago! I had quite a scare about him. He disappeared from New Orleans for about a month and no one knew where he was. Now it comes out that he was visiting Grandma who has married again with the funeral baked meats of her late lamented hardly beginning to cool. It seems she has promised him, Poppins, a condominium (high-rise apts.), but with the re-marriage, Poppins is understandably anxious about the estate.

Rose is thriving in Key West, and all those who tolerate me at all are rallying about. For a long while she has been giving all possible distress signals about the situation at Stony Lodge: always packs everything she can get in her suitcase when she comes to New York for a visit. The last visit she was in a desperate physical state. Unable to hold anything in her stomach. She said the food at the Lodge was "too foul to eat." She would have gone into a steady decline if I hadn't taken her away and strictly *entre nous* I don't intend to have her go back there. Billy opposes my taking her to Europe on the *QE II*—which sails May 5th—but I think where Rose is concerned my instinct is better. She is no trouble at all. She still considers herself to be the Queen of England as I discovered when I asked her where she wanted to go in Europe. She said, "To England." I asked her why and she said, "Because I'm the Queen." I told her I felt that Parliament could handle the British Isles as well as could be expected, that there were many bombings, etc. She seemed to consider the matter seriously, in silence, and hasn't brought it up since.

So!—Billy assured me some time ago that you were going to join me in Cannes but you have made no reference to this so I wonder . . .

I am taking Madam Sophia with me: she has shaped up wonderfully in Key West, has more charm than any dog I have had. We will be at the Hotel Majestic which has a pool. I feel that Rose would be happy there. If any complication developed I could fly her at once to a good clinic in Switzerland.

Of course a lot of my plans have to be correlated with yours, so would you call me at once here in Key West, collect—(305) 294-6769—when you receive this special delivery in Tunisia. Please don't construe this as any kind of pressure. You must do what is best for you and your family. I believe the festival only lasts a week. I can visit you whenever, wherever is convenient to you if Cannes is stout. I am more and more inclined to emigrate permanently to Europe, get that little farm and raise goats and geese . . .

Much love always, Tenn

[*Added in handwriting*] Tell Franco to "break a leg"—that means good luck in American theatre.

————

"I JOINED Tennessee in Cannes, where he was honorary president of the film festival jury. He arrived with Madam Sophia and refused to go anywhere without her. That meant that we could not attend the first-night party in his honor. They were terribly annoyed. I realized that this was going to

30 ème **FESTIVAL DU FILM**
CANNES 76

At the Cannes Film Festival, 1976. Tennessee was the honorary president of the jury that year and insisted on bringing his dog, Madam Sophia, everywhere he went.

"Tennessee and Madam Sophia in the gardens of the Hotel du Cap, Cap d'Antibes, where we stayed during the Cannes Film Festival, 1976"

become impossible, unless we moved to an hotel with a garden. We decamped to the Hôtel du Cap. The move was an enormous success. Madam Sophia won everybody's hearts. She adored going up and down in the glass lift, and would wait, on her own, until a lift man took her for a ride.

"One evening, before a very grand premiere, everyone was in evening clothes. Among them was a very elegant woman in a long white organdy dress with diamanté embroidery which caught the light and glistened as she moved. Madam Sophia decided that this apparition must be some sort of dangerous animal, and began stalking her, so stealthily that the victim didn't notice. Tennessee and I, among others, were helpless with laughter.

"Languidly, the unfortunate woman sat down in an armchair. This was too much for Madam Sophia, who took one enormous leap and landed, one hundred and ten pounds of her, sprawled in her lap. To everybody's astonishment, she was delighted: 'C'est un chien magnifique!' She evidently had not noticed that her organdy dress was completely ruined for the grand gala.

"Tennessee refused to sit in a box with any of the other judges, saying that it made him nervous. We would be constantly hounded by the press, lying in wait for us everywhere. Melvyn Bragg was working on a profile of Tennessee for British TV. Tennessee's attempts to dodge them and to enter through the side doors, which were nearly always locked, drew far more attention than that he was trying to avoid.

"We had a wonderful time."

Tennessee had by now bought a house for Rose in Key West.

1431 Duncan Street
Key West, Fla.

June 22, 1976

Dearest Maria:

Our discussions of the *Memoirs* was over-shadowed in Cannes by the fantasy of the festival but your letter, received yesterday, registered very strongly and clearly. You are so right to object and I am now able to understand your objections. I don't have a copy of the book but I see how it makes no sense about us. Next time we meet I will show you the original manuscript and the cuts which were made to meet their commercial standards. I don't say that it was an easy work to deal with. Sometimes they must have felt like they had a sizzling hot potato pie in their hands. But they were inordinately strict about length and date of publication.

I am enclosing a first-draft of a section chiefly concerned with us which I think must be put into the English edition if it is to appear.

It is probably a little stilted in the present draft, it needs to be given more specifics and more liveliness and humor.

Keith [Baxter] has received rave notices at the Shakespeare theatre in Canada, and so has Maggie Smith. Billy has assured me that Jerry Hellman will fly up there to see Keith. He was covered by both Clive Barnes of the *New York Times* and by *Time* magazine both of which raved about him and I have wired him that he is now completely established as an international star. I don't feel that I have to go to Canada as there was never any doubt in my mind that he was the ideal man for King.

Rose got up at 4 a.m.—I had to make her coffee and provide her with cigarettes. Our gardener has quit and Rose spends an hour and a half, morning and evening, pouring a glass of water over each plant—nothing will deter her. Her opinion of Madam has greatly improved. At first she described her as "a wicked beast" but she now finds her "as good as gold."—I think the discipline you gave her at the Hôtel du Cap has resulted in this transformation.

The Twerp has been on speed for about two months and during that period has eaten only about three meals—when he was briefly out of the stuff. From the look of him he will soon be released from the law of gravity.

Now Anne Meacham is in Key West with Pat Carmichael whom she expects to direct her in England as "the celebrated soubrette." She does create for herself more problems than she solves!—but is a good friend and a fine actress in roles that suit her.

Love, 10

P.S.—The key to my studio mysteriously disappeared for several days. Leoncia just now found it. I fear that the Twerp, having access to the unlocked studio, found this letter with the presumptuous reference to Pat Carmichael and Anne, since just after I wrote this letter I had dinner with them and the whole table talk was about the normalcy of their relations, how people sometimes mistook them for dykes but they had only the purest and most professional of an association.—As if I really cared!—What I do care about is the difficulty that poor Anne will encounter in trying to sell Mme. Carmichael—yes, it now seems she has a husband somewhere—to London actors and a management for the production of *The Latter Days of a Celebrated Soubrette.* Since I had never heard tell of Mme. Carmichael, I doubt very much that her renown has extended to London.

Dear Ruth [Brinkmann]!—She has finally written me a letter in which she enclosed a clipping that says Vienna has discovered—in her, Ruth—the "ideal Williams actress."—Suggest you destroy this letter as it is full of caustic remarks due to the strain of conditions at the old home-place.— Latest development is that Rose now refuses to eat—when I called in a doctor she said to him, "I will not accept any medications from you or anyone but Cornelius Williams"—the latter being our father who was laid to rest in Old Gray about twenty years ago . . .

In the enclosed piece of writing for the London edition of *Memoirs* I have put brackets in charcoal pencil about a possible cut since I know how publishers love cutting. I'll be back in N.Y. this week-end and will find where this new piece can best be inserted. You may be able to help me. Of course I'll also study all the references you object to and write the London publishers that they must be deleted.

Remember me kindly to all you regard as deserving, including Her Majesty the Queen, H.R.H. Princess Margaret—even your daughters and their dogs. (A clout in time saves nine.)

Love always, Tennessee

———

"KEITH BAXTER was baffled on an occasion when he and I were following my daughter along a pavement in Vienna. Natasha knew perfectly well that she had been annoying me for two weeks—never getting up, refusing to learn any German, and not having her expensive Parisian boots reheeled being among her many transgressions. The sullen way in which Natasha was slopping along on her heels was the final straw. I swung my handbag around on its long strap and gave her what must have appeared to be a totally unprovoked clout on the head. Keith was stunned. 'But she didn't do or say anything, Maria!' Natasha was not in the least surprised but managed to squeeze two crocodile tears from her slit eyes. Three minutes later, she and I were cramming Sacher torte into our mouths at a coffee house, the best of friends.

"That perplexed Keith still further.

" 'Russians!'

"Tennessee admired Maggie Smith very much as an actress—although this may not have been apparent to the audience at the first night of her *Hedda Gabler*. Tennessee had been given a box, and Pulcheria was very keen to go with her godfather. Knowing that his behavior in a theatre audience was unpredictable, I mischievously let her go instead of me.

"Tennessee had the habit of falling asleep, and decided to fetch a bucket of ice to press onto his forehead. He clattered back into the box, tripping up and disturbing the rapt audience. He pressed the ice into his brow, which slithered down onto the heads of people sitting in the stalls. He loudly apologized. The audience hissed to him to be quiet. But then, to Pulcheria's mortification, he began roaring with laughter at the most tragic moments. 'Of course *Hedda Gabler* is a comedy!' he insisted. When Maggie Smith shot herself, he howled. One critic gave him a personal review the next day. Maggie has been noticeably glum about him ever since."

———

[Enclosed with the preceding letter was the following typescript. Handwritten at the top of each page is "T.W. for Maria."]

"Who is there to care beside yourself?" I exclaimed silently last night as I lay sleepless, turning over and over in my mind various unsatisfactory solutions to some very difficult problems which had to be resolved in the next few days.

What a flat-sounding word [friendship] is for what becomes, later on in life, the most important element of it! To me the French word for this deep relationship, probably all the deeper because it exists outside and beyond the physical kind of devotion, is much more appealing. It covers a broader spectrum and surely its depth is greater. The word is *l'amitié*—apologies for assuming that some of you might not know that.

That which we call and think of as "love" is often a promiscuous word in more senses than one. In all but the rarest cases in my experience I am afraid that it has depleted more than replenished the reservoir of my emotions, and in quite a number of cases it has also polluted and debased—and never mind if I come on as what I am, a man who is still a child in the shadow of a Protestant rectory.

L'amitié never involves a material transaction. You don't see it in a shop-window with a price tag attached to it or close beside it, and it requires no exertion of will to animate it with the breath of spirit. It is a consecrated thing and it is devoutly to be wished for, because, if it is real as opposed to artificial or trivial, it can endure until death, and Miss Elizabeth Barrett Browning was convinced that it lasted after. I think she is right to the extent that it lasts afterwards in the heart of the survivor.

Now for an insertion of a less serious nature, that bit of comic relief which I think is essential to a book of my memoirs.

Upon a crossing of the Atlantic on the *QE II* I was stalking up and down the arcade of little shops on both sides of B deck in search of a gift for a lady toward whom I felt this ineffable emotion which I have been discussing as though it were effable. The jewelry shops had been depleted of gold ornaments by those passengers who descend upon them like crazed birds the moment their doors are opened the day after embarkation. The only really attractive thing left was a heavy necklace of braided silver, the sort of necklace that, in fashionable circles, is called a *collier*. I have always loved silver: it says something to me that gold doesn't say, and this does not mean that I have never heard or read the renowned "Cross of Gold" speech by the renowned William Jennings Bryan, now chiefly remembered for his last-ditch stand in East Tennessee against Fundamentalist interpretations of the origin of man. I love silver because you see it less conspicuously. It has a moon-glow reticence about it. It looks much better on a summer throat than does gold. And so I bought it for the lady, since it was summer—I believe it was usually in winter that I had presented her with golden bangles.

I was disconcerted by her laughter when she unwrapped this gift and her mock-serious remark: "So I have descended from gold to silver in your esteem!"

It's no good using phrases like "moon-glow reticence of silver." You are forgiven, possibly even understood, but when you shy away from verbal expression of this certain sentiment, *l'amitié*, you would do well to think twice about silver necklaces till they start appearing on the throats of those ladies who are said to be contemplating libel suits against an American writer not safely mentioned, now, in any season at all.

All right, not terribly funny, would not serve a stand-up comedian in Vegas. But I do have just a bit more to say about *l'amitié*.

It is a delicate feeling, of course, and of course it is frangible and most certainly of all it must not be neglected. And yet it is long-suffering. It survives many unavoidable separations without disrepair, since it does not depend on physical presence as much as a carnal attachment. Extended absences of one from the other do not affect it, probably because these absences are a material element and this feeling that I call *l'amitié* has so little concern with material things.

I have been told and have no reason to doubt that *l'amitié* can exist between two men as well as between a man and a woman, but in my case it has occurred usually always with someone of the opposite gender.

I have had many close friendships with men which were without any sexual connotations, God knows. But I have found them less deeply satisfying than those I have had with a few women.

Of these women, the most important has been with [my dearest friend] Maria, as both Maria Britneva or as the Lady Maria St. Just.

In the American edition of my memoirs this richly sustaining attachment was, for some reason, reduced by the editors to the point where it seemed to be little more than an acquaintance, practically unexplained.

Despite her exceptional gifts as an actress—until her marriage to Lord Peter St. Just she was kept under contract by London's most prestigious management, H. M. Tennent, and had appeared in important roles with Sir John Gielgud and Dame Edith Evans and their like—she had not acquired a prominent name in the theatre or film industries of the States and, alas, the publishing firm that brought out these memoirs in America apparently had the usual hang-up concerning "names." They had heard of my friends Anna Magnani and Margaret Leighton because of their stateside appearances, but when Maria came to America it was usually to help me through the rigors of a stage production in which she didn't appear.

I always press the panic-button for Maria when I have a play coming up. The last time I did it was when *The Red Devil Battery Sign* was running into trouble out of town: in Boston, of course, and, also predictably, under the controlling power of a certain impresario whose initials are D.M. [David Merrick].

Maria could not save the abortive D.M. production but she made it possible for me to survive it.

The play did not stop there nor did Maria's commitment to it.

In a crucible of fury, I wrote the play once again and it was presented the following winter in Vienna's English Theatre with an all–English and American cast which included Maria in a leading role.

She and Keith Baxter and the American actress Ruth Brinkmann, under the direction of Franz Schafrenek, gave the revised play a production which won a theatre work of mine the first great notices—aside those given to revivals—that I had enjoyed since 1961 when those "two Limeys" Margaret Leighton and Alan Webb gave poetry and truth to *Night of the Iguana*.

And so *l'amitié* is a long, long word of great consequence in my life. . . .

Hotel Elysée
60 East 54th Street
N.Y.C.
(in 10 days)

July 24, 1976

Dearest Maria:

This letter on an electric typewriter at the Jerry Hellmans' at Malibu may be interrupted at any moment by the arrival for lunch of Michael and Pat York. I do wish you were here. Last night there was a gala dinner attended by most of the local literati and intelligentsia such as Isherwood, Don Bachardy, Joan Didion and her husband, a stately scientist engaged in the study of the speech-methods of dolphins, etc. Excellent champagne and wine.

Jerry Hellman is the movie magnate who is supposedly trying to mount a stage-production this year of *Red Devil*. He is quite nice—looks marvellous for a man nearing fifty. His wife takes nude photos of him and I regret to report that he has some white pubic hairs. She is also quite a gifted painter.

Right now I am between secretary companions, the inevitable split with the "Twerp" having occurred some weeks ago in Key West. I came to the Coast with one of Andy Warhol's kids, no one else being immediately available. He is an ex-hustler turned photographer. I became annoyed when he announced that photography was the one art of tomorrow, that it would replace all painting and literature. I said, Well, thank God Renoir and Van Gogh didn't have a Kodak. My annoyance increased when he began cohabiting with another young rip-off artist at my expense. I really exploded when he locked Madam for several hours in his clothes-closet. Then I told him to hit the road, bought him a ticket back to New York—but since he left for the air-port in my rental car and the rental agency hasn't reported its return, he may have decided to tour the country.

Well, I am now through with all these rip-offs and am searching desperately for a *serious* secretary with only the stipulation that he be socially presentable and a sympathetic care-taker.

While I am in Malibu, poor Madam is staying in San Francisco with Andrew Lyndon.* I called last night to check on things. Andrew, drunker than usual—if possible—tried to get Madam to speak to me on the phone but she refused . . .

There is a little black-board and piece of chalk outside my bedroom here for memos. I just wrote "Tennessee Slept Here 2 nites with 9,999 cats." Actually there were not quite that number but their presence was noticeable.

I do hope to see you very soon.

All best love, Tennessee

[*Added in handwriting*] *Could not bring her here because of the cats which are very ill-natured. Is there no possible way to get her to England without quarantine?! She needs Wilbury & Wilbury needs her . . . Liz Taylor kept her dog in yacht on Thames.

Later: back at Elysée

Well, you've heard about the fate of dear Madam.—I found this letter returned to me here. The Malibu hosts filched it from my ms. case. I now have a different producer who has produced plays in both England and the States. He is selling his California estate and settling again in London in about two weeks. I hope to follow shortly with new travelling-companion [Dick Ellis] whom I think you'll approve, a well-bred poet but highly competent and reliable. He's visiting his mother in Denver and will pick me up here just after Labor Day and we'll rest up on an island till the producer wants me to join him.

What an appalling summer it has been, but another season approaches that can only be better. Is Peter all right again? My sympathy to him.

Much love always, Tennessee

———

PETER had been suffering from a serious depression.

Tennessee had been assured that the hold of the aircraft in which Madam Sophia was to travel back to New York was air-conditioned, but it was not, and upon arrival the dog was found dead of suffocation.

The Eccentricities of a Nightingale, the revised version of *Summer and Smoke,* was produced at the Morosco Theatre, New York City, on November 23, 1976, directed by Edwin Sherin, with Betsy Palmer and David Selby.

Tennessee wrote an article for the *New York Times,* published on November 21, in which he discussed the search for "artistic purity" that had initiated the revisions.

. . . This purifying process began back in 1951 during a Roman summer when I was working against time to remove from *Summer and Smoke* the many things which offended me before it went into rehearsal as an H. M. Tennent production in London. . . .

I arrived in London with what I considered, quite correctly I think, was practically a new work excavated from the mouldering debris of its predecessor. As usual, I was met at the airport by my longest-surviving friend of the female gender, then a young actress under contract to H. M. Tennent, Maria Britneva, now known non-professionally as the Lady St. Just. When I told her that I had arrived with a work purified of all but its humor, poetry and passion, though retaining a pair of protagonists known as Miss Alma and Dr. John, she had to deflate my elation with the news: "But we are already deep into rehearsals with *Summer and Smoke.*"

Observing my crestfallen look, she said, "Oh, never mind. Give me the new play and I'll put it safely away till—"

She didn't specify when, but some 10 or 15 years later, she produced *The Eccentricities of a Nightingale,* which I had actually forgotten by this time. "I'm going to put this in your overcoat pocket, and I want you to read it tonight if you're sober enough," she informed me. It looked very pretty, all in pale blue type, and I was so happy with it that I read it through non-stop that night.

Space, not time, is of the essence, I believe, and so I now leave it to you who must be its true mentors, at the Morosco on Tuesday.

Hotel Elysée
60 East 54th Street
New York

November 23, 1976

Dearest Maria:

A thunder of silence between us since you left me with the last and worst of the three hired companions of summer, '76. Mr. John O'Rear has now returned to California with a thousand dollars severance pay which was a bargain I'd say.

This evening *Eccentricities of a Nightingale* opened. I don't know whether successfully or not, as immediately after the performance Bill [Barnes] and Faye Dunaway and I went to a recording studio where her rock 'n' roll boy-friend whom we met once in Boston [Peter Wolf of the J. Geils Band] was cutting a new album. Then I cut out while she and Billy remained to drink Dom Pérignon and I turned off my phone. I am booked out at 11 a.m. this morning on American Airlines to the Morning Star Beach Hotel on St. Thomas, Virgin Islands. It has the loveliest stretch of Caribbean swimming and beaching I've known. The Twerp who's been in attendance a while says he will not go but I have an alternate companion who works for a living (free-lance writing, including a recent interview with Gore) who said today he would be available. Of course I hope the Twerp adheres to his resolution to stay here. He has been on "speed" for weeks and is afraid it would be unobtainable in the Caribbean. Really such a sad case. I'm sure that in your heart, which is wide as the sky, you must share my pity for him.

I have to be back here December third to be inducted [as a lifetime member] into the American Academy [of Arts and Letters]—immediately afterwards I plan to fly to England alone. I hope that Persson or you can get me into the Berkeley. As I wrote Keith this afternoon, one of my principal objectives is to acquire a duplicate of Madam Sophia. She haunts me. I am "marble constant." Purchasing her facsimile in England would by-pass the quarantine.

I invited Tatiana and Igor to the opening tonight but couldn't find them afterwards.

I doubt that I will ever make a home again in the States, not if my new work catches on in England. The only real tie is Rose. I might be able to find a place for her in Switzerland.

All best love as always, Tenn.

Madam Sophia

"THE USE of the phrase 'marble constant' (a quotation from Shakespeare's *Antony and Cleopatra*) had originated from the sculptor Tony Smith. Describing Maria's loyalty to Tennessee, he had said, 'Maria, you are marble constant.'

"Igor Schvetzoff, Tatiana's cousin, was a ballet teacher who had written a best-selling book, *Borzoi,* about escaping from Russia by walking to Siberia in his ballet shoes."

On January 9, 1977, Tennessee complained in a letter to a mutual friend that "although my last letter [to Maria] was rather urgent, I got no response. I sometimes suspect this friendship and concern for me is all a myth that she has constructed. However, this is a suspicion that I'd love to discuss as there's no one else whom I can look to in times of emotional stress. I am also troubled by the possibility that maybe she received a bad report from the hospital and hasn't felt like writing on that account."

––––––––

[Letter from Maria to Williams, in reply to a letter that has evidently been lost, January 7, 1977]

Darling Tennessee:

I was so pleased to get your letter just now. I am immediately writing, otherwise old Father Time takes over and nothing gets done. Guess whose pen this is? Yours, from Sheaffer. Luckily I whipped it into my handbag, otherwise that would have been lost. I like the end of your letter. "I love you as ever, but not because you are icy." I am icy, but only to little twerps. That's the best news, that the Twerp has twerped off. All he contributed was to muck up your visit to London and stop business being done.

It's Russian Christmas today. I went to Church last night. Beautiful service, everyone gets anointed with holy oil. I helped an old lady of ninety into church, who was blind, and deaf. She said, or rather yelled, "Who are you? I know your voice." I said, "Born Britneva." "Ah, yes. I loved your mother," and in the same breath, yelling, "The first time I ever went to church in St. Petersburg, I was six years old and it was during Holy Week." All the congregation hissed at her to be quiet. I thought it was very beautiful, that cry out for her youth, suddenly, like that, when one knew that this would probably be the last time she would go to church. Poor soul.

Well I'll post this quickly. I'm just off to Wilbury.

Love and kisses. The Frog seems okay. Don't be so suspicious.

Love, Maria

1431 Duncan Street
Key West, Fla.

February 6, 1977

Dear Child of God:

I have little to report of a startling nature except that I am actually going to have a new play, *Vieux Carré*, presented—more or less—as the hounds of spring appear on winter's traces. I received a breathlessly exhilarated call from Billy [Barnes] this eve stating that he has resumed his piano lessons for the first time since he was twelve. Did you know Billy was over twelve?—And also that the new play has the following bookings on the road. A week in New Haven and *two* weeks in Boston, a couple of New

York pre-views and an opening late in April—this is despite the fact that we have no star name like Quinn—but it is a play of considerable charm and has been cast with the actors precisely fitting the parts.

However, if you can read a bit between the lines, you may understand why I propose to stay with this venture through rehearsals and through the first audience-exposure in New Haven and then cut out on the Concorde again for points east of everywhere but Mandalay . . .

Now about Burt Shevelove [director of *Red Devil Battery Sign*]. This does present a problem as the great American director of serious drama Joe Hardy is truly enthusiastic about *Battery,* loves the Round House idea, loves Baxter. The credits of Shevelove are *A Funny Thing Happened on the Way to the Forum, The Frogs* by Aristophanes—performed by nude boys in the Olympic sized swimming pool at Yale—and that he is now about to revive *Merton of the Movies*—a killer-diller of the early twenties—at a Hollywood playhouse.

This birthday stationery that Mary Poppins afflicted me with is finally nearing exhaustion—and as for Poppins, I have heard indirectly that she is embarked upon a career as a printer's apprentice in a place called Punte Grande [*sic*], Florida. I must call her soon and find out if she has discovered that June does not come immediately after January.

The Twerp re-appeared. His little misadventure on Half Moon Street and his vacation in Vera Cruz have greatly altered his personality in some respects. He seems to have come mysteriously into a great deal of the hard stuff—surely not through transactions related to cannabis!—and is buying nearly all the groceries and picking up nearly all the restaurant bills. I have a new male English bull puppy who is a holy terror. I mean unholy. I had to build a kennel for him to exercise in. Otherwise he is constantly chewing on any exposed appendage of my body, devouring my tubes of paint, and mistaking the house for a public lavatory.

You-know-who will never again set foot on English shores, but I hope that I shall.

Much love, Tennessee

———

BURT SHEVELOVE, after visiting Vienna, said that he would direct *The Red Devil Battery Sign* in London.

Because of the considerable public conjecture concerning the real circumstances surrounding the death of John F. Kennedy, the time seemed appropriate for a production of the play, whose themes are similar.

This and *Orpheus Descending* are Tennessee's only two plays with political connotations.

———

[*From Gore Vidal to Maria, handwritten letter from Ravello, Italy, April 15, 1977*]

Dear Pig:

Saw the Bird in L.A. and he was able to stop the endless flow of self-pity long enough to tell me of your operation—Do they give you treatments? Are they the best? Wisest? We are here for summer—perhaps our last in these parts—Italy crumbles unpleasantly. Bought a house in L.A. but not happy at prospect of living there—

Love from G

[*Envelope postmarked Key West*]

April 15, 1977

Dearest Maria:

To coin a phrase, all hell has broken loose here. There was a big drug bust on the Keys a week ago and all the "smokers" have had to go on pills, among them the Twerp, of course. Last night and this morning he was totally and pathetically "bananas." He threatened suicide yesterday and had confiscated enough of my prescription pills to accomplish the act. This morning he was drinking on top of the pills and was completely raving. Poor Leoncia is wild-eyed, the animals are in shock, and the Twerp has left for a female doctor's office. I called her from my studio and warned her what to expect, that he was going to attempt to score for strongest Valiums and for Seconals. I told her that there must be no police but that a hospital must be alerted, as he is capable of violence in this state. She seemed to understand and to be prepared: I won't know anything more till six p.m. as I've turned my phone off. This hysterical alcoholic, Viola Veidt, is trying to set the brutal local police on him. I had to turn them away last night.

They had to delay opening of *Vieux Carré* till May 5th because of the set which is too complicated for any theatre I've ever seen. Don't ask me why these matters are not dealt with in advance. The Broadway theatre is finished, in my opinion. I believe I have given them one last play which is lovely: but after that, I want to produce only in England: then a season of repertory in Australia.—Trying to get that subsidized and organized.

Last word I heard about *Battery* was that Vanessa Redgrave was seriously interested. I think she'd be marvelous. The "conspiracy" surrounding Kennedy's death is breaking wide open again, with oil billionaires in Texas, such as W. E. Hunt, now implicated by a suicide note from someone who was involved.

I've received a lovely letter from Keith but must delay answering til I get his address in New York.

All love, Tenn.

Later: Thanks to Valium tablets, placed in my care, kept locked in studio and doled out one every four hours to relieve "anxiety," things are back under control here. Twerp has quieted down miraculously, but these improvements are only temporary, I know from experience. I also know the identity of the chief drug-peddler on the Keys. He is allowed to operate without interference because he has an old bitch of a mother probably in collusion with him, [and] runs a big restaurant here as a front. I have the authoritative reports on him from two of his former clients, one of whom was taken for ten thousand on a cocaine deal. He has been trying to lure me to his restaurant, called me on the phone and asked why I didn't drop by. I told him he was the root of all evil on the Keys. When I am not here, he sleeps in my house with criminal types—with Twerp's permission. The new district attorney, at Viola Veidt's instigation, has been inviting me to dinner. He wants me to put the finger on this peddler whom I am quite certain he knows—so I politely decline the invitations. It is impossible to know which, if any, of the law personnel can be trusted.—It is Watergate and the Kennedy conspiracy on a small scale.

The weather is lovely this past week, unaffected by events below. I will be flying North in a few days, soon as my nerves are repaired from the recent tempest.

Hope to see you for the pre-views which start April 22.

Love, 10

———

ON MAY 11, 1977, *Vieux Carré* was first produced at the St. James Theatre, New York City, directed by Arthur Allan Seidelman, with Richard Alfieri as the Writer, Tom Aldredge as Nightingale the Painter and Sylvia Sidney as Mrs. Wire. The production closed after five performances.

Maria had flown to New York to be with Tennessee. "The play was in no fit state to be shown. The scenery was only half up, and the actors, except for Sylvia Sidney, barely knew their lines. I felt that Tennessee's advisers were very much at fault in allowing this production to go ahead.

"*Vieux Carré* was produced in London, however, with great success."

———

[*Handwritten note to Lord St. Just, on paper headed* Red Devil Battery Sign]

Dear Peter:

I observed in a newspaper that you've just had a birthday and take the occasion to wish you many more.

Also to thank you for your kindnesses to me in London, over many years. *En Avant!*

Affectionately, Tennessee

1431 Duncan Street
Key West, Fla.

July 28, 1977

Dearest:

Getting a "massive dose of rest and seclusion" here, which is what I needed. Feeling much better, almost well enough to undertake another play production. I believe the Twerp has run out of those speed tablets he wangled out of some witless doctor in Brighton, as his appetite has returned with a bang. When I got up for lunch, he had prepared three courses, the entrée a huge red snapper. I told him I couldn't stuff myself at noon—just had ice tea and a salad of mozzarella and tomatoes.

We spent the night in Washington. There was no reservation at the Watergate so we passed the night at the Madison downtown. My charming friend Edmond took us out to a discreetly gay restaurant. Twerp still had his speed at that time and Edmond, who is employed by a psychiatric clinic, gave him a good scare. Called up the clinic and said he had an emergency patient for immediate commitment.

I called Natasha's apartment but no one answered. I will make more persistent efforts to contact her when I go to New York this coming week to get my new version of *Vieux Carré* typed up and dispatched to . . . the director who . . . told me in London that he needed another week with me there to set things up for the production he plans in December, when I will be back from the Australian gig.

Don't worry about Natasha.

If I find that I can afford another round trip on the Concorde, I may pop back over to England. This time I could rest and work at Wilbury and perhaps [Keith] Hack could join me, the condition being that he change his clothes. He's a delightful person but he seems to be imitating the life-style of the early Brando or the Lower East Side hippies: the out-fit which he wore whenever I saw him had acquired a rancid odor: I had to sit across the room from him.

Barnes says that the Australians are paying my round-trip passage to Sydney and a per diem of fifty a day. I'm sure they will be more reliable in their payments than was Personne. Have you heard any recent report of his activities, in or out of gaol?

I am in a dilemma, not right now but impending. I can't take the Twerp to Australia as he seems to expect: it would hazard the whole expedition. Yet it will need a travelling companion for all the island-hopping involved. Edmond hinted that he was not satisfied with his present employment and I may be able to engage him for Project Kangaroo.

Wouldn't it be nice to have Christmas in England this year?

No other news at present except that Windham and Campbell have received a 25 thousand dollar advance on the commercial publication of the letters. [*Tennessee Williams' Letters to Donald Windham, 1940–1965* was first published in 1977.] Since Floria [Lasky] appears to be totally complacent about this situation, I am going to change to Arnold Weissberger who feels that I have good grounds to secure a court injunction against these miscreants, Les Soeurs Biches.

I hope you'll soon be exercising your high-voltage talents in luckier ventures than the past one.

Much love, Tennessee

[*From Key West*]

September 1, 1977

Dearest Maria:

The house is under siege from without and within. There is a hurricane in the Gulf of Mexico which has brought rains that are flooding the grounds and inside there is the Twerp, sweating as if he had a mortal fever from the drugs he's been taking, ups and downs. So it's impossible here. I think I will have to fly back to Europe: a couple of days in London and then down to Tangier or Marrakech. Unfortunately there is no one to go with me. Despite his good breeding and charm, my friend Edmond won't do as a travelling companion. He got in touch with Bill Barnes (who happened to be in Washington the week-end we arrived there) and told him that I didn't trust him and that I was in a state of derangement. Of course I do have periods of questioning Bill's judgement in my professional life. An aging writer prey to Perssons, Windhams, Campbells and to his own constant apprehensions, paranoiac or not, is bound to feel like a creature that is backed into a corner. In my undisturbed moments I still look to Bill as to a sort of final protector. I guess that you are the only person whose loyal friendship I have never doubted.

This is a crucial time of my life. I had a medical examination in New York with disheartening reports. I am developing a cataract on my right eye, now, the one that I regarded as my good one. The doctor said it would "mature slowly" but I notice each day that without my high-power glasses I see more dimly. Also alarming hypertension. Of course sometimes I wonder if I want to go on under such circumstances. When Tatiana and I visit Rose, I am ashamed of myself. She has such amazing strength of spirit: we can't keep up with her when she is walking about the grounds at Stony Lodge. And I feel that Mother, at 92, has expiated all of her dreadful but unintentional mistakes. Dakin and I are back on amicable terms. He is running again [his previous campaign was for the Senate] for governor of Illinois and this time he is getting a much better press. Almost as if he were being represented by Margaret Gardner. His interviews are witty and amusing and touching: every evening he visits Mother and gets her to eat a little.

I've had phone conversations with Natasha which are reassuring. She thinks she'll return to England in two months. Maybe you'd like to join me in New Orleans where I have to go to make new arrangements for the rental property and maybe we could persuade Natasha to fly back to England with us. Hope springs eternal. . . . . . .

I'm getting her a new typewriter to replace the one you loaned me.

Remember me to Peter. I hope he knows that my own problems make me feel close to his.

Love to Keith Baxter. Billy says that Sherin wants to put on *Battery Sign* at the theatre in Buffalo where we saw Jon Voight in *Streetcar*. I wouldn't be interested unless Keith were accepted as King.

Love, 10

———

MARGARET GARDNER, who worked for the Rogers & Cohen public relations agency, had been engaged by Tennessee to promote *The Red Devil Battery Sign*. After it closed so abruptly (although through no fault of hers), she returned Tennessee's check. He was extremely impressed by how honorably she had behaved.

––––––

[*Undated*]

Dearest Maria:

I haven't written to you in quite a while because I am in a stubborn state of depression and didn't want to burden you with it. I've almost stopped talking to people, a condition I haven't been in since the seven years of almost clinical depression after Frankie's death. I have no suitable companion here in Key West, just a crazily narcissistic young man. It takes him an hour to prepare himself to his satisfaction to go out. This evening, for instance, he couldn't find a black headband, and accused me of confiscating it. He is still out at 4 a.m.

I get about two hours sleep a night. So it goes. Abominably. I don't pity but despise myself. Some drastic step has to be taken. I think I should go up to a hotel (with swimming-pool) near Rose's lodge. It would not be necessary to talk much up there, unless I found a psychiatrist to talk to.

If I can hang on till spring comes, I'd go to Europe and we could go to Russia together to collect my royalties, which are said to be a lot. Of course the greatest advantage would be being with you. You know that you and Janie [Smith] are my greatest friends.

Please light a candle for me since I am afraid that I have only a prayer at this point.

Tatiana's courage and gallantry make me feel so weak in comparison. The death of Igor [Schvetzoff, her cousin] almost killed her but she still goes to visit Rome.

There are rare people who make you believe in God. I think continually of them so that I can go on.

> With much love as ever, Tennessee

[*Undated*]

Letter II

I'm enclosing the long letter I'd lost in Key West. As you'll see from the contents I was about to sink into another bad depression but now I'm pulling out of it, due mostly to few days rest in a delightful hotel in Pascagoula, Mississippi on the Gulf Coast. I will be too busy, now, to relapse. I'm leaving tomorrow for St. Louis where there's a lot of action. I give a reading at Washington University there for the Oliver Evans Fund, attend a ceremony at which Mother received a citation from the mayor as "Literary Mother of the Year." Then go to Chicago with Dakin to publicly endorse him in his latest political campaign, this time for governor. Bill Barnes wants to know what I'll say. I assured him that I would think of something suitably amusing but not embarrassing to him.

Last night I had dinner at Oliver's charming apartment. That fantastic eighty-five year old woman Ardis Blackburn is taking beautiful care of him. He is surrounded by all his Oriental art objects and mementos. Ardis prepared a lovely meal. Tonight I'm entertaining them at dinner. I had the impression that Oliver is distinctly better than when I last saw him about six months ago. I believe you saw him then, too. They are such a beautiful pair of people. They have two views from the apartment, the back looking out on a cemetery and the front on City Park and the bay. I told him to only look out the front windows.

Oliver's improvement is despite a most peculiar physician. At a recent social occasion he denounced Ardis as an old dyke, broke her spectacles and tried to throw her out of the car going home.

What a bewildering world this is!

I'll call you from New York hoping to hear good news concerning your domestic problems.

With my love, 10

1431 Duncan Street
Key West, Fla.

December 2, 1977 ["Nov. 1977" deleted]

[Added in handwriting]
Note: This letter discovered unmailed

Dearest Maria:

Your letter emanated such sparks of Russian volatility that the postman brought it straight in the door and handed it to Leoncia, who came lumbering out to the lunch-table in the patio with it, a fearful gleam in the glass eye as well as the "good" one.

Twerp: "What does she say about me, what does she say about me?"

Tenn: "Not a word."

He's gone off to get a lawn-mower with Leoncia and the dog in his '61 Triumph, loudest thing on wheels since that Jeep without a muffler that terrorized Roman streets in '48. Very crestfallen that you had disregarded his existence. I yelled after him, "What are you gonna do with the dawg?" He said he was gonna chain it to the steering-wheel of the car. My guess is that the dog will arrive any moment dragging it up to the gate: unfortunately it has a home-coming instinct as well as a lust for blood (preferably mine), cunningly timing his attacks to moments when I'm trying to have a phone-conversation: all of them lately have been interspersed with outcries of pain. He first snatches off my shoes so it is quite impossible to kick him without losing a foot. Leoncia sits at the kitchen table with a big stick in her hand, clever girl. My dear cat Sabbatha only appears in the hours just before daybreak when I get up to work, utters a whispered mew. I have to set her food on a wooden table back of the house which is too high for the fanged monster to jump on.

After giving me his word via the phone in New York, the book review editor of the *Times* now refuses to take my phone-calls. His secretary says, "Oh, Mr. Shapiro has just stepped out." Apparently she means out the window, for though I leave a message for him to call me collect, he doesn't. It's undoubtedly a conspiracy, perhaps associated with the Kennedy assassinations. (Two "asses" in that word.)

All my love, Tennessee

[*From* Androgyne, Mon Amour, *published 1977*]

A DAYBREAK THOUGHT FOR MARIA

A daybreak thought
I may die
no reason not
nor reason why

Yet still live
moments through
sky now turning
lighter blue

City woke
as if God spake
"Cities wake
at daybreak."

Daybreak makes
living wake
and tired move
more to prove

"I live still
ten stories high
with it moving
still am I."

As if God thought
"Let him go
through at least
one daybreak more."

[*On letterhead British Airways Concorde, postmarked Atlanta, January 8, 1978*]

Dearest Maria:

I called you in London yesterday. Some breathless old hag shrieked: "Lady in Roma, Roma!"—so I guess you've extended your vacation through the New Year. It must have been very lovely. I watched midnight mass on TV, hoping to catch a glimpse of you and fellow celebrants.

Of course I'm anxious to know if you left the script for Helen Montague [producer] to type. It is still in a fluid state. I think I've re-written the ending exactly as Keith [Baxter] would want without any pain or displeasure on my part.

I left my new play *Tiger Tail* in Atlanta to visit Oliver in the hospital. He had suffered another stroke. The out-look is far from bright. That ancient lady companion of his is about to desert him: I guess she is justified as she has stood by valiantly for a long time and looks a wreck herself. But what to do about Oliver now? He must have constant attention. Under the circumstances we all agree—except Oliver—that he should return to the very superior nursing-home where I'd got him located when I was last here. I feel that we must prepare ourselves, all of our adult lives, for the unavoidably difficult end of an active life. That is especially hard for Oliver: he has always been such a hedonist, prodigal by nature. Threw his inheritance from his father to the winds by purchasing and restoring with fabulous antiques an historical house in the Quarter which he could not maintain. Purchased a white Cadillac convertible. Laid away nothing for the future which he apparently thought would be nothing but a continual ascent to more glory.

An improvident grass-hopper or cricket with great charm. Now we are stuck with his dilemma. It is heart-breaking. Immediately after my play opens in Atlanta I must return here to give a benefit reading for him to 2,500 people, most of whom won't understand a word that I'm croaking. The price is inflexible, $2,500, but I intend to interrupt the reading to make an appeal, pass a plate or basket for a "paper shower." New Orleans is a city of great wealth.

I think I've got a winner in *Tiger Tail,* the play trying out in Atlanta. The cast is perfect, it is delightfully funny folk-comedy. It remains to be seen if Billy will bring it into New York. The only two real plays (unless you count Neil Simon) are closing this month. And all the rest is just a crock of . . .

In Atlanta I'm staying at the tallest hotel in the world (72 stories) which is called the Peachtree Plaza and is sort of a Disneyland. Hope you'll call me: COLLECT!

Twerp is behaving incredibly well, has done days without dope, but is eating so much he is almost a chubby. He delivers me to Atlanta and goes on the next day to Key West.

Must get cracking for the air-port. Did I tell you that the Concorde—after all the rush—was delayed an hour because of mechanical difficulties?

Was too exhausted to eat the gourmet dinner, just slept the whole way across.

Love and a lovely New Year, 10

———

"NEIL SIMON was not Tennessee's favorite playwright. During rehearsals of *Red Devil Battery Sign* in Vienna, Tennessee was forever taking my script, which was very irritating. I finally wrote, in huge letters, on my script, 'THIS IS *NOT* TENNESSEE WILLIAMS'S SCRIPT.' Later, I discovered that Tennessee had added, in brackets: 'It is Neil Simon's script.' "

Tiger Tail, a stage version of the film *Baby Doll,* was first performed at the Alliance Theatre in Atlanta on January 19, 1978, directed by Harry Rasky, with Elizabeth Kemp as Baby Doll, Thomas Toner as Archie, Nick Mancuso as Silva, Lorrie Davis as Ruby Lightfoot and Mary Nell Santacroce as Aunt Rose Comfort. The play did not move to New York.

Creve Coeur was first produced at the Spoleto U.S.A. Festival at the Dock Street Theatre in Charleston, South Carolina. The official first night was June 5, 1978, but critics had seen the play on June 1. Shirley Knight played Dorothea and Jan Miner (replacing Geraldine Page on two weeks' notice) played Bodey.

Tennessee had begun to take his painting more seriously, and it pleased him very much that some of his work was exhibited in Charleston.

Later that summer, Tennessee travelled to England for the London production of *Vieux Carré,* which opened at the Piccadilly Theatre on August 9, 1978, directed by Keith Hack, with Karl Johnson as the Writer, Richard Kane as Nightingale the Painter and Sylvia Miles as Mrs. Wire. Although the production had poor reviews, the performance by Sylvia Miles was praised, and the play was more successful in London than in New York.

While Tennessee was staying with Maria at Wilbury Park, he wrote this letter to James Laughlin:

August 13, 1978

Dear J.:

This distillation of your poetry has been a great joy to me and to Maria. You've never shown an adequate confidence in the unique quality and beauty of your work. Please recognize it and take deserved joy in it as I always have.

I have very little time as I must return with Maria from Wilbury Park to London to cope with an hysterical leading lady and an irate narcissan of a leading man.

For once, perhaps for the first time, I cut a play beyond expectations, the scene involving these two.

Sometimes I feel that I should confine the Theatre of Tennessee Williams to my studio in Key West, for there's little time or strength left.

Very briefly and truly, I want to say this. You're the greatest friend that I have had in my life, and the most trusted.

With love, Tennessee

———

[*On letterhead British Airways Concorde, postmarked Key West*]

August 31, 1978

Dearest Maria:

I'm just writing to find out if you received a long letter I wrote a couple of days ago. The Twerp claims he mailed it but I strongly suspect he didn't as I've always insisted on mailing letters to you myself. I'm afraid it's pretty obvious that his intention is to isolate me from everybody. I see no one here in Key West (can't even obtain an art-model) except his little group of addicts and pushers.

We came here by way of St. Louis as I had received alarming reports about Mother's condition from an actress who had visited her there. There has been an awful regression, both in her and in Dakin. She is barely able to sit up, makes ineffectual efforts to feed herself. Dakin neglects his law-practice, such as it is or isn't, to be with her: has set up a sizeable bar in the kitchen of her little suite: has turned to a drunk. Mother thinks the suite contains several animals, including a horse. She talks to them. I suppose she is in no pain, but it was shattering to see her in this state.

I return to New York on the 16th to resume work on *Creve Coeur* under Hack's supervision and to sign a rather tacky photo-biog called *The World of Tennessee Williams* [by Richard F. Leavitt]. The text was written by an old friend of the Windham type, almost as malevolent but not such a gifted writer.

After the book-signing on the 18th I will either fly out to visit Andrew Lyndon in San Francisco—he recently tried to kill himself—heart-break over a hustler who had priced himself out of the market—or I'll return to London, if the situation re: *Vieux Carré* seems to justify it. Have you received any reports? Do you see Michael Garrity? If only I could import a few nice people here. Twerp's design is becoming fairly clear. He wishes to take the place over as a club for himself and his dangerous cronies.

If I go back to London it might not be too late for a week in Venice with you.

Much love, 10

[*Added in handwriting*] If threatened mail-strike goes into effect tomorrow, I will try to phone you again.

Billy [Barnes] told me he was not leaving ICM [International Creative Management; Tennessee's agency, formerly the International Famous Agency (IFA), became International Creative Management, Inc. (ICM), in 1974. When Bill Barnes left ICM, he was replaced as Tennessee's agent by Mitch Douglas] till first of year. A reprieve.

———

GARRITY was an Australian painter in whose London studio Tennessee painted his *Portrait of Maria—Amitié Amoureuse*.

———

From left: Maria, Tennessee, Tony Smith, Jane Smith and Pulcheria in Key West after the disastrous run of *Clothes for a Summer Hotel*, 1980. It was the last time Maria visited Key West.

[Telegram from Maria to Tennessee, from St. Moritz, December 31, 1978]

MAY THIS YEAR BRING YOU HAPPINESS AND SUCCESS MY DARLING THINKING OF YOU WRITING KEY WEST RETURNING LONDON MONDAY LOVE MARIA

ON JANUARY 5, 1979, Frank Fontis, Tennessee's gardener in Key West, was shot dead in his house. A pile of Tennessee's original manuscripts was found under his bed.

On January 8 and again on January 14, the house at 1431 Duncan Street in Key West was ransacked.

Creve Coeur, revised and retitled *A Lovely Sunday for Creve Coeur,* was produced at the Hudson Guild Theatre in New York City on January 21, 1979, with the Charleston cast except for Jan Miner, who was replaced by Peg Murray as Bodey. The reviews were again unfavorable, and the play closed after thirty-six performances.

Throughout the winter Tennessee worked on *Clothes for a Summer Hotel,* his play about Zelda and Scott Fitzgerald.

Tennessee's friendship with Truman Capote had been soured when excerpts from Capote's "novel-in-progress," *Answered Prayers,* were published in *Esquire* in 1975 and 1976. They contained references to "a chunky, paunchy, booze-filled runt . . . America's leading playwright."

––––––––

[Sent to Maria, with handwritten postscript]

Capote wrote an incredibly vicious piece about me in his serialized novel— this was to be my reply but Billy persuaded me to preserve a "dignified silence." I enclose it for your possible amusement.—Can never stay mad long, it is so boring!

TO TRUMAN CAPOTE BY COURTESY OF *ESQUIRE*

As you know, dear Truman, all encounters between us of the slightest consequence have been recorded in my book of memoirs: you are too memorable a creature for any meaningful moment with you to have slipped my mind. Unhappily these meetings were not of the sort on which I am tempted to expose myself but you have been vastly more accessible to observation in your recent work "Unspoiled Monsters." You have allowed me to plumb completely, however shallowly, the uttermost depths of your being. I understand you have granted the same privilege to other acquaintances. What a generous nature you do seem to have! Do you remember your stay at the Pier House some while ago? That genial host, Mr. David Wilkowski, had photographs of us both hung side by side in his cocktail lounge but yesterday I asked him if he would kindly remove one or the other. The one of you was taken down, but when I go there for lunch today, I'll ask him to put it back up, since it's the only photograph of a writer beside which a recent photo of myself looks "reasonably presentable" in contrast. . . .

––––––––

ON JANUARY 28, 1979, Tennessee and a visiting writer had been victims of an attempted mugging in Duval Street in Key West.

––––––––

1979

[*From Maria to Tennessee, a surviving typewritten letter from Wilbury Park, dated February 24, 1979*]

My dearest Tenn:

I was so sorry to read in the paper of the scuffle you had. I hear though that you are fine and everything was alright. I have been expecting a call from you.

Natasha has started to study at the Sorbonne in Paris and I have found her the most delightful little flat, and she seems very happy at the moment. I'm very worried about Tatiana who seems to be very weak and depressed but I hope she will recover. I want to come over to the States soon so keep in touch. Peter has been to Russia and said it was the most beautiful country he had ever been to—so why don't we all go? When are you coming to New York? I don't want to miss you when I come. I think the news of the Twerp is rather sinister. Lying low and pretending to be a goody-goody doesn't convince me that any good will come of it.

Wilbury is beautiful—the snowdrops are coming up—Mishka [the golden retriever] loves the snow—and so do I. For goodness sake, darling, do write and take care of yourself. Pulcheria is here with her young man who is 6'10". They are at the moment painting the North Hall—he does not need a ladder.

Still trying to find some staff here which is a nightmare.

Love and be good and *careful!* Maria

———

IN THE spring of 1979 Tennessee worked on revisions to *Goforth,* a new version of *The Milk Train Doesn't Stop Here Anymore,* for the English Theatre in Vienna. The production never took place.

Maria and Peter were planning a dance at Wilbury Hall on July 7 for Franco Zeffirelli, whose film *The Champ* was opening in London, and for their daughters' coming of age.

———

[*Handwritten, postmarked Key West*]

June 21, 1979

Dearest Maria:

In just about 2 weeks now you'll be "at home" for Katya, Natasha and Franco and I'm sorry I will miss this gala occasion as I can't go abroad till after July 17 when I must meet old Roger Stevens [the producer] and José Quintero in Washington, concerning production of *Clothes for a Summer Hotel,* play about Fitzgeralds (Scott and Zelda) which seems to interest people more than anything I've done in a long time. After that I shall fly to Venice, spending a night at London airport hotel where I hope you'll visit me. If not there, we'll surely meet on the Continent. Sylvia Miles is going to play *Goforth* (based on *Milk Train*) at Vienna's E.S. [English Speaking] Theatre. She'll be all right and we hope will transfer to London in fall. So I'll be in Europe a long time. So far no travelling companion. Edmond may have that honor briefly.

I'm afraid Rose's transfer to Key West is fizzling out. Her companion is a *liar* and *common*! Forgets to give Rose her tablets, allows her to smoke continually despite her bad cough and uses Rose's house mainly to entertain her equally common boy friends.

Rose loves the house but wants to return to the Lodge. I will take her back when I go to Massachusetts in a week for a production of *Camino.* Rose is patient and sweet and so tragic. Of course the house I bought (duplex with lovely location and pool-patio) is an excellent investment.

Today I shall try to make reservation at Cipriani or Excelsior in Venice. Finally realize the Twerp can't travel with me.

I've taken off almost 15 pounds and may appear more enticing to prospective escorts here or abroad. Eat nothing but fish and veg!

I love you, I long to see you. Rose wrote our grandmother a single-sentence letter yesterday. It went: "Dear Grand. I hope you are not dead. Have heard such."

Awful how death haunts those of later generations—the escapes are work and travel, and a few friends surviving—

Somehow I anticipate a beautiful late summer.

Hope *Champ* is a triumph in London. I loved it so much, identified so completely with the desperate struggle for a "come-back."

A bientôt, dear girl! Tennessee

Write me at N.Y. apt., 484 W. 43, Apt. 44 N.3.

————

TENNESSEE bought the apartment, at New York City's Manhattan Plaza, and sold it soon afterwards.

"I'd told Tennessee that I felt that it was a tremendous mistake to remove Rose from the familiar environment at Stony Lodge, and that it would be impossible to find anybody to care for her properly in the house at Key West which he had bought for her. Tatiana Schvetzoff agreed. In retrospect, however, it was a very good thing that he did move her. He was subsequently able to dine with her every other day and to visit her daily."

Rose and Tennessee, 1981

[*Handwritten letter undated, postmarked San Juan, July ?, 1979*]

Dearest Maria:

This is the tail feather of a pink flamingo, dropped as it fled from me in rage or panic. The great white swans were equally hostile although accepted bits of bread. *Bit* the hand that fed it.

I am going in old San Juan for an acqua puncture—trust it will cure me totally of a lifetime of self indulgence.

Love, 10

[*On letterhead Pier House Inn and Beach Club, Key West, postmarked November 5, 1979*]

1431 Duncan Street
Key West, Fla.

October 1979

Dearest Maria:

So often this fantastic summer I've been at a loss for words, written or spoken.

I've kept shuttling back and forth between here [Key West] and New York.

Only positive accomplishment is getting the Twerp back to Boone County, West Virginia.

He gets $150 a month to stay away, which is just a fraction of his demands—well-worth the relative peace on the compound, even the creatures seem relieved.

I just returned this evening and found your letter. I'll see Rose tomorrow. You're probably right about her as you usually are about things. I don't think, though, that Stony Lodge is the place now. It's deteriorated. They were serving junk-food such as hot-dogs for lunch. I'll have to look into other places for her.

It seems incredible I haven't been to England in so long. But a comfort that you're planning to join me here. The Washington (Kennedy) honors are on December 3rd. [The Kennedy Center ceremonies were held on December 2.]

The National Theatre has expressed interest in producing *Clothes for a Summer Hotel*. The letter came from a director I haven't met. Of course I'd prefer to have it done by Peter Hall whom I know. Perhaps you and Lord Goodman could feel him out on the matter: I think he's the greatest director in the English-speaking theatre, bar none.

Will continue this in the morning.

With all my love, 10

Madame Gilberte Paul, the French lady who replaced the Baptist evangelist freak as Rose's companion, has just turned in her notice. The French are a very cold people. I don't know where to turn next. I doubt that there's a suitable companion for Rose on this island. She wants to go back to New York, she said at dinner.

Do you think Tatiana, whom Rose loves and who seems to care for Rose, would be willing to stay with her down here? The wonderful climate might relieve her arthritis as it does mine.

I think it's time for you to stop worrying about poor Natasha. Obviously she just doesn't know what to do with herself. Many young people seem to be like that now: and who can blame them, society being in such a state of confusion?

Maybe Natasha would also like to be here with Rose, I mean if Tatiana can come down. There's a swimming pool in the patio of the house, it's on a very nice residential street, there are three bedrooms downstairs: the upstairs apartment is still unrented.

By early March the play [*Clothes*] will have opened on Broadway. Then I will have found the right sanitarium in which to leave Rose while I go abroad for a long vacation.

Dakin wishes to join us in Washington in order to declare for the Presidency in 1984. I hadn't believed he was serious until he re-iterated the intention in a letter.

Rose has a piece of two of my plays, *Summer and Smoke* and *Orpheus Descending,* and has a nice little fortune of her own. My accountant assures me that—although Dakin is trustee—he's not able to draw on it.

Mother still survives in a nursing-home in St. Louis.

Audrey Wood still weaves cunningly malign webs at ICM—she is peddling a musical by my younger agent, Mitch Douglas. There has been a sort of dynastic succession. Audrey chose Barnes to succeed her. Barnes chose Douglas.

Sounds like that old child-hood game: "The cat takes the rat, the rat takes the cheese, the cheese stands alone."

[*Added in handwriting*] C'est tout pour maintenant!

10

[*From Maria to the Swedish ambassador to the Court of St. James's, October 4, 1979*]

My dear Ambassador

I wonder whether you would be kind enough to forward the enclosed letter to the Committee of the Nobel Prize in Sweden.

I wonder why the most distinguished dramatist writing in English, Mr. Tennessee Williams, who has given vast pleasure to enormous audiences throughout the world over many, many years and in fact is still writing magnificently at the age of sixty-nine, is not nominated for the Nobel Prize, and on this score I would suggest he be nominated.

Yours sincerely, The Lady St. Just

TENNESSEE referred to Lilla van Saher in the *Paris Review,* 1981, as "the last of the crepe-de-chine gypsies." He went on to say that her imperious treatment of the press during his 1955 Stockholm visit had put the Nobel Prize forever beyond his reach.

My agent in Scandinavia, Lars Schmidt, said, "You know, you've been nominated for the Nobel Prize, but now it's finished." The scandal was so awful, the press having been abused, and they associated me with this awful woman. Well, after all, one doesn't have to get it. It'd be nice because it's a lot of money, isn't it? I could use that, if I could get it.

Maria was with Tennessee for the first Kennedy Center honors on December 2, 1979, not December 3 as he writes. Along with him, Henry Fonda, Martha Graham, Aaron Copland and Ella Fitzgerald were honored for their lifetime contributions to the arts. The event was so emotional that Fitzgerald, sitting in the box next to Tennessee, began to cry.

"Tennessee lent her his handkerchief to wipe her tears, and when she handed it back he gazed at it and, not thinking of mascara, whispered to me: 'Look, even her tears are black. I must keep this handkerchief forever.'

"Kazan gave a wonderful speech about Tennessee, who received an enormous standing ovation.

"Mrs. Carter, the President's wife, unexpectedly appeared in Tennessee's box. I was scrabbling for my shoes. Tennessee was catching forty winks. She invited us to join her in the President's box, where the President congratulated him warmly."

Rehearsals for *Clothes for a Summer Hotel* began in January 1980. Tennessee interrupted rehearsals to go to Key West, where, on January 24, 1980, the Tennessee Williams Performing Arts Center at the Florida Keys Community College was officially inaugurated by the first performance of a play written in 1969, *Will Mr. Merriwether Return from Memphis?*

The first performance of *Clothes for a Summer Hotel,* directed by José Quintero, with Geraldine Page as Zelda and Kenneth Haigh as F. Scott Fitzgerald, was at the Cort Theatre, New York City, on March 26, 1980. New York Mayor Edward Koch proclaimed the day Tennessee Williams Day. Pulcheria and Maria flew to New York for the first night.

"Tennessee told us: 'They call it Tennessee Williams Day today, and then

This gesture accompanied Tennessee's rallying cry, "En avant!",
which he always used to end his journal entries.

annihilate my play tomorrow.' That is what happened. The play received
an ovation from the first-night audience and everyone thought it was going
to be a success, but the reviews in the morning were terrible. Tennessee had
had great misgivings over the casting of Scott and Zelda Fitzgerald, and the
fact that the critics had attended the preview performances only came as a
blow.

"There was a news strike on, but in spite of all this, business began to
pick up, and the box office was quite busy. However, with no possibility
of advertisement, the production survived for only fourteen performances.
It was Tennessee's last new play on Broadway."

At the party Vassilis Voglis gave for Tennessee after the first night, the
atmosphere was jubilant.

"Kazan and his [second] wife Barbara [Loden] were there. We decided
that, whatever the reviews on TV and radio, we were not to say anything
to Tennessee if they were negative. He was really enjoying himself. However, unable to contain his malice, the latest travelling companion whispered
to Tennessee that the reviews had come out and that they were damning.

Tennessee flew into an awful rage, kicked him out of the party, and never saw him again."

After the play closed, Maria took Tennessee down to Key West with Pulcheria.

"He was in no condition to travel alone. Rose met us, with their cousin Stell [Adams], at the airport. Rose was dressed all in white, and I've never seen such joy on anybody's face as when she saw her brother.

"Jane and Tony Smith were in Key West already. Tony was in a very bad condition, with diabetes and cirrhosis of the liver—he was to die later on that year. He and Jane had rented a nasty pokey little house from a local resident whom Tennessee referred to as Texas Kate.

"Tennessee collected his mail and took us all to a very grand place on the beach for dinner. He was reading the letters during the meal. Perusing one letter, he kept on putting it nearer to the candlelight in disbelief. 'What is it, Tennessee?' It was a letter from the ex–travelling companion, who had, unexpectedly, sent a bill. The last item read: 'Five hundred dollars: For having had to have dinner every night with Lady St. Just.' It cheered us all up immensely."

———

Key West

May 17, 1980

Dearest Maria:

Many, many thanks for the Reactivan. It has been of enormous help, now, while I am struggling against reduced energy to finish what may be important work of my late years.

I have been called again to THE WHITE HOUSE to receive what they call their highest award conferred upon civilians, THE MEDAL OF FREE-DOM. Of course I've invited too many guests, for the eight or ten allowed. Texas Kate wants to come. She's made it fairly clear that she also wants me to pay her expenses. Frankly, her financial exploitation of Jane and Tony—having made them pay highest hotel rates daily for their stay in her house here—has sort of alienated me from this lady. I only really want Jane and Tony to come. I talked to Jane yesterday. She will be there. She thinks that Tony can make it, but I reminded her how sick he was after the Kennedy awards. Still. If he really does want to come there, it would be lovely.

I do hope that Rose and Stell can come. Rose will probably feel that is the first American President—or that Rose of England has overcome the States. But she will conduct herself with her usual grace, I am sure.

Christ, time's going so fast! I have given so little in return for so much from you, little Mary. I don't mean material things. Your loyalty, your beauty.

Believe me, I know how deeply I am indebted to you for your shining spirit.

Love, Tennessee

ROSE did attend the ceremony, and behaved perfectly.

Tennessee's mother, Edwina Dakin Williams, died on June 1, 1980. She was ninety-five.

[*On letterhead San Domenico Palace Hotel, Taormina, Sicily, postmarked June 25, 1980*]

June 1980

Dearest Maria:

I am writing on an Italian Olivetti which has a radically different keyboard than ours so you may observe some peculiarities in the typing.

This has been a vacation with considerable peculiarities too: Henry [Faulkner] does not know or won't face the extent of his sickness and disability: he careers wildly along the Corso singing in loud falsetto, stopping every attractive boy on the way to make sexual proposals in the crudest language, and since we are usually together, both of us are regarded as the most freakish stranieri ever to hit Taormina since the German Baron Wilhelm von Gloeden. I suspect the Baron had a far more brilliant time of it on the letto [bed]: the Sicilian boys—at least those here—have to avoid public scandal that would naturally result from accepting such flagrant solicitation. It doesn't much matter as I am absorbed in a play [*The Everlasting Ticket*] and Henry gives me good technical instruction in painting. In that department I did him a good turn yesterday when we were at the gallery where he exhibits: he remarked that he intended to paint a lot of flower pictures; I said, "Henry, a rose on canvas is never as lovely as the real flower." The proprietor of the gallery shouted, "Thank God you told him that, his flower pictures are almost impossible to sell except for small sums to poor borghese."

He wanted to share a room with me and had assured the management that I, being rich, would assume the whole shockingly inflated cost: after three sleepless nights—he coughs and groans at night—I had to insist that he be evicted.

I gave him five hundred dollars and he has now gotten a studio for habitation and boys—talks of staying here through the summer but I am heading back to Key West in a week. Will continue with pen—this keyboard is driving me crazy:

[*Added in handwriting*] I have—won't! Henry is shouting at the door

Love, 10

———

THE PLAY *The Everlasting Ticket* was dedicated to the memory of Joe Orton. It remains unpublished.

———

[*Manuscript of prose poem dedicated to Maria, undated*]

The animal is the comforter and the betrayer. He stays half-way between you and the dark that you shrink from, he watches you from the periphery of your firelight as though to guard you from the dark that he bears with him contentedly, trustfully, never glancing back at it, knowing it's there.

Your stolen firelight, the lighted circle you crouch in, is what he regards with suspicion, believing it should have been left an undisputed mystery of the gods.

And yet his longings remain so familiar to you that you mistake them for yours, obliging them continually, unthinkingly, and being only a bit disconcerted, at times, by the chance discovery that his hunger, and his satisfaction, appeases your heart . . . And this confusion has no right to exist, for certainly his night eyes, with their expressionless, soulful phosphorescence, have no relation to your eyes that in the morning will open to face each day's bland reassurance of a simple existence continued among your kind.

For not as you are now will he be startled by the fault of his heartbeat. Nothing in him has ever dreamed of forever. That's a conceit for which you gave up humility and comfort, dropping them on the grand marble stairs of the gods when you fled them at midnight with your theft of a cognizant heart. Perhaps, no, probably.

Mysteries should have been left where he has left them, not completely unknown but known without knowing, the way that he knows death, and in this way being your comforter as well as your betrayer.

But the animal is your betrayer as well as your comforter. He is constantly waiting for you to complete that circle which returns you to him. He knows

that circle, better than you he has measured the radius of it and knows you'll
return when there's nothing else to return to. He knows without knowing
he knows, which is doubtless the way that it was meant to be known, and
when you return to the animal crouching a little outside of the firelight he's
never trusted . . .

[*Surviving letter from Maria to Tennessee, from Wilbury Park, July 27, 1980*]

Dearest 10:

How lovely it was to see you, and you seemed, in spite of your trip, to
be in very good form. Also what a marvellous surprise when I had my car
cleaned out to find crumpled in the corner an enormous birthday-present.
In fact, it was so enormous that I felt I had to share it with you. I bought
you a gold pen which will arrive via a friend. I gave it to him last week,
and he should have sent it to you by now. I know you will lose it in a
second, but it is rather nice, even for a second, to have a gold pen to match
your golden heart.

Peter and I took your advice, and we went to the Hotel du Cap, where
everybody asked after Madam [Sophia], and was horrified to hear that she
was dead. It was nice to see all the familiar faces of the staff and we were
marvellously looked after and Peter became much, much better. In fact, we
are thinking of going back for a refresher course.

Will write a longer letter. Much love, and thank you.

Maria

[*Address on envelope The Inn at Denman Place, 1733 Comox Street, Vancouver, B.C.,
Canada*]

October 14, 1980

Dearest Maria:

Here I sit on the 27th floor of a high-rise hotel in Vancouver, British
Columbia, on the west coast of Canada. The view is magnificent, I see the
Pacific Coast studded with mountainous little islands and the harbor full of
great freighters and little sailing boats, it is probably the most beautiful city
next to Venice that I have ever been in. The occasion is the definitive
production of *Red Devil Battery Sign* being staged by a brilliant director.
He is particularly good on script and the play is now tight as a fist, cut to
80 pages, about twenty less than it was in England, every superfluous bit

eliminated. I have had a very strenuous program here. Since my expenses are paid by the theatre and I am receiving a weekly salary of 2,000 dollars from the University of British Columbia, I have been having to address classes in all departments of theatre, sometimes twice daily. At first I thought I couldn't cope with it and took flight to San Francisco: rested only a couple of days and returned. Which was fortunate, as the brief defection made it apparent to them I had to have more personal attention and they introduced me to congenial young people who see that I don't get bored. The opening date is October 18th: I leave the next day for Chicago where a triple bill of short plays will be in rehearsal at the Goodman Institute. Then in mid-November Gucci shoes is bringing me to Rome via Concorde and London for a gala re-publication of *The Roman Spring of Mrs. Stone* which, it seems, they've come to regard as flattering to Rome. I will take the new script of *Red Devil* with me. I wondered if you could join me in Rome. We could fly down together from London. After the Roman gig we could take the play to Russia. I think it might be attractive to Russian theatres, and it is one of the very few plays of mine that were written after an agreement was reached permitting American playwrights to receive royalties outside of Russia. I hope that a lot of past royalties accrued before the agreement are still being held in Russia but those would have to be spent there so we could live very sumptuously and acquire some becoming new furs. If this seems practicable to you, perhaps you could discreetly enquire about what theatres to contact in Moscow and how to obtain visas.

I received a sweet letter from Jim in Key West, enclosing a society clip of the Key West paper, mentioning Rose as having been at an art-exhibit. When shown the clipping Rose said: "I did not attend it and so was not present"—apparently she is on her high horse. I will have two weeks rest at home before the trip abroad.

I have re-written *Clothes* and hope to submit it to a theatre in England. It is much shorter: I have eliminated the exposition.

I have no idea what is going on in your life.

Much love as ever, Tennessee

[*Added in handwriting*] Will call you from Chicago or New York, next stops on the *seemingly* endless itinerary.

————

THE NAME *Tennessee Laughs* was given to a triple bill of the one-act plays *A Perfect Analysis Given by a Parrot*, *The Frosted Glass Coffin* and *Some Problems for the Moose Lodge*. The first performance, directed by Gary

Tucker, was at the Goodman Theatre Studio, Chicago, on November 8, 1980; *Some Problems for the Moose Lodge* received its world premiere.

———

[*International telegram*]

DECEMBER 25, 1980

DEAREST MARIA,
TRUST YOU ARE ALL ENJOYING A LOVELY CHRISTMAS, HOPE TO BE OVER SOON AS I FIND A RIGHT HOSPITAL FOR ROSE, WILL CALL WHEN CHANNELS ARE FREE. LOVE TO YOU ALL,   TENNESSEE

———

PULCHERIA Katya Grenfell had married the conductor Oliver Gilmour, the son of Sir Ian and Lady Caroline Gilmour.

———

[*From Key West*]

March 6, 1981

Dearest Maria:

Natasha and Pippo [Pischotto, an assistant to Zeffirelli] came through with the medications from London. Another batch of them were sent by Dr. Mitchell at the Wimpole office. Please thank them for me. I had suffered a great loss of energy which they've restored.

I leave this coming Sunday for Orlando to give what I hope is my last public reading: afterwards on to Chicago to attend the rehearsals of probably my last new play.*

By the middle of April I ought to be on my way to Europe, via London.

I believe I've found a perfect psychiatric nurse, now, for Rose. She has wonderful credentials. The oddest thing about it is that she's the sister of the kindest male friend I ever had before Frankie. I don't want to leave Rose in the sanitarium when I go abroad. She needs and surely deserves a well-trained, sympathetic companion in her house here.

I gave a big farewell party for my friends in Key West last night and it seemed a great success. I let the caterer take care of it all and just sat in the patio and enjoyed it.

In some ways this has been a sad spring. I made the mistake of bringing a companion from Vancouver, Canada. He is highly efficient but cold as a fish.

I hope that Jane [Smith] will fly to Europe with me. The Goodman

Theatre in Chicago is giving me a big 70th birthday party—both Vass [Vassilis Voglis] and Jane are coming.

Did you and Peter go to St. Moritz? Are Pulcheria and her Oliver [Gilmour] getting happily through the hazards of forming a new relationship? It's always difficult at first.

My address in Chicago is c/o the Goodman Theatre, 200 S. Columbus Drive, and I hope to hear from you. I'll be in some hotel suite but still not certain which. Let me know where I can reach you.

Much love as always, Tennessee

[*Added in handwriting*] *Fortunately a good one, both humorous and tragic—*A House Not Meant to Stand.*

―――――

ON APRIL 1, 1981, *A House Not Meant to Stand*, an expansion and a revision of the one-act play *Some Problems for the Moose Lodge,* was produced at the Goodman Theatre Studio, Chicago, directed by André Ernotte, with Peg Murray as Bella and Frank Hamilton as Cornelius. Tennessee further revised the play and it was produced again at the Goodman Theatre (the main stage), with the same director and cast, on April 27, 1982. It ran for forty-one performances.

On April 30, 1981, Audrey Wood suffered a massive stroke which left her in a coma until her death in December 1985.

In May, Pulcheria's daughter Natalia was born.

"Whilst I was with Pulcheria at the hospital, I told Tennessee to wait in a restaurant around the corner with Vassilis Voglis for news of the birth. Eventually I telephoned the restaurant, and Tennessee was called to the phone, where I gave him the news.

"Solemnly, Tennessee held up two fingers. 'Twins?' Vassilis asked him. Gravely, Tennessee shook his head. 'No. Two heads.' And then roared with laughter. Vassilis had completely believed him.

"Tennessee visited his god-daughter and the baby in hospital with flowers and gifts."

In the autumn of 1981 Oliver Evans died.

Tennessee's last new play to be performed in New York was *Something Cloudy, Something Clear,* in August 1981 and again in February and March 1982 at the Jean Cocteau Repertory, directed by Eve Adamson, with Craig Smith as August, John Arndt as Kip and Dominique Cieri as Clare.

―――――

When he painted, Tennessee used old magazines as a palette.

[From Key West, undated, March 1982]

Dearest Maria:

The fact that I write letters to you so seldom is not that I don't think of you daily: it is that this bone-trouble, so vaguely diagnosed, in my right shoulder compels to take powerful pain killers after my short writing-periods are finished each day and the effect on the nerves is such that it is difficult as hell to write a reasonably cheerful letter. And who wishes to hear lamentations?

Of course in the evening the wine at dinner casts a comforting spell: sometimes a bit riotous. I am regarded as somewhat eccentric in Key West as I shout remarks to all who attract my attention on the street. I must be trying to replace dear Henry Faulkner. Remember him?

He was killed in a car-accident (instantaneously, thank God), and to my surprise he has actually left me his farm in Kentucky. The lawyers have notified me. The house, a little outside of Lexington, is called "Falling Timbers." I hope that is not a description of its state of repair. Well, I think shall pay it a visit soon as the unprecedented cold winter has past. If the timbers of the house are really falling I shall just inspect the property and stay at a lovely hotel in the city which has glass-domed pool.

Rehearsals begin March 23 at the Goodman Theatre in Chicago. The play does not have an attractive title but unfortunately it's the only one that could be pertinent: *A House Not Meant to Stand*. It is to be directed by a noted Belgian director [André Ernotte] and the Goodman always gives you—on its main stage—a lovely set and very talented actors.

There is to be an intimate little birthday party for me, they say, on the 26th [of March]. I do wish you'd be there. I'm sure that Janie [Smith] will. It is a dark and beautiful play with a great deal of comedy in it, the usual Williams mix.

I want to do my important work (spent 3 years on it) in London. It needs that special intelligence that the English bring to theatre.

A curious advance last night. Being somewhat inebriated, I was having some difficulty descending the stairs from the roof-top of our wildly popular disco bar. I was about to take a tumble when a short, dark young man grabbed hold of me. I turned to thank him and it seemed that I was looking at Frank Merlo. He drove me home and stayed the night. He is pure Sicilian. He has the first real warmth, humanity, and tenderness that I have encountered in a man in these years since Frankie left us. Still more startling, he lives in Chicago and promises to be with me. He has a master's degree in English literature and when we got home we sat by the lighted pool and he recited Shakespeare's sonnets.

I had begun to turn completely against all "gays," and was killing them off in my plays, all except Trigorin.

Gave a public reading of a story I thought was finished a few nights ago. Well, it may be finished but the pages were out of sequence and full of inserts. There was too big a crowd for the amplification system and the rude ones kept shouting "Louder." Finally I got up and said I would leave if they did not shut up. I am happy to say that they did. The story is a scandal but very funny. It is called "The Donsinger Women and Their Handy Man Jack"—I don't think your grand-daughter should be exposed to it yet. It came out of my visit to Texas with the notorious Texas Kate. She had a young gigolo with her and insisted that we all go to "the ranch" on the Guadalupe. A nightmare! Icy cold and nothing to eat but venison *sausage*!

I had a bit of cosmetic surgery done on my eyes but I am not satisfied with it. I think the surgeon was a sadist or homophobe, as I received no local anaesthetic, nothing, and it was the most physically excruciating experience of my life.

Perhaps I will have it corrected in London.

If I carry out my plan to go back to Bangkok, I must look—if not ravishing—at least noticeably better.

Is it true that there is a Concorde that flies directly from London to Singapore in 8 hours?

Must close with that question. The news is coming on!

Much love as always, Tenn

AT THE END of his life Tennessee was working on his free adaptation of his favorite play, Chekhov's *The Sea Gull*, which he called *The Notebooks of Trigorin*.

Tennessee sent the following poem dedicated to Maria:

TO MARIA

You would not understand.
I can't explain.
The negative. Half of my blood seems to have
sprung from that and it's become a sort of cooling rain,
a season of monsoon to which I'm comfortably used,
since if you could or were inclined to see
I'm sure you'd see that what it offers me
is the assuagement of a fever
otherwise quite difficult to contain.
The negative. Oh, once
I did attempt to speak but what I spoke
seemed only to confuse the subject more.
I believe I said I am a furtive cat, unowned,
unknown, a scavenging sort of blackish alley cat
distinguished by a curve of white upturned
at each side of its mouth which makes it seem to grin
denial of its eyes,
The negative: unhomed.
It is too intricate for me to say.
I can't explain.
If I reached out my hand its bones would break.
If I should call you back and you should turn
it would be useless, no, I can't explain.

My smile is meaningless, our meetings burn
and homelessness is long and cooling rain.
Do you understand? I can't explain. . . .

————

[*From Key West?*]

April 26, 1982

Dearest Maria:

You've probably guessed, being no fool, that I am not well. At first it was severe arthritis in my right shoulder and arm that made me sleepless. They gave me periodic cortisone shots for it and it has now subsided but the sleeplessness continues. It's now six a.m. and I am wide awake.

Dear Vanessa Redgrave called me this afternoon. She wants me to read with her in Boston on Friday and of course I shall. I don't understand her political affiliation but that doesn't matter. She's the greatest actress of the English speaking theatre and now that [Keith] Hack is out of the picture she intends to do *Stopped Rocking* she says, and since my own agents make no effort to arrange productions, I told her to please arrange it through hers. Did you see her magnificent performance in *My Body, My Child*?

I have a play [*A House Not Meant to Stand*] opening in Chicago on Tuesday [April 27]: am casting another play in New York on the 28th, something for the "Miami Festival"—strikes me as a sort of con-game, but I have a play that I want to develop there so I'll go.

On June 10th I'm receiving an important honor [an honorary Litt. D.] from Harvard University.—After that? Release from this situation here. A highly efficient and totally inhuman sonovabitch who stays out all night, every night.

Fortunately I met a young Sicilian in Chicago who wants to travel. He is so much like Frankie that it's phenomenal. Precisely the same height and the same warm nature. I plan to go with him directly from Chicago to the Vanessa occasion in Boston.—And I want to spend a month, after June 10, in England and then in the Hotel du Cap.—Maybe that would get me together a bit.

Rose had pneumonia on top of her emphysema. She's out of the hospital now and back at the Lodge. I suspect that my continual worry about her has much to do with my sleeplessness.

I hope to see you in London, come early summer.

With all my love as ever, Tennessee

[*Postmarked Charleston, May 15, 1982*]

Dearest Maria:

I heard from the con-man tenant occupying my Key West home (rent-free) that you had called yesterday. Well, I am now in a Charleston, S.S. hotel, checking up on the Enfant's condition here. I tried to get London from my hotel room but each time was informed that all circuits were busy so unless I devote the morning to that fruitless and frustrating effort, I shall have to get this letter to you by special delivery, or whatever way the postal service operates most rapidly.

What's going on, Your Ladyship? I hope that you are contemplating a trip to the States. The whole upper story with twin bedroom and bath is at your disposal, Leoncia is ever more precious, and my English bull-dog Cornelius, my beautiful Persian, Topaze, and my parrot, Juanita, are all thriving, or were when I left home yesterday morning. It is cooler than it is here in Charleston, and I can accompany you back to England en route to Chichester and then some pleasant watering hole in the south of France, or whatever is most familiar and appealing. I think my Sicilian friend, the look-alike of Frankie—he loves poetry and literature but can get only a short vacation from his business-firm in Chicago—might fly over with us and stay a little while.

I will be back in Key West in a few days: please call me collect—(305) 294-1430.

Perhaps you can persuade the "squatter" to find lodgings elsewhere: I suspect him of confiscating some of my scripts but have no certain evidence as yet.

On June 6th I am supposed to be at Harvard to receive an honorary Doctor of Letters degree [June 10]. I already have one from a relatively obscure college in Hartford, Conn.

It is very hard, indeed, for me to continue a career in theatre in New York. I do have a good play running in Chicago.

I had been out of touch with Janie [Smith] for sometime. Finally called her: reached one of her daughters who assured me she was well and would return my call but I left before she had a chance to. The "squatter" was driving me up the wall onto the ceiling. I think my strategy will be to simply locate another place for him and book him into it.

The Enfant does much better in Charleston than anywhere else. He is unable to afford much drugs on the weekly stipend I give him but manages well, has a nice little apartment, is simply but neatly dressed and has even completed a long new novel which contains no reference to you.

I could not consider removing him from here as it seems to be his only favorable environment.

Since I am probably the only person who has ever shown him any kindness he has put himself out enormously to please me: loaned me this little Olivetti and a box of typewriter paper. Engaged me a beautiful room with an ocean-view.

Did you know that I gave a reading in Boston with Vanessa Redgrave? This seems to have incurred the fury of my agents. They no longer forward my mail and make no effort to set up new American productions for me. Fortunately I make a living off productions abroad.

Well, my dear girl, I must suspend these rather bleak communications *pour le moment* and do a bit of work on a play called *The Lingering Hour*—the twilight of the world which I hope I am managing to make somewhat poetic despite its subject matter.

With all my love, Tennessee

I shall probably return to Key West Monday, May *17th*. Do call me on Tuesday, please.

UNFINISHED and unpublished, *The Lingering Hour* is also called *The Negative.*

[*Handwritten note on letterhead British Airways Concorde, undated*]

Confession may be good for the soul, even necessary if the soul is to survive—it is certainly not easy. Nothing worth while is.

With love as ever 10

IN THE LAST weeks of his life, Tennessee revisited the places with the happiest personal associations for him: London, Rome and Taormina. He told Maria that he would never return to Key West.

He had intended to spend Christmas at Wilbury but, deeply depressed and unsettled, cancelled at the last moment. Maria offered to fly out and accompany him to England. Although she was very concerned, she was unable to contact him, until she suddenly received a telephone call from New Orleans, saying that he was coming to England the following day. Arriving in London, he was untypically hasty in leaving the airport and

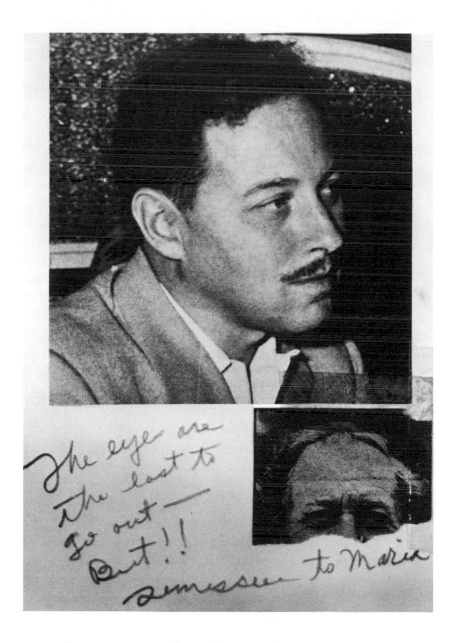

"Tennessee gave me this card in 1971 when we were in Vienna for Christmas. He made it from two photographs; the picture of his eyes was cut out of a newspaper."

missed Maria, who had arranged to meet him. Later, he dumbfounded her by saying that he had thought she hadn't waited for him.

They spent a week constantly in each other's company, seeing Harold Pinter's triple bill at the National Theatre, *Other Places,* and meeting the playwright Christopher Hampton, whose work Tennessee greatly admired.

"Tennessee's mood was very withdrawn, and punctilious in a way that he'd never been before. He was early for every appointment with me, as though he didn't want to miss a second of any contact. I'd say, come for dinner at eight, and he'd be there at seven. He gave me a bundle of papers, saying that he'd photostatted them, and that he wanted me to have them until we next met.

"He telephoned me at about eight one morning, saying that he was leaving for Rome, and asking me to join him at his hotel for breakfast. I had been very disturbed by his whole aura during this visit. I asked Natasha to take me to the Berkeley and telephoned the hall porter to reserve a second seat on Tennessee's flight. I took my passport, and prearranged with Natasha that she was to ask Tennessee while I disappeared from the breakfast room for a few minutes whether he would not like me to accompany him, so that he wouldn't have to travel alone. I didn't wish to embarrass him in any way.

"When I returned to the breakfast table, Natasha discreetly shook her head no. Tennessee wanted to be alone.

"I took him to the airport, where we had a glass of red wine together. I kissed his hand.

"That was the last time I saw him."

―――――

[*Handwritten note, undated*]

Even very fat people get thin in the grave.
Pensée pour le jour

TW

―――――

TENNESSEE WILLIAMS died at the Elysée Hotel, New York City, on February 25, 1983. That evening, thirty Broadway theatres dimmed their lights in his memory.

There was some initial doubt about the cause of death, and so the police confiscated his suitcase. It was later established that he had choked on the cap of a bottle of eye drops. When the estate's lawyer, Michael Remer, went to collect the suitcase from the police precinct, a policeman asked, "Is it *the* Tennessee Williams?" Mike said, "Yes." The policeman said, "I'm proud to be carrying his suitcase." Mike said, "It's so sad, isn't it?" The policeman said, "Not really. Think of what he left us."

Tennessee's two great loves had been his work and his sister Rose. In his will, he entrusted the care of both to Maria.

After a ceremony at his graveside, and before the interment, the mourners drove back to St. Louis. Maria took a car to the cemetery. The sextons were lowering the coffin. Alone, Maria buried her friend.

Index

Index

Gardner, Ava, 187
Gardner, Margaret, 361–2
Garrity, Michael, 368
Gasperi, Alcide de, 97
Gauguin, Paul, 240
Gazzara, Ben, 107
Gershe, Leonard, 303
Gielgud, John, xviii, xix, 13, 30, 37–39,
  43, 90, 112, 169, 170, 177, 190, 258,
  350
Gilmour, Natalia, 384
Gilmour, Oliver, 383, 384
Ginsberg, Allen, 205
Giving It Away (Osborne), 205
Glass Menagerie, The (Williams), xix,
  3–5, 7, 10, 18, 26, 78, 90, 192, 202,
  236, 331
Glenville, Peter, 45, 46, 48, 71, 273, 274,
  279, 280, 282, 295, 303
Gloeden, Baron Wilhelm von, 379
Gnädiges Fräulein, The (Williams), 190,
  192, 297, 312
Goforth (Williams), 371, 372
Goldman, Dr., 209
Good, Joan, 320
Goodman, Lord Arnold, 244, 264, 273,
  286, 374
Goodman Theatre (Chicago), 382–4, 386
Gorky, Maxim, 112
Gourevitsch, Dr., 95, 138
Graham, Martha, 376
Granger, Farley, 78, 81, *illus. 84, 85*
Grass Harp, The (Capote), 55
Graves, Robert, 93
Greenwich Theatre (London), 320, 321
Grenfell, Natasha, 170, *illus. 171, 172,* 188,
  198, 207, 218, 228, 229, 233, *illus. 293,*
  322, 335, *illus. 339,* 375, 392; at
  Sorbonne, 371; in Thailand, 279; in
  U.S., 359, 361, 383; in Venice, 298; in
  Vienna, 333–4, 347; in Zeffirelli film,
  338
Grenfell, Peter, *see* St. Just, Lord
Grenfell, Pulcheria, 150, 170, *illus. 171,*
  172, 188, 198, 207, 218, 224, 229, 233,
  294, 295, *illus. 339, 369,* 371; attends
  theatre with Tennessee, 347–8; birth of,
  146–8; birth of daughter of, 384; good
  luck picture by, 245, 250; marriage of,
  383, 384; in Thailand, 279, 280; in

U.S., 376, 378; in Venice, 298; in
  Zeffirelli film, 338
Grigoriev, Serge, xvii
Group Theatre (New York), 37, 58, 240,
  241
Guardino, Harry, 195
Gunn, Thom, 203
Gwynne, Fred, 317

Hack, Keith, 360, 367, 368, 388
Haigh, Kenneth, 376
Hall, Peter, 57, 74, 151, 374
Hamilton, Frank, 384
Hamlet (Shakespeare), xviii
Hampstead Theatre Club (London), 195,
  266, 280, 289
Hampton, Christopher, 392
Hardy, Joe, 356
Harper's magazine, 216
Harris, Elizabeth, 193
Harris, Richard, 193
Harris, Rosemary, 289
Harrison, Rex, 281
Hartford, University of, 277
Harvard University, 388, 389
Harvey, Lawrence, 160, 177
Hayes, Helen, xix, 305, 312
Headley, Ed, 280, 287
Healy, Jo, 192, 254, 276–7
Heat (film), 271
Hedda Gabler (Ibsen), 247–8
Heggen, Tom, 27
Helen Hayes Theatre (New York), 170
Hellman, Jerry, 346, 350–1
Hellman, Lillian, 178
Helpmann, Bobbie, 26
Hemingway, Ernest, 96
Hepburn, Katharine, 161
Herlie, Eileen, 221, 225, 230–3, 244
Hero Continues, The (Windham), 164
Hewes, Henry, 120
Hoctor, Dr., 124
Hoiby, Lee, 226
Holman, Libby, 163
Hopkins, John, 306
House Not Meant to Stand, A (Williams),
  384, 386, 388
Huddle, Elizabeth, 336
Hudson Guild Theatre (New York), 369
Hunt, W. E., 358

399

Index

Photographic Credits

A NOTE ON THE TYPE

The text of this book was set in a film version of a typeface named Bembo. The roman is a copy of a letter cut for the celebrated Venetian printer Aldus Manutius by Francesco Griffo. It was first used in Cardinal Bembo's *De Aetna* of 1495—hence the name of the revival. Griffo's type is now generally recognized, thanks to the research of Stanley Morison, to be the first of the old-face group of types. The companion italic is an adaptation of the chancery script type designed by the Roman calligrapher and printer Lodovico degli Arrighi, called Vincentino, and used by him during the 1520s.

Composed by ComCom,
A Division of Haddon Craftsmen, Inc.,
Allentown, Pennsylvania

Printed and bound by Halliday Lithographers,
West Hanover, Massachusetts

Typography and binding design by
Dorothy Schmiderer Baker